Andrew Ten Brook

American State Universities

Their Origin and Progress - A History of Congressional University Land Grants

Andrew Ten Brook

American State Universities
Their Origin and Progress - A History of Congressional University Land Grants

ISBN/EAN: 9783337232931

Printed in Europe, USA, Canada, Australia, Japan

Cover: Foto ©Suzi / pixelio.de

More available books at **www.hansebooks.com**

AMERICAN

STATE UNIVERSITIES

THEIR ORIGIN AND PROGRESS

A HISTORY OF

Congressional University Land-Grants

A PARTICULAR ACCOUNT OF THE

RISE AND DEVELOPMENT OF THE

UNIVERSITY OF MICHIGAN

AND HINTS TOWARD THE FUTURE OF THE

AMERICAN UNIVERSITY SYSTEM

BY

ANDREW TEN BROOK

CINCINNATI
ROBERT CLARKE & CO
1875

CONTENTS.

PREFACE.

THE preface to a book is a device in order that its author may say, in regard to his work, something which ought to be known and still could not well be put together in a connected way in the body of the work. It may have reference to the origin of the work, or its plan and purpose, or to the authorities consulted, or anything personal to himself or others who may have been concerned in its production, or to all these.

This book did not originate in the author's conceit of his own special qualifications to prepare it. He was repeatedly urged to write a series of sketches of early university history for the *University Chronicle;* this he did, the articles numbering in all about twenty. These were favorably referred to in the Detroit and other papers, and several of them were stolen and published as original in a New York periodical. Dr. Haven, at that time president of the University of Michigan, on several occasions urged their elaboration into a volume, and supported his advice by words which seemed indeed too flattering, in regard to the author's qualifications for such an undertaking. As the facts brought out in these articles related solely to an earlier period than that of Dr. Haven's first connection with the University, his words were taken as expressing an unbiased and honest, though perhaps mistaken conviction, that the author was the right man for this work. Dr. H. gave furthermore this sound advice : " Trust your own judgment and do not submit your work to others for opinions by which to be governed ; they will only confuse your own mind." His opinion has not been asked and was never offered, and the work, with the exception of two or three chapters which contain no references to the personalities of the present time, was submitted to no one for an opinion until after its completion.

The original plan embraced only a history of the University of Michigan. Reflection, however, led to a change. The attention which the subject of University education is now receiving

throughout our land, the fact that in a large portion of the country
this enterprise is either not yet inaugurated at all, or is only in an
incipient stage, and that everywhere the public mind is awake to
any suggestions which the study of our history may bring out,
led to the determination to attempt a work of more than a mere
local interest. It will still remain as first intended, a history of
the University of Michigan, not, however, now as a single
phenomenon, but as part of a system yet to extend itself over the
whole country, if not the whole continent.

The question of State Universities is of difficult solution, and
deeply concerns the people of every state. If this question has
anywhere been solved, the work ought to be spread out for inspection. As preliminary to this, it seemed proper to survey the
early condition of the old States as to culture ; then that of the
new ; then of congressional action as it concerns all these States
in common ; then insert that particular solution of the problem
which should seem to be most nearly and satisfactorily completed, with suggestions as to its future completion in the Universities of our land. This is just what has been attempted, with
what success, the reader is to judge.

The difficulties which have been encountered in one State, are
in general those which may be expected in any other, their variations being rather in extent and complication than in character.
These will arise chiefly from the elements which are present, and
must be provided for. All shades of political and religious bigotry, and fanaticism, ignorance, infidelity, and all the various
prejudices against education or any particular forms and grades
of it, must be so considered as to be either canceled or accom-
modated. The manner in which this has been accomplished in
one instance, will show how it may be in another. It has therefore been deemed important to give a view of the religious public
as related to irreligion and indifference, and of the religious
denominations as related to each other, as also of the attitudes of
politicians ; and just in the proportion that this is fairly and faithfully done, will be the value of the work to those who have these
battles still to fight.

The articles above referred to can not in any proper sense be
regarded as the basis of this work. Scarcely a dozen pages have
been used as printed in those sketches. The most extended passage of the work which has ever before been printed, is that on
self-education, in the fourteenth chapter. This was prepared for

an educational convention, where it was read (the writer himself not being present) by Dr. Haven, and received such decided commendation as to furnish one of the encouragements to this work. The editor of an educational journal, who was there on the occasion and obtained possession of it, afterward furnished the author with a printed copy; his manuscript he never saw again.

The author knows of no obligation which he has to acknowledge to others, except in general that he has conversed with Presidents Haven, now of the University of Syracuse, in the State of New York; Angell, of the University of Michigan; Folwell, of the University of Minnesota; and Read, of the University of Missouri; and believes that he found evidence of their concurrence on the main features of the plan which he has sketched of the future University. But as his system has never been submitted for the approval of these gentlemen, or any others, he pledges no one for it. Dr. Read, who is perhaps the real Nestor of State University labor in this country, having been in this work in Ohio, Indiana, Wisconsin, and Missouri, and being now near the end of fifty years of service, has furnished some valuable hints, in a conversation which has occurred since the manuscript was finished.

As to the authorities which have been relied upon for facts, they could in all instances have been given. In regard to much of the work, memory has been able to run its lines with perfect accuracy from one to another of those stakes which documents have fixed, and yet this has seldom been used without confirmation.

There is but one chapter the documentary authority of which needs special explanation—the review of events from 1844 to 1851. On his retirement in the latter year, the author was requested by his friends to prepare a statement of the facts which led to this step, the publication of which one of those friends chose to take mainly upon himself. This paper was sent on from Utica, in the State of New York, soon after the author's arrival there in December of 1851, and placed, together with certain correspondence, which supported its statements, and was to be printed with it, in the printer's hands. Within a few days the action of December 31st of that year took place, and was announced to the author, as stated in the chapter in question. This led to correspondence and some delay, and as he never had any special desire to publish anything on the subject, it was dropped;

the manuscript was not returned to the author, and when desired, about four years ago, for this work, could not be found. Mr. Kendrick, to whom it had been entrusted, long since deceased, had probably not thought to obtain it from the printer, as the author had never asked for its return to him ; but the original rough draft still remained in the author's hands, containing references to the correspondence, but without the letters themselves, so far as they had been sent away. This draft has been largely the authority on this part of the history. An interval of more than twenty years has removed the little desire which the author even then felt for any personal vindication, and taken from the matter all its interest except as a history of the University, for which purpose alone it it has been used, and simply because the facts relate to a class of difficulties which must in some form be met in all state institutions ; and this has been done not without grave doubts as to whether it would not have been as well for the author's name, had he left out this portion of the history ; but that it could not have been properly a history of the University without this account of the greatest difficulty ever encountered in establishing it, decided his course which he submits to the reader's candid judgment.

In the first place, then, because he was urged to the work, and then because he felt a deep conviction that if properly executed it would be important to an interest scarcely second to any in our country, he has completed and now sends it forth, commending it to the fair and kind consideration of a generous public.

UNIVERSITY OF MICHIGAN, *May*, 1875.

AMERICAN STATE UNIVERSITIES.

CHAPTER I.

Sketch of the Early Progress of Higher Education in the Atlantic States.

ECCLESIASTICAL organization in New England was, from the beginning, quite complete, and included everything pertaining to schools as being but a part of religion itself. The introduction of an educational system into these colonies may therefore be deemed substantially contemporaneous with their settlement. It was of such character, too, and so energetically prosecuted that education suffered little, if any, deterioration in passing from Old to New England. It was, indeed, even more diffused on this than on the other side of the ocean; for the classes which in the old country were uneducated, were not represented in the new. The settlements were large enough to maintain their primary schools. Single families seldom passed so far from these centers as not to be within their reach. Thus common school instruction at least was provided for all.

Higher schools, too, had an early beginning. What afterward became Harvard College was established but six years after the settlement of Boston, the general court having increased the amount raised by private subscription by an appropriation of £400. Every town of fifty families was obliged to support a school, and the same general state of facts existed throughout New England. Classical schools followed in regular succession. These were modeled after the grammar schools of England, in which the founders of the colonies had themselves received their first

(1)

classical training.   The scholars of New England's early days learned in these schools to write and speak Latin ; so that if scientific teaching was nearly unknown, discipline was secured by a more thorough instruction in the ancient languages, and especially the Latin.   Grammar schools were very early established at Boston, Dorchester, Cambridge, New Haven, Salem, and Hartford.

In 1763 the oldest of the so-called academies, the Dummer School, at Byfield, was founded.   Philips' Academy, at Andover, soon followed, as also similar institutions at Leicester and Exeter.   These were designed for public use, and provided no special advantages to the towns in which they were located; nor is it unworthy of note that those which were made free to all—that is, were not founded for the particular accommodation of those living near them—succeeded, while the restrictive ones failed.   Of the earliest charters, some contained express provisions against localization, and justified the State appropriations to them by the equal freedom of all to their advantages.

The academies in Massachusetts were designed to be a part of the public school system.   There was indeed a plan which contemplated one in each county.   The State appropriated lands in Maine toward the endowment of some of these; and not the least interesting fact in regard to this subject is, that the man who was most prominent in this endowment by the State of the high schools of Massachusetts, Nathan Dane, was perhaps, more than any other man in Congress, the author of the system by which lands have been appropriated in the western Territories for education. In the pursuit of this policy, fifteen academies were incorporated in Massachusetts prior to 1797, seven of which had received donations of lands in Maine, and the principle involved in such gifts from the State had become settled.*

The other New England States were, according to their resources, about as forward as Massachusetts in the work

---

* An excellent account of the academies of New England will be found in the report of the Commissioner of Education for 1867, p. 403-432.

of education. As early as 1701, the law of Connecticut required every parent to see that he had no child or apprentice in his household who could not read the word of God and the "good laws of the colony." The system embraced a common school in every town of seventy families, a grammar school in the four chief county towns to fit pupils for college, and a college, to which the general court made an annual appropriation of £120.

We shall scarcely find an instance in which educational matters were in a more unfortunate condition than in New York during the first two centuries of its existence as a colony and a state, New Jersey, Pennsylvania, and Delaware being included in the same statement. This was not so much on account of the indifference of the people, or because the support of schools was not regarded as an obligation of the government, nor was it because the colonists were unwilling to contribute voluntarily to this object; but grew out of unsettled proprietary relations, or perhaps it will be better explained by the fact that the colony was settled by merchants who were more intent on making money than on building up its best interests.

In 1649, complaint was made to the States-General, that, although contributions had been collected for a school, the money had been dissipated,[*] and no school built. Their answer was, that the church wardens had had charge of the money.[†] Neither complaint nor answer determines where the fault lay, but they both show the destitution of schools.

In 1656, forty-seven years after the settlement at New Amsterdam, there were but three schools in the entire province of New Netherlands. These were at Manhattan, Beverwyck (Albany), and Fort Casimir (below Philadelphia, on the Delaware). There were, indeed, no persons qualified to teach who were not otherwise occupied, and if there had been, the people were too poor to pay them, though anxious to have their children taught. This state of things existed, too, in spite of an injunction of the

---

[*] Documents relating to the Colonial History of New York, Holland Docs., Vol. I., p. 300. [†] Id., p. 423.

Dutch West India Company, to the effect that the colonists, whether independent or under patroons, should make provision for the support of ministers and schoolmasters. If the colony had been under the States-General directly, instead of a mere mercantile company, the case would have been quite different; schools would not have been allowed to fall into neglect; not immediate interests, but permanent results would have determined action. A Latin school was indeed started in 1659, previous to which time classical teaching was not to be had nearer than Boston. This school was not indeed very successful under its first master, but became so eminent under his successor, Luyck, who entered upon its superintendence in 1661, that children were sent to it from Fort Orange (Albany), South river (the Delaware), and Virginia.

When the province fell into the hands of the English, in 1664, the king's commissioners were instructed to "make due enquiry what progresse hath been towards ye foundacòn and maintenance of any college schools for the educacòn of youth."*

The relation between the Dutch colonists and their English masters was probably unfavorable to any school system. Their ecclesiastical differences increased the difficulty. Zealous churchmen held that the English Church was established in the province. The few Episcopalians of New England had been viewed with jealousy, and treated with some severity, as representatives of the persecutors from whom the Puritans had fled. Not finding congenial homes among the Congregationalists there, they sought to establish themselves in New York.

The colonial assembly took some action, in 1747, looking toward a college—that is, made an appropriation of £1,800; † but the entire legislation of that period, attended as it was with frequent arbitrary adjournments by Governor

---

* Documents relating to the Colonial History of New York, Vol. III., p. 53.

† Id. The authorities consulted on this subject are O'Callaghan's History of New Netherland; Brodhead's History of the State of New York, first period; and especially the Documents relating to the Colonial History of New York.

Clinton, shows a want of harmony between these Dutch people and their English rulers, which will account for much of inefficiency in every branch of the government. The college was, however, founded by royal char-, ter, in 1754. This was to be an Episcopal seminary. Correspondence between Rev. Dr. Johnson,* who became its first president, and Bishop Sherlock and Archbishop Secker, shows what the plan was in relation to its religious character, and this plan was in general carried out, though its religious features were tolerant and catholic. Indeed it could not well have been otherwise, as there was but about one churchman to fifteen so-called dissenters.

It is a matter of curious interest, that Dr. Johnson, in one of his letters to the archbishop, describes the college work. The description is in these words: "The president's business here is to oversee and govern the college, read prayers, moderate in disputations, and prescribe exercises, and to hold commencements, and give degrees; and besides, to act the part of tutor to one of the classes (I have often two); all of which the vice-president must do in my absence, and be always one of the tutors, living in a collegiate way, at a common table, at the expense of about six shillings sterling per week for mere board." The salary of the president, together with his perquisites, was, in 1760, about £650. Dr. Johnson urged a grant of land for an endowment, and the Lords of Trade reported to the privy council in favor of one of twenty thousand acres, in the immediate vicinity of New York.

The early school advantages of the States of New Jersey, Pennsylvania, and Delaware did not differ enough, as already intimated, from those of New York, to make a separate treatment important for our purpose. They were all, at first, the same; and when they passed severally into the hands of different proprietors, their action in regard to schools was, in general, of the same kind—it was

---

* The Life and Correspondence of Dr. Johnson, by Rev. E. Edwards Beardsley, D.D., has just been published.

*in*action. William Penn, and afterward Benjamin Franklin, expressed themselves strongly in favor of education by the State; but still Pennsylvania, in common with the other States here grouped with it, remained without a system of public instruction.

In relation to the means of culture of this period, the Swedish scientific traveler, Kalm, employs the following language: "On one side of this building (the Town Hall), stands the library, which was first begun in the year 1742, on a public-spirited plan, formed and put into execution by the learned Mr. Franklin. For he persuaded first the most substantial people in town to pay forty shillings at the outset, and afterward annually ten shillings, all in Pennsylvania currency, toward purchasing all kinds of useful books. The subscribers are entitled to make use of the books. Other people are likewise at liberty to borrow," etc.

"The building of the academy is in the western part of the town. It was formerly, as I have before mentioned, a meeting-house of the followers of Whitefield, but they sold it in the year 1750, and it was destined to be the seat of an university; or, to express myself in more exact terms, to be a college; it was therefore fitted up to this purpose. The youths are here only taught those things which they learn in our common schools; but, in time, such lectures are intended to be read here as are usual in real universities." *

Dr. Franklin obtained subscriptions for this academy in 1749. He had some correspondence with Governor Colden, of New York, the same year, on the subjects of college instruction, and some soon afterward with Rev. Dr. Samuel Johnson, whom he desired to obtain as head of the school, but who did not accept the place, because he had a similar offer in New York. In 1751, he gives an account of the academy, as follows: "Our academy is beyond expectation. We have now above one hundred scholars, and the number is daily increasing. We have excellent mas-

* English translation, Vol. I., p. 44-46.

ters at present; and as we give them pretty good salaries, I hope we shall always be able to procure such. We pay the rector, who teaches Latin and Greek, per annum, £200; the English master, £150; the professor of mathematics, £125; three tutors, each £60."

The provinces further south really made at first more adequate provision for education. In 1692, the legislature of Maryland passed an act for the encouragement of learning, and four years later King William's free school was established. In 1723, schools were started in all the counties. To these, State aid was given in money, and lands were appropriated in each county for the use of the teachers. Such pupils as the visitors should designate for the purpose were to be taught gratuitously. Among the means of supporting the schools were a poll tax of twenty shillings on negroes and Irish (Catholic) servants imported into the province. These county schools were not of the primary, but of the higher grade. As early as 1782, the school for Kent county had made such progress as to apply to the legislature for a college charter, which application was followed two years later by a similar one in behalf of the King William school at Annapolis, both of which were granted, and the names Washington College and St. John's College applied to them severally. The same act which chartered them also united the two under the title of " The University of Maryland," though each retained its separate character and location. But this system, so promisingly started, failed of any considerable success, chiefly because its government was vested in a board of visitors, to whom appeals could be made from all disciplinary action of the faculty, and of course the latter lost the respect of the students. Though the interests of these local institutions were clearly diverse, the two were treated as one, and such became the general dissatisfaction with their working that the State withdrew its aid in 1805,* and increased its appropria-

---

* Mr. Sparks in N. A. Rev., Vol. XIII., p. 338-342.

tions to the county schools, so that some received as high as $800 a year.

In New England, a public school system had grown up with the very first settlement. This had been fostered and perfected, and had remained without any interruptions in its practical execution, which was not strictly true anywhere else. The very first settlers in Virginia, which was the leading province, and afterward the leader among the States, intended to establish a university, and endow it with lands, and had a good prospect of effecting this, which was, however, defeated by the massacre of 1622, some other causes also concurring in the production of this result. It was just seventy years after this time that the first steps toward the realization of such a plan were taken. William and Mary College was founded in 1692 by King William and Queen Mary, they having given £1,985 14s. 10d. and 20,000 acres of land toward its endowment, one penny per pound on tobacco exported to the Plantations, with some other sources of revenue from the crown, some private subscriptions—the celebrated Robert Boyle being one of the large donors—and some provincial aid. It had a powerful influence in the early history of Virginia.*

Even in the time of the Revolution, there was an application to the House of Burgesses to aid the Academy of Hampden Sidney. This they did so far as to grant the right to raise money by a lottery, but the heavy drafts of the war forbade direct appropriations. This was in 1777. In 1783 this institution was incorporated. One of the arguments used in the appeal for aid was that the war was in the way of their going to the English universities for edu-

---

* This is scarcely less true in later days, in illustration of which the case of the late President Dew may be adduced. He was professor of political economy, history, and metaphysics, from 1827 to 1836, and thence to his death, in 1846, president. He died in the forty-fourth year of his age. His work on the restrictive system, published in 1829, is supposed to have affected the tariff of 1832, and John Quincy Adams regards his argument on domestic slavery as inaugurating a new era in our country. His posthumous work, "Ancient and Modern Nations," published six years after his death, is perhaps his ablest.

cation, and the college at Williamsburg was so near the seat of war as to cripple its usefulness.

But with these highly creditable movements toward higher education, there was no school system. The great statesmen of Virginia—the State most influential in later colonial times, and especially during the Revolution—perceived, indeed, and admired the excellencies of the New England system. Patrick Henry wrote to John Adams: "It shall be my incessant study so to form our portrait of government, that a kindred with New England may be discerned in it; and if all your excellencies can not be preserved, yet I hope to retain so much of the likeness that posterity shall pronounce us descended from the same stock." Richard Bland Lee, speaking of the institutions of New England, declared them "the wisest the world had ever seen."

In 1779, Wythe and Jefferson reported a bill, prepared by the latter, for a school system in Virginia, to be supported by taxation according to property. The great statesman may speak for himself. In a letter to Dr. Priestly, dated January 27, 1800, he says:

"About twenty years ago, I drew a bill for our legislature, which proposed to lay off every county into hundreds, or townships of five or six miles square. In the center of each of them was to be a free English school. The whole State was further laid off into ten districts, in each of which was to be a college for teaching the languages, geography, and surveying, and other useful things of that grade, and then a single university for the sciences.*

---

* Those who regard Jefferson as their model statesman might do well to consider his plan. Nearly a century has passed since he proposed it. His native State has not even yet attained to its standard, and no State has transcended it, though all have of late been rapidly advancing in the direction which it indicates. In some quarters, however, an opposite movement is started. The legislature of Ohio is at this time (December, 1874) discussing the question of the right to support higher education by taxation. A judicial decision has just been given in Michigan as to the constitutional right to collect taxes for the teaching of the higher branches, especially the foreign languages, in the schools supported by taxation.

It was received with enthusiasm; but as I had proposed that William and Mary, under an improved form, should be the university, and that was at that time pretty highly episcopal, the dissenters after awhile began to apprehend some secret design of a preference to that sect."

The adoption of the system seems to have been left to the option of the county courts, and it never went into effect—perhaps, as has been hinted by Mr. Jefferson himself, because the judges were wealthy, and feared the taxes.

How earnestly the great statesmen of that time were enlisted in placing the cause of learning on a firm foundation, will further appear by a reference to plans for a national university at the capital, in which Washington was greatly interested. One of the forms in which this subject was presented through Mr. Jefferson, was that of a proposition from M. D'Ivernois, and the professors of the University of Geneva, Switzerland, to remove in a body to the United States, and establish a university. This was most probably designed to be a Virginia, rather than a national school; though perhaps the central and leading position of Virginia led these men to include both in one. Mr. Madison even proposed in the Constitutional Convention to give Congress the power to establish a national university at the capital. It is not our purpose to enter into any details on this subject, the interest in which, at that time, as shown by Washington's and Jefferson's references to it,

---

The two questions are indeed quite distinct; the one regarding the propriety of passing laws providing for taxation to support higher schools, the other being a question of existing constitutional law. No point is better established by facts than that it is vital to primary schools that they be but part of a system which shall embrace the highest grade of scientific and literary culture. It is the old fable of the "Stomach and the Members," the latter complaining at the enormous expenditure upon the former, without benefit to them. But as in the one case, so in the other, the withholding of these supplies must be quickly felt to the extremities. Nearly a century of progress has been lost by some of the States, less by others, from their not holding the position which they had occupied at the beginning of the Revolution, and advancing from it. It is to be hoped that the lesson will be learned, and no retrograde movement ever again be allowed.

and correspondence in regard to it, appears strange when viewed retrospectively through more than a half century of apathy.

The failure of Jefferson's school system, introduced in 1776 into the legislature, including, as it did, the advancement of William and Mary College to the rank of a university, and the subsequent failure of a plan for importing an institution of that rank from Europe, led finally to the inauguration of the measures which partially succeeded; for no man ever pursued a purpose with more determined perseverance than did Thomas Jefferson that of establishing a system of education in Virginia.*

If we pursue our way southward from this great central colony, we shall scarcely find the interest in schools to diminish. North Carolina may be regarded as varying too slightly from Virginia in its early educational history to merit separate treatment in so brief a sketch as we propose. Let it suffice to say, that the constitution of this State, adopted in 1776, made it the duty of the legislature to establish a school, or schools, for the convenient instruction of youth, with such salaries to the masters, paid by the public, as might enable them to instruct at low prices. It required also the establishment of one or more universities. Though no great results were realized, the theory, which, after a long period of inaction, with its sad consequences, is now becoming well-nigh universal, is here found in most decided expression.

South Carolina had some early, as she has had some later, features to distinguish her from her sisters. In this colony, culture received its first impulse from one Dr. Bray, whose liberality provided for libraries, not only in Charleston, but in other parishes also. Assuming the management of these, the legislature in 1700 provided for their care, and in 1710 and 1712 started a free school in Charleston, giving

---

* The authorities used on the schools of Virginia have been chiefly Burk's History of Virginia; Jefferson's works, especially Vols. I. and IV; Cabell's History of the University of Virginia, and Madison's Debates in the Federal Convention.

£100 to its preceptor, while the country schools received
£10 from the treasury, to which sums private donations
were added. This did not provide a support for education,
and more at this time went to Europe from South Carolina
for their collegiate training than from any other colony.
The want of other provision was increasingly felt, and in
1769 a bill was introduced into the legislature for founding
a provincial college. Aristocratic prejudice, however,
stood in the way of this project, and it was dropped, and
not realized until 1785, when the Revolution had prepared
the way. Three colleges were established on the same
day. All these, and one for which the city of Beaufort
obtained a charter in 1795, soon descended to the rank of
grammar schools, and the legislature in 1801 established
South Carolina College on a liberal plan, paying its president $3,500, the professors $2,000, and the tutors $1,000 a
year. Up to 1820, the State had expended upon this institution $286,000. Some of the men connected with it have
spoken even better for it than this amount of expenditure.
Dr. Maxy, successively president of Brown University and
Union College, was its president from 1804 to his death in
1820, and the late Dr. Lieber was long there.

This State expended with equal liberality on lower
schools, $302,000 having been drawn for this purpose from
the public treasury from 1812 to 1820; but corruption, or
gross neglect, was found in the use of this money—in one
year $40,000 having been drawn, and no account given of
its use. There were other similar instances, and of course
the schools languished, or died out.

Georgia was later settled than most of the sisterhood of
States. She has indeed the remarkable coincidence with
Maryland, that there elapsed just one century from the
time that Maryland's charter passed the great seal to the
time when that of Georgia was confirmed—the former being in June, 1632; the latter in June, 1732. A period,
therefore, briefer by one century, intervened between the
founding of this State and the era of the Revolution, much
beyond which latter epoch we have not designed to em-

brace in this sketch of scholastic culture in the Atlantic States.

Oglethorpe, the father of Georgia, was educated at Oxford, and some of his colonists had received their education in the English universities. His intimate friend, George Berkeley, afterward Bishop of Cloyne, whose favorite scheme of a college in Bermuda, for which he had been promised by the British prime minister £20,000—the price of some lands in St. Christopher*—came to America in order to carry out his plan. After he had lived two years in Newport, and scattered money and books in Rhode Island and Connecticut for the purposes of learning and religion, he found, through the Bishop of London, that Sir Robert Walpole did not intend the money should be paid over, although the amount proved to be £90,000, instead of £20,000, and he returned home; but Oglethorpe, doubtless with the good bishop's aid and concurrence, managed to secure some of this money "for Georgia."† The sum of £10,000 from the price of the St. Christopher lands was voted by Parliament "to the 'Trust' for establishing the colony of Georgia, in America, to be applied toward defraying the charges of carrying over and settling foreign and other Protestants in said colony."

Here is a hint of the benevolent character of the colonization of Georgia. In this feature it is distinguished from all the American provinces. James Oglethorpe moved, in Parliament, a committee to visit the jails of England, where he had himself observed barbarous treatment of persons imprisoned for debt. The result was the chartering of a board of trustees for the settling of such of this class in America as should be accepted for the purpose. The colony was called Georgia, in honor of the king, George II., and Oglethorpe benevolently gave himself to its interests. But others than the debtors of England were drawn to it. The persecuted Christians from the valleys of Salzburg,

---

* Wright's ed. of Berkeley's works, Vol. I., p. 10.
† Stevens' History of Georgia, Vol. I., pp. 78, 105.

the Vaudois from Lombardy, Count Zinzendorf's United
Brethren, the Protestants of the Swiss cantons, those of the
Highlands of Scotland, and the dispersed Israelites of Por-
tugal, all sent of their people to this asylum, so opportunely
opened. This feature of the colony doubtless drew thither
John and Charles Wesley and Whitfield, where the latter
built his orphan house—in keeping with the general spirit
of the whole movement.

Such, with an intermingling of English gentlemen, were
the elements of the first colonization in Georgia, and all
who believe that Providence awards to great movements a
harvest of the nature of the seed sown, will perceive in the
exceptionally thrifty and enterprising character of the
people of Georgia a new verification of this law.

The persecuted Protestants from the continent doubtless
had schools. The beneficent character of the enterprise
itself naturally drew some English clergymen with it, and
these did some teaching, especially of a religious nature,
which is generally the best foundation for mental development. John Wesley had a school while in Georgia, and
started a Sunday-school half a century before Robert
Raikes projected his system in Gloucester, England, and
eighty years before the starting of the first school on
Raikes', plan in America.

There was less time in Georgia than in the other original
colonies, between the settlement and the Revolution, for the
development, on the one hand, of culture, or, on the other,
for the begetting of that indifference to mental improvement
which is the natural growth of the privations and hardships
of pioneer life. It is a trite saying, even in the mouths of
the unlearned, that "no effect is without a cause." It is
equally clear that there is no cause but will produce its
effect, and the succession—not to take one side or the other
of the metaphysical question involved—will be practically
interminable. We could doubtless find in Georgia the elements originally introduced, or collaterally added, which
have naturally produced what has followed. We have referred to the benevolence in its founder's plan. We may

not be able distinctly to detect the fruits in history, but the seed has not been lost. As this aspect is peculiar to Georgia, so we find another such quite worthy of our regard. The fifty-fourth article of the constitution of 1777—made in the midst of the war of the Revolution, and but a little over forty years from Oglethorpe's first landing on the grounds of his new State—provides that every county shall establish and keep up a school at the public expense, and this provision grew out of what had previously existed in the public mind, and was perhaps already in process of realization.

The movement for higher education did not stop here. The legislature, in 1785, developed almost at once a university to crown their school system. In an act which had been previously passed, there was a section which ran as follows :

"And whereas, the encouragement of religion and learning is an object of great importance to any community, and must tend to the prosperity, happiness, and advantage of the same : Be it therefore enacted by the authority aforesaid, that the county surveyors, immediately after the passing of this act, shall proceed to lay out in each county 20,000 acres of land for the endowment of a college or seminary of learning, and which said lands shall be vested in and granted to his honor the governor for the time being. And John Houstoun, James Habersham, William Few, Joseph Clay, Abram Baldwin, William Houston, and Nathan Brownson, Esqrs., and their successors in office, are hereby nominated and appointed trustees for the said college or seminary of learning, and empowered to all such things as to them shall appear requisite and necessary to forward the establishment and progress of the same, and all vacancies shall be filled by said trustees.*' And the said county surveyors shall, within six months of the passing of this act, make return to the trustees hereinbefore mentioned of all

---

* Stevens' Georgia, Vol. II., p. 353.

regular plats of all such tracts as they shall have laid out and surveyed by virtue of this act."

On this basis was a college or university placed at the head of the school system of the State, the whole endowed with magnificent land grants, and provision made for its perpetuation. The further development of this system lies outside of the limit prescribed to this survey of culture in the Atlantic States. Indeed this limit has already been transcended in case of this last born of the original thirteen ; for it was not until 1801 that this institution was placed in its present site, and its president made the head of the educational system of this Empire State of the South.

In this rapid survey, it has appeared that each part of this extensive line of settlements has shown its own peculiar features, and developed its own form of culture. The New England colonists left the mother country in quest of greater religious freedom. Their religious system was put first, and carried with it a school system as perfect in organization, and administered with equal vigor. This formed an active leaven, which, at a later day, was to spread to other parts. In New York and its neighbors— New Jersey, Pennsylvania, and Delaware—settled by merchants, with the necessary infusion of other elements, we have seen religious and mental culture, though not neglected, still struggling more slowly into life. In Maryland again has appeared a religious colony, though quite unlike those of New England, and developing itself naturally from its elements. We have seen Virginia and the Carolinas settled with English gentlemen, with an admixture of the laboring classes ; the difference in the characters of the settlers on the James river and those on the Hudson perhaps having somewhat to do in fixing the commercial center of the country at the mouth of the latter, and not at that of the former. In Georgia is seen a colony of beneficiaries under their chief benefactor, with some English gentlemen of means among them. Minor peculiarities have appeared, as in Rhode Island, settled with exiles from the exiled Puritans ; Hollanders and Swedes mixed with the

English on the Hudson and the Delaware, and remaining perpetual factors in the production of the result; as also the French Huguenots in Carolina, and the Puritans in Maryland. But everywhere there was a considerable infusion of men who had received in the European universities a liberal culture, which they desired to reproduce on these shores. Early action was full of promise. Probably at a period from just before the Revolution to the end of it, the average position of the colonies in regard to higher education, relatively to the age and to population and wealth, was quite as good as it is at the present time. Massachusetts had its Harvard; Connecticut its Yale; New Hampshire its Dartmouth, endowed with forty-four thousand acres of land; Rhode Island had Rhode Island College, founded mainly by donations from the Baptists of America and England; Maine its Bowdoin, endowed with one hundred and fifteen thousand acres of land; while academies were scattered thickly throughout New England, with land endowments. In New York, Pennsylvania, and New Jersey, the beginnings of Columbia and New Jersey Colleges and Pennsylvania University had been well made. Maryland had its county academies, and its university made up of Washington and St. John's Colleges. Virginia had William and Mary, and Hampden Sidney Colleges, with other schools. South Carolina had an inceptive system of schools, with a university at its head, on both of which the State was expending largely; and Georgia had its county system, headed by an embryonic university, based upon large land grants.

Most of the colonies established or aided these institutions, by gifts of land or money. The principle of State support to higher learning was not merely accepted, but was the prevalent one. A period of decline, however, in the desire, and perhaps in the means of culture, followed that which we have now reached in our inquiries. Intercourse with the mother country was for a time cut off; resources were diminished; the spirit of intellectual progress was repressed in the toils and privations of pioneer

2

life; the people, scattered over an immense surface, lost each other's aid in the work.   The introduction of slaves by Great Britain into the colonies, so diluted the population to be educated as to greatly augment the difficulty. From these causes combined, soon after the close of the Revolutionary war, outside of New England, if not even within its limits, there had arisen, or was arising, a comparative apathy, which, on the wide and ever-widening frontiers, continued for a generation to increase.

The praiseworthy movements referred to as having been made, or rather planned, in some States—as Maryland, Virginia, the Carolinas, and Georgia—have been treated as part of the history of culture, and rightly; for they were honest pledges of a magnificent future, of which circumstances forbade the redemption—they may still be redeemed.   Indeed, such is now everywhere the ruling tendency.

Nor should our favorable reference to the schools of New England be turned into a complimentary opinion in regard to their character.   They generally embraced but few branches, and the teaching was often of a low order. They were, however, the elements of that noble system, out of which has grown the present one by the natural laws of development, and perhaps judged by the character of the discipline received, rather than the number of studies pursued, their comparison with the present age might not be against them.

But those views of education which we find to have prevailed just before the Revolution, survived in a class of men, of which Nathan Dane, Manasseh Cutler, George Washington, Thomas Jefferson, and James Madison are fit representatives, and from these ripened and bowing heads, just before they fell into the earth, seeds were gathered and sown in the broad western fields just in time to save them.   These germinated, endured a half century's winter, and are now beginning to yield their perpetual succession of golden harvests throughout these extensive regions, and the fruits are even borne back to those parent States which furnished the seed; nay, even to those transatlantic lands whence all originally came. We now, therefore, pass in our inquiries beyond the Alleghanies westward; take a view of the fields in which this seed was sown, and observe the process of its germination and its growth.

CHAPTER II.

The State of Culture in the West at the Commencement of the Congressional Land-Grant Policy, and subsequently.

IT has been intimated that the chief elements of western culture must be sought in the Atlantic States, which furnished the settlers for the West. For this reason, the educational and social progress of the older States has been passed in review. Its western movement must now be followed. This will run in but slight variations from the parallels of latitude; for, if people change their homes, their love for all the attributes and surroundings of those they leave, will lead them to seek as many of these as possible in those to which they shall remove, and especially will this be true in regard to climate and productions. The quest of health or of wealth, the course of a road or a river, or other circumstances, will sometimes deflect their line of march a few degrees to the north or south of their native parallels; but instances of greater deviation are somewhat rare, the rule remains unchanged, and we shall, in tracing the westward advance along this entire line, which we have just surveyed, extending from the St. Lawrence to the Gulf of Mexico, find that the civilization of the West has the same lineaments of character and shades of coloring as appear in the Eastern States of the same latitudes, varied only by difference of resources, new combinations of the elements, and the privations and hardships endured in the western settlements.

The picture given above of culture in the old States was designed to be that of about the period when the movement to the westward in real earnest began to develop itself; but it needs a few additional strokes in the nature of generalizations to complete it. The Revolution, as stated above, intervened and greatly changed the prospect, and more in some parts than in others. The school system in New England had advanced so far toward completion as not to be destroyed or very seriously interrupted or disturbed by the war. Primary instruction was provided for, academies and grammar schools were extensively established, and Harvard and Yale had been so far endowed that they were capable of doing efficient work in those days of simple habits. Rhode Island College was already in successful operation. The irregularities of the revolutionary period left here no permanent traces of injury. Rhode Island College must indeed close its doors for a time, that its halls might be used for barracks and its president serve in Congress, but they were to be opened again without enduring loss to the enterprise. So in each other case. The whole educational structure was there, too firmly built to fall into decay, even if portions of it should not be used for a time. It was ready, with but slight repairs, for use again.

Nowhere else was there a complete system. Kings (afterward Columbia) College, in New York ; Nassau Hall (afterward Princeton College), in New Jersey ; William and Mary College, in Virginia ; the county academies in Maryland and Georgia, and a somewhat similar class of schools in South Carolina ; a few grammar schools in different parts of this extensive region ; sometimes a log hut built by the planters, or perhaps by the boys' who were to be benefited by it, in which some Scotch or Irish, or even native American pedagogue, in addition to the common branches, taught the ancient languages and other studies preparatory to college, and with no public common school system,—these made up the ante-revolutionary school provisions for education.

Several other facts still further increased the difference in school advantages between New England and the States south of Delaware Bay. Slaves were indeed introduced by the mother country into all the provinces, and quite as much in the South as elsewhere, against the protest of the

colonists.   But slavery was unprofitable in the North, and
seemed to be otherwise in the South; hence slaves were
greatly multiplied in the South, and disappeared from the
North.   The people of New England lived in cities and
villages made up of merchants, mechanics, and professional
men, with small farmers around them, each holding generally only as much ground as himself and his sons could
cultivate, thus forming just the kind of community in which
schools are most easily maintained.   Nor is it immaterial
to add that New England was peopled by those whose chief
motive in seeking homes on these shores sprung from a
great, nay, the greatest of social and educational impulses—the desire of religious freedom.

On the contrary, in the South, the tendency which arose
naturally from the kinds of fruits sought in cultivation, was
to large plantations, and to only so much of manufacturing
or mechanical labor as must be performed near the places
where its products were to be used in the farming work,
other manufactured articles being transported from a distance, or not used at all.   Population was thus sparsely
spread over large surfaces, and the constant increase of the
colored race, who were not to be educated, operated in the
same direction, becoming a kind of diluting process upon
the European population, and increasing the difficulty, if
not the desire, of maintaining schools.   Nor were the peculiar dialect, habits, and notions of the negroes without
their influence upon the children of their masters, excepting
where a thorough education came in to neutralize this effect,
nor perhaps even there.   The motives, too, which led to
the founding of the colonies west and south of the Hudson,
with the slight exception of the Catholics in Maryland and
the Huguenots and Salzburgers in the South, were commercial.   The social and religious questions were second-
ary, and this fact has been clearly traceable in succeeding
generations.

People so situated could not but suffer an abatement of
their educating forces as the result of a war like the American Revolution.   If they could not maintain schools in

peace, they of course could not in war. The Southern
States did not soon, if ever, recover entirely from the shock
so far as to establish such common school systems as they
might have had but for the war. Scattered over immense
territory, much of which was wilderness—the effect of this
dispersion largely increased by the presence of a class,
which, from the nature of their relation, was not to be educated, a universal school system not having been established immediately after their arrival in the country—the
necessities of pioneer life and of war had accustomed the
great body of the people to do without education, and had
introduced upon the stage of action a generation which
knew little of its value.

This condition of things will be found to have affected
largely the state of early culture in the West, and especially south of the Ohio. The considerable admixture of
an element, either cultivated or desirous of culture, had
little power to remedy the evil. The men of high culture,
elevated character, and large views, of which there have
always been many who were equal to the best of their
brethren in the North, were relatively too few to provide a
leaven active enough to transform entire communities.
This could only be effected by a very slow and gradual
process. Indeed, actual retrogression was an almost necessary result of the hardships and privations of pioneer
life.

A brief picture of the West will here be drawn preliminary to a view of the provisions which Congress has made
for education in this section of our country, beginning with
the Northwest, which has been most favorably situated for
the effective employment of provisions for education.

No colonizing movement westward was ever made with
so fair a prospect, so far as concerns the formal organization of the colony, and the moral worth and intelligence of
the colonists, as that made in 1788, under the direction of
the New England Ohio Land Company.

General Rufus Putnam had been offered the place of
surveyor of public lands in the West, but was not ready at

the time to enter upon the work on account of other engagements, and used, therefore, his influence to obtain the place for his friend, General Benjamin Tupper, which latter made an attempt in 1785 to reach the field of his expected labors, but Indian troubles were in the way of his success, and after his return, he visited his friend Putnam, at the latter's residence in Rutland, Massachusetts, and fully succeeded in enlisting him in a great scheme of settlement, which others, to whom he had hinted it, deemed too visionary for serious consideration. It was in the year 1786 that the two visited together the scene of their future pioneer life, and they doubtless made, during this visit, no little progress toward maturing their plans.

Before proceeding to details of this enterprise, it would be well if the chief figures connected with it could be made to rise and stand before our readers, so as to impress them with their characteristic lineaments; but the strokes of our pencil must be few, and the reader's imagination must be left to fill up the meager outline. The general portraiture of the officers and soldiers who came out of the Revolutionary time, after fighting its battles, is one which we almost instinctively draw, whether correctly or not, and refuse to have it dislodged from our minds. Simple in dress, manners, and all the habits of social and domestic life ; made frugal by necessity ; inured to toil and hardship ; large numbers of them impoverished by the war, and too proud to settle down among those inferior to them in energy, enterprise, and endurance ; taught by the greater sufferings of the camp to bear, what they naturally supposed to be the lesser ones of frontier life, they were prepared for this movement, though doubtless, as in all such cases, with but an imperfect estimate of what they would really have to endure. None need be told how largely the first settlers of the wilderness after the Revolution, were of those who had fought its battles and won its victories.

Of those who went on in person, General Putnam was doubtless the most prominent. In the engineering department of the Revolutionary army, he superintended the

construction of some of the fortifications, and especially
those at West Point. He had enjoyed about as. good advantages for the study of military engineering as the times
afforded. A common soldier in the old French war, from
1757 to its close in 1760, he had learned what observation
would naturally teach an apt scholar in the interesting
battle-grounds and fortifications of that contest, and from
its close, for seven or eight years, had diligently followed
his trade as a millwright. The science and art here
brought into exercise, were as nearly allied to those of
constructing military works as any then known, and he
had employed his leisure during this period in augmenting
his stock of scientific and practical knowledge, surveying
and navigation being among his acquisitions—the former of
which became of great use to him, as it was to his more
illustrious friend, who commanded in chief the Revolutionary army.

Thus was he educated for his work as a military engineer, in which department he remained through most of
the war with the rank of colonel, having received his
appointment as brigadier-general not until near its close.
Washington's confidence in him, and friendly feeling toward him, are pleasantly testified, in a published correspondence between the two. The soldier, the military
engineer and commander, the mechanic, the man by
the very necessities of his past life prepared for every
labor and inured to every kind of hardships, combined
with desirable moral qualities and found all united in one
person, furnish most excellent material for a leader in the
pioneer life of the West, and such was Rufus, Putnam.

Rev. Manasseh Cutler may be regarded as the most
active agent of the company, especially in its preliminary
measures. Mr. Cutler was a man of no ordinary mental
ability by nature, to which had been added not only a thor-.
ough college education, but also a full course of preparation both for the bar and the pulpit, and very creditable
attainments in the exact, as also in the natural sciences; to
all which was superadded a highly creditable Revolution-

ary record.   He never went on with the colonists, though
he paid them a visit during their first summer in the West,
but spent his days in his New England home. Washington
honored him, in 1795, with the offer of a place on the bench
of the Northwestern Territory, which he declined ; he accepted, however, a seat in two successive Congresses—
1800 to 1804.

Colonel Return J. Meigs, who was afterward in the service of the government for his whole life, and at one time
as Postmaster-General, was one of this colony, as was also
General James M. Varnum, whose name is found among
those of the very first class which graduated from Rhode
Island College. He had been in the Continental Congress,
and was also, at the establishment of the territorial government of the Northwest, one of the judges, but died soon
after.   These are but a portion of those connected with
this movement who have become historic ; among which
should not be omitted a name, than which few have been
more deservedly prominent in the West and in the entire
country—that of Lewis Cass, who, as a young man of
eighteen years, settled in the year 1800, and began the
practice of law, at Athens, among these New England
colonists.*

The inquirer into the history of the settlement of the
Northwest will not fail to observe that a Providence quite
above human wisdom had ever been watching over it.
The French towns on the lakes, the Detroit, the Wabash,
the Illinois, and the Mississippi, had indeed maintained an
existence, but showed no signs of progress, developed no
spirit of enterprise, and evinced no capacity for it.   In
1755, Great Britain offered, on certain conditions, to cede
to France all the lands west of a line running through
Western Pennsylvania to the last of the mountains of Vir-

---

* The influence of this colony on higher education in Michigan has been
by no means small. The mention of four names, which will be met again
in the course of our narrative, will suffice to show this. Lewis Cass, William Woodbridge, Austin E. Wing, and Warner Wing may all be reckoned
as having belonged to this settlement.

ginia which descend toward the ocean; and if this offer had been accepted, whatever might have been the ultimate fortunes of these regions, French colonies would doubtless have been planted all over them, and would have entered, to a much larger extent, as an element into their civilization. Furthermore, not only did George III., soon after the treaty of Paris, in 1763, issue a proclamation forbidding his governors in America to grant titles to " any lands beyond the heads or sources of any rivers which fall into the Atlantic ocean from the west or northwest;" but the contest in regard to the ownership of vacant lands, which began to wax warm soon after the opening of the Revolutionary war, led Virginia to enact, in 1779, "a law to prevent settlements on the north side of the Ohio river."*

While Kentucky, therefore, was being rapidly settled from Virginia, the Northwest was kept free for such a movement as this—free, too, for the action which Congress took in the ordinance of 1787, that neither slavery nor involuntary servitude should exist there, thus making this the only part of our country east of the Mississippi in which slavery never existed.

The time had come for the settlement of this region, and a people was ready for it. The opening was grand, and Providence seems to have held it in reserve for the leadership of the impoverished and unemployed officers and soldiers who had just come out of the war; nor has there ever been a time when, relatively to the whole population, so many were inclined, not to say that their inclination was wise, to accept such an offer.

The men referred to above as leaders of this colony were worthy of the mansions since reared upon the ground which they helped to clear with their own hands; but we must first see them in their log huts, dressed in their homespun linsey-woolsey—the material grown by the men, the texture and garments wrought by their wives and daughters—or encamped, as necessity often required, in the open

---

* Burk's History of Virginia, Vol. IV., p. 374.

air, occupied in preparing and defending homes for another generation.

The company which had its origin in the visit of the two veterans to the West was formed at the "Bunch of Grapes" tavern in Boston, in the beginning of March, 1786, a meeting for the purpose having been regularly called by a circular, which Messrs. Putnam and Tupper had issued on their return. This missive called for a delegate from each county in the State of Massachusetts, and the response was as follows: Winthrop Sargent and John Miles, from Suffolk; Manasseh Cutler, from Essex; John Brook and Thomas Cushing, from Middlesex; Benjamin Tupper, from Hampshire; Crocker Sampson, from Plymouth; Rufus Putnam, from Worcester; John Patterson and Jelaliel Woodbridge, from Berkshire; and Abraham Williams, from Barnstable. Over this delegation Rufus Putnam presided. The details would be wearisome, though of great interest; the articles of the association would admirably illustrate the character of the men engaged in the movement, but would occupy too much space in this work. Let it suffice to add that a year was employed in maturing the organization of the company, and in March, 1787, another meeting was held, by which Manasseh Cutler and Winthrop Sargent were delegated to represent the company before the Congress of the Confederation. The journal of the former preserves the account of the negotiation.

Dr. Cutler, on his way to New York, where Congress was in session, remained over Sunday, the 30th of June, in Middletown, Connecticut, where Samuel H. Parsons, one of the directors of the company, lived, and drove into the metropolis, on the Bowery road, on the afternoon of the 5th of July. He was provided with letters to all whom he needed to see, and had indeed many more than he could use; but he personally saw every member of Congress, as well as the committee, with which he was more immediately concerned. At his first meeting with the committee, the parties were so far apart in their views that he cherished little hope of final success.

The price at length agreed upon for the land was one dollar per acre, and the amount which they expected to take was 2,000,000 acres. Of this price, one-third was remitted in consideration of waste lands and reservations. What the terms suggested by the committee, which so depressed Dr. Cutler's hope of success, may have been, we find no means of ascertaining; but when it is remembered that some of the companies which treated with the State of Georgia for Mississippi lands, in 1789, expected to obtain them at about one cent per acre, and that a magnificent attempt was made to obtain at about the same price 20,000,000 acres in Michigan, by negotiations with Congress in 1796, we perceive in the case before us what it really is—a company of upright men, planning a great enterprise, which they never lose sight of in their desire of personal aggrandizement; while, in the other cases, we see bold speculation seeking personal ends. The one class, in a purchase of 2,000,000 acres, were willing to pay at a rate nearly equal to that which the individual settler has paid the government from that day to this; the others sought to obtain the same at about a hundredth part of that price. The course of the one has been followed by beneficent results, which have spread and are spreading all over the land; that of the other has left naught but an inheritance of disputed titles and frauds and feuds to after generations.

While Dr. Cutler was in New York, Congress had under consideration a plan for the government of the Northwest. It was a new problem in American statesmanship to provide for governing sparsely settled districts lying outside of the self-governed States, and probably no statesman of the time foresaw the momentous line of consequences which action on this subject must draw after it. It is pleasant to know that a bill for this purpose was submitted to the chief agent of the first colony of Anglo-Americans which was to settle in this territory. Dr. Cutler says in his diary, under date of July 10th:

" As Congress was now engaged in settling the form of government for the federal territory, for which a bill had been prepared, and a copy sent to me (with leave to make remarks and propose amendments), which I had taken the liberty to remark upon and propose several amendments, I thought this the most favorable time to go to Philadelphia. Accordingly, after I had returned the bill, with my observations, I set out at seven o'clock."

Dr. Cutler was much in the company of Nathan Dane, the reputed author of this bill, and one of the chief actors in the endowment of Massachusetts academies with Maine lands, by which latter policy he showed the same views which appear in this legislation for the Northwest. In this fact we find good ground for the impression that the ordinance for the government of the Northwest, and the contract with this company, came from the same minds, and were parts of the same general plan—the former of which passed Congress on the 13th, and the latter on the 27th of July, 1787.

The agent of the company was not only consulted in regard to the provisions of the ordinance of 1787, but the opinion which prevailed in the highest circles in regard to the character of the elements of this colony will give probability to the view that their influence prevailed in preparing a government for this first federal territory. It will suffice to cite the words of Washington. He says:

"No colony in America was ever settled under such favorable auspices as that which has just commenced at the Muskingum. Information, property, and strength will be its characteristics. I knew many of the settlers personally, and there never were men better calculated to promote the welfare of such a community."*

Of the Anglo-American population of the Northwest, these were almost the first, and far the most important in character, of those who were to be the subjects of the government by this action established in that wide and wild region, and to form the nucleus around which its future was to gather, and nothing could have been more proper

---

* Letter to Richard Henderson; Sparks' Washington, Vol. IX., p. 385.

or more promising of wise counsels, than to consult them as to the provisions of that government under which they were to live, and spread the blessings of civilized life over this waste.

Mr. Cutler set out for his home on the same day on which his bill became a law, and no time was lost in setting forward the preparation for an early realization of the company's hopes. He had a large wagon made, and covered with black canvas, on which, some say, were painted in white letters the words, " OHIO, FOR MARIETTA ON THE MUSKINGUM ;" and doubtless some words were so painted, but the word " *Marietta*" involves too serious an anachronism, for this name was not given to the place until the 2d of July, 1788, and that proposed by Dr. Cutler him_ self, and actually borne by the town up to that date, was Adelphia.* The emigrants, then forty-five in number, having fired a volley as a farewell salute, set out from Dr. Cutler's house, in December, 1787, and afterward augmented to sixty, reached a place called Sumrill's Ferry, on the Youghiogheny river, about thirty miles above Pittsburg; in February, 1788, where they remained until the beginning of April, and constructed a boat to carry them to their destination, which they reached on the 7th of that month.

General Arthur St. Clair, who, at the time of the legislation just referred to, was president of Congress, and had, in the following autumn, been appointed governor of the Northwestern Territory, arrived at the mouth of the Muskingum on the 9th of July; and the judges—Samuel H. Parsons, of Connecticut; James M. Varnum, of Massachusetts (both directors of the company) ; and John Cleves Symmes, of New Jersey—had reached the place before him. Dr. Cutler paid them a visit during this first summer, having made the entire journey, occupying twenty-nine days, in a sulky.

But the details of this movement, interesting as they are

---

* *Vide* Walker's History of Athens County, Ohio, p. 87.

in themselves, have but an incidental connection with that scholastic culture, the development of which in the West, in one of its aspects, it is the purpose of this work to trace. In the very laying out of the place, they betrayed the Puritan, both in its better features and its pedantry. In the first name of their new city—Adelphia—Dr. Cutler designed to express the desire of his heart, that it might be the center of a great brotherhood. In memory of the unfortunate queen of France, they changed it to Marietta—an attempt at blending her two names in one word. The large public square was called Quadranaon; the small one, Capitolium; the street from the landing to the square, Sacra Via; the fort and its inclosure, Campus Martius.

Dr. Cutler had provided that the two college townships should be near the center of the first million and a half acres which should be paid for by the company—less than a million was ever paid for—lest the realization of this cherished hope should be too long delayed. But there was delay; for it was not until 1795 that this land was surveyed. The county in which it was situated was called Athens, also one of the townships and the village where the university was to be located, by which a significant hint of the great intellectual enterprise there to be inaugurated was sought to be conveyed. In 1800, Dr. Cutler sent on a draft of a charter which he had himself prepared, and in 1802 it was, after some modifications, passed by the Legislature of Ohio, which that very year became one of the United States. The land was to be leased, not sold; its price was fixed at $1.75 per acre, making the income, at six per cent., a little over $4,000 per annum, which is understood to be about the amount now realized.

This may be deemed, so far as the establishment there of a university is concerned, almost a failure. It is indeed an honor to have founded the first college west of the Alleghanies, as also to have given to the country Thomas Ewing as its first graduate; it is not only an honor to those who caused it, but an inestimable blessing to the whole country, that a precedent was then established by which a university might spring up in every new State of our Union, and it is this alone which places the importance of this first Congressional grant, for such a purpose, quite above our power of estimation. Almost a century has passed away, and nothing worthy of the name of a university has been realized on the spot first chosen for this enterprise ; perhaps nothing can be there accomplished, as the present tenants of the land really feel themselves about the same as its owners in fee simple. The very movers in the work, long ago discouraged, established a college at their beloved Marietta, and there is a plan now contemplated for transferring the fund to the State institution at Columbus.

Reasons for the failure of this first attempt of its kind are not wanting, without impeachment of the wisdom of the men connected with it. Human sagacity had not, as yet, anticipated that progress which should make $4,000 a year so utterly inadequate to support the institution, or $1.75 an acre an insignificant price for land. But more than this could not have been fixed as the capital, since settlers could obtain land in fee simple for even less, and would rather deem it a hardship that they and their posterity should pay interest perpetually on that amount, than consent that it should ever be appraised anew.*

The movement was half a century too early. Education is a luxury. It comes after bread in the struggle of life. Those in whom the desire is strongest and most earnest, will place it next to bread, and many will pursue it when the world would say that they had not yet secured a supply of their animal necessities ; it must nevertheless be ranked among the luxuries. The contest for the wants of the body

---

* Dr. Reid, now president of the University of Missouri, was once professor in this institution; occupied the best house in Athens, and paid on his property an annual tax of about fifty cents, which was supposed to represent the interest on this valuation, and no additional taxes could be levied on the property. This really makes the leases of these holders incalculably better than freeholds. More could not be charged without a revaluation. He claimed that such ought to have been made, and refused to stay in an institution which was condemned by its policy to remain perpetually stationary.

was a long and severe one in Ohio, and before it was generally decided, its severities had proved well-nigh fatal to
those higher aspirations with which the New England colony had set out in 1788.   A generation born in the wilderness, and knowing little beyond its toils and privations, had
succeeded the one which came fresh from their comfortable
homes in the East.   Toil had chilled their aspirations.

There was another large purchase, similar in most of its
provisions to that of the Ohio Company, and made nearly at
the same time, by John Cleves Symmes.   Symmes was one
of the territorial judges, and an able and upright man, but
he labored under difficulties greater than were naturally to
be anticipated, and which in the end proved too great for
him ; for, in addition to those which were common to the
whole West, were some which were peculiar to his purchase.

There was to have been a university also on the Symmes
purchase, and some have blamed him, doubtless unjustly,
for the failure.   His difficulties were insurmountable.   He
never had the whole amount of land which required him,
by the contract, to make the university reserve.   When it
came to making the location of the institution, there was
not one whole township remaining within his purchase ; it
was therefore located outside of his tract, to the west of the
Great Miami, at Oxford, Butler county.   Thus these two
universities, the earliest growth of Congressional legislation of this kind, established in the occidental Athens and
Oxford, failed to make their respective sites worthy of the
renowned names they bear ; they have, however, an importance in the history of American State universities much
beyond their rank as educational centers, and all who know
the facts will be glad to assign them that rank.

Imperfect surveys, and consequently bad titles ; sickness,
and all sorts of discouragements of settlers on his lands ;
desertions of their purchases, and removals from them,
with attempts to recover their money :—these extraordinary
trials which he had to encounter, and more still, the violent
outbreak and persevering prosecution of Indian hostilities,

affecting him in common with all others; these must be the apology for Symmes' failure. The tendency to a general movement of the whites westward alarmed the Indians, and made them feel that unless this were promptly and decisively arrested, they must inevitably, and soon, be driven from their present homes and hunting-grounds, and then successively from others, until the pale faces should overspread the whole continent. They acted under the impulse of this conviction. The settlers were driven to the protection of the forts; stragglers were picked up in great numbers by the ambuscades of small marauding parties; the attempts of the general government to put them down under General Harmer, in 1790, and Governor St. Clair, in 1791, having resulted in disastrous defeats, only emboldened them, and consequently checked immigration and crippled the settlements. For five years did the settlers live in one continued attempt to dodge the rifle-balls of the savages, and not till the year 1798 did the adult male white population of the whole Northwest, including the States of Ohio, Indiana, Illinois, Michigan, and Wisconsin, rise to the number of 5,000. And yet, during this period, the New England colonists persevered in keeping up some kind of schools, not unfrequently taught even by some man of liberal education,* in any room which could be obtained for the purpose. Here knowledge was pursued under difficulties, and only by the few; the great majority had too many other cares to do much in the way of mental improvement.

The British government, up to 1795, held certain military posts in the Northwest, and there were not wanting those who thought that they stirred up the Indians against the western settlers. The final victory of General Wayne on the Maumee, in August, 1794, occurred in sight of the garrison occupying one of these posts, and the correspondence between its commander and the American general showed at least what the latter thought of the influence of these

---

* *Vide* the Hildreth's Pioneer History.

English garrisons upon the savages. Jay's treaty of 1795 provided for the surrender of these military posts on the 1st of June, 1796. But this treaty contained provisions which were so distasteful to members of the House of Representatives, and to many throughout the country, that they came near taking action which would have virtually annulled it, and left the West exposed to the cruelties of an exterminating Indian warfare. At this crisis, Fisher Ames made, in committee of the whole, one of his most powerful speeches in support of the following resolution : "*Resolved*, That it is expedient to pass the laws necessary to carry into effect the treaty lately concluded between the United States and the king of Great Britain." The vote taken after the speech, in committee of the whole, was a tie, and the chairman decided the question in the affirmative, and the final vote in the House was nearly as close.

A few passages from this speech will indicate the state of things : "The refusal of the posts (inevitable, if we reject the treaty) is a measure too decisive in its nature to be neutral in its consequences. From great causes we are to look for great effects. A plain and obvious one will be, the price of western lands will fall ; settlers will not choose to fix their habitation on a field of battle. Those who talk so much of the interest of the United States should calculate how deeply it will be affected by rejecting the treaty ; how vast a tract of wild land will almost cease to be property. . . . No, sir, it will not be peace, but a sword ; it will be no better than a lure to draw victims within the reach of the tomahawk. On this theme my emotions are unutterable. If I could find words for them, if my powers have any proportion to my zeal, I would swell my voice to such a note of remonstrance, it should reach every log house beyond the mountains. I would say to the inhabitants, Wake from your false security ; the wounds yet unhealed are to be torn open again ; in the daytime your path through the woods will be ambushed ; the darkness of midnight will glitter with the blaze of your dwellings. You are a father—the blood of your sons shall fatten your cornfields.   You are a mother—the war-whoop shall wake the sleep of the cradle."   '

The treaty was just saved, and as its result and that of the treaty of Greenville, peace and thrift began, but progress was necessarily slow.   Roads were almost unknown. Marietta, Cincinnati, Detroit, Vincennes, Kaskaskia, and the few other small settlements scattered over this immense region, were each other's nearest neighbors, and there were no roads by which the inhabitants could conveniently reach each other.*

An account of the French settlers at the various points

---

* The late Judge Burnet, of Cincinnati, one of the most eminent of the earlier members of the bar of that place, in his "*Notes on the Northwest,*" has given us a series of graphic and really beautiful pictures of this life in its higher circles, if indeed higher and lower can be predicated of it, consisting largely of accounts of his journeys with members of the bar and bench over this vast territory.   They traveled on horseback, and the first requisite in a horse offered for sale at that day was that he be a good swimmer; for scarcely a road had been constructed or a bridge had been built.   Besides the saddle-bags, which each of the company must carry on his own horse, one horse must be used to carry common baggage, such especially as they might need in camping out for the night.   They sometimes swept away the snow to make their beds.   Panthers, attracted to their camping-places, came around and were kept at safe distance by the glare of their fires.   In one instance, a wild cat was ejected from a deserted hunter's cabin, that they might occupy it for a night.   Again, they would ride all night in order to escape the discomforts of lodging out, and in such cases they walked and lead their horses by turns, one at a time, as guides for the rest of the company.   The judge, while in one instance acting thus as guide, in attempting to go by a new path from Chillicothe to Marietta, suddenly stepped down a ledge of about three feet, in which step his more prudent horse declined to follow, and, on retreating, he perceived that there was an abrupt turn in the path, which he had failed to make.   A few days later, the company returned by day, and found that the next step would have sent him over a precipice of about fifty feet, where the tops of the trees growing from beneath but reached the level of the plain on which they had stood.   Again they enjoyed the hospitalities of the Indians, for this was all after the peace of 1795, and sometimes quite to surfeiting; for, on one occasion, the son of Governor St. Clair being of the company, an old squaw, who felt some effects of the fire-water, repeatedly kissed him, and showed him other attentions, calling him the "big man," quite reconciling the rest of the company to their lower rank, and inducing them to hasten on and travel all night, in preference to accepting the proffered hospitalities of the Indians.

of the West, with incidents showing the expedients which
they adopted to meet the emergencies of forest life, would
be interesting, but its connection with culture in the West
is scarcely intimate enough to justify its introduction into
the direct line of narrative.

A colony of these people established themselves on the
Ohio, near the Muskingum settlement, where they built
their little cabins, and hacked and dug, and sung and
danced, in contempt of fearful privations. They were relieved by government in 1795, by a grant of 24,000 acres,
and in 1798 by one of 12,000, and finally either scattered
to other French colonies, as Detroit,* Vincennes, and Kaskaskia, or, becoming acclimated and inured to labor, remained at their point of original settlement, where the
county still bears the name of Gallia, and the county-seat
that of Gallipolis, as a monument of this history.†

Without money, without any practical skill or knowledge
in forest life,‡ these artisans had been transferred from the

---

* Peter Desnoyers, one of the most prominent citizens of Detroit, once
marshal of the Territory of Michigan, and in 1839 state treasurer, was one
of the colony settled originally at Gallipolis.   •

† In 1790, Joel Barlow, distinguished as the author of the patriotic poem
entitled the "Vision of Columbus," circulated in Paris proposals for the
sale of lands in the West at five shillings per acre, "which promised," says
Volney, "a climate healthy and beautiful; scarcely such a thing as frost in
winter; a river called by way of eminence 'The Beautiful,' abounding in
fish of enormous size; magnificent forests of a tree from which sugar
flows, and a shrub which yields candles; venison in abundance, without
foxes, wolves, lions, or tigers; no taxes to pay; no military enrollments;
no quarters to find for soldiers." Purchasers became numerous; individuals and whole families disposed of their property, and in the course of
1791 some embarked at Havre, others at Bordeaux, Nantes, or Rochelle,
bearing title deeds to land. Five hundred settlers, among which were not
a few carvers and gilders to his majesty, coach-makers, friseurs and
peruke-makers, and other artisans and *artistes* equally well fitted for a
backwoods life, arrived in the United States in 1791-2; and acting without
concert, traveling without knowledge of the language, customs, or roads,
they at last managed to reach the spot designated for their residence, after
expending nearly or quite the whole proceeds of their sales in France.

‡ The following was their plan for getting rid of the great buttonwoods
on the Ohio: They collect what axes and hatchets they can for hacking
down the monster, and prepare to quicken its fall by tying ropes to the
branches for those to pull upon who are not occupied with the hacking.

capital of the world of fashion to the depths of an American wilderness, where many a problem quite new to them
presented itself for their solution.

These early settlers—Anglo-Americans, as well as foreigners, and especially the farming population—just lived,
and nothing more. This is sufficient to account for the
want of educational progress, even in those families which
had been well educated in the East; and when it is borne
in mind that this class of settlers had been diluted before a
school system was introduced with perhaps ten times their
bulk of people, of little or no education, it will be clear
that the leaven of learning worked as early and as well as
was possible under the circumstances. Their disadvantages
were great, compared with those of Michigan and Wisconsin of thirty to forty years later, whose settlers were not
indeed superior to these first Ohio colonists, but they began
their settlements at a time when development was too rapid
to allow the spirit of the first settlers to be extinguished in
the trials of pioneer life; while, on the contrary, in case of
the early New England colonists in Ohio, before they had
been able to crystallize their culture in schools, churches,
and other social forms, a new generation, which had been
born and had received its scanty training amid the hardships of these frontier settlements, had come upon the
stage.

Thus the tree is worried down. But there is a more difficult problem. It
can not be cut in pieces, nor removed whole. They therefore hack off the
limbs, dig a ditch the entire length of the trunk, and sink it. Other illustrations of their skill and originality could be given.

But the toils and trials of these people did not kill out their characteristic
light-heartedness. Twice a week, though no condition could have been
more forlorn than theirs, they came together, and they had not far to
come; for, instead of building in the scattered manner of the Americans, they had two rows of log cabins, about sixteen feet square, while at
one end was a larger room, to be used as a council-chamber and ball-room,
to dance off their cares and sorrows. Malaria and Indian warfare augmented the sadness of a condition quite sad enough without either. The
Indian scout, who lurked around and listened to music more strange to
him than it was even to the Yankee neighbor, reported to his fellows of
the forest that they should be attacked by the whites soon, for he had seen
them dancing the war dance.

The intelligent and educated labored long and hard to introduce into Ohio a school system, but with almost hopeless odds against them, growing out of the state of things pictured above. There is a touching anecdote in illustration of this remark. Hon. Ephraim Cutler,* who was one, of the colony, an account of which is given above, being a member of the Ohio Senate in 1824, stood by the side of Mr. Guilford when the vote upon a bill introduced by the latter providing for a free common school system was taken, and announced as passed, a result for which he had labored thirty-five years. He exclaimed aloud : "*Lord, now lettest thou thy servant depart in peace, according to thy word, for mine eyes have seen thy salvation.*" Tears filled many an eye in that chamber.

If we could, in imagination, lift ourselves to a position of observation above the scene of this great drama, so as to embrace a view of the whole stage from the Monongahela to the Mississippi, and a period of about sixty years, beginning with the establishment of the Moravian missions on the upper waters of the Muskingum, in 1770, we should combine the elements of a picture of wilderness life, which could seldom have been drawn without transcending the facts of real history. In the foreground stands the veteran Zeisberger, the ablest and the noblest of missionaries to American aborigines, with his coadjutor Heckewelder, and their swarthy band of disciples around them, their noble leader still peaceful and faithful at the end of a life of eighty-seven and a missionary service of sixty-two years. In this section of the picture is seen the martyrdom of ninety-two Moravian Indians at the hands of their white brethren, brought up under the influence of Christianity.† Then appears the noble band of New England colonists

---

* Mr. Sparks, in an article in the N. A. Review for July, 1838, gives the anecdote quite circumstantially, and applies it to Rev. *Manasseh* Cutler, the first agent of the colony, who never lived in Ohio, and had died one year before this occurrence. Ephraim Cutler was his son. See Walker's History of Athens County, Ohio, p. 393.

† Life of Zeisberger, by Schweinitz, 1871.

on the Muskingum, with the powerful train of influences which prepared their way before them, and followed after them. Here and there, over the whole stage, appear gathered companies of the Gallic race, mingling their gayety, like the orchestra, with the various scenes of the tragedy. A rush of all classes then passes before us, when apparent stillness and deep shadows begin to settle over the whole theater, ever and anon broken by voices of alarm and distress and the glare of burning huts. The savage warriors appear, their determined spirit driving successively two armies from the field, and then yielding to a third. Then gradually the shadows lift themselves; the light begins to shine upon the scene; the cornfields, the meadow lands, and finally the fruit orchards, with large barns, and here and there stately mansions, villages, and churches, begin to diversify the landscape. School-houses, small to the eye, large in significance, are seen; other evidences of advancement, in a work dear to the New England colonists, have been seen multiplying; and when the venerable Ephraim Cutler stands in the Senate chamber, in 1825, and, at the announcement of the result of the vote, explodes the profound emotions of his soul, which have been accumulating force during the progress of the drama toward this end, and we see the responsive tears glistening throughout that legislative chamber, we feel that we have passed the first important stage of this enterprise, and are assured of its further and rapid development and consummation.

The state of culture in the territory south of the Ohio is distinguishable from that on the north of that river, in several respects, and calls for a separate treatment. The chief differences, however, have been indicated in the account given above of education in the Atlantic States at the time when the westward movement began; but these differences developed into modified forms in the West.

Aside from the few French and Spanish settlements in the Southwest, the first organized colony within the limits of what is now a western State, was that on the Watauga river, in Eastern Tennessee. This State and Kentucky

did not differ greatly in the period, or character, of their
early settlements; nor did the grade of culture in the first
settlers of Alabama and Mississippi offer any so marked
variations from that of the States between them and the
Ohio as to require distinct notice in so general a view as
that sought to be presented in this work. The climate and
the peculiar agricultural productions of the more southerly
portions of this great region did indeed encourage larger
plantations and greater numbers of slaves, and so led to
some incidental modifications of social life and of culture;
but these are not such as to be material to the purpose of
this chapter, which is to describe in general terms the
elements which higher education had to work upon when
Congress began to make appropriations for it.

Daniel Boone, the great Kentucky pioneer, visited the
Watauga valley as early as 1760, where there stands on
Boone's creek, in sight of the stage road leading from
Jonesboro to Blountsville, a beech-tree, with this inscrip-
tion: " D. BOON CILLED A BAR ON TREE IN THE YEAR
1760." *

The six nations of the Iroquois claimed the ownership of
the land in Eastern Tennessee and Kentucky, and in the
treaty of Fort Stanwix (Utica, N. Y.), in 1768, conveyed
the same to the King of England. . This emboldened the
people in their disregard of the royal proclamation against
settlements west of the mountains. Emigration immediately
began from the adjacent parts of Virginia and North Carolina, caused largely by the oppressions which were then so
rapidly developing themselves in the mother country's treatment of her colonies, to the Watauga and Holston rivers.
These settlers, cut off from immediate relations with the
government of North Carolina, to which, though without at
first even knowing it, they belonged, formed a kind of government of their own, called the "Watauga Association."

---

* Ramsey's Annals of Tennessee. It is one hundred and fourteen years
since this inscription was made, and the tree is now covered with the names
of others who have felt ambitious of the honor of placing their names by
the side of Boone's.

The entrance to this region from Carolina was by the valley of the Watauga; from Virginia, by that of the Holston. The first permanent settlement was in 1768, and the organization was probably formed in 1769. This point was also the place of rendezvous for those who designed to pass the Cumberland Gap, and penetrate the depths of the wilderness beyond, whether on the north or south of that line, which afterward separated the States of Tennessee and Kentucky. The territory on one side of this line was the extension westward of North Carolina, and belonged to that State; while that on the other was, in like manner, a part of Virginia. On the breaking out of the Revolution, the people on the Watauga and vicinity applied for annexation to North Carolina, showing that they did not know that they were in that State. Their petition was received in August, 1776; but there is no record to show that it was acted upon. As this settlement did, however, send delegates to the provincial convention, which assembled at Halifax in the following November to form a State constitution for North Carolina, they must have been deemed entitled to representation as a part of that State. Be this, however, as it may, the people of both these territories felt dissatisfaction with the treatment which they severally received from the parent States, and acted as if scarcely conscious of obligations to any transmontane government, taking steps which were at least revolutionary in their tendencies, and prophetic of early independence. This independence was brought about finally, as will appear, by processes very unlike in the two instances.

The people of North Carolina's western territory felt that the mother State was without true maternal interest in them; and the latter felt, on the other hand, that the daughter was extravagant, and without due filial piety. In a fit of this feeling, the State legislature, in 1784, passed a hasty and ill-digested act, providing for the cession of her western territory to the confederate government, which act rather increased, than allayed, the irritation, because the people settled in these wilds, though quite willing that the cession should be made, perceived that the action had not been taken in good spirit, and that the terms were such that Congress would not accept them, and they would therefore be left in a kind of orphanage. This state of unrest, impatience, and turbulence continued for six years. During this period, three successive conventions were called with reference to the forming of a State government, and doubtless, as well in these conventions as in many a local meeting of these pioneers, there was a great expenditure of rhetorical and oratorical power, more Demosthenian in vigor and sense than in polish. But the constitution was formed, and the short-lived State then brought into being was called Franklin, or, as some have it, Frankland.

This history can be thrown together in few words, in a way to intimate the inharmonious course of things during the initial period of Tennessee's existence. Its government was by the Watauga Association from 1769 to 1777; thence to 1784, it was a part of North Carolina; from this time to 1788, it was the State of Franklin; thence again to 1790, it was a part of North Carolina, and then it was ceded to the United States, and subjected to a territorial government of the general character of that inaugurated two years earlier to the northwest of the Ohio, which was continued until 1796, when it was admitted into the Union. During this entire period, the government was doubtless supplemented by what was called "regulation," varying little from what we now call "Lynch law."

It was otherwise with Kentucky, the history of which as a dependency of Virginia ran by no means smoothly. At first, it was a proprietary government under Mr. Henderson, who pretended to have purchased one hundred miles square of the Cherokees, and was employing Boone and others for his purposes; and it was never ceded to Congress as a territory. The people carried on their own contests with the parent State and among themselves, having no direct relations with the general government until admitted as a State, in 1792.

Returning now to the time when the settlement of this

region began, we may take a brief survey of the elements
of culture then introduced into it, and observe how far they
flourished under fostering care, or died from neglect.

In no section south of the Delaware Bay, if indeed any
south of Long Island Sound, had an educational system
become so rooted and grounded before the Revolution as
to stand the shock of that period without suffering enduring
harm. A seven years' war set them back more than can
well be estimated. The pioneers of the Southwest had
very little of those elements which made up the emigrants of the New England Ohio Land Company. The
southern movement preceded, the northern followed, the
war; the southern had in it more of the roving disposition, which had not been disciplined to the love and labors
of a settled home. Many in both parts, but more south
than north of the Ohio, were not really so much in search
of new and fixed habitations, where they might develop the
highest improvements of which our race is capable, but
were really, though unconsciously, retreating before the
march of civilization and culture.

Daniel Boone, generally regarded as the leader of the
first company which settled in Kentucky, though Finley
had really preceded him and explored the way, probably
had no scholastic training. He was a native of Pennsylvania, but early removed to North Carolina. He could
doubtless read, but his inscription on the beech, as given
above, will show that he was quite unpracticed in the art
of writing, and his perpetual wanderings will satisfy us that
he could not have read much, even if he had once learned
to read, and that he felt so little the value of learning as to
be content to take his family beyond the advantages of
schools. He has indeed given the world a brief narrative,
which is executed in the beauty of simplicity, yet there can
be no doubt that some other hand was employed in giving
its final shape to this production.

The same may be said of James Robertson as of Daniel
Boone, and yet no name stands higher than his in the early
annals of Tennessee. And these are but typical men. As

to education, they were the rule; the better educated the
exceptions. They did not emigrate in order to secure
higher culture, nor did their companions or their successors
to any great extent. Those of them who had such desires
did not give them predominance over the grosser ones.
Indeed, emigration to the West put it out of their power to
promote higher education. The hopes of great advantages
from this removal were indeed high, but they were vague,
and were seldom set upon definite objects. They made no
adequate allowances, for the obstacles to be met. Cheap
lands and abundance of room were, with a restless desire
for wandering and change, the chief motives, and no definite estimate was made as to whether intellectual advantages would be greater or less. Those exceptional men,
who, in mental strength and understanding, tower above
the masses, will generally be more noticeable in an uneducated than in an educated community, and so we find it in
these Western States.

The hopes of emigrants to the West always proved more
or less fallacious. Their increased wealth was in land
merely, which was wealth only for the next, and, in some
instances, only for a still more remote generation. The
land was productive, but there was no market for the produce; the people were long too poor to construct roads,
and roads would not have made markets—they would only
have connected places in similar condition. Steamboats
did not come into use until about forty years after the settlement of Kentucky and Tennessee, and the market down
the Mississippi, from its various branches, by sailing vessels and rafts, was of little value, as produce must be carned
a second time in the labors and risks of transmission. The
people were therefore in no condition to make any great
progress, intellectual or otherwise, for want of ready money.
Travelers represent them as living mainly in their log
houses far into the present century; perhaps we may safely
say for an average of thirty years in case of those who removed west not later than the beginning of this century,
and this was long enough for them to lose all taste and de-

sire for mental improvement, and time would be required again for these to spring up.

This poverty, and its effects upon mental improvement, were greatly increased by sickness, from which settlers in new and uncultivated regions have scarcely ever been exempt. The people of every locality would deny the prevalence of sickness in their midst, and point to some neighboring place as thus afflicted; but, in truth, sickness was everywhere. Discouragement necessarily followed the hardships and privations of the western settlers. Homesickness was superadded. Everywhere was stagnant water, from which generations of vegetable growth, alternately covered and exposed, were ever sending forth their miasmatic poison into the atmosphere. The people not only breathed the malarious air of these pools, but drank their water. Bilious fevers and agues were the natural consequences. These the people knew not how to check, and were as often worn out by them in body and spirit as they were successful in rising above them. Men felt ashamed to return to their old homes; few could have done it without losing their property in the West, and having to begin anew in the East. They preferred to continue the contest, and bequeath it, or the triumph over it, to their children. Sometimes the one, and again the other, was the result. When any did return, they often found that their old neighbors had outstripped them in progress.

Nor have doubtful land titles been without an unwholesome influence upon the early prosperity, and of course the culture of the West. This has already been referred to in the case of the settlers on the Symmes Purchase in Ohio. The case was worse, because more extensive, in Kentucky. The Transylvania Company's tract is perhaps the most noted instance of this; but it is true in general that all the early land companies and all the squatting had a tendency to introduce confusion into surveys, and so into titles, and inflict upon the western pioneer some of his most tormenting trials. The instances of different deeds claiming the same land were by no means infrequent. These spread

apprehensions all around and greatly diminished the immigration into some sections. Men often found that they
did not own the land they had paid for.

The westward movement begins before the temperance
reformation. Bad water, home-sickness, all shades of discouragement, and those tedious and depressing fevers already mentioned, all sought their relief in the common use
of alcoholic drinks. The whisky made from fruits and
grains which had no market, was cheap and universally
used, and even the religious conscience of the day did
not forbid this use, unless carried to the evident disturbance of reason.

The intelligent travelers who visited these regions during
the periods embraced in this sketch, testify to the views
here presented. Michaux, who sketches his journey from
Philadelphia, by way of Lancaster, Pittsburg, Wheeling,
Marietta, Maysville, Lexington, Nashville, Knoxville,
Greenville, and Jonesborough into North Carolina, is one
of those who may be deemed worthy of special confidence.
He traveled partly on foot. until he reached Pittsburg;
thence down the Ohio to Maysville (then called Limestone)
in a skiff, and thence mostly on horseback. He shows not
the least disposition to improve his narrative by exaggera-
tions, but simply states what he saw. Being a foreigner,
things struck him as the same would not strike an American who saw them every day and regarded them as normal.
Michaux found the people, even in Western Pennsylvania,
still living in their log-houses, and to a great extent even
the villages were built of logs, and so throughout his
journey. After he reached the Ohio his lodging over
night was very generally in log-cabins of a single room,
where he slept on the floor. Bacon, venison, and corn or
wheat bread was the chief living. Of course the taverns
could furnish beds, but had seldom better tables. The
universal whisky-drinking and collecting of the people at
the taverns seem most to have struck him. In Wheeling
and Lexington he paid two dollars a week for the best board.
He says that the merchants of Lexington carry on nearly

all the commerce of the country, receiving their goods from Baltimore and Philadelphia in thirty-five to forty days, by wagons, at a cost of seven or eight dollars per hundred-weight for transportatiou. When it is remembered that this was twenty-eight years after Henderson began his Transylvania settlement, and more than thirty years after a government had been organized in Eastern Tennessee, and that previous to 1790 there had been as many as 20,000 new settlers yearly entering the country, it will be a little surprising to those who have observed the rate of progress only in more recent times, that such remained in 1802 the condition of things in these regions. Mr. Burnet makes the case almost as strong, if not fully so, in the Northwest, including Ohio, Indiana, and Illinois. In regard to the habits of drinking mentioned, he says that of the great number of lawyers who were his associates in those scenes which he narrates in his notes, he alone had escaped falling a prey to this universal habit.

In a historical sketch of culture like this, the power to draw a word-picture which shall aid the reader's imagination to take in the whole field at a glance, is the historian's highest and rarest gift, and is greatly to be coveted. In the absence of this, however, the reader must be content with the effort of humbler talents.

Taking the whole region west of the original thirteen States, or, in general, west of the Alleghanies, at about the year 1830, this picture will in the main be true to the facts; for, while in a few places improvement had reached a stage quite in advance of that here indicated, over the larger extent of the country there had been no such progress.

With no tools but axes and augers, and no material but forest trees, log huts were put up in the wilderness and furnished. These were the first dwellings of all pioneers. Some had indeed brought on articles of furniture; others had only what they had made. Bedsteads were constructed by boring holes in the logs to support the rails at three corners, while a crotched stick driven in the ground gave

4

support to the fourth. Floors they sometimes had, and
again none; these were at first made from puncheons split
and hewn from the bass-wood or tulip-tree. Blocks split
out, hewn smooth on one side, and furnished with legs,
served as chairs, and longer ones formed benches, uniting
the utility of several chairs in one. Tables were easily
constructed on the same general plan, and also shelves to
answer the purpose of a pantry, the puncheons being supported by pins driven in the logs. Pegs served to hang
articles of dress upon. A garret, reached by a ladder from
the corner of the room, combined all the purposes of store,
lumber, and sleeping rooms.

Cooking utensils of cast-iron had indeed been brought
on to some extent as prime necessities; but many domestic
utensils now deemed necessary, were either not used at all,
or were made of wood. Tin cups, as drinking-vessels,
were a luxury which many could not afford. All articles
which could be hollowed out or coopered, were easily made,
and abounded. A wash-bowl was dug out in the top of a
stump, near the door.

The backwoodsman had his pocket-knife and his hunting-
knife, which must do service at the table; and as the knives
were less in number than the persons in a family, they must
be used in turn, while metallic forks were not ranked
among the necessary articles of table furniture.

The wardrobe was simple. Flax and wool, grown on
the farm, and spun, woven, and made up in the house, produced a uniformity of material, and of cut, fit, and finish
unknown in recent times. Shoes were by no means general, or even common. The women, at least, went about
their work without them. When they wore them, they
were the low-quartered, heavy cowhide shoes, and in summer these were worn without stockings. Moccasins of
dressed deer-skin were much in use; and the so-called
moccasin awl, made of the back-spring of a pocket-knife,
was attached to every hunting-bag.

Gala days, and especially weddings, were occasions of
great display, which, of course, must consist in something

else than finery in dress and equipage and costly entertainments. Let the reader fancy to himself a party assembled
for such an occasion a hundred miles from any merchant,
milliner, dressmaker, shoemaker, blacksmith, or saddler.
The ladies are in their linsey gowns; the men in their
hunting-shirts, breeches, and leggins of the same fabric.
If there are buttons, rings, or ruffles, they are relics in the
family, and are not in harmony with other articles worn.
The horses are unshod, saddles and bridles extemporized;
and yet all, both men and women, are mounted and proceeding from the house of the bridegroom to that of the
bride, which latter they must reach for dinner at twelve
o'clock. When within about a mile of the place, two
young men are selected for a race to bring the bottle, which
the successful one bears and offers to each of the company.
Their way is often beset with ambuscades, either friendly
or hostile; trees are felled across it, grape-vines wreathed
over it, and guns discharged to frighten horses. If ladies'
wrists are sprained, or even worse disasters occur, a hand-
kerchief is bound over the wound, and the matter lightly
treated. Dancing and drinking occupy the afternoon and
night, except with those who are disabled and borne from
the field.

Two days' work of the men build a house for the young
couple, after the model given above, and a new family
starts on the same scale as that of the parents.

Such was the extreme destitution of all means and facilities of commerce. Money was little used, and came to be
little needed, as people then lived. The States earliest
settled were longest in acquiring a commercial character.
They became inured to live almost without commerce.
There were indeed some schools, but they scarcely carried
the people far enough to give them a relish for further
study. A few wealthy planters, though these were not
numerous among the early settlers of Tennessee and Kentucky, could have their private schools, or send their sons
and daughters away for education; but the body of the
people had no basis in their culture, or in their financial

standing, for education, and before such condition could be attained, the funds which Congress had provided became permanently crippled in their power; for people, among whom the educated, and those who understood the management of educational funds, were so few, could not, if ever so well disposed, take care of these and apply them to their uses. We should rather wonder that anything had been effected, than that no more had been done. Land was deemed worth little, when all could have what they needed; nor was there any immediate prospect of a market which should make the school grants available for founding and supporting schools.

It was very early thought by some, whether correctly or not, that this frontier life tended to degrade civilization and lead back toward barbarism. The question was discussed in Washington's administration, whether emigration ought for this reason to be encouraged. Hildreth,* in treating the subject of the public land sales, as discussed in Congress in 1796, says: " A certain number of the members from the older and more settled States were very doubtful as to the policy of extraordinary encouragement to emigration, tending as it did to increase the backwoods population, rude, unsocial, and discontented, whose insubordination and violence and threats of secession had already occasioned so much trouble, expense, and anxiety."

This view must be admitted to be correct, and at the time here referred to, the tendency had but just begun to be developed; but this statement must be made, not as a reproach to Western settlers, but as showing the necessary result of the privations and perils of pioneer life.

The religious sentiments of these western communities had indeed been largely developed, and had attained in some places and periods to great power. Religion and education have in all ages gone hand in hand, but in these days, whatever a few learned clergymen may have thought and felt, or a few learned men in any other profession,

---

* History of the United States, 2d series, Vol. I, p. 625.

there was wanting any such culture as to be in sympathy with higher education, nor was there then the necessary commercial power; there was no money. Efforts were indeed made, early and praiseworthy, at founding institutions. In 1785, in the first legislature of the State of Franklin (Tennessee), there was preliminary provision made for a university, in an act passed for the promotion of learning, and Martin Academy sprung from it. This was started by Rev. Samuel Doak, who graduated at Nassau Hall in the days of Dr. Witherspoon. The school was kept in a log house on his own farm, and near the present site of Washington College, in the neighborhood of Jonesborough, in East Tennessee, In case of Kentucky, it is also found that the parent State was not altogether without thoughtfulness in regard to higher education in her western territory; for, in the year 1780, the legislature of Virginia enacted " that 8,000 acres of land within the county of Kentucky, late the property of British subjects (viz: Messrs. McEnzie, Collins, and McKee), should be vested in trustees, as a free donation from the Commonwealth, for the purpose of a public school or seminary of learning, to be erected in said county, as soon as its circumstances and the state of its funds should permit." Whether this grant laid the foundation of the present University of Transylvania, at Lexington, we have at hand no means of ascertaining. But the difficulties of backwoods life led to decline rather than progress after this date.

Many French and Spanish settlements had early been scattered along the Mississippi and its branches, in anticipation of the arrival of the Anglo-Americans, who by degrees settled down by their side. Illustrative instances of this were found on the Red and Arkansas rivers, in what is now the State of Arkansas, about 1820, where the distance asunder of the settlers was still such that combined with their almost total want of any aspirations after mental improvement, or anything higher than a life without labor or care, left them to pursue nothing but hunting and fishing, trade with the Indians, and the rudest beginnings of agriculture. Deterioration, where there was any room for it, was for a long time the rule, to which the exceptions were not numerous. Louisiana was still more preoccupied by the French, with too little admixture of Anglo-Americans to supply an effective leaven. Alabama and Mississippi, both originally belonging to Georgia, had similar foreign elements, while Florida had a still larger and longer continued prevalence of these; in the latter there being more Spaniards than French, while in the others there were more of the latter. Shades of difference there were in the various parts of this extensive western country, the highest intelligence being in Ohio; but the same general facts were true. Land bore too low a price to make that appropriated by Congress for higher education of much value for that purpose, even if the funds could have been well administered; much less could they be made available to this end in the hands of men without the needed experience, and especially, as was everywhere true of the great majority which must rule the more intelligent few when the former were without sufficient intelligence to form a basis for experience.

In looking over this whole field, it will appear that in no one of the States to which reference has been made, have there been any such resources of intellect, culture, and material progress as could be reasonably expected to bring forth a respectable university from a Congressional land-grant made for the purpose. The brief general explanation is that the problem was in all these instances too hard a one to be given for solution to communities of their stage of advancement. It was offered them from forty to seventy years before they had attained to such grade of mental and material progress as to be able to solve it. In more appropriate words, they had needed the benefits of universities for all these years in order to prepare them to found and manage such.

During the early part of this period, aside from the depressing effects of pioneer life upon education and culture, there were embarrassing difficulties growing out of the unsettled state of government, both state and national. The powers of government were not settled. What belonged to the town meeting, what to a convention called by some political leaders in the community, what to the state, and what to the general government, seems to have been a question upon which the minds of the people were not clear. Washington's entire administration was disquieted in this way. The whisky insurrection is as good an illustrative instance as can be chosen, for the double reason that it shows the loose views entertained of the powers of the government, and because the outbreak in this particular question points to that pernicious habit of drinking which everywhere prevailed. The seat of this movement was in Western Pennsylvania, but it extended east of the mountains also, and into the neighboring States of Maryland, Virginia, Ohio, and Kentucky, and numbered in the organized opposition to the excise law a future Vice-President of the United States—Albert Gallatin—with not a few men of prominence, and with no small sympathy from such men as Jefferson, the great founder of American democracy. The violent agitation in regard to Jay's treaty, and the relations of our country with the French Republic, furnish other appropriate illustrations of this unsettled state of things.

The people have been found mostly with simply their land and what they grew upon it, with almost no market for their produce—grain stacks standing unthreshed for years; people living in their log huts and running barefoot, even sometimes in the villages, much more in the country; discouraged, sickly, disappointed in their hopes, without any element among them sufficiently numerous and vigorous to lead them in the path of intellectual progress. We have found this state of things extending in some instances half a century, into the period since Congressional grants for education were made.

Though the French and Spanish settlers of the West and Southwest form a relatively small element in the civil-

ization of these regions, they were not altogether without
their influence, and others of them, as well as those of Detroit, which is reserved for another place, ought perhaps
to have had a passing reference. The general facts, however, which shall be given of the French settlements of
Michigan, may be deemed true of all those north of the
Ohio. The chief of these were at Kaskaskia, on the Mississippi, and Vincennes, on the Wabash. These were settled from the North, and intercourse between them and the
French settlers on the lakes was frequent, and their habits
were doubtless much the same.

The French and Spaniards who settled south of the
Ohio, including those on the Gulf of Mexico and those on
the Mississippi, entered the country through the gulf.
Of these colonies, New Orleans is the chief of those of
French origin, and the mother of most of them. Only
this can be said to have produced a permanent result upon
the civilization of the country around it. It has perpetuated the language and manners and customs of the French
people, while even Detroit has now almost lost them, so
far as any influence upon the character of polite society is
concerned. French gayety in New Orleans probably did
not vary from that which existed in Detroit, further than
the very different climatic influences, and the presence of
the colored race, and constant intercourse with the mother
country, would naturally cause.*

In this chapter, indeed, little has been said of universities, or schools of any other grade; the search has been
for the elements from which they might spring, the soils in
which they might flourish. Neither have been found favorable in the period to which the inquiry has been confined.

---

* Besides the references already distinctly made, it will be sufficient to
add that the following works have been chiefly consulted in the preparation of this chapter, viz: Ramsey's Annals of Tennessee, Burnet's Notes
on the Early Settlement of the Northwestern Territory, Nuttall's Travels
in Arkansas, Albach's Annals of the West, and all the volumes of the
Ohio Valley Series.

Failure has been found attending the honest and praiseworthy efforts made under the first Congressional grants—
those in Ohio.   We now pass to a review of the history of
these grants themselves.

CHAPTER III.

Congressional Land Grants for Universities,

How the general government of the United States became possessed of its immense territory, including the right of both soil and jurisdiction, and the several subordinate questions connected with the use of this territory, offer matter of profoundest interest to the historical inquirer. It is well known that the original charters of the several colonies which established themselves upon our eastern coast formed their title-deeds to the lands described in them. All that these charters claimed belonged to them. But these were made out when the geography of the country was little known, and were therefore difficult of interpretation, and quite irreconcilable with each other. Different charters seemed to convey the same lands to different companies. Some of them were fortified by claims founded upon conquest and some kind of occupation; but still these claims were of so doubtful a nature that any persistent effort to extend jurisdiction over much of this territory, or to convey the lands to purchasers, would have led to long and perhaps armed contests. Nor is it unworthy of mention, that States having no claim to lands beyond their immediate and admitted jurisdictions, and having nevertheless borne an equal part in the war of independence, deemed these claims of others as carrying with them unjust advantages; and it is even said that some of the States entertained thoughts of seizing their respective shares. The State of Maryland will furnish an example. She for some time withheld her assent to the articles of confederation on account of the disadvantages of States having no lands outside of their own limits, as compared with those which laid claim to such, representing that Virginia, in case her right to the lands she claimed were admitted, could, by their sale, pay the expenses of her government without taxing her people, and thus draw away the best of the population from those neighboring States which had no such resources, and maintaining also that Virginia's claim to these extensive possessions was without any good foundation.

The disputes between Pennsylvania and Connecticut had become so serious that as early as July, 1775, they were laid before Congress. These, too, related to land claims, and doubtless in many ways coming evils of this kind had begun to be foreshadowed.[*]

Here were evidently the elements of endless conflicts between the several States, and perhaps between each of them and the general government, whatever form it might in the end assume, and it was important to make early provision against these impending strifes.

It was not, however, on the doubtful validity of these charters, nor on the ground of any title which Congress ever claimed to these lands, that their cession was urged. The reasons brought forward were of quite another kind. Our weak and imperfect government, in carrying on the war, had found the provisions for the common expenditures very inadequate, not only for the increase of the forces, but for paying those already in the field.

As early as April 29, 1778, Congress[†] made definite proposals to such foreign officers and soldiers as might be disposed to enlist in the service of the colonies, among the terms of which was the offer of lands, and as Congress had no lands of its own, it was, by resolution, " recommended to the several States having vacant lands, to lay off, with as much expedition as possible, a sufficient quantity of such lands to answer the purposes expressed in an address which had been sent out, and for these lands no charge was to be made against the United States."

---

* Secret Journal of Congress, Domestic Affairs, Vol. I., p. 24.
† Id., pp. 70–74.

Action of this kind was followed, in 1780, * by a distinct proposition to the States to cede a portion of their vacant lands to the general government, and the payment of the public debt and the further prosecution of the war were understood to be the purpose in view ; nor is there any evidence that the Congress of the Confederation, while it foresaw and deplored the evils likely to grow out of the existing claims of some of the States, ever itself claimed the ownership of any part of the soil, or any governmental jurisdiction over any of its population, except as should be arranged by treaty with the States owning these lands and acting as independent powers in conveying them.   The cessions were urged in order to provide for common wants, though the arguments were doubtless enforced by apprehensions of internal troubles.   It is also intimated that special terms of favor were stipulated to the future population of the territory which should be ceded, which terms related to education, morality, and religion.

The territory lying north of the Ohio and east of the Mississippi river was the first and the princpial tract contemplated in the proposed conveyances.   This was mostly claimed by Virginia, whose claim rested partly upon her charter, indeed, but more upon conquest and occupation. The facts connected with the claim as a conquest are of transcendent interest, bringing before our minds, as they do, one of those instances which often surprise us in history by showing the narrowness of the chances of incalculable losses and gains.

In January, 1778, Lieutenant-Colonel George Rogers Clark † received a commission from Patrick Henry, as Governor of Virginia, with reference to the occupation of the country northwest of the Ohio, which he in a most marvelous manner accomplished by taking Kaskaskia and other posts on the Mississippi, and Vincennes on the Wa-

---

* American State Papers, Public Lands, Vol. I., p. 96.
† Colonel Clark himself wrote an account of this expedition, which has been published by Robert Clarke & Co., Cincinnati, 1869, and is a most interesting fragment of Northwestern history.

bash, carrying with them the whole Northwest. This region was erected by Virginia into a county named Illinois, embracing all the chartered limits of Virginia to the northwest of the Ohio. The British Commissioners at Paris insisted on the Ohio river as their boundary, and the Count de Vergennes favored this claim, but the continued occupation by General Clark's forces decided the question in our favor, and made this whole region a part of the United States. This conquest can not, however, be deemed to add much support to Virginia's claim, as that colony merely authorized the expedition, without furnishing its men and supplies. In any case, however, the title to this region would not have been deemed perfect without cessions also from New York, Massachusetts, and Connecticut. The last-named State made indeed an early offer, and perhaps the earliest one, to convey to the general government her title to western lands, but it was on terms not acceptable to the latter, and no transfer was ever made until in 1786, and it was not fully completed until 1800. In the former year, this territory, with the exception of a tract extending 120 miles west of the Pennsylvania line, and from the parallel of the 41st degree of north latitude to Lake Erie, was conveyed to the Confederation. On the excepted portion the State of Connecticut established an office for the sale of these lands, and from this State all buyers derived their titles. The government was also administered by Connecticut, and although this became a great inconvenience to the people after Congress established a government in the Northwest, yet they could not do otherwise than submit to it and refuse submission to the government established by Congress, without endangering the titles to their lands. Under the pressure of these difficulties Connecticut ended her jurisdiction, and Congress accepted it, in 1800.

Virginia made her offer of cession in 1781, which was accepted by Congress in 1783, and New York and Massachusetts readily yielded their claims. Thus the title of the United States to the Northwestern Territory, mostly derived from the State of Virginia, was complete, though the rights of Connecticut were not fully ceded until 1800, as already stated. Virginia had, indeed, in order to complete the provision of bounty lands for her Revolutionary soldiers, reserved about 3,500,000 acres between the Miami and Scioto rivers in Ohio, but without right of jurisdiction, and Connecticut had reserved the quantity indicated above, and sold it for the support of her common schools.

In 1790 the contract was completed between the General Government and the State of North Carolina, by which the sovereignty and soil of Tennessee were transferred to the United States, except—and this was true in all other ' cases—the actual previous grants and sales made by North Carolina were to be held as valid. In this contract it was made a special condition that this was to be accepted toward the payment of North Carolina's part of the public debt, according to the usual proportion of the States. This will further show the ruling purpose of the cession, and both this and the case of Connecticut will show the freedom of the States in their negotiations.

Kentucky was a part of Virginia until 1790, and in 1792 was admitted into the Union on equal terms with the original States, without any previous transfer of the right of jurisdiction, and of course without vesting any right of soil in the United States.

Georgia having previously made an unacceptable offer, ceded in 1802 the whole of what now forms the States of Alabama and Mississippi, except a small portion which was obtained by the purchase of Louisiana, both as to soil and jurisdiction, to the general government of the United States; yet, in view of certain expenses which had been incurred, perhaps in the extinguishing of the Indian titles, the State was to receive from the first sales of these lands the sum of $1,250,000. As our government inherited from the State of Georgia some remains of one of the most momentous and exciting agitations which ever afflicted the earlier stages of our development, it is quite in place to refer to this here, and especially as it relates to the subject now under consideration.

About the year 1788, a company calling itself " *The Combined Society*," its members sworn to secrecy, was formed for the purpose of speculating in Georgia lands. As they could not well labor for their end and still keep their secret, this escaped and defeat ensued. This, however, stirred up cupidity in all directions. Other companies were formed. In November, 1789, three such, called respectively the South Carolina, the Virginia and the Tennessee Yazoo Companies—the second of which was headed by Patrick Henry—applied to the legislature of Georgia for grants of land. To these, a Georgia company was afterward added. Such was the persuasive force of the considerations offered by the petitioners that all other business was set aside, and in a few days a bill was rushed through, which disposed of 20,000,000 acres of land, included in the present States of Alabama and Mississippi, for $207,000, or slightly over one cent an acre, the Georgia company alone failing of a share in the purchase.

But these companies did nor meet the requirements of the law, and so did not secure the benefits of their contracts, though suits in equity were instituted in order to compel the State to confirm its grants.

In 1794, the attempt was renewed in the legislature. The several companies which applied, were the "Georgia Company," the "Georgia Mississippi Company," the "Tennessee Company," the "Virginia Yazoo Company," and the "Georgia Union Company," with General Twiggs at its head, which alone applied for about 23,000,000 acres, for which they offered $500,000. Though this was the best offer made, it was thrown out, and the sale made only to the other four companies. But the governor—Matthews—vetoed the bill; though being waited upon by a committee, he was persuaded to sign it in a modified form, the result of which was to sell to four companies 35,000,000 acres for $500,000.

Details, which could be obtained even to surfeiting,. would be out of place here. Let it suffice to add, that of the senators in Congress—James Gunn and James Jackson —the former remained in Georgia laboring to aid the specu- lators, so that he did not take his seat in the Senate until four days before the term of the Congress legally expired. The other senator was in his place, proof against specu- lators, bribes, and arguments. Georgia was surging with excitement; the neighboring States which furnished the purchasers sympathized deeply in it, and the whole country felt it. Mr. Jackson resigned his seat in the Sen- ate of the United States in order to accept one in the legis- lature of Georgia, and lead an attempt to wipe out the stain which his State had received from this act. The problem was not easy; the money had been paid over. But Mr. Jackson, the head of the committee before which the matter came, produced such evidence of fraud as to bring both Houses to the almost unanimous conviction that the contract should be deemed null and void from the be- ginning. The so-called rescinding act passed the House by a vote of 44 to 3, and the Senate by one of 14 to 4. A resolution purged the records of all traces of the act of 1795. All that could be separated from other records was torn out and solemnly burnt in front of the State-house door, the members of both Houses forming a ring around the place; and it is even reported that some were unwilling that common fire should kindle the flame, and so used a sun-glass to call fire down from Heaven.

But the roar of the receding storm, with its echoes and re-echoes, was scarcely less than had prevailed during the legislative action. It soon became indeed less violent, but was more widely spread. The purchasers had claims which they continued in various ways to urge until the State conveyed her lands, and with them this contest, to Congress, where, for a generation afterward, the agitation was kept up.

The title to the territory of Florida having been several times changed, became vested finally in the United States

by a treaty of purchase made with Spain and ratified in
1821, which completed our ownership of all the unoccu-
pied lands to the east of the Mississippi, within the limits
of any organized State government, and not yet formed
into States.

This work of cession once begun, though no constraint
beyond the pressure of the public conscience, was ever used,
furnished a pledge that it would be completed, if it did not
indeed create a necessity for its completion ; and this was a
happy solution of giant evils, which had, previously to the
close of the war, begun to cast their shadows before them,
and threatened to develop themselves into uncontrollable
dimensions. It might perhaps be shown, if this were the
place for it, that this one simple measure, introduced apparently for a minor purpose, and one which it did little
toward accomplishing, stands foremost among those influences which have elevated the central government to its
present high position. Centralization, as we now have it,
would have been impossible without some measure of this
kind.

No State of the Union, though several of their original
charters claimed to the Pacific, has ever set up any claim
to lands lying west of the Father of Waters. The treaty
of 1763 between France and England had made that river
the line between their North American claims. A region
extending from the Spanish possessions on the south to
the British on the north, and from the western bank of the
Great River indefinitely toward the setting sun, bearing the
name of the Louisiana Territory, and belonging still to
France, was purchased by President Jefferson of the con-
sular government in 1803. Whether by right of this indefinite purchase, or by that of subsequent explorations
and discoveries, such as those of Lewis and Clarke, the right
of the soil, so far as no earlier titles existed, and of jurisdiction, was finally established to the United States over
their present extent of territory, except the later acquisitions of Texas, New Mexico, and California. Of these,
the first having acquired independence, became, by its own

5

act of treaty in 1844, a member of the Union ; while the
other two became such in 1847-8, by treaties with Mexico.

Returning to a point of time near the completion of the
first of these cessions, we find that the first great instal-
ment of this territory was but fairly in the hands of the
Federal Congress, when they began to provide for its government.   This provision appears in the ordinance of 1787,
in which it is declared that "religion, morality, and
knowledge, being necessary to good government and the
happiness of mankind, schools and the means of education shall forever be encouraged."   This ordinance was
passed on the 13th of July, 1787, and on the 27th of the
same month, Congress provided for the sale of 2,000,000
acres of land in southeastern Ohio to the New England
Ohio Company, at one dollar per acre—one-third of which
price was to be remitted as an allowance for bad lands,
and reservations, of which there were the following :

Two entire townships of good land for the purposes of a
university.

The lot No. 16 in every township, or fractional part of a
township, to be given perpetually for the maintenance of
schools within said townships.

The lot No. 29 in every township, or fractional part of a
township, to be given perpetually for the purposes of religion.   .

The lots Nos. 8, 11, and 26, in each township, or fractional part of a township, to be reserved for the future disposition of Congress.

Such provision was the more easily obtained from the
general readiness which existed in all the colonies to appropriate lands to educational uses.

In pursuance of the policy indicated in the grant to the
Ohio Company, in 1794 a patent was issued to John Cleves
Symmes for 248,000 acres between the Great and Little
Miami rivers.   The contract embraced the same amount
as that with the Ohio Company as above, and in it was
reserved one entire township for the establishment of an
academy or seminary of learning.

Thus was the first precedent of this kind established in the true spirit of the ordinance of 1787, by setting apart a portion of the public lands for the perpetual mental and moral improvement of the people who were to occupy these lands. Other grants followed, so that before 1821, they had been made to Louisiana, Indiana, Illinois, Michigan, Mississippi, and Alabama. Moreover, the State of Tennessee received, in 1806, a special donation of 200,000 acres for the endowment of two colleges in the State and an academy in each county; and Connecticut received, in 1819, an entire township for the education of the deaf and dumb. It has since become the policy of Congress to make grants to all the new States, and this has been done with such uniformity that particulars need not be given.

A question had been fermenting in the public mind, which came to open agitation in Congress as early as December, 1818, when a proposition was made to appropriate 100,000 acres of land to each State, the number then being twenty-three, for the endowment of a university. There are no traces of any petitions to this end; but the subject was referred to the committee on public lands, and an adverse report was brought in, which admitted, indeed, that it might be well for Congress to endow a *national* university, but claimed that so far as the States were concerned, they should furnish such endowments for themselves. It claimed also that even should it appear that Congress ought to provide for State universities, the method proposed was the most objectionable one of doing this, as it would put it in the power of these great corporations to impede the progress of settlement in the States where their grants were located, and diminish the value of adjacent lands. The report also objected to grants or sales of large tracts, either to individuals or corporations. Two years later, in 1821, a resolution was introduced into Congress calling for inquiry into the expediency of granting to the old States lands corresponding in quantity with those granted to the new States and Territories for educational purposes. The report which this called forth took the ground that, as

these proposed grants would have to be located in the new
States and Territories where alone Congress owned lands,
and this would impose upon them a great burden in the
form of tracts of land exempt from taxation, and controlled
as to their settlement by distant corporations, it would be
unjust. It claimed further, that the grants made in the
West were rather sales than donations, since their freedom from taxes was a kind of equivalent for their value.
The committee—Mr. Thomas, of New York—does, however, suggest that it would be just to grant for educational
purposes a certain per centum, and to each according to
its population, to those States which had as yet received
nothing. During the same session there was a movement,
led by the State of Maryland, to call for grants to the
older States substantially equal to those which the newer
ones had received. This was claimed, not as a favor, but
as a right. The Maryland memorial contains the whole
history of the public lands so far as concerns the rights of
the several States to them. It was sent to the other States
interested, and nearly all of them forwarded similar claims,
and made the pressure upon Congress very heavy.*

This question was discussed again in 1829, on a bill for
the appropriation of lands for schools in some new States.
Mr. Branch, of North Carolina, afterward Secretary of
the Navy, claimed that these grants were pure donations,
and that the old States should, in regard to them, be made
equal with the new. Mr. Hendricks, of Indiana, and Mr.
Benton, of Missouri, maintained, as was done in the debate of 1821, referred to above, that these were not donations, but that they were a part of the compacts by which
the new States were received into the Union, which compacts they claimed were really to the prejudice of the new
rather than the old States; and Mr. Benton added, that
" if the senator from North Caro ina had in his own State
vacant lands and wished to appropriate them to the purposes of education, he would not object; but he did ob-

---

* See Appendix A.

ject to an appropriation within the limits of the State which he had the honor to represent for those purposes in North Carolina."* Here is stated, probably, the principle upon which Congress has acted. No lands were appropriated to schools in Kentucky, although a new State, because Congress never owned lands in Kentucky.

The question suggested above has, indeed, never been settled. An extreme view of the rights of the older States is taken in an article in the New Englander for August, 1854, from which the following is extracted:

" Of late the Western States claim the entire right to these lands, and the Eastern States, partners in the firm of States, and originally constituting the entire firm, are smiled at for their superannuated simplicity, when they assert that these lands belong to the United States, and not to the West alone. . . . . This treatment of the old thirteen States is neither just nor honorable."

The action of Congress does not sustain this charge, since it has been taken by an immense preponderance of members from the old States. This view attributed to the western people is seldom heard in the West, though it might be supported by good reasons, and certainly the facts of history will hardly support the doctrine taught by the New Englander.

The old thirteen States owned the soil within their chartered limits. This they doubtless sold to private persons, and applied the proceeds to the payment of the public indebtedness, or established funds, the incomes of which might support educational or religious institutions, or at least, the lands being their own, they could have used them for these or any other purposes, according to their respective wishes. Nor is this a mere theory unsupported by facts. Trumbull, in the appendix to his history of Connecticut,† states the fact in regard to the support of schools in that State as follows : " For the support of these schools the legislature

---

* Benton's Abridgment of the Debates, etc., Vol. X., pp. 238, 239.
† Vol. II., p. 547.

have appropriated very ample funds : One from new lands,
sold by the then colony many years since—the other from
lands in New Connecticut.   These lands, called the Western Reserve, sold for $1,200,000."

The same has been done by other States, as shown in a
previous chapter ; perhaps most largely by Georgia, which
did, indeed, establish academies throughout the State.
Connecticut—whence comes this charge of unjust and dis-
honorable claims on the part of the West—after using up
for her own purposes all her lands at home, created a fund
for the perpetual support of her common schools by the
sale of those she held in the Northwestern Territory.   The
unbiased mind, in view of our entire history in this respect, will therefore scarcely claim that the old States
should share *equally* with the new ones of the West in the
proceeds of the sales of the lands within the limits of those
new States themselves.   Indeed, it would not seem to be a
deviation from the analogy of the old thirteen States, if
the general government should appropriate to the improvement of each new Territory destined to become a State, all
the lands within its limits, less the amount necessary to
pay the expenses of the territorial government and those
of the original acquisition.   But the history of our country
shows many instances, doubtless, of inequality, not to say
injustice, in the legislative and administrative distribution
to its various sections and States, both of burdens and favors.   We can not read a chapter of American history, or
indeed of any other, without meeting such.   It can never be
otherwise.   It is, however, neither wise nor magnanimous to
call up too minutely these old scores from this distant past, to
be used in detail in order to affect future legislation.   We are
in great danger of erring, in any attempt to institute historical inquiries with the hope of finding a rule of exact
and rigid justice for such cases.   Connecticut acted wisely in
securing a school fund from her western lands, as did also Virginia in providing bounties for her Revolutionary soldiers,
and Georgia in obtaining in the same way more than a
million of dollars in money ; nor should we plead that any

one of these States acted unjustly or dishonorably in making their terms of cession, or urge upon Congress, in any future distribution of public lands, to be very much affected by these ancient or by any more recent differences. Such could indeed be found large and numerous, but they could never be adjusted. While there is much feeling against giving these lands to wealthy corporations, there would be a wide-spread gratification in seeing them all and rapidly given away to create funds for the permanent progress of civilization and improvement—more freely, to be sure, for the use of States or future States in which they are situated, but not to be limited to them. Ohio and Tennessee, for instance, received their grants when there were no precedents for their use, and they have proved of little value. Who would object to other gifts to these States? There may be other such. Michigan, and some of the newer States, have used theirs well. Who would object to their receiving a reward for their fidelity from the general government?

No one can hold the scales so as to weigh out minute and absolute justice to all the States and Territories in this matter. This, in taking our whole history from the beginning, would be quite impossible. It can only be approximated.

Dropping here this general view of Congressional grants for education, the grants for Michigan claim attention.

Congress, by an act making provision for the disposal of the public lands in the Indiana Territory, and for other purposes, approved March 26, 1804, appropriated an entire township of land to each of the three divisions of that Territory in which the several land-offices were then established. In the following year, one of these was organized into the Territory of Michigan, which, of course, became entitled to the grant. By the treaty of Fort Meigs, concluded with the Indian tribes of the Northwest, September 29, 1817, by Governor Cass, on part of the government, there were reserved six sections of land—one-half to go to the "College of Detroit," the other to St. Anne's Catholic Church in that city.

To those who have felt the beneficent influence of these grants, it will be a matter of profound interest, as preliminary to an account of educational grants for Michigan, to learn of an escape from the toils of corrupt land speculators, which occurred in the year 1796. · The attempt at corruption was made by Messrs. Robert Randall and Charles Whitney, in 1795–6, their purpose being the purchase, at about two and one-half cents per acre, of the entire southern peninsula of Michigan, they themselves taking the responsibility of securing the extinction of the Indian title to these lands. These men, and especially Randall, made corrupt approaches to members of Congress, offering to the latter their share of the plunder. But on the 6th of January, 1796, the House resolved—78 to 18—that Robert Randall had been guilty of a contempt and breach of the privileges of the House by attempting to corrupt the integrity of its members, and should be called to the bar, reprimanded by the speaker, and recommitted to custody until further orders from the House. Whitney was discharged; not because he was innocent, but because he was either less guilty or less prominent, and on some technical grounds.*

These grants to Michigan, just touched upon here, were for some time in hibernation, while a population was collecting and getting ready to use them, and they will be dropped in our narrative until a survey of this intervening period shall have been taken.

It has been the purpose in this chapter to show how Congress became possessed of lands, and then how these have been given for the noble work of education. In pursuit of the facts relating to this subject, we have been incidentally led to perceive those workings of divine Providence which achieve other and vaster results than its human agents had intended or foreseen. Our feeble colonies were

* See Benton's Debates, Vol. I.

in the most pressing need of means to carry on the struggle for independence, and pay its expenses when ended. Some of the States held by doubtful and conflicting titles the only property which promised ever to be equal to this need. The request of Congress that this property might be consecrated to the relief of the common necessity did not meet an immediate response from these States. In the meantime, conflicts between the members of the confederation began to develop themselves—black clouds thickened upon the country's horizon. States without lands protested against claims which, if admitted, would reduce them to insignificance and raise some of their sisters to empires. Cessions at length were made, and the confederation, designed at first only to keep together independent States for times of external peril, and which might have proved scarcely more than a rope of sand for this purpose, began to illustrate its capacity for the direct government of the sparse populations settled upon these ceded territories. A model system was gotten up for the Northwest, in which the means of mental, moral, and religious improvement were promised, and the subsequent carrying out of the system redeemed the promise by generous land grants for education.

The example once set, all the States followed, as we have seen, with their cessions of territory, which must be governed from the common center. In the meantime, the weak confederation became a constitutional republic, gradually but surely absorbing the powers of the States, and developing—whether for weal or for woe, statesmen may settle, if they can—its tendency toward centralization, until it has already become one of the strongest governments on this globe. During this progress, purchases of native tribes and of foreign powers, together with explorations and the events of war, have fixed its present limits, and given it the ownership of immense tracts of land, never of much value, and now scarcely of any at all, toward the revenues for which they were at first so earnestly sought. Wisely and happily gifts were made from them for education to those States to be formed out of them. Unhappily, Congress had no precedents to guide them·in fixing the terms of these grants, and the States none for their administration, and in consequence there have been embarrassing conditions on the one side, and squandering on the other. In administering the gifts for higher education, with which this work is chiefly concerned, there has finally been one instance of a somewhat marked success, in which others are following with the prospect of attaining to or transcending its ample measure; while others, which had become crippled, are recovering, and the States which had been careless, delinquent, or corrupt in the administration of the grants made them, are beginning to feel their obligation to restore, supplement, and wisely administer them. Leaving Congress to look over the past and determine how the vast national domain can be most justly and beneficently distributed for the best good of the whole country, and to the several States the determination of their respective duties in regard to the use of Congressional grants, this work drops for the present this general view, and turns to that particular institution, the birth of national munificence, which has thus far best accomplished its purpose.

CHAPTER IV.

Michigan's Early Condition as to Culture and Education.

In taking a view of that university system which is likely to prevail in most of the United States, it seems fit that a somewhat particular history of the earliest instance which has as yet proved eminently successful should be given; for in such an one will doubtless be found all the problems which have yet appeared or may hereafter present themselves for solution in the other States.

An inquiry into the antiquities of an institution so recent in its origin as the University of Michigan, seems not at first view to offer any points of special interest or difficulty. The subject is, however, fraught with an interest as deep and beset with questions as perplexing as almost any class of archæological studies. As an infant never makes a record of its own birth, or takes note at the time of the contemporary events and surroundings of its infancy and childhood, so this infant institution has neglected to record many facts connected with its origin and early history, and especially with the train of its antecedents, and left to the keeping of a many-tongued tradition those which, could they now be summoned forth from their partial oblivion, would be invested by the fame of the university with the charm of a tenfold interest. Men most earnest in their work, and much more, those whose connection with a work is rather accidental and official than from love to it, often forget to provide for the perpetuity of some portions of their records; and it is only when great measures of success have been achieved that a desire arises to look after the forgotten sources of grand results, and then they are often sought in vain.

A few contemporaries of the very first movement toward

higher education in Michigan are, indeed, still living, as
are also some of the prominent actors in the organization
of the present system; and a majority of the latter, now
deceased, were personally known to us of the present day.
Yet it has not, in many instances, been found possible to
fortify recollection with such written statements as have
seemed desirable, and this fact has greatly strengthened
the determination to make immediate use of both reminiscences and written notices before still more of them shall
have perished.

Higher education in Michigan may be traced back
almost to the fountain-head of the Anglo-American history
of the Territory, to a period when the French population
was largely in the majority. Beginning necessarily so
near the time of our first settlements, it would doubtless be
unsatisfactory to the reader if this account were not introduced with a picture of those early settlements in their
social and educational lineaments. Nor can a passing reference to the mere physical features of our State, as related to the theater upon which our great scholastic drama
is being enacted, be deemed out of place, since the construction and scenical appointments of the stage do, indeed, have much to do with the success of the play.

The first permanent settlement within the present limits
of Michigan was at Sault Ste. Marie, where a mission was
established in the year 1668, by the Jesuit father, James
Marquette, who, in the following spring, was joined by
Claude Dablon, of the same order. Other members of
this society had preceded them as voyagers and explorers,
and had made some attempts at the evangelization of the
savages; but these labors had been spasmodic, and their
results were transient. As early as September, 1641, two
Jesuit fathers—Raymbault and Jaques—had reached this
same point from Montreal, by way of the Ottawa river,
Lake Simcoe, and the Georgian Bay, and had quickly satisfied themselves of the adaptedness of the place for gath-
ering the Indians into a settlement, whether for purposes
of evangelization or traffic, for which latter, as well as the

former, the Jesuits always had a keen and practiced sense. They learned from these savages of a lake above called Gitchee Gomee (the Great Water), the south shore of which other members of the order afterward explored, as also the whole upper peninsula, at a period when the lower peninsula was as yet unvisited by civilized man. Claude Allouez, however, 1666–75, traveled over this region, and taught its wandering people with more enterprise and perseverance than any of his predecessors had done. Nor were his explorations barren of scientific results. Allouez knew of the copper mines, which were first worked almost two centuries later. These were not lost sight of for a century after Allouez's time; for, under date of August 25, 1687, M. Denonville, the governor of Canada, writes to Colbert, the French premier, proposing the construction of barks above and below Niagara Falls, on Lakes Erie and Ontario, for the transmission of the copper to France. Nor were they unknown in the following century; for Sir William Johnson, in a letter to the Earl of Hillsborough, dated December 23, 1768, states his perfect assurance that large quantities of copper ore are to be found on Lake Superior, very rich, and capable of being easily and cheaply reduced. And yet this element of Michigan's future wealth was afterward lost sight of and did not begin to be developed until the present school system had been planned, and was already in process of realization. Allouez and Marquette made, in 1688, the first map of this region, embracing only parts visited by themselves. This was published in 1672, and is mentioned by Foster and Whitney in their report as being, under the circumstances, " a remarkable production.*

Although the very name of Jesuit has become a by-word and reproach, both in Catholic and Protestant lands, this can not extinguish the inquirer's interest in them, which often rises to admiration, when beyond the utmost verge

---

* Documents relating to the Colonial History of the State of New York, Vol. IX., p. 344, and Vol. VIII., p. 141.

of civilized life he finds the foot-prints of the Jesuit fathers, and finds no others ; and this is true here.

Marquette probably visited Mackinaw in 1670. In the following year the mission there was established and named after the founder of the order, the Mission of St. Ignace. This may therefore be assigned as the date of the settlement of Mackinaw, while the founding of Detroit, which place was destined to throw its two predecessors quite in the shade, can not be placed earlier than 1701, more than thirty years later than the other two.

Several considerations concurred to determine these points of settlement. The stinted resources of savage husbandry, and the uncertain products of the chase, formed but a precarious subsistence for the Indians, and needed to be supplemented by all possible facilities for adding fish to their other supplies. For this purpose the places chosen were the very best on the line of the lakes, and were at the same time on a convenient thoroughfare of trade and travel to the cities of Montreal and Quebec. Officers, merchants, missionaries, and Indians often performed this trip at the expense of a month's time each way, and perhaps with less manifestation of impatience at delays than the passengers by railroad now show in passing over the same distance in less than twenty-four hours. These settlements, too, were at suitable distances in that cordon of fortified places which the French government was establishing in order to compete with the English for the sovereignty of the whole country. By the choice of these posts, therefore, the purposes of the missionary and the merchant, together with those of the French government and its savage allies, were all subserved.

The intelligent reader will not greatly err in his estimate of the type of character formed in these settlements. The European must descend toward his brethren of the forest full more than he could even hope to raise them toward himself. Those middle men between the merchants and the savages, called by the French "*courreurs des bois*," were not less at home in the wigwam of the savage, than in civilized life; nor was it decidedly otherwise with the merchants and missionaries. The former sometimes even intermarried with the Indians, and the latter lived in close and constant relations with them, going whithersoever they went, and dwelling where they dwelt.

The habits which had become traditional in these settlements since the end of the 17th century, were but slowly and slightly modified, when, in 1760, the results of Wolfe's victory on the Heights of Abraham reached the distant west, and brought Detroit and Mackinaw under English rule. The French population and garrison readily took the oath of allegiance to the new sovereign; little was changed beyond the commander, and the social and business routine remained undisturbed. The Revolutionary war did not reach these secluded points, which were still deemed to belong to Canada, until the victory of General Wayne on the Maumee, in 1795, established our government over them. Nor could this event introduce any rapid process of change in the social character of the little communities on our Michigan frontier.

The changes in social life from the early middle ages of Europe have not been so great as they were in Detroit and Mackinaw during the first half of the nineteenth century. Indeed, the transformation in life and manners has not been less than in the physical aspect spread out before the observer's eye. The first settlement on the present site of Detroit, made by M. de la Mothe Cadillac, in 1701, was chiefly a fort, and the place itself was called in honor of a minister of Louis XIV., Fort Pontchartrain. The town was surrounded with a stockade, which was from time to time extended. The old fort was near where Cooper's block now stands, on Jefferson avenue. Various changes continued to be made, but still with the main features unchanged, until after the period of the American occupation, within the recollection of persons still living. The dwellers outside of the stockade, who cultivated the soil, occupied farms laid out with a frontage of twenty-three to fifty-eight rods on the river, with a depth of four hundred and fifty-two rods, or about one mile and a quarter, which depth was in some few instances doubled. There were but about four hundred and fifty of these farms in the whole Territory, in 1806. These were along the water, from Lake Huron to the Raisin, and about Mackinaw, and the Indian title was as yet extinguished to little more than this narrow strip. Odd as were the shapes of these French farms, the burdens descended from the feudal times, to which each owner was subject, would strike still more strangely our American sense of free proprietorship.*   .

In 1796, the eastern boundary of the town, as inclosed in the palisade, began on the river at Griswold street, the western at Cass street, ; but these lines approached each other, so as to leave on the north side but the width of the fort proper, which extended from Fort to Lafayette street. Between the fort and the river, near where Congress street now is, crept a small, sluggish stream, called the River Savoyard, which discharged itself into the Detroit, near where the Central Railroad depot now stands. This stream was large enough to float canoes, and from the beautiful esplanade, parties of officers and their ladies were wont to embark and move down upon the broad bosom of the Detroit, meeting in their way the tiny craft of the Indians, and the more substantial ones of the Canadian boatmen, their oars keeping time to their wild songs, and the whole presenting a picture, the traces of which have now well-nigh faded from the memories of the living.

The dwellings were of one story, with dormer windows, and built of hewn logs, and the furniture was doubtless even more rude. Housekeeping was indifferent, and none of the domestic arts had risen above the lowest demands of civilized life. Fleeces of wool, instead of being spun, were used for stopping cellar-windows in winter, and in such like ways. Sewing was the chief occupation of the women, and they earned not a little by making simple garments for the Indians. The out-door labors of hus-

---

* See Appendix B.

bandry and the mechanic arts were equally rude. The
manufacture of lumber was by the toilsome process of
whip-sawing. The windmill—the first step above the
hand-mill of the ancients—was the only means for grind-
ing grain. The people made cider, which is referred to
by a French traveler as being bitter as gall—a fact easily
explained by the suggestion that it was made of crab-
apples, which grew abundantly in the woods. The implements, processes, and motive power in agriculture could
not be described in detail; but if the reader will take the
small native horse, rigged out with a harness in which elm-
bark and ropes of tow are chief constituents, he will not
be much out of the way by completing the list on the same
scale of advancement in the arts.

In the winter, while intercourse with their eastern neighbors of the lower lakes and St. Lawrence was interrupted
by the congealment of its watery channel, and the Indians
were pursuing their game in the depths of the forests, the
people resigned themselves very much to pleasure-seeking.
About three miles above the limits of the old city, there
was an extensive marsh, called "le Grand Marais." This
came down to the river bank, and in the fall was covered
with water, which, in winter, became ice, and forming a
connection with that on the margin of the river, made a
continuous ice-road, capable of being used for sleigh-riding,
even when there was no snow.

On the margin of the Grand Marais, the young men were
accustomed to build, late in the autumn, a temporary
structure, with stone chimneys in the two ends, fit it up
with rude tables and benches, and then on each Saturday
morning of the winter, vehicles crowded with young people of both sexes, with their baskets of crockery and provisions, drove to the so-called " *Hotel du Grand Marais.*"
Miscellaneous pastimes on the ice, or otherwise, doubtless
occupied those not employed in the preparation for dinner;
but dinner over, the dance began, and was kept up until the
discharge of the evening gun at the fort warned the party

6

that it would be prudent to return. After morning mass on Sunday, the young men found their way back to the field of the previous day's exploits, and consumed the remains of the feast. Balls and parties in town, and sleigh-riding upon the ice, occupied the rest of the week, and of the earnings of the business season, little or nothing generally remained when that season again returned.

With the opening spring, though the instincts of human nature remained unchanged, the occupations of the people suffered a revolution. The Indians, with their pack-ponies laden with peltries, filled the streets—the miniature horses, looking as if they might stagger under their loads, still maintained a firm footing, while their savage masters staggered under invisible burdens. The "*courreurs des bois*," and the merchants themselves, were going and coming, as were also the voyagers from point to point, on the long watery way of the rivers and lakes. Only the days, however, were given to business, and the pleasure-loving instincts of the people, for which little or no escape was provided in books and schools, found relief in general evening visiting, to which the younger portion of the people added promenading, together with sailing and rowing upon the beautiful Detroit, when the moon or a bright star-light favored, while almost the sole recreation for the day-time, during the season of business, was an occasional barbecue in a grove near Baby's windmill. The officers and men of the garrison, with little actual service, would have supplied a leaven of indolence and gayety, if such had indeed been wanting, but there were always enough of these social elements.

Some Scotch and English families, attracted by the offer of land grants to settlers, together with rations for a limited time after their arrival, had settled along the Detroit, and even the St. Clair, as at Grosse Point and Newport, during the period of British occupation. These and the French all remained and formed the body of the population, long after the flag of the Union waved over the fort. The very first American merchant established himself in Detroit, in

1799; but he, together with a long line of successors, must rather conform to the traditional social life, than make any violent efforts to bring it to their own standard.

By an act of the 11th of January, 1805, Congress organized Michigan into a separate territorial government, of which William Hull was made governor, and Augustus B. Woodward, Frederick Bates, and John Griffin, judges, and the people were anxiously waiting the arrival of these men as a great event in their history, when, on the 11th of June of the same year, the town within the stockade, excepting one small wooden house and one brick storehouse, was burnt to the ground. Furniture, having been repeatedly removed to escape the spreading flames, was finally saved only by being thrown into the river, whence it was picked up by skiffs and canoes employed to convey it to the other side.

This conflagration will not be surprising, when it is borne in mind that the town of Detroit, properly so called, occupied but about two acres of ground, which was entirely covered with buildings of the most combustible kind, the streets or lanes which separated them being but fourteen or fifteen feet in width. This narrow limit was inclosed by pickets.

On the very next day, the new territorial officers arrived at the scene of desolation. Infancy, illness, and old age had been provided for among the neighboring farmers; the bulk of the people were to dwell in tents, under the guns of the fort, in which latter the governor and his suite had their lodgings.

In October following, an official statement of the burning of the city and the suffering condition of the people was forwarded to Washington, and Congress, at its next session, passed an act authorizing the governor and judges to lay out a new city, which should include the site of the old one and 10,000 acres of the adjacent lands. It is said that there were at that time but eight legal titles* to real

---

* Judge Woodward's letter, Amer. St. Papers, Pub. Lands, Vol. I., p. 282, etc.

estate in the entire Territory ; for which extraordinary state
of facts Congress provided in the same act, by empow-
ering the territorial officers to give titles to lots in the new
plat to all who had either owned or occupied houses in the
old town before the fire, making similar provisions also for
the farmers—including in them not only those who had
sworn allegiance to our government, but also all who were
not in active allegiance to any other power, and giving the
entire adjudication and execution to the governor and
judges. This movement probably resulted in a revolution
in the plans and prospects of the town and people of Detroit greater than has ever occurred to any other in this
country, which had existed so long and became so far developed.

As was hinted above, there were other settlements in
the Territory besides Detroit. These were, however, so
connected with it, and so subordinate to it, as not to call
for separate description. The upper peninsula has also
been referred to as a part of Michigan, which, however, it was not until 1836. According to the interpretation which its own people put upon the boundary as established by Congress, a narrow strip of land on the south,
taking in the site of the city of Toledo, belonged to Michigan, the jurisdiction of which the settlers themselves
owned. Owing, however, to the ignorance of the geography of this section at the time, this boundary proved
difficult in practice. Ohio claimed this strip. The dispute
known as the Toledo war arose, and was settled at Washington by giving the land to Ohio, while Michigan was in-
demnified by the gift of the upper peninsula, itself large
enough for a State. Wisconsin, which, from 1818 to 1836,
had been attached to Michigan for the purposes of government, was at this time separated, and the boundary became
as it has since remained.

Some might seek to find in the natural features and
capabilities of this Territory an explanation of the early
beginnings and rapid development of its educational institutions ; but theories of this kind are often more fanciful

than sound. With her boundless pine-forests and her immense advantages for agriculture, permeated with streams supplying the hydraulic power for the manufacture of their products, and surrounded by navigable waters to bear them to distant markets, Michigan would have possessed the elements of great wealth if railroads had never came into use; but these resources lay still undeveloped at the time when the work of higher education, even in its present form, was inaugurated, and the only effect which they could have was to call upon this theater the people, and summon into life the enterprises by which it would ultimately be fostered and extended.

If, therefore, about the time when a little company of sages sat in the Flemish town of Ghent, negotiating the treaty which took its name, the genius of civilization had explored our whole land to the west of the Alleghanies in search of a theater upon which to develop most rapidly a great educational system, would he have discovered any reasons for selecting our beautiful peninsula for that purpose?

CHAPTER V.

Early Organization for Higher Education in Michigan, and their Contemporary Events.

THE Anglo-American element in the population of Michigan gradually increased, but was long in obtaining a controlling influence. Nothing will better impress this upon the mind of the reader than to learn that no Protestant religious worship was instituted in the Territory, so as to remain subsequently uninterrupted, until 1816. This fact will be deemed sufficiently significant, when it is borne in mind how fully Christian worship has ever kept up with our frontier settlements. It is indeed known that Daniel Freeman and Nathan Bangs * each preached in Detroit in the spring and summer of 1804, and that the Methodist Conference had, as minister in charge there, in 1809, William Case.

There exists also a tradition, descended from that day, to the effect that some Methodists, perhaps under the lead of a lay preacher from Canada, attempted to hold evening religious services, both in Detroit and on the Rouge, six miles below, and that these were disturbed and broken up by the attendance of some young people, who generously supplied candles, having quills charged with gunpowder inserted in them, which, by their explosion, generated feelings and utterances not in entire harmony with the purpose of the meetings.

In the winter of 1815–16 the leading Protestant people of Detroit, without reference to their ecclesiastical relations— Governor Cass himself being prominent in the movement—

---

*Afterward Rev. Dr. Bangs, of New York. For the information in regard to these three men, we are indebted to Rev. Dr. Pilcher, of Detroit.

wrote to the professors of the theological school at Princeton, to send them a young man whom they could recommend as a suitable candidate for the pastorate of the congregation. In response to this letter, John Monteith, who was to graduate in June following, although he had already been designated for a college professorship elsewhere, was named, and acknowledged the paramount claim of Michigan, by setting out for Detroit immediately after the commencement at Princeton. On his arrival we find two men standing in such relation to the people, and to the future cause of education in the State, as to call for some special notice.

Gabriel Richard was born in Saintes, department of the Lower Charente, France, in 1764, and educated for the priesthood. He came first to Baltimore, in 1792, where were several of his own religious order, the Sulpicians; thence, in December of the same year, he went to take the pastoral care of the Catholics in Illinois, at Prairie du Rocher, Kaskaskia, and the vicinity, whence he came on to Detroit in 1798, and had accordingly been there about a score of years, when the first movement toward higher education in Michigan was inaugurated. After so long a residence in this little place, not only as chief representative of the priesthood, but much of the time as vicar-general, performing episcopal functions, it may well be supposed that he had become the best known person in Detroit. He was faithful to his church, discharging his pastoral duties as he understood them, and his faithfulness to other public trusts was not less marked. Tradition has kept numerous anecdotes which illustrate his character.

In the discharge of duties to the public, he had a self-forgetfulness which amounted to a misfortune. It made him fruitful in expedients to accomplish public ends, thoughtless of those which keep one out of trouble. In the struggle for building St. Anne's Church, in order that the work might go on, he once issued due-bills, for which he kept some blanks on hand. Some one got hold of his blanks, filled them out, and put them in circulation to the

amount of seven or eight hundred dollars, which he redeemed as they were brought in. He next conceived the
idea of making seines, for fishing in the Detroit river.
These were even sent to Eastern markets, and the basement
of the church was completed as the result. This was soon
after the fire of 1805.

It was a curious incident which led to his remaining in
Detroit, instead of returning to France; for in 1805 he was
called to return to his native land, where his brethren
thought that the d.sordered state of religion required his
presence. In the temporary chapel, where the worship
was held after the fire, he published his intention to return
to Europe. The trustees made use of a calumny, which
had been circulated against him, had a writ served upon
him, and, as a consequence, he spent his life in Detroit.

He had been as absolute and unquestioned in all matters
of his parish, as if it had been in the Pyrenees; but he had
seen settling around him a class of people more cultivated
than his own, and including most of those connected with
the government, who did not sympathize with his religious
teachings and ritual services, and for whom he could not
minister satisfactorily when they felt most deeply the need
of the consoling offices of religion. In 1807 the Protestants
of the place invited him to preach to them in English, and,
though he well knew that he could not meet all their wishes,
he undertook the work, and every Sunday at noon delivered at the Council-house a religious discourse of such
general nature as he deemed adapted to his audience.

Father Richard called on the young Monteith soon after
his arrival in Detroit, and welcomed him with sincere cor-
diality to the performance of services which he felt himself unable to render. On the occasion of one of his
earliest calls at Mr. M.'s boarding-house, he was invited to
remain at tea, and requested to ask a blessing at the table.
He replied that he was unaccustomed to that service except
in the Latin language, which he would use, if agreeable.
Mr. M., however, thought it not well to employ a language
unintelligible to those at the table. Another incident,

however, will show that at a later day he did learn to pray
in English so as to be understood. It occurred in the
legislative council, where he used, as nearly as one who
heard his broken English could report it, these words:
" *O Lord, bless dis legislatif council, and enable dem to
act for de peple and not for demselfs.*"

Father Richard once excommunicated from his church
a man who had been legally divorced, and had married
again. This man had combined the two occupations of
carrying on the tillage of a little farm and the keeping of
a little store near the city. He was feeble in health, and
dependent upon the labor of others to harvest his grain,
and upon their custom to support his trade. But such was
the fearful nature of the ban, that no Catholic ventured to
go near him, and he was left to suffer. He was, however,
not to be beaten ; he sued the priest for the damage result-
ing from this state of things, and obtained a judgment for
about $2,200. It was in the days of imprisonment for
debt, and as Father R. had nothing to pay, he was taken
to jail, but was of course bailed out. In the meantime he
had been elected territorial delegate to Congress, and the
question was raised whether he could derive any advantage
from the law exempting members from arrest for debt.
Relying, though without any good reason, upon this provision, he went on to Washington, and his friends had to
provide for the payment of the judgment. Notwithstanding those good qualities which made him so well known
in Detroit, he was careless of his finances, and was ever
getting into trouble as the consequence.

Father R., moved mainly by the desire to benefit his
people religiously, established a printing-press in the city,
and published a small paper, called " *Essai du Michigan,*"
which was not indeed sustained, but the press was useful
in printing the religious works needed by the Catholic
people, and the matter called for by the territorial government. Mr. Girardin, in a paper on Father R., recently
read before the Pioneer Society of Detroit, resents as unjust and malicious, an intimation that he was not in favor

of the education of the masses. Mr. Girardin's proofs that he was favorable to this, will, however, fall short of satisfying most readers, as they consist mainly in his efforts at the education of young men for the ministry, and in the establishment of a young ladies' seminary.

It was in 1823 that he went as territorial delegate to Congress. He showed an intelligent interest in the affairs of the Territory, and is regarded as having procured the construction of the great roads leading from Detroit—the Pontiac, Fort Gratiot, and Grand River roads. As he was always getting into financial troubles, so the same self-forgetfulness, when duty seemed to call, made him careless of life itself. When the cholera raged in Detroit, in 1832, he, with characteristic disregard of danger, moved freely among his people, ministering to their spiritual and temporal wants, was taken with the disease, and died, being about sixty-eight years of age, and having spent thirty-four years in Detroit.

Mr. Monteith was a man of another order of mind and of culture; but if his life had even been one of more diversified incident and adventure, too little of it was spent in our Territory to entitle it to be sketched for this work. His talents and education prepared him for the work of instruction to which his life, after the few years spent in Detroit, was mainly given in the discharge of the duties of a professorship in Hamilton College, in the State of New York. His chief distinction in Michigan was as standard-bearer in establishing the first Protestant congregation, and in the inauguration of our educational work. Had he chosen to remain in Michigan, his influence in educational matters would have been large and salutary.

These two men, representing in these wilds the two general sections of the Christian world, were to labor together in the opening of the work of public education in that region which has since become the State of Michigan, and this work began within a few months after Mr. Monteith's settlement in Detroit.

Hon. Augustus B. Woodward, one of the judges of the

Territory from 1805, seems to have been the organizing mind among the members of the territorial government, and was probably the author of the following :

"AN ACT to establish the Catholepistemiad, or University of Michigania.

"*Be it enacted by the Governor and Judges of the Territory of Michigan*, That there shall be in the said Territory a catholepistemiad or university, denominated the Catholepistemiod, or University of Michigania. The Catholepistemiad, or University of Michigania, shall be composed of thirteen didaxum or professorships : First, a didaxia, or professorship of catholepistemia, the didactor or professor of which shall be president of the institution ; second, a didaxia, or professorship of anthropoglossica, or literature, embracing all the epistemum or sciences relative to language ; third, a didaxia, or professorship of mathematica or mathematics ; fourth, a didaxia, or professorship of physiognostica or natural history ; fifth, a didaxia, or professorship of physiosophica or natural philosophy ; sixth, a didaxia, or professorship of astronomia or astronomy ; seventh, a didaxia, or professorship of chymia or chemistry ; eighth, a didaxia, or professorship of iatrica or medical sciences ; ninth, a didaxia, or professorship of œconomia or economical sciences ; tenth, a didaxia, or professorship of ethica or ethical sciences ; eleventh, a didaxia, or professorship of polemitactica or military sciences ; twelfth, a didaxia, or professorship of degitica or historical sciences ; and thirteenth, a didaxia, or professorship of ennœica or intellectual sciences, embracing all the epistemum or sciences relative to the minds of animals, to the human mind, to spiritual existence, to the Deity, and to religion, the didactor or professor of which shall be vice-president of the institution. The didactors or professors shall be appointed and commissioned by the governor. There shall be paid from the treasury of Michigan, in quarterly payments, to the president of the institution and to each didactor or professor, an annual salary, to be from time to time ascertained by law. More than one didaxia or professorship may be conferred upon the same person. The president and didactors or professors, or a majority of ·them assembled, shall have power to regulate all the concerns of the institution ; to enact laws for that purpose ; to sue, to be sued ; to acquire, to hold, to alienate property, real, mixed, and personal ; to make, to use, and to alter a seal ; to establish colleges, academies, schools, libraries, museums, athenæums, botanic gardens, laboratories, and other useful literary and scientific institutions consonant to the laws of the United States of America and of Michigan, and to appoint officers, instructors, and instructrixes in, among, and throughout the various counties, cities, towns, townships, and other geographical divisions of Michigan. Their name and style as a corporation shall be "The Catholepistemiad, or University of Michigania." To every subordinate instructor and instructrix appointed by the catholepistemiad or university, there shall be paid from the treasury of Michigan an annual salary, in quarterly payments, to be from time to time ascertained by law. The existing public taxes are hereby increased fifteen per cent. ; and from the proceeds of the present and all future public taxes, fifteen per cent. are appropriated for the benefit of the catholepistemiad or university. The treasurer of Michigan shall keep a separate account of the university fund. The catholepistemiad or university may prepare and draw four successive lotteries, deducting from the prizes in the same fifteen per cent. for the benefit of the institution. The proceeds of the preceding sources of revenue, and of all subsequent, shall be applied, in the first instance, to the acquisition of suitable lands and buildings, and books, libraries, and apparatus, and afterward to such purposes as shall be from time to time by law directed. The honorarium for a course of lectures shall not exceed fifteen dollars ; for classical instruction, ten dollars a quarter ; for ordinary instruction, six dollars a quarter. If the judges of the court of any county, or a majority of them, shall certify that the parent or guardian of any person has not

adequate means to defray the expense of suitable instruction, and that the same ought to be a public charge,
the honorarium shall be paid from the treasury of Michigan. An annual report of the state, concerns and transactions of the institution shall be laid before the legislative
power for the time being. This law, or any part of it,
may be repealed by the legislative power for the time
being. Made, adopted, and published from the laws of
seven of the original States—to wit, the States of Connecticut, Massachusetts, New Jersey, New York, Ohio, Pennsylvania, and Virginia—as far as necessary, and suitable
to the circumstances of Michigan, at Detroit, on Tuesday,
the 26th day of August, in the year of our Lord one thousand eight hundred and seventeen.

" WILLIAM WOODBRIDGE,
" *Secretary of Michigan, and at present acting Governor thereof.*
" A. B. WOODWARD,
" *Presiding Judge of the Supreme Court of the Territory of Michigan*
" JOHN GRIFFIN,
" *One of the Judges of the Territory of Michigan.'*

This legislation did not suddenly spring up without antecedent facts in the public mind to give rise to it. The subject had been more or less agitated in the community.
The contemporary numbers of the Detroit Gazette, a
weekly newspaper which began its career about two months
before the date of the act establishing the catholepistemiad,
contain evidences of this fact. This little sheet prudently en-
deavored to adapt itself to all classes of the people. The
French population was still quite in the majority throughout
the Territory. Many of them had emigrated from France in
the reign of Louis XIV. Of these, some had been of the
higher classes, and being cut off from all immediate intercourse with their own country, they were still handing
down from generation to generation the French language
of the age in which they had left their native land, as they
are, indeed, still doing in some of those retired parts on
the Canada side of the river, where the pressure of the

Anglo-Americans has not dislodged or corrupted it. The Gazette, in deference to the wishes of these people, was divided between English and French in its advertisements, editorials, and communications. Under date of August 8, 1817, is an editorial in the French language on the subject of education, from which the following is translated :

"Frenchmen of the Territory of Michigan! You ought to begin immediately to give an education to your children. In a little time there will be in this Territory as many *Yankees* as French, and if you do not have your children educated, the situations will all be given to the *Yankees*. No man is capable of serving as a civil and military officer unless he can at least read and write. There are many young people, of from eighteen to twenty years, who have not yet learned to read, but they are not yet too old to learn. I have known those who have learned to read at the age of forty years."*

This contributes to a view of the state of things in Detroit, by stating the writer's idea of the smallest amount of education which would enable his countrymen to compete successfully with the " Yankees," informs us that many of them were without these essentials, and invites them to enter at once upon their work of preparation, hinting a word of encouragement even to those who might have lived forty years without making the beginning.

The earliest numbers of the Gazette, in consequence no doubt of this movement, are much occupied with brief articles, both original and selected, on the subject of education. One appears from Montesquieu, showing the necessity of intelligence and virtue in republics, and one from Howard, the philanthropist, setting forth the relation between intel-

---

* "Français du Territoire de Michigan! Vous devriez commencer immediatement à donner une education à vos enfans. Dans peu de temps il y aura dans ce Territoire autant de *Yankees* que de Français, et si vous ne faites pas instruire vos enfans, tous les emplois seront donnés aux *Yankees*. Aucun homme ni est capable d'etre officier civil et militaire à moins quil ne sache lire et ecrire. Il y a plusieurs jeunes gens de 18 à 20 ans, que n'ont pas encore appris à lire, mais ils ne sont pas trop vieux pour apprendre. J'en ai connu qui ont appris à lire à l'age de 40 ans."

ligence and virtue, ignorance and crime; and these are the
straws which show to us of this day, in what direction the
current was then setting in.

But how exceedingly small and isolated the community
in which this work began! The exact population in 1817,
the period now to be pictured, is not known. The whole
Territory in 1810 contained 4,762 souls; in 1821, 8,896;
probably, therefore, in 1817, 6,000 to 7,000. The tonnage
of Michigan vessels, in 1816, in the foreign trade was $430\frac{68}{95}$;
in the coasting trade, $59\frac{10}{95}$—the largest of which might
easily have been the measurement of one small vessel.
The expectation of the arrival of the first steamer at Detroit,
was heralded by an editorial of the Gazette in the following
language: "We learn with pleasure, by a gentleman from
Buffalo, that the steamboat may be expected the first week
in August." It was not, however, until the 28th of that
month that the editor could announce the arrival of that
"elegant" structure. This vessel, called from the Indian
Chief of that name, "Walk-in-the-Water," began at that
time her regular trips, forming an era in the history of the
Territory. Detroit had then a total population of 1,110
souls, occupying 142 dwelling-houses.

We learn from an editorial of the Gazette of February
20, 1820, that two years previous to that date, all the
goods consumed in this whole western country, were either
"boated" up the Mississippi, or "wagoned" over the
mountains from Philadelphia, and that these enterprising
Detroit people began at this time to think that by the canal,
of which De Witt Clinton was then urging the construction,
their goods might come, perhaps with advantage to themselves, from New York by way of Buffalo and Lake Erie.
The Indians were still a main element of the population.
The best church in the vicinity had been built chiefly by
the Hurons, or Wyandottes, as they were sometimes called,
and on special occasions they filled it. The French people,
which were but little in advance of them in intelligence,
were still in the majority. Few of their men could read or
write except those intended for mercantile life; singularly

enough more of the women than of the men were able to read, which fact is accounted for by their more general attendance upon the mass for which they thus prepared themselves. There was, however, little reading even among those who had acquired this accomplishment. An inquiry was instituted about this time in order to know how many of these French people had the Bible in their own language; most of them, on being asked, claimed to have it, but when produced, it proved generally to be the litany, or some collection of prayers, and even Father Richard had only a Latin Bible until one in the vulgar language was given him by the Protestant pastor. They felt little obligation to observe the Sabbath, otherwise than to attend mass once, until the commencement of Protestant worship, almost immediately after which, an ordinance in regard to Sabbath observance was passed, and was generally respected.*

---

* The most of this account of the intellectual and religious condition of the French people of Detroit is taken from a manuscript of Rev. John Monteith, kindly furnished for this purpose by his son, late superintendent of schools in Missouri. It is replete with interesting statements of facts, the use of which in this work would be foreign to its design. There is, however, one too interesting to be omitted, and so is thrown into this note:

Mr. Monteith, on his way up the lake, in 1816, was passenger in a little schooner called the " Union," having among his fellow-passengers Captain Root, and Lieutenant Clark and wife, and Colonel McNeil and wife, all of the United States army; the wife of Colonel McNeil being a sister of Franklin Pierce, afterward President of the United States. This little craft, thus respectably laden, was old, and had always been under the same command, that of Captain Ruff, who related to this company, among other perils of himself and his little vessel, that he had once had the celebrated traveler Volney for a passenger, and had in the passage encountered a severe storm, which had well-nigh driven his schooner upon a shoal near the Canada shore. To use Mr. Monteith's words: "There was much solemnity and prayer, and especially among the females on board. But some were greatly agitated, and none more so than Volney. When the danger seemed to be very near, he ran to his trunk, and seizing his gold pieces, he filled his pockets with them, and coming to a traveling companion, he expressed his satisfaction that he had secured his money. His friend remonstrated against his folly in so doing, and said, ' If you are cast away, you will sink to the bottom like a stone!' Volney saw his mistake, and emptied his pockets. But then he was in greater distress

On the 16th of August, 1817, James Monroe, then in the first year of his administration as President of the United States, on a tour of inspection of the fortifications on the northern frontier, arrived in Detroit. A telegraphic message, which for speed was doubtless sent on horseback, had previously announced to the citizens that the presidential party had reached the mouth of the river, eighteen miles below. The people were occupied for about a week in the festivities connected with this extraordinary visit, in all of which Judge Woodward, the author of the act for the establishment of a university; Mr. Monteith, its first president, and, of course, Governor Cass, were prominent; and as the whole population of the town could not then have formed so numerous a company as would gather now at the depot of almost any town on the Central Railroad, to obtain a sight of so distinguished a personage, and as such an occurrence could scarcely be expected again for a lifetime, it may well be supposed that the body of the people was stirred by this event.

Governor Cass and General Macomb accompanied the President to Washington, traveling through the woods of Eastern Michigan and across Ohio. As the act above quoted was passed just after this party left, the reason will be apparent why the signature of Governor Cass is wanting to it. Six days before the publication of this act—that is, on the 20th of August—Judge Woodward invited Mr. Monteith to an interview on the subject of a university, and early in the next month the diary of the latter contains the following entries:

---

than ever. In his agony he threw himself down on the deck, making his final appeal to the Hearer of prayer, which he had probably before never attempted. 'Mon Dieu! Mon Dieu! que ce que je prai, que ce que je prai.' The wind, however, changed and bore the vessel from the shoals, and the danger vanished."

As Volney was in this country from 1795 to 1798, and most likely visited the settlement of his countrymen at Detroit, it seems not at all improbable that eighteen to twenty years before, when this schooner was new, he might have been a passenger upon it.

7

" *September 9th.* A bill has just passed the territorial legislature establishing a university. In order to carry out its provisions, commissions have been made out for its officers. That for the office of president, and six others, embracing so many separate professorships, have been offered to John Monteith, and six commissions, embracing so many other professorships, are offered to Gabriel Richard, the Catholic bishop of Michigan. The commissions have been accepted, and the institution is ready to go into operation."

" *14th.*—James McCloskey is this day appointed superintendent of the buildings of the university."

" This corporation," adds Mr. M., in the manuscript referred to above, "proceeded to secure a site for a school in this city. They drew the plat of a building, let it out by contract, and in the course of about a year had the lower story occupied with a systematic English school, and a portion of the second story with a classical school, and another with a library."

The statutes enacted for the carrying out of this plan began immediately to be published in the Gazette.

When the catholepistemiad was founded, the great Napoleon was only in the second year of his exile. His marvelous career was still fresh in the minds of admiring Americans, whose warm and wondering regard for the great man was much enhanced by certain recollections of our own war with Great Britain, then just closed. It is suggestive to observe in the columns of the Gazette of this period, the deep interest with which items of information relating to the Bonapartes, and especially the exile of St. Helena, are given. Governor Cass and Judge Woodward, as public and learned men, and contemporary with that exciting revolutionary movement at the head of which Napoleon had placed himself, and doubtless in deepest sympathy with it, must have understood the system organized under the name of the University of France, and certainly this act looks very much like an attempt to copy it in Michigan. It makes the university include in itself all the primary and higher schools, and gives all legislative and executive control over them into the hands of its president and professors. It is true that this act declares itself to have been " made, adopted, and published from the laws of seven of the original States, so far as necessary and suitable to the circumstances of Michigan at Detroit;" but this statement is introduced only in order formally to meet a requirement of the act from which the territorial government derived its authority to legislate, and probably this main feature of the system existed in no one of the seven States mentioned.

Higher education must, in the end, direct and control the lower, and it ought to do so ; for while the latter employs itself mainly with simple facts in detail, the former teaches the principles or theories into which accumulated facts have been generalized, and those books and systems of teaching, which should be used in the common schools, can be well prepared only by those who have mastered the highest generalizations. But whether the lower schools should be thus formally subjected to the control of the faculty of the highest grade of schools, or whether free competition should be left to work out its legitimate result, is more doubtful. It is perhaps better that neither the university nor its graduates should have any other advantage than that which well-trained talents naturally give them in a free competition for positions as teachers, and this must, in the end, diffuse throughout the lower schools the principles taught and the spirit generated in the university, unless, indeed, the latter fails to realize the only purpose worthy of it.

The professors of the catholepistemiad began, in accordance with this provision, by taking the whole work of lower education into their hands. A few specimens of their legislation may not be devoid of interest. *Statute third* made provision that the pupils in the primary schools should be instructed in reading, writing, English grammar, and elocution. The *fourth, fifth,* and *sixth statutes* enacted the establishment of primary schools in Detroit,

Mackinaw, and Monroe; while the *twelfth* provided, that
as soon as practicable, the following books should be used
in these schools, viz: Murray's Grammar and Spelling-
book, together with his English Reader and Exercises,
Walker's Elocution, and Walker's Dictionary.

It is evident that as early as September, 1817, the new
university had three primary schools under its direction,
whether it found them existing or called them into being,
and had selected books for them which were not then in
use, and most probably were never all of them introduced,
but merely named as the goal to which this aspiring institution was striving to attain. Although it is not beyond
doubt, we may reasonably suppose that these were the only
primary schools then in the Territory; and if so, we might
guess with tolerable accuracy its educational statistics.

Statute fifth provided a course of instruction for the
pupils in the classical academies: The French, Latin, and
Greek languages, antiquities, English grammar, composition, elocution, mathematics, geography, morals, and ornamental accomplishments; and further enacted that the
Sacred Scriptures should constitute a portion of the reading,
from the beginning to the end of the course. The two
next following *statutes* provided for the establishment of a
classical academy in Detroit, and named the trustees and
visitors of the same; and *statute fifteenth*, published in
the Gazette of October 24, 1817, enacted the establishment
of a college in the city of Detroit, to be denominated the
"*First College of Michigania.*"

As the university in this its first form did not last long,
nor achieve much, it will not be necessary to pursue its
course in detail. The governor had the appointment of the
president and professors, and doubtless before leaving with
the presidential party, had concurred in the appointments
as carried out soon after by Judge Woodward. As the
salary of a professor was $12.50 a year, and one of these
men had seven and the other six professorships; one of
course received $87.50, and the other $75 a year.

They had, however, other professions, and little to do in
the work for which these salaries were provided, and as
they probably received in addition tuition fees when they
did any teaching, they were doubtless well enough paid,
and both enjoyed that high regard so generally accorded
to worthy clergymen and teachers in frontier settlements.
It should not be overlooked that, while one was a Presbyterian and the other a Catholic clergyman, they seem to
have agreed in providing that the Scriptures should be read
throughout all the schools under their charge from the
lowest to the highest.

The law in which this institution originated, provided
for fifteen per cent. increase of the taxes for the support of
the enterprise, and also allowed of the drawing of two lotteries in its aid. But the interest of the people is best
shown by a private subscription, raised in the very beginning to the sum of $3,000. The amount obtained by the
sale of the land grant, made in the treaty of Fort Meigs in
1817, was more than $5,000, all of which is supposed to
have been expended in the educational work in Detroit, in
addition to what was raised from tuition and subscriptions.
How much the subscriptions were increased afterward is
not so evident from the published references to the subject.
One of the most interesting ways for an old resident of
Michigan to spend half an hour, is in reading over the
names of the subscribers to this fund and the amounts of
their several subscriptions, as published in the Gazette of
that day.

Statutes 13 and 14 recite equally interesting facts, viz:
That certain sums of money had been sent on from Montreal and Mackinaw, in 1805, for the relief of the sufferers
by the fire of that year; that these had not been paid over
because the holders could not obtain satisfactory security
to relieve them of their responsibility, and that the sufferers
themselves expressed the wish that this money should be
given to the university; and they then provide that the university shall receive this money and become security for

satisfying the claims of the donors, should any ever be preferred.

On the 30th of April, 1821, the governor and judges passed an act for the establishment, in the city of Detroit, of an institution to be called the " University of Michigan." This act repealed that in regard to the catholepistemiad, and gave all the schools which the latter had established, and the funds which it had acquired, into the hands of the new organization. This charter continued to the corporation substantially the powers conferred by the act of 1817, except the provisions for taxes and lotteries. The board might establish such colleges, academies, and schools, depending upon said university, as they should deem proper, and the funds should permit. They were to have the charge of the township of land granted by the Congressional act of March 26, 1804, making provision for the disposal of the public lands in the Indiana Territory; also of the three sections reserved in the treaty of Fort Meigs, concluded September 29, 1817. This act was in the ordinary language of such charters instead of the pedantic terms of the charter of the catholepistemiad. It bore the signatures of Lewis Cass as governor, John Griffin as one of the judges, and James Witherell as secretary of the Territory of Michigan.

During the closing days of the first organization and the opening ones of the second, events of deepest interest were transpiring in our country, in regard to one of which —the Missouri Compromise—the views entertained in our new Territory are not unworthy of record here, since they are not foreign to the history of higher education. The Detroit Gazette of February 25, 1820, holds the following editorial language : " If, in expressing our wishes on this great question, we could suffer our feelings as citizens of Michigan to be warped by a desire to hasten the prospective welfare of this Territory, we should say, let Missouri enjoy her slavery ! Let her citizens eat the bread of idleness, while their corn-fields are moistened by the sweat of the

black man's brow! For we well know that to a country
where slavery is tolerated the hardy yeoman of the Eastern
and Northern States will never emigrate. . . . Let,
then, the right (what a right!) of holding slaves be extended to the people of Missouri, and from the date of that
charter, never will an emigrant from the non-slaveholding
States press the soil of that country with his foot." Still in
the beginning of 1821, Mr. Sibley, the delegate of Michigan in Congress, having some reference to the desired action for education in the Territory, wrote : "The Missouri
question has excited so much interest, that nothing else
can be done." When the elements of the Northwest were
in process of collecting, the people of Missouri, looking
forward to wealth and greatness, chose to plant in their
fertile soil the institution of slavery, while the people of
Michigan, for the purpose of fostering intelligence and
virtue, were intent upon planting in their Territory institutions of learning. The one, anxiously and unwisely seeking wealth from the richness of its soil, obtained even this
result but very inadequately ; the other, seeking the ends of
mental and moral elevation, gained these, together with
physical thrift. The one which ought to have been twenty
years ahead in development, is full twenty years behind—
a difference which is, however, rapidly disappearing, and
destined not distantly to pass away, under the regenerating
influences which now prevail in Missouri.

The new corporation carried on from 1821 to 1837 the
work of education begun by its predecessors, including the
classical academy, and in the early part of the time a Lan-
casterian school. By these successive boards the educational spirit was kept up, and transmitted to the university
as now organized. The three organizations have been one
institution in three stages of development. This has even
been judicially declared. In an action of ejectment brought
by the regents, to recover certain lands which had been
deeded by the governor and judges in 1825 to the trustees
of the University of Michigan, the Supreme Court, at its

January term in 1856, decided that the plaintiffs were entitled to receive and hold the lands. The three are, therefore, in law, as they certainly were in spirit, one and the same institution. The earliest management of the fund, which has made the third stage of development possible, will form the subject of the next chapter.

CHAPTER VI.

Grant of the Present University Fund and its Administration by the Board of Trustees.

In the chapter on land grants for college education, two were referred to as having been made for Michigan ; one by Congress, in 1804, consisting of an entire township ; the other, a reservation in the treaty made with the Indian tribes at Fort Meigs, in 1817, of three sections. Both of these grants, for the location of neither of which any measures had as yet been taken, together with all the funds and schools which had belonged to the "catholepistemiad," became, by the charter of 1821, the property of the institution. The government at Washington recognized this board as the responsible administrator of the grants provided for by that charter ; at least the board instituted at once the necessary measures for locating these lands. At its second meeting, which occurred June 20, 1821, on motion of Hon. Austin E. Wing, the following action was taken :

"*Resolved*, That his excellency, Lewis Cass, and Mr. Sibley, be a committee, whose duty it shall be to communicate with the Secretary of the Treasury of the United States on the subject of the location of the college townships in this Territory, and that he be urged to hasten the location of the same."*

Mr. Wing did not include the Fort Meigs reservation in this resolution, and the reason is incidentally brought out in a letter of Mr. Crawford, Secretary of the Treasury,

---

* It is a remarkable and very interesting fact that the three men—Messrs. Cass, A. E. Wing, and Woodbridge—who had most to do with the procuring of the grants for Michigan, were from the New England colony in Ohio, of which an account has been given above.

dated September 8 following. In this the secretary
acknowledges the receipt of a letter from Governor Cass
of April 28th preceding, and replies to the same, authorizing
the governor to locate the reservations of this treaty.
Messrs. Wing and Lecuyer, as committee for this purpose,
made personal examination of the country, and reported
their recommendations, in accordance with which selections
were made on the river, a little below Detroit, and in Farm-
ington, Oakland county; and government patents for the
same were issued May 15, 1824. Thus twenty years after
the first, and seven years after the second of these grants,
the first lands came into the possession of the board.

One of the results of the inquiries set on foot by Mr.
Wing's resolution, was to show that the provisions of the
act of 1804 would be difficult of execution. The time had
been long since its passage. It was understood that the
lands must be selected from those of which the Indian titles
had been already extinguished at the time of the grant,
and no general extinction of these titles had taken place
until the treaty of Fort Meigs, in 1817. There were still
other difficulties growing out of the changes since 1804,
and new legislation by Congress was deemed necessary, in
order that the lands might be advantageously located. In
order to meet this state of the case, a committee, consisting
of Messrs. Woodbridge, Sibley, and Williams, was appointed to memorialize Congress in behalf of the board,
setting forth the facts and praying for the appropriate action. Their memorial was read and approved at the meeting of December 10, 1823, and, together with a draft of a
bill embodying its substance, was sent to Washington, and
Congress finally responded by an act,* approved May 20,
1826, giving to the Territory of Michigan for a " seminary
of learning," two entire townships of land, with liberal
provisions for the location of the same in detached sections,
or smaller quantities. This act was read in a meeting of
the board, held August 1, 1826, and such was the en-

---

* See Appendix C.

thusiasm that at this very meeting, Mr. Wing and Dr. Brown were appointed a committee to examine the country and report fully their opinion in regard to the location of these two townships of land. They were also authorized to associate with themselves, as a member of the committee, a surveyor to accompany them.

The first act of the board, by way of authorizing the committee in relation to locating the two townships, was under date of May 11, 1827, and in the following words:

"*Resolved*, That the committee heretofore appointed to examine and report their opinion in regard to the two townships of land granted by the United States to this institution, be authorized to locate such tracts at the mouth of Swan creek, on the Miami river, in this territory, as may seem to them expedient," etc. The river now known as the Maumee, was formerly called the Miami, and sometimes, in order to distinguish it from another of the same name, the " Miami of the Lakes." Around the point where Swan creek discharges itself into this river, now stands the city of Toledo, on that strip of land which then acknowledged the authority of the territorial government of Michigan, but as the result of that contest, known as the "Toledo war" has, since 1837, been a part of the State of Ohio. At this point the committee did select lands, which are described as river lots 1, 2, 7, 8, 9, and 10, amounting to 916 acres, but accepted them for two sections, or 1280 acres, and as early as the 7th of July following, a letter from the general land office, at Washington, declared these lands reserved and appropriated to this purpose. Thus the University of Michigan, many years before it had any actual existence, had, in less than one-fiftieth part of its lands, the possibility at least of a much larger fund than is yet possessed by any educational institution in America.

But these lots were too tempting a bait to speculators, and the shrewdness which had selected them, proved unequal to the task of holding them to the proper moment. Major William Oliver, in behalf of himself and others, visited Detroit repeatedly from 1828 to 1831, and impor-

tuned the board to convey to him lots 1 and 2, in exchange
for other property near them. In August, 1830, it was
voted inexpedient to make the exchange ; but on the 4th
of January, 1831, the board voted, seven to two—the two
negatives being the votes of Messrs. Brown and Desnoyers—
to make the exchange with Mr. Oliver, giving him lots 1
and 2, containing 401½ acres, in exchange for 3 and 4, and
some other adjacent lands, amounting in all to 777 acres.
The conveyances were made out on the 7th of February
following.

In 1834, however, Mr. Oliver began to manifest a desire
to purchase back the lots which he had exchanged for these
university lands, and on the 24th of October of that year,
the board voted to sell them to him for $5,000, Messrs.
Desnoyers and Williams voting in the negative—thus making it quite clear that the latter would have added another to
the negative votes on the question of the exchange with
Oliver, had he been present at the meeting of January
4, 1831. In connection with this action, the board voted
also to ask Congress to carry it into effect, showing that
the action of Congress was necessary in order to perfect
the conveyance, which action, unfortunately for the university, was taken, and the board, at its session of May 5,
1837—the last but one it ever held—"authorized and required their president to remise, release, and quitclaim to
William Oliver, his heirs and assigns, the several parcels
of land mentioned and described in an act of the Congress
of the United States of America, entitled 'an act to authorize
the conveyance of certain lands belonging to the University
of Michigan, approved March 22, 1836.'"

Thus the trustees of our university fund received $5,000
for more than 400 acres of land, making about 2,000 city
lots in what is now the best part of the city of Toledo.
This was their first and last sale from the two townships
granted in 1826.

By an anticipation of about a dozen years, the whole
unfortunate history of the Toledo university lands may be
closed up in a few words. The land mentioned above as

river lots 7, 8, 9, and 10, were many years ago already within the city limits, and, according to a survey of 1848, contained 621 acres. They were sold mainly in 1849 and 1850, and a small portion under litigation as late as 1855, bringing an average of somewhat over $19 per acre, or about $3 per acre less than the average sales of 1837. The Toledo lands, which might have brought the university some millions altogether, brought about $17,000.

While all will regret the unfortunate transactions with Mr. Oliver, it must nevertheless be admitted that this board did a great work in locating the lands granted by the act of 1826. They reported twenty-three sections selected and acknowledged by the general land-office as set apart and reserved for the university, leaving but twenty-nine sections to be chosen by their successors; and having done what has been briefly narrated in this and a previous chapter, at a session held on the 18th of May, 1837, they made all the arrangements for closing up their business and transferring their trust, or rather a part of it, to the newly appointed board of regents of the University of Michigan, the history of which will follow, and on that day virtually expired, after an existence of sixteen years, which, added to the four years of the catholepistemiad, make twenty years.

These trustees, however, discriminated between that part of their trust which related to the grant of 1826 and that which related to the administration of funds derived from other sources. The amount paid over to the regents—a little over $5,000—was designated simply as the proceeds of the sale of lands to William Oliver. They had sold lands to about the same amount from the Fort Meigs reservation, made in 1817 for the "College of Detroit," which they had probably expended, as already hinted, in the educational work in that city. Part of this was doubtless represented in their property in Detroit, of which they made no transfer. On the contrary, they took measures for the investment on interest of all funds except those received from Mr. Oliver for the Toledo lands. They also authorized the leasing of the academy building for five years to the regents, for the purpose of procuring the establishment of a branch of the university at Detroit, as also another piece of real estate for a term not to exceed thirty years, so strictly did they discriminate between the grant of 1826 and all other property in their possession. Thus it appears that the identity of the two corporations of 1817 and 1821 with the university board as organized in 1837, was adjourned over to a judicial decision of nearly twenty years later. The record of this action is the last made by the board of 1821.

We of this generation, in view of all the facts of this history, will, after all, praise these men for their noble work, rather than blame them for their one great blunder. The future lay to them, as it does to us, beyond the range of certain vision.

In our account of Michigan's early condition, we omitted any reference to the general progress of its settlement by immigration from the Eastern States. This scarcely began in earnest before 1830; the height of the removal excitement was in 1836 and 1837. The settlers built log huts, with scarcely any tools but axes, and often lived in them without chimneys, doors, windows, or floors, drank "mud-hole water," used hickory bark in place of candles, and suffered privations similar to those detailed in our account of the earlier settlements of Ohio, and the further South. But in Michigan this state of things was exceedingly brief; it never became normal; few became inured to it and satisfied with it; seldom was a community long enough in such condition of destitution as to lose the remembrance of the school advantages they had left in the East, and the desire and ambition to renew them or rise above them in their western home. This state of things presented Michigan, as also other States of its latitude which were settled at the same time, or later, at immense advantage compared with the earlier settled States of the West and Southwest. We may not, therefore, give very much credit to our people for their rapid progress in industrial pursuits and education. These settlers came from New

York and New England. The former had had its school system since 1820; the latter from its first settlement, beginning in 1620. Their sons carried the best spirit of their native sections with them to the West, where they determined to reproduce the educational advantages which they had left in the East, or an improvement upon them, and their early agricultural and commercial thrift enabled them to effect this before their spirits had been cooled. The very parents who once sat together in such log huts, as we have described above, occupied with their sewing and knitting, shelling corn and basket-making, reading and conversation, by the snapping blaze of the hickory bark, have sat in their own parlors by gas-light, received the visits of sons at home during the vacations of their own State university, and listened to the music of the piano, played by daughters, while all the signs of physical thrift have surrounded them.

CHAPTER VII.

Organization of the School System and Administration of the Endowment Fund.

THE formation and development of the present higher educational system in Michigan owe much to the discipline which had been gained in the work carried on from 1817 to 1837. Though few of the men engaged in the earlier movement were on the first Board of Regents, much also is due to a class of educated minds, mainly from New York and New England, distributed among the early settlers of the Territory. Nor were there wanting some of those happy coincidences which often surprise the historical inquirer in the prosecution of his investigations. To this last-named class belong the circumstances which introduced into the State constitution the provision for a superintendent of public instruction, assigned his duties, and made the first appointment to the place. ·

Hon. Isaac E. Crary had recently married, and brought with him his wife to board in the family of Rev. John D. Pierce, of Marshall. A translation of Cousin's report upon the Prussian educational system had just fallen into his hands, and being a member elect of the Constitutional Convention which was to sit in Detroit in the spring and summer of 1835, and feeling some responsibility in the providing of a system for Michigan, he read the work carefully over, conversed with Mr. Pierce on the subject, and it was agreed between them that a similar provision ought to be introduced into the State constitution. Mr. Crary was himself made chairman of the committee on education, and reported a clause giving the charge of the schools into the hands of a superintendent, as nearly like in powers to the Prussian minister of education as the genius of our government seemed to allow.

There was delay, growing mainly out of the boundary contest of Michigan and Ohio, in effecting an agreement between Congress and the State as to the terms of the latter's admission to the Union; but the State assented to those fixed by Congress rather than be kept longer out of the sisterhood, the assent being given in a convention assembled at Ann Arbor, on the 15th of December, 1836. The conditions of this contract are not important.here, except the following:

"*First*. That section numbered sixteen in every township of the public lands, and where such section has been sold or otherwise disposed of, other lands, equivalent thereto, and as contiguous as may be, shall be granted to the *State* for the use of schools.

"*Second*. That the seventy-two sections of land set apart and reserved for the support of a university, by an act of Congress approved on the 20th of May, 1826, entitled an act concerning a seminary of learning in the Territory of Michigan, are hereby granted and conveyed to the *State*, to be appropriated solely to the use and support of such university, in such manner as the legislature may prescribe."

It is indeed maintained, and with reason, that this legislation has no validity, because Congress had already settled the terms of the grant, and could not make other and different terms. Nevertheless, this action is important as a help in the interpretation of the mind of the parties at the time when it was taken.

These provisions were first suggested by the State convention,* and not by Congress, and their advantages in that particular, which was of most importance, are apparent. The original plan of Congressional grants for education, was that those intended for primary schools should be conveyed not to the States, but to the *townships*, and ad-

---

* Journal of the State Convention of 1835, p. 219.

8

ministered by them; that the university lands should be all in one tract, and that both should be leased, not sold. The grant, or rather reservation, made for a university in Athens county, Ohio, in 1787, was upon these conditions. But the act of 1826 gave to Michigan the right to locate its university lands in detached parcels. It is claimed for Mr. Crary, by his friend, Rev. J. D. Pierce,* that he introduced into the Congressional ordinance of admission a provision to convey the primary school lands to the State, and not to the several townships in which they were situated, and that this passed in Congress unobserved, and thus changed the policy. If this is true, he doubtless, also, in a similar way, added the clause which conveys the university lands to the *State*, to be used as its legislature should prescribe—that is, as the event proved, by selling instead of leasing them. Thus gifts, which otherwise would have been nearly useless, became great educational funds.   .

Congress passed the act admitting Michigan into the Union on the 26th of January, 1837; but previously to that date quite a body of statutes had been formed for the future State, the legislature having begun its work as early as the autumn of 1835, and corresponding executive action had been inaugurated.

Mr. Crary, just before leaving home to take the seat to which he had been elected in the first Congress in which Michigan was represented as a State, addressed a note to Governor Mason requesting the appointment of Rev. John D. Pierce as Superintendent of Public Instruction, which was accordingly made and confirmed July 26, 1836, and an act approved two days later defined the superintendent's duties. The provisions of this act, so far as they relate to the subject of this work, are as follows:

Section *first* provides that "it shall be the duty of the superintendent of public instruction to make out an inventory of all the lands, and all other property, if there be

---

* Michigan Teacher, Vol. IV., No. 5.

any, according to the best information he can obtain without personally viewing the same, which have been or may be set apart and reserved for the purposes of education in this State, with a statement of the location and condition of said property."

Section *second*. "The superintendent shall give his views, in writing, to the legislature on or before the second Monday of January, 1837, relative to the disposition of said property."

Section *third*. "He shall prepare and digest a system for the organization and establishment of common schools and a university and its branches."

Section *seventh*. "He may hold correspondence with such members of literary institutions as he may deem proper."

The superintendent's first report was laid before the legislature in January, 1837, a few days previous to the passage of the act admitting Michigan into the Union. It is elaborate in its discussions, and full and detailed in its recommendations of plans for primary and higher education, and for the administration of the school and university funds, and proposed also the further defining of the superintendent's duties. It states, too, the condition and prospect of the funds, and argues the question fully and well in favor of selling, instead of leasing the lands. This report furnishes the basis of the whole educational system, the germ from which the future was to be developed. In accordance with its recommendations, the law providing for the organization of the university was passed, and a board of regents appointed, which proceeded immediately to establish branches, and take other measures looking to the early opening of the central institution. Only the management of the fund will be treated in this chapter, the reader, however, being requested to bear in mind that during most of the period covered by this narrative, the work of instruction was being prosecuted with large measures of success.

The superintendent, in his first report referred to above, which was made before the passage of the act authorizing him to sell the university lands, made the following estimate of the fund which their sale would create:

"At $15 per acre, 20,000 acres of the seminary lands would sell for $300,000, and it is more than probable that the first 20,000 would average as high as $20 per acre, which would amount to $400,000. The interest of $300,000 would be $21,000 per annum, while $28,000 would be the annual interest of $400,000. With such an income, how easy to lay the foundation of a university on th'e broadest scale, and place it on high and elevated ground at the very commencement of its career of light, usefulness, and glory. The balance of the seventy-two sections— 26,080 acres—would undoubtedly sell as soon as the funds would be needed, at the same rate. If for $15 per acre, they would sell for $391,200, the interest of which would be $27,384 per annum. If for $20 per acre, the sale would amount to $521,600; the interest would be $36,512. We have then this result: At $15 per acre, the whole would amount to $691,200, with an annual income of $48,384; at $20 per acre, it would amount to $921,000, with an annual interest of $64,912. It is not apprehended that the amount can in any event fall short of the lowest estimate, while it is believed, judging from the decisions of the past and the indications of the future, that it will exceed the highest computation."

By an act approved March 21, 1837, the superintendent of public instruction was authorized to sell at auction so much of the university lands as should amount to the sum of $500,000, none of which were to be sold lower than $20 per acre—the principal to stand for a term of years, bearing interest at seven per cent., payable annually. The money to be raised by these sales might be loaned to counties, not more than $15,000 to any one, nor for less than ten years. If there should be any left after the demands of the counties should have been supplied, it might be loaned to individuals. In both cases some provisions in regard to security were added. The interest was to be made payable to the State treasury. The superintendent was to give bond in the sum of $100,000. It appears by the report of this officer that the sales made in 1837 in pursuance of this enactment, were at an average price of $22.85 per acre, and their amount was $150,447.90—certainly a good beginning, both in legislation and execution. A series of acts, however, followed, which wrought great depreciation to the fund and embarrassment to the board.

The first legislation tending to disturb the progress of the work, was approved March 20, 1838, and authorized the release of sixteen sections, which had been located for the university in 1830. The conditions of this release were that Congress should assent to it, and grant the same number of sections elsewhere, which should be certified by a person named in the act, to be of equal value with the original sixteen sections, less the improvements made by the settlers. These conditions would, indeed, seem to be both just and safe; nor do we know that the result was otherwise. But such legislation is hazardous. The occupants of these lands had doubtless settled upon them after they had been taken for the university; otherwise their pre-emption right would have been sufficient without legislation. If such precedent had been established, then settlers could have driven the university from every section of land which might have been located for it.

Difficulties, too, were always arising between the purchasers of university lands and the superintendent of public instruction. To adjust those which had already arisen within the first three years after the sales commenced, a commission was provided for by the legislature of 1840. Major Kearsley represented the board of regents before this body, and in July of the same year, reported the settlement of forty-two claims, not all, however, to the satisfaction of the board.

The single case of most imminent peril to the fund, is that in which Governor Mason, on the 17th of April, 1839, interposed his veto in behalf of the interests of our then infant institution. Previous to the passage of this "*act for the relief of certain settlers on university and state lands*," the board remonstrated against it, but without effect. Their consternation will appear from this, that at a meeting held on the 13th of April, just after the act was passed, resolu- tions were introduced for the suspension of the work of instruction in the branches, and that of building at Ann Arbor, which had just been inaugurated. These resolu- tions were laid on the table, the governor himself voting for such disposition of them. A gleam of hope now ap- peared in another quarter—the governor had not signed the bill. The regents sent him an earnest protest against his approval of it, and four days later, he returned it with his reasons for withholding his assent, as follows:

" I return without my signature, to the house in which it originated, a bill entitled ' an act for the relief of certain settlers on university and state lands.' In refusing my sanction to the provisions of this bill, I am governed by an imperious sense of public duty, urged upon me by the solemnity of my official oath. The determination I make is a painful one. It has been formed, however, after ma- ture and anxious deliberation, and can not be resisted.

" The ostensible object of the bill is to secure to certain settlers on public lands their just rights under the pre-emp- tion law of Congress, which is alleged to have been inter- fered with by the state. Does this bill meet the object in- tended, and are its provisions limited to the designs of the legislature?

" I will not permit myself to inquire into the equity of the claims of these settlers. I do not stop to ask how far the eager hopes of the people of Michigan in an institution fraught with benefits to thousands yet unborn, are crushed by the measures proposed to me. The pre-emption law was framed for the protection of the bold and daring pio- neer, who leads the march of civilization, and proclaims to the world the unknown beauties and hidden resources of our western wilderness. For the protection of such men was the law designed, and if the applicants under the bill before me, are entitled to the right of property to the lands in question, not even for the holy purposes of education should that right be disturbed. How far, then, these claimants come within the spirit and intentions of Congress, I leave the legislature to determine. To the representatives of the people properly belongs the decision of all such questions. Appreciating, as they ever should, the high interests committed to their charge, I am bound to believe that such claim, under this bill, has undergone the most rigid scrutiny, and that none other save a disinterested sense of justice, an anxious desire to protect the rights of the citizen, and a high sense of what is due to the character of the state and our institutions, could have induced your sanction to the measure proposed in the bill before me. If, then, a mere question of expediency were involved in the bill, it might become my duty to yield to it my unhesitating assent. But my solemn convictions sanction no such conclusion.

"By the first section of the bill, you propose to sell at $1.25 per acre *any lands located for university purposes*, if it is proven they were occupied and cultivated as pointed out by the pre-emption law of Congress, before their location by the State. Where is the necessity for this unlimited provision, releasing all lands located for university purposes, whether heretofore claimed by individuals or not? What is the object of this wholesale temptation to fraud and perjury? The applications before you have emanated from that highly respectable class of settlers whose rights are affected by the locations on the Niles and Notawassippi reservations, and on the Grand and Muskegon rivers. The relief asked by these claimants should have been extended to them whenever their claims were found to be meritorious. I am anxious to afford that relief, and I regret that their rights have been jeopardized by a wholesale species of propagandism, in search of adventurers to claim your public lands.

"The Congress of the United States ' has granted and conveyed these lands to the State, to be appropriated *solely* for the *use* and support of the University of Michigan.' The State has accepted these lands, and the constitution

enjoins that the legislature shall take measures for their
protection and improvement, and also provide means for
the *permanent security* of the funds of the institution.
These are the solemn conditions by which the State holds
this sacred trust; and yet, by one single enactment, you
place all the lands thus held in trust in market at $1.25 per
acre, no matter what their value when located, or how
claimed. Yet, it may be said, they are protected by the
provisions of the bill from all illegal claims. What is that
protection? The feeble barrier of an oath, held out with a
bribe for its violation by bad and wicked men. Can this be
a faithful administration of the trust committed to us? Is
it the appropriation of these lands *solely to the use and
support of the University of Michigan*, as required by
the compact with the United States, or their *protection and
improvement*, as enjoined by the constitution?"

This message impressed the members of the legislature .
with a strong, though somewhat vague and indefinite
sense of something which they had almost unconsciously
done, and they made no attempt to pass the bill over the
veto. The friends of the university again breathed more
freely, but, disturbed by the recollection of this action, and
the fear which it brought with it that similar legislation
might again occur, they hoped only with a trembling solici-
tude in regard to an uncertain future.

The language of this paper is in some places wanting in
clearness and exactness, in place of which, expressions
akin to declamation are substituted. As a specimen, the
following words, at the end of the third paragraph, may be
cited: "I regret that their rights have been jeopardized
by a wholesale species of propagandism, in search of adven-
turers to claim your lands." If these words have a definite
import, they are meant to intimate that fictitious claims
were gotten up in order to justify what some wished to accomplish; that is, the throwing of all the university lands into
the market at $1.25 per acre—the severest charge ever
made in regard to the administration of this fund, and,

coming from such a source, it was probably well founded. The veto saved the fund.

Mr. Mason, when this occurred, was but about thirty years of age. His name is scarcely known to most of the younger generation in Michigan. But if he had never done another act for which his memory ought to be cherished, this alone would entitle him to perpetual and grateful remembrance. The spirit and evident sincerity of his utterances, quite as much as the force of his arguments in this message, carried conviction to the honest minds among those to whom it was addressed, and such check to a certain tendency in our legislation, that nothing so sweeping was ever again attempted.

There was, however, a very persistent tampering with the price and sales of the lands. The legislatures of 1838 and 1839 had extended the time of payment to purchasers, and so caused embarrassment, but had not directly diminished the fund or its income. By an act of March 25, 1840, however, $4,743\frac{12}{100}$ acres of university lands were sold, at an average price of $6.21* per acre, to persons who had settled upon them, making an aggregate of upward of $65,000 less than the minimum price of the lands as it then stood, or somewhat over $78,000 less than these lands would have brought at the average price of the sales of 1837; and this amount seems to have been paid as a premium for squatting upon the lands without buying them. This is always a loose and generally a rascally way of doing business relating to lands which have been surveyed and brought into market. The presumption is that these squatters often, if not always, knew that the lands had been taken for the university, and that they relied upon the prevailing feelings which settlers cherished against allowing for any purpose the continued existence of these unsettled and untaxable lands, to secure their purchase at any price they might choose to offer.

By similar acts of legislation, sales were soon afterward

---

* Session Laws for 1840, and Superintendent's Report for 1841.

made at $17, $8, $19, and $15 per acre ; and then, in 1841, the minimum price was reduced to $15, and, in 1842, to $12 per acre, and in the latter instance the act was made retrospective. It constituted the county judges and county surveyor an adjudicating board, with power to appraise anew lands already sold ; and in case a lower price should be fixed upon them than that at which they had previously been sold, if not below $12 per acre, the superintendent of public instruction was to credit the purchaser with the difference. This *ex post facto* legislation unsettled the whole past. All the contracts for university lands made previously to 1842 were annulled by it, in case the appraisers should in any way be influenced to put upon them a lower price than that at which they had been sold. It was much the same as if $12 had been originally made the minimum price. The details of the application of this law to the previous sales need not be given, even if that were possible. The superintendent's report for 1843 shows $34,651 either returned or credited to purchasers. At this time the sales on contract amounted to $220,000, but had been reduced by forfeitures and relief legislation to a little over $123,000,* showing $93,000 less than the contracts, or a loss of $27,000 more than all the sales of the first five years after those of April, 1837. This does not include the effect of the regular reduction of the minimum price in 1841 and 1842.

The question of the reduction of the price for future sales is indeed quite distinct from that of relief legislation, and yet the moral principle involved is not substantially different. It is clear that when the legislature determined, in 1837, that no university lands should be sold at a lower rate than $20 per acre, they made a contract with the regents of the university that the latter should have at their

---

*Mr. Shearman, on page 93 of his School Law of 1852, says $137,000, which Dr. Tappan has followed in his Memorial of 1855; but in a table, in the appendix of the same work, he says $123,209$\frac{80}{100}$. Although the latter number has been placed in the text, we are, on reflection, more inclined to regard the larger as the true one.

disposal a fund of not less than $921,000, and justified them in laying their plans accordingly. When the first sales brought $2.85 on the acre above the price fixed, the hope was encouraged of a capital of more than a million. And this can scarcely be regarded as less than a contract, both with the regents and the people of the State. Nor was there any necessity for a breach of this promise upon which the board had already begun to act.

It is indeed true that speculation, and its consequent expansion of the paper currency, had raised prices above what could be immediately realized after the reaction set in; but it was certain that the lands would, at no distant day, return to the price fixed. It was the *price* which had been established, not the time of its realization; and time should have been left to work the fulfillment of contracts and the accomplishment of hopes, rather than that the former should have been broken and the latter blasted at such fearful expense of complicated evils as must necessarily be incurred. The legislature did not wait a single year to see whether their price would prove too high. They began at once to interfere with it; and yet subsequent facts showed that the lands would have risen in the market to the price put upon them, before any pressing needs of the university would have called for their sale.

So far as the reduction of the price has been made retrospective, it has operated by the wholesale as relief to purchasers, and has always been unjust to the university fund, and all concerned in it. The State, soon after accepting this trust from Congress, determined the lowest price at which this property could be sold, did it freely, accepted the responsibility as trustee of realizing that amount or more, and published this, so that Congress which gave the fund, the regents who were to administer it, and the people who were to enjoy its benefits, might understand what to expect. As has already been shown, this fund could not justly, by any legislation, be brought below the amount thus solemnly pledged, and the obligation of the trustee receives an additional element when contracts of sale have actually been made; and yet, for a long time, it was rather the rule than the exception to grant relief from the terms of these sales, or to sell on special terms to those who had settled without previous purchase upon these lands. The instance in 1840, stated above, in which four thousand seven hundred and forty-three acres of land were sold to settlers upon it, by special act, is one in which the result was made to depend upon their own testimony and that of their neighbors, and the report of the same year shows the natural consequence. Forty-three acres sold by free contract with the superintendent, brought $24.96 per acre, or a little over four times the amount obtained for choice lands sold to settlers by special legislative provision. Thus the sales of 1840 brought the university a little over $30,000, instead of about $96,000, which they would have brought if the legislature had not interfered to nullify its own original contract. Such special legislation continued for many years. There is one instance of a sale as low as two dollars per acre. In 1843, a provision passed the legislature for relief to twelve purchasers in Oakland county—the oldest and richest farming section of the State —by which a new appraisal was to be made, with the limitation that it was not to fall below five dollars per acre, or one-fourth of the minimum price established in 1837; but the report of the following year does not state that the relief was realized, and we may therefore presume the contrary. Thus everything relating to the fund was to unsettle it.

No price was so low that the purchaser might not hope for its reduction; none so high that he might not feel safe in offering it, if deemed necessary in order to compete successfully with more conscientious bidders. The result can not be given in its details, nor would the reader be willing to wade through these. But a fund which the trustee pledged at about a million of dollars—which its legally constituted administrators accepted at that, and planned their action accordingly, thereby justifying the people in expecting the beneficent influence of this amount—finally settled down at about $450,000, and there remained until a happier epoch in legislation dawned upon the university.

In another class of legislation having reference to the university fund, the legislature and the regents have acted concurrently. The chief instance of this kind, and perhaps the only one which we need to notice, is the notorious $100,000 loan. While the regents continually protested against that succession of acts stated above, as tending to imperil the fund and cripple the work, they, on the other hand, sought this loan, by a resolution offered by Mr. Schoolcraft on the 3d of March, 1838. This contemplated the raising of $150,000. As a fund of about $1,000,000 had been virtually promised, the board naturally desired to anticipate its income, and hasten forward the work already inaugurated in the branches.

We may look upon this action from the distance, and find in it much to censure as premature and imprudent, as bringing into peril the university fund, as threatening to strangle at its birth the great enterprise which it proposed to hasten into life and into a full development of its beneficent career; even the closest scrutiny and most careful investigation of facts will rather increase than diminish the number and strength of the grounds of censure; and yet, after all, there will be found reason to believe that the very boldness of the act and the incentives to exertion generated in the straits into which it brought the board, really saved the institution, and contributed to make it what it is. The loan, once obtained, was soon exhausted; embarrassments followed; legislation was wild; the extravagant and crude notions with which the board set out received a check; they felt the need of other counsels, and sought them; they were conscious of fault in getting into trouble, and put forth the more strenuous efforts to get out again. These efforts doubtless reached the legislature, and checked that reckless course which, unchecked, would have annihilated the fund.

This loan seemed to supply a stimulus to exertion, which proved an antidote to apathy and crude, reckless, vague,

and extravagant notions in regents, legislators, and state
executive officers. The careful student of the facts will,
therefore, learn to look over this history, observing acts
which are to be censured and those which are to be commended with much the same feelings, seeing, as he must,
how all these things, under a higher supervision, have
worked together for the production of their grand result.
There is no one thing in the financial history of the university which has been the subject of so persevering and so
interested discussions and action as this loan, and yet nothing is shrouded in so much mystery.

By acts of legislation approved April 6, 1838, and February 28 and March 11, 1844, the following general provisions were made : *First*, for the issue of certificates of a
loan to the university of $100,000 ; *second*, for the receiv-
ing of certain depreciated State obligations at par in payment for university lands, *provided* the amount thus received
should not exceed the principal and interest of the $100,000
loan, and *provided*, *further*, that the whole amount of the
purchase money should be paid down at the time of the
purchase ; *third*, for relieving the university from the direct
payment of the principal and interest of this loan ; and
fourth, for receiving certain real estate in Detroit, viz., the
female seminary lot and building, for $8,095, toward this
indebtedness.

This loan was negotiated through the Bank of Michigan,
and was to run twenty years, viz., from July 1, 1838, to
July 1, 1858, and a premium of $6,000 was received upon
it by the university.

By examining the annual reports of the finance committee of the board of regents, it can be seen just how rapidly
the payment under the law of 1844 progressed. The following extract from the message of Governor Felch for
1846 will show the progress up to that time :

"The university fund, at an early day of its existence,
became indebted to the State for a loan of $100,000, and
the interest of this debt has been liquidated from the interest received annually on the fund. The acts of the legis-

lature, approved February 28, 1844, and March 11, 1844, authorized the state treasurer to receive certain property, and state warrants belonging to the university fund, and to credit the same on this loan, and also authorized the sale of university lands for internal improvement warrants, which were to be paid into the state treasury, and credited in like manner. The effect of these provisions has been materially to aid in relieving the fund from its embarrassments. The amount received by the State, under these provisions, and credited to the university fund, is $56,774.15, leaving due to the State from that fund, for principal, $43,225.86."

The above extract shows that in less than one-half of the twenty years, it had been reduced to about $43,000, and Governor Ransom's message of only two years later, shows the debt already brought down to a little over $20,000.

The following extracts from a report of the finance committee of the board, found in the records of the meeting of December 23, 1852, will sufficiently set forth the final extinction of the debt:

"It is the duty of the committee to call the attention of the board to an act of the legislature approved February 28, 1844, entitled 'an act for the receipt of obligations of this State in payment of university lands;' and also to an act, No. 83, approved March 11, 1844, entitled 'an act for the relief of the University of Michigan.' Under the provisions of these acts, treasury notes and warrants to the amount of $100,000 were received from purchasers of university lands, except $8,095 paid in real estate, and perhaps $7,000 in interest warrants paid directly to the State by the regents. On this sum the university has received but six per cent., in place of the ordinary legal interest of seven per cent."

It is then clear that the State executive knew of the progress of the payment of the debt, and that the board of 1852, though not quite exact in their statement, seemed to have at the time known that it had been paid. How did any doubt ever arise on this subject? In answer to this question many things could be said, all showing a tendency to an oblivion of the facts, with nothing to necessitate their remembrance, and with some things directly tending to keep up or renew even the impression of the university's indebtedness. The loan was for the university, was taken for twenty years, and was not therefore due until 1858, and it was not to be supposed that a six per cent. indebtedness would be paid before its maturity. The stock was not to be redeemed until 1858, and without decisive evidence to the contrary, it would naturally be supposed that, as it was the university's loan, the university had it to pay. Rotation in office and distribution of responsibility were such, during that period, as not to hold attention to this point. The board, in 1851, became elective by the people, and all the members entered and retired at once. But two regents were upon the board of 1852 who had previously been upon it. All were new in 1858. Succession in the State executive, both chief and subordinate, was still more frequent, and although each did his work with substantial accuracy, yet no one was responsible for communicating to his successor an exact understanding of the system upon which he had acted. Furthermore, by the legislation of 1853 and 1855, it became temporarily indifferent to all the purposes of the State executive offices whether the debt, principal or interest, had ever been paid or not, and by act 143 of 1859, it became permanently so. There was, therefore, no absolute obligation to investigate this matter, where alone it could have been settled, and speculative attempts at its settlement have only led to profounder confusion. The statement extracted above from the report of the finance committee of the board, made in 1852, is the last which has approached the truth.

President Tappan, in 1855, memorialized the legislature for the *remission** of the debt. He based his petition on the ground that the loan was a violation of law (meaning doubtless the compact with Congress); claimed that the

---

* Senate Documents for 1859, No. 1.

principal of the university fund could not legally be touched for buildings, or for any other purpose; that the entire expenditure upon the branches had been contrary to law; that the university had overpaid the interest, having paid seven per cent., or $119,000 in seventeen years, while the State had paid but six per cent., or $102,000, and he does not intimate in all this that the principal, or any portion of it, had ever been paid.

Governor Bingham, in his annual message for 1857, takes substantially the same view, as follows:

"Soon after its (the university's) organization, a stock of $100,000 was issued by the State, to raise money to construct buildings for colleges and professors' houses, to be redeemed out of the sale of the lands granted by Congress 'for the support of a university, and for no other purpose whatever.' The act authorizing the issue of the stock pledged all the disposable income from the university fund for its redemption. This has been deemed such a perversion of the income of the fund from its original design, that the legislature for several years past has authorized the payment of the interest from the general fund. The principal is now about becoming due, and I respectfully recommend that it be paid from the treasury of the State, so that this noble institution, in the prosperity of which every citizen of Michigan feels a deep interest and pride, shall be entirely relieved from embarrassment and debt."

The board of regents which came into office on the 1st of January, 1858, memorialized the legislature* under date of December 21st of the same year, and taking for granted, indeed, that the debt had not been paid, but still quite ignoring that question, they prayed for the enactment of a law to the effect that the university should "*receive permanently the interest on the whole amount of the proceeds of the sales of the lands granted by the United States to this State for the use and support of a university.*"

---

* Senate Documents for 1859, No. 1.

The ground upon which the board placed this application was that Congress did not give this fund for the *establishment* of a university, but for its "use and support"
when established; that the fund itself was' for this latter
purpose alone, and could not be touched for any other;
that it no more belonged to the Congressional grant made
for a university, either from its principal or its interest, to
put up buildings, than to the primary school fund to erect
school-houses; and that the language in which the State
accepted the trust, implied the understanding and hearty
indorsement of this condition. Only on this last point
issue may be taken with the opinions of the memorialists.
They have indeed rightly interpreted the words of. the law;
the legislature may be presumed to have entertained the
meaning ascribed to them, and we may justly regard this
as the true intent of the law, because it is the only natural
interpretation; but those whose memories embrace the
early part of our university history, and who know the
spirit of the State government and legislation of the time,
will feel quite sure that there was no design on the part of
those who acted in our State affairs to make any appropriations to the university fund, nor had it ever occurred to
them that there was any on the part of Congress to require
it. The law holds a meaning which existed very dimly
and indefinitely, if at all, in the minds of the Congressional
legislators, and which never occurred to the people of the
young State for which that law was made.

Within about a month after receiving it, the legislature
responded to this memorial, and other solicitations to the
same effect, by the following enactment:

" *The People of the State of Michigan enact,* That the
auditor-general be and is hereby required to credit to the
university interest fund, interest from and after the 31st day
of December, 1860, on the entire amount which has heretofore been or may hereafter be received by the State for
university lands sold or contracted, and to draw his warrants
upon the state treasurer for the same, who is hereby re-

quired to pay the same to the treasurer of the university upon his application therefor, from time to time, as the said interest may accrue, and be required for the use of the university. Approved February 12, 1859."

This action would seem to show that the view presented in the regents' memorial, and the other extracts given above, prevailed in the legislature. The question of payment or non-payment by the university of the loan, however, as one of fact, was evaded in this act and left to the auditor-general, and his decision, though singularly enough it seems not to have been thought of at the time, is an acknowledgment that the board had paid the loan—it gave them the interest on $100,000 *more* than the sum upon which they had prevously been entitled to receive interest.

How the error in regard to the payment had become current—how it could have found place in the minds of regents, president, and heads of the executive offices of the capital, is matter of curious interest, and yet not difficult of explanation. In the regents' estimates and statements of expenses was usually found an item of $6,000 for interest on loan, which would naturally be regarded as decisive proof that they had not paid the principal. It is true that the very first report of the finance committee made after the law of 1844, providing for the payment of the principal, went into operation, explains the matter fully. This report shows, indeed, the item of $6,000 interest, but shows also that the State returned the interest on that portion of the loan which had been paid. But overlooking this and the executive references to the payment of the principal, all—even the president and later regents— seemed to take for granted, from the fact that the loan was not yet due, and $6,000 was annually reported as interest paid upon it, that it remained due from the university. Even the auditor-general, in deciding the " entire amount which has heretofore been or may hereafter be received by the State for university lands sold or contracted," was not, as stated above, aware that he was at the same time decid-

ing that the university had paid this debt. He furnished
the premises, but did not draw the conclusion.*

As to the interest which the regents paid upon the loan,
notwithstanding the confusion which has run through the
whole matter, it can be shown almost to a dollar.† President Tappan says, indeed, in a memorial already referred
to, that the university paid seven per cent. for seventeen
years, making $119,000. The interest, however, was
paid but fourteen and one-half years, and was but six per
cent., making $87,000, which, by some other items, was in-
creased to about $89,600, paid by the university as interest
on the loan.

It was doubtless the design of the legislature of 1859, to
treat the whole matter of the loan as if the State had originally given the university $100,000 for buildings, and
they actually did what they supposed to involve this result.
In order to do this, however, they should have refunded all
the interest paid by the university, together with interest
upon the sum up to the time of refunding it. As this interest was paid from 1838 to 1853, the medium time to 1875

---

*The present auditor-general, Mr. Humphrey, as we learn by a corre-
spondence with him, is acquainted with the state of the facts, and we are,
indebted to him for confirmations of the views here offered, and also for
some facts.

† The following is a substantially accurate statement in detail :
Interest on $100,000 from July, 1838, to January, 1853, four-
teen and one-half years, at six per cent.   .   . $87,000 00
Less one year's interest on bond redeemed in 1852,   .   .   60 00
                                                                    ‾‾‾‾‾‾‾‾‾‾
                                                                    $86,940 00
The university paid an average annual exchange of *about* $80
    in New York, ...   1,160 00
The university lost the difference between six and seven per
    cent. on the amounts received and credited upon the loan
    from 1844 to 1853. As the earliest payments were much the
    largest, this may be estimated to have averaged $75,000, at
    one per cent. for nine years, ...   6,750 00
                                                                    ‾‾‾‾‾‾‾‾‾‾
                                                                    $95,730 00
Then the university received :
    As premium on this loan,   .   . $6,000 00
    As interest on premium,   .   .   .   38 50   6,038 50
                                                                    ‾‾‾‾‾‾‾‾‾‾
Loss of the university by the loan, ... $89,691 50

would be thirty years, and the amount of the university's loss, at simple interest, would be about $278,000.

The sum of $35,900 was expended upon the branches, and, beyond all question, in violation of the Congressional provisions, so that this amount, with thirty-two years of interest added to it, making $115,000, or, at compound interest, about $285,000, may be justly deemed to be due from the State to the university. This was precisely the same as it would be now to expend university money upon union schools.

There is a curious episode in the history of the loan as viewed from the side of the regents. Immediately after the act of April 6, 1838, authorizing it, the board took measures for its negotiation by appointing Major Kearsley, one of its members, its agent for this purpose. Some inquiries had been set on foot in the East by Governor Mason and others, the issue of which the agent waited first to learn, and suitable offers in other quarters not having been received, the terms stated above were concluded with the Bank of Michigan. The board probably never thought that any charge would be made for this service of their agent. He did not leave Detroit. Perhaps half an hour's time taken from business moments settled the terms, which were, indeed, very favorable. The regent now presiding over the finances of the board would not think of making a charge for stepping into a bank in Ann Arbor, Grand Rapids, or Detroit to negotiate the sale of building warrants; but Major Kearsley claimed remuneration; continued to bring the matter up every year, until long after the statute of limitation had put an end to his legal claim, if indeed he ever had any, expressing the hope that this statute would not be pleaded against him. Committees at various times recommended the payment of some small amounts, the largest being $250. A commission of three persons was once appointed at Major Kearsley's request, but nothing came of it except some expense. The board had counsel fees to pay. We have not found that any settlement was ever made of this claim. The motive of the

major in bringing it forward was always a matter of curious
speculation, never satisfactorily settled. The prevailing
opinion seemed to be that he cared more about a recognition of his great service than about the insignificant addition which the highest amount he ever claimed would
bring to his ample fortune. His attempt to collect the pay
for his half-hour's service cost him probably more than a
thousand times the labor which he had expended upon the
original service, and the board much more, if their time is
to be reckoned, than the amount of the claim at its highest. It was before the board at least fourteen years, and
then in 1850, just before the expiration of his term of
service as a regent, it was brought before the legislature,
where he was handled with no little severity ; and in abatement of his merits, it was pleaded that he had for considerable times been in the receipt of $500 a year as chairman
of the building committees of the board. Thus ended a
matter, the history of which shows one of the less favorable idiosyncrasies of a man who labored long, and, in the
main, wisely and well in the interests of the university. It
would perhaps but illustrate the same feature of his character, if the remark were made—and Dr. Williams would
doubtless accept the responsibility of it—that the surest
way to obtain anything from Major Kearsley was vigorously to protest against it. The value of his services can
scarcely, however, be too strongly stated, notwithstanding
the truth of the above, and the further fact that he was one
of those who voted for the exchange and sale of the Toledo
lands. He was the Cerberus who guarded the entrance to
the university fund. His appearance before the commission mentioned above as having been appointed to settle
the claims of purchasers, and his preparation of a review
of the bearings of legislation on the fund, are prominent
among his services. But his great merit was his ceaseless
vigilance at every moment of peril to the interests of the
institution. It is scarcely too much to say that if he had
not been present to growl at the approach of danger to its
finances, there might not have been either professors or

regents here now to growl at him.   Probably, at least, no
man ever did more than he for the safety of the fund.

The administration of the finances, as carried on by the
board, will demand but a brief consideration in closing up
this long chapter of financial history, and will relate mainly
to the building and other initial work at Ann Arbor.   We
have seen the fund beset with perils and making its hair-
breadth escapes, until we have become used to them.   By
these some of our readers have been taught to expect more
such, and others, perhaps, to suppose that the supply of
material must have been already exhausted.   There is
another such, however, and of precisely the kind to be expected from the analogy of the initial history of almost all
colleges.

The legislature, in the organic law of the university approved March 18, 1837, authorized the board to procure
the most appropriate plan for buildings, which, when approved by the governor and superintendent of public instruction, was to be adopted by the regents.   Mr. Pierce,
the superintendent, shall himself state the result :

" One other question of great interest fell to my lot, solitary and alone, to decide, the decision of which, for the
time being, created much ill-feeling, and brought down
upon me a storm of denunciation.   Indeed, so intense was
the excitement, that an indignation meeting was proposed
to be called at Ann Arbor.   The occasion was this : The
legislature passed an act authoring the regents to procure
a plan for buildings.   They employed an architect from
New Haven to draft one ; that plan, if approved by the
governor and superintendent of public instruction, should
be adopted.   The one prepared was truly a magnificent
design, and would, in that day, have involved an expenditure of half a million, if not more.   It was accepted by the
regents and approved by the governor.   It was presented
to me.   Most respectfully, yet decidedly, I refused it my assent, and gave as a reason that it would absorb so much of
the university fund as would cripple it in all time to come ;
and urged further that a university did not consist in build-

ings, but in the number and ability of its professors, and in its other appointments, as library, cabinets, and works of art. The result was, the regents receded, and the present plan was adopted, and the university started into being. Twenty years after, or more, at the house of Dr. Denton, one of the medical professors, in company with President Morgan, of Pennsylvania, the doctor, in referring to my course in refusing my assent to their plan for building, and the bitter feeling incited against me at the time, remarked that, while he was unwilling to give me credit for so much sagacity as seemed to be implied in my action, yet he would truly say that it was the best thing that had ever happened in the State. My reply was that I was just as well satisfied then as now that its adoption would have been fatal to the institution."[*]

Here was an expenditure provided for, which actually exceeded the whole amount ever realized by the sale of the university lands in the thirty years following. The plan of the principal building which was to absorb this fund now hangs in the Museum—a monument, in connection with the above statement, of another of the university's marvelous escapes, the hero of which should be duly honored for it, not only while his gray hairs shall wave in the winds before us, but by the generations which shall follow each other after his form shall have been covered by mother earth.

The injudicious transactions of the board, however, viewed in their financial bearings, come almost entirely, so far as their plans are concerned, within the first two years of their existence, though some of them were not executed until later, and to all of these the $100,000 loan made in 1838 is fundamental. From this were built four professors' houses, at an expense of about $32,000, which have been a constant source of annoyance, and have never yielded a fair income on one-third of the investment, and the plan embraced the surrounding of the grounds on three sides with such houses. Two buildings were also erected for dormitories. It may, perhaps, be justly claimed that even at the time of the erection of the first of these structures, light enough had been diffused to make it clear that no money should have been expended for such a purpose. These, however, did not cost very much, and, in course of time, have been easily turned to other and more necessary uses. Within about one year from the organization of the board, a professor of botany was elected, and was immediately under pay, but without services to perform. The sum of $5,000 was placed in his hands for the purchase of books, of which he brought with him, on his return from a European tour, about 3,700 volumes. His salary continued a year and a half at $1,500 per annum—an amount which the salaries did not reach again for about sixteen years. This can not be called good financiering. The opposite was shown in case of two other professors, Drs. Houghton and Sager, who were elected years before their services were required, but it was on the stipulation that they should not receive any pay until they should be called into service ; and this arrangement gave the university the advantage of these gentlemen's superintendence of the putting up of the collections in natural history. The regents paid from the loan $4,000 for the Baron Lederer collection of minerals, which seems a large amount to pay in anticipation of the existence of both an endowment and an institution, and yet as this was nearly all that was expended for such purpose, it can not well be deemed injudicious.

In a previous chapter it was stated that the old board of trustees, in resigning their trusts to the board of regents of 1837, made a discrimination between the Congressional grant of 1826 and property which had been derived from other sources, delivering the former to the regents and retaining the latter. This consisted chiefly if not wholly of the so-called academy lot on Bates street, in Detroit, which had doubtless been purchased with funds obtained by subscriptions, and by the sale of the Fort Meigs reservation. The regents claimed this property, acquired a title to it by

decision of the Supreme Court in 1858, and sold it for
$22,010. This forms what is now called the reserve fund,
which is accumulating for the use of the library.

A review of these transactions from the beginning, with
the purpose of better understanding their real nature and
bearings, and fixing the ultimate responsibility for them,
would be an appropriate close of this history of the administration of the university fund.

To return for a moment beyond the period of the organization of the State, a shrewd policy on the part of the
old board located lands on the site of the present city of
Toledo, as already related. These alone, kept to the right
time, would have formed an endowment fund for a great
university ; but they were sold prematurely, and this well-
founded hope was thus blasted. This transaction was in
violation of no pledge of the State, for the State had then
no existence. No minimum price had been set upon the
lands, and of course no distinct obligation was violated.

The first legislation in regard to the fund was good, but
was followed by a system of general and special reliefs,
involving ever a lurking element of injustice. There is,
however, no evidence of corruption, nor do we find good
reason to suspect anything worse than prejudice, want of
due appreciation of university education, if not indeed an
unconscious dislike of it, and various mixed motives, such
as a desire on the part of legislators to please constituents,
without carefully weighing the interests which must suffer
as the effect. While some were thus operating to relieve
their friends at the expense of the university, some friends
of the university were unconsciously co-operating with them
in the hope of relieving the embarrassments of the institution
itself. But the need of relief was itself brought about by
the joint action of legislature and regents, in making the
loan, spending it, and pledging the fund for the payment
of principal and interest, all of which was afterward admitted to have been in violation of the terms of the grant. This
review should not therefore be made for the purpose of dispensing censure to those who have had the administration

of the trust. They all stand acquitted and unsuspected of corruption.

In 1837, a price was fixed on the university lands, for less than which none were to be sold. The first offered in the market brought, as above stated, nearly $3 an acre above this price—thus, indeed, giving a pledge to the regents and the people of a fund of about $1,000,000, and justifying expenditure accordingly. But the legislature began at once to violate its own pledge, by putting down the price, granting reliefs, and selling on special terms. Contracts for university lands were not regarded as ordinary transactions bearing that name. They seemed to settle nothing. Buyers neglected payments, in expectation of relief. The only plausible argument ever offered for this general policy was, that it hastened sales, which, indeed, it may have done, but it delayed payments, and led to all kinds of tampering with contracts. The attempt to create a market was premature. The stimulus applied in this direction even by the law of 1844, authorizing the receipt of depreciated State paper for university lands, though of very considerable immediate effect, but slightly hastened a demand which would have arisen without it. The sales of 1843 amounted to but $1,900; those of 1844 were $32,000; but in 1845 they declined to $17,000; in 1846, to $9,000, and then within three years after the demands of the law were satisfied, and purchases must again be made on a specie basis—in 1853 they rose to $34,000—all showing that the effort to quicken sales by tampering with prices was useless; that even the impulse given to them by this only act of considerate and judicious legislation in that direction, was really brief and comparatively unimportant, and that had the price been steadily maintained where it was first fixed, the sales would have been completed just as soon. All attempts of all kinds, except this one, at hastening sales, are to be condemned as breaches of faith, though unintended on the part of the State toward the university, to which the entire difference between a fund of $450,000 and one of about $1,000,000, together with more than a score of years' interest on that difference, is to be charged. This, at simple interest, amounts to $630,000, to which is to be added $265,000 for losses by the loan as stated above, and $110,000 for illegal expenditures upon the branches—giving, in 1872, the not inconsiderable sum of $1,005,000 as due from the State to the university, in fulfillment of the obligations assumed in 1837. From this should be deducted, however, $215,000, the principal represented by the $15,000 paid annually by the State to the university since 1867, leaving $790,000 as the amount by which the State may be deemed to be still in arrears to the university. As these figures were made in 1872, they are not disturbed by the legislation of 1873, which gave the university $13,000 for a deficiency, and the twentieth of a mill tax for the future.

To sum up this whole matter, if that line of argument pursued by President Tappan in his memorial presented to the legislature of 1855, is at all valid, it calls for an amount not less than that indicated above, from the State to the university, in order to restore the losses by unconstitutional and the various forms of relief legislation during the thirty-eight years now past since the organization of the institution. And this argument is indeed sound; trustees are bound to make good to its purpose the fund intrusted to them, even though that purpose were quite foreign to their own interests. But this fund was not given for an object indifferent to the interests of the State, but for its highest weal—for one which it should provide for from its own funds, if nothing had been given for it, so that the obligation is stronger than this argument presents it; and especially since the university has been made a part of that system of free schools established in the State, the State ought to support it without any reference to a fund granted by Congress.

This argument drawn from the indebtedness of the State as trustee of the fund is not, however, the one by which the regents of the university should endeavor to support any appeals which they may deem it necessary to make to the State legislature. It is indeed proper to relate these facts as matter of interesting history, which the people may like to look back upon in future years and future ages, that they may know what the university has struggled* through. Nor can it ever be viewed otherwise than that the State is bound in some way, and at some time, to restore, with interest, what the fund has lost by its management. But the guardians of this institution may fairly rise to a higher plane in their applications for aid. They should take a ground more consistent with their own dignity, and with a proper respect for the State legislature and executive than is implied in any attempt to merely call up old scores, and reckon their present value from interest tables. It is too much like claiming " the pound of flesh," because it is due by contract, instead of asking for what the university needs, in order fully to sustain and develop its character as head of a great system of free schools, every other part of which is supported by local taxation. This, therefore, not being local, but the consummation of all the local schools, should, by the State, be kept up with the demands increasingly made upon it. The State legislature seems to have come at last to this principle, which, indeed, is almost identical with that which was set forth in the bill establishing the catholepistemiad in 1817. The institution has proved its beneficent character, and has gradually brought the legislature to perceive this and act accordingly.

The University of Michigan is, as yet, greatly in advance of any other of the State universities ; but there are other States which recognized earlier and more fully the obligation to support their universities, and which, in proportion to their resources, will probably be found to have made larger appropriations for this purpose.

The reader can scarcely regard the financial history of the university otherwise than as a series of providential deliverances,* by the turning of human errors and over-

---

* This remark in regard to providential escapes might be illustrated by incidents outside of university history. One in regard to the common school lands may be given as an example. In the administration of Gov-

sights to account for good, and as the financial condition
of the institution is fundamental to all else in its development, its friends will surely feel, as they pass this history
in review, a deepened gratitude for that marvel of success
which it has achieved—a gratitude greatly increased by a
view of the numerous perils which have beset its pathway
to this crowning glory.

---

ernor Felch, some gentlemen, when the location of the capital was under
consideration, and it was supposed that it might be made upon or near
the school section on which it now stands, were on their way to the land-
office, at Marshall, to enter the section for purchase. The governor,
knowing nothing of this, but yet thinking that such a thing might occur,
sent a message to Marshall, asking the register of the land-office to withdraw this section from the market. The speculators and the message
were on the same train, which was so delayed as not to reach Marshall
until the office was closed. The register received his mail at his house in
the evening, and when he went to the office the next morning, he found
the two gentlemen waiting at the door for admission, only to be informed
by how narrow a chance they had failed of a great speculation, at the expense of the school fund.

CHAPTER VIII.

The Branches—Rise of Union Schools.

THE history of the university fund has been traced with as little reference as possible to the actual work of instruction. It will now be necessary to return to the period and work of organizing the forces of the institution. This, as already stated, was in 1837. Not far from the year 1833 a great impulse was given to immigration into the Territory, and its population at the time of its admission into the sisterhood of States had reached about 175,000, while the city of Detroit had not far from 8,000 souls. The body of the inhabitants was made up of the more intelligent and enterprising of the middle class of New York and New England, but more from the former. The views and feelings of these settlers in regard to higher education may be inferred from their action as it shall appear in our narrative.

The law for the organization of the university was approved March 18, 1837; two days later, that which located it on such ground—not less than forty acres—as the regents should select in or near the village of Ann Arbor, an interior town, with a population at that time of about 2,800. On the 21st of the same month the Senate confirmed the governor's choice of a board of regents. The following are the names: Isaac E. Crary, Zina Pitcher, Lucius Lyon, Thomas Fitzgerald, John J. Adam, Robert McClelland, Samuel W. Denton, John Norvell, Henry R. Schoolcraft, Ross Wilkins, Michael Hoffman, and Gideon O. Whittemore. Before the first meeting Mr. Fitzgerald resigned, and John F. Porter was appointed in his place. The *ex-officio* members were the governor, then Stevens T. Mason; the lieutenant-governor, Edward Mundy; the justices of the Supreme Court, William A. Fletcher,

George Morrell, Epaphroditus Ransom, and Charles W. Whipple; and the chancellor, Elon Farnsworth.

The obvious and just criticism made upon the composition of this board was, that while there was not a man in it to whom a positive objection could be made, it was without a single educator; it had on it but two members of the old board of trustees—Messrs. Norvell and Wilkins—neither of whom had been long enough in the service to know much about it; it was moreover made up almost exclusively of the prominent politicians of the time. They had not the leisure for their work as regents; they had not bestowed the necessary thought upon the subject committed to their care so as to be able to digest plans; no practical educators were as yet in the field to help them, and politics had preoccupied most of their minds. It was feared that men of this class would be less decided and independent, especially in a new State, settled with various elements from abroad, whose politicians had not yet become fully acquainted with each other and with the temper of the people upon whom they must act.

These men were in the Senate and House of Representatives in Washington, or in the legislature of the State, or the State executive or judiciary—all except Messrs. Pitcher and Schoolcraft—or, if they were not at the time, had been in these places, and were expecting to be again. At least, justly or unjustly, this was the criticism offered; nor was there ever any one objection in the public mind against the university which was so tenacious of life, as that it would be controlled and destroyed by politics and politicians. The board themselves, sensible men as they were, felt the need of another class of men to share with them this responsibility. The error being perceived, was in a few years corrected. Some clergymen were appointed, so that all the religious denominations of any considerable numbers in the State were represented on the governing body; but it took many years to remove the apprehensions which the religious public had felt.

The board, made up of the men whose names were given

above, held its first meeting at Ann Arbor, on the 5th of June, 1837, and following days. They chose a site for the university, and received without remuneration from the Ann Arbor Land Company the proper conveyance, on condition that the university should be located upon it. The ground conveyed was that upon which the buildings now stand, was forty acres in area, and was part of what had been known as the Rumsey farm. The remains of a peach-orchard were upon it, and years afterward some professors' families were supplied with fruit from these trees; while the whole ground around the buildings, as late as 1845 and 1846, waved with golden harvests of wheat, which the janitor had been allowed to grow, for the purpose of putting the ground in a proper condition to be left as a campus.

Dropping further reference to the other business done at this meeting, we shall trace, in the remainder of this chapter, the history of the branches from their establishment, which dates from this meeting, to their final suspension.

The superintendent, in his first report, had recommended provision for a branch in each county of the State, so far as they should comply with certain conditions. The counties were to furnish buildings, and then share equally with the regents in the support of these schools. The legislature enacted in general that which the superintendent had recommended. These branches were to be aided also, in regard to libraries and philosophical apparatus, from the university fund. Although Mr. Pierce was in most respects a conservative man, it will be perceived that this plan presupposed a fund immensely greater than his own highest estimate. With a territory which might ultimately be divided into about a hundred counties, each of which could have its branch on terms so easy that none would be likely to remain without them, each of these to have a department for the higher education of females, as also a normal and agricultural department, thus providing for institutions, from which it was absurdly hoped that colleges would spring up in all the counties—giving the State about

10

a hundred colleges with a university at their head, the latter of which was to support itself, and pay half the expenses of the former, from a fund of about $1,000,000.

According to the original law, the special authorization of the legislature was required, in order that the regents and superintendent might establish branches, but at the first meeting of the board, they applied for such change of the organic law that academic branches could be instituted without special legislative action, and that there might be but two agricultural schools in the entire State ; which was immediately granted, and on the same day—June 21, 1837 —the board resolved to start eight of these academies, as soon as possible, and for this purpose gave the committee on branches discretionary power, and appropriated $8,000 to pay the teachers, $500 of which was first to be given to each, and the remainder to be distributed among them, according to the average numbers of pupils in attendance. Arrangements were made for raising money in the several counties where branches were to be located ; a special agent—Dr. R. C. Gibson—was employed to visit different parts of the State, in order to arrange for putting branches into operation, and especially to find the most eligible places for such. The first was opened at Pontiac, of which George P. Williams, then a professor in Kenyon College, Ohio, was made principal, at a salary of $1,500 a year—an amount which, after his transfer to the central institution, he did not receive until after a service in the latter of fifteen years. Four other branches were started within a year—at Monroe, Detroit, Niles, and Kalamazoo —the principals being paid from $1,200 to $1,500 a year. Experienced men from other institutions were placed over these schools, viz : Rev. C. W. Fitch, for Detroit, also from Kenyon College, and Rev. Joseph Whiting, for Niles ; and without being more specific in details, branches were afterward started at Tecumseh, Romeo, White Pigeon, and Ann Arbor, and such men as Rev. John Pratt, of Granville College ; Rev. Rufus Nutting, of Western Reserve College, Ohio ; Rev. J. A. B. Stone ; Professor C. H.

Palmer, afterward regent, the Messrs. F. O. Marsh, now acting president of Denison University, Ohio, and E. Fish, both graduates of the first class which went forth from the university, were principals.

In tracing the history of institutions, we often find the germ of the whole future wrapped up in the actuating principles of their founders. This may be true in regard to the University of Michigan, and a brief review of some of those principles may be of interest, as serving to account for results.

The annual report of the regents, made at the close of the year during which the work of instruction at Ann Arbor was begun, states some views which had operated in the management of the branches, and foreshadowed those which were to prevail in the establishment and prosecution of the work in the university proper. This report was doubtless written by Mr. Schoolcraft, noted for the most extensive researches ever made into the history, manners, and customs of the North American Indians, and bears the names of Henry R. Schoolcraft, Zina Pitcher, and George Duffield. That part of it which is pertinent to our present purpose is as follows:

"In organizing a board of regents to carry out the views of the legislature in the establishment of a university, it is conceived to have been the primary object of this body to extend its benefits as widely, and at as early a period, throughout the state, as the wants of the community and the means at their disposal would admit.

"And their attention was therefore called at an early day to the location and establishment of branches of the university at suitable points, where the branches of a classical and English education, preparatory to the entrance of the students into the parent institution, should be taught. This object has been steadily pursued, not only from its being the appointed means for preparing classes for their final collegiate course, but from the additional consideration, that, in a new and hastily settled community, it would be one of the best and most practical means of arousing attention to the value and importance of the plan of education submitted to the people in the organic act, and of thus preparing the public mind to appreciate and foster it. To this end the most competent men were sought as principals of the branches, liberal salaries paid them, and every facility afforded in connection with the citizens of the respective sites of the branches, to render the means of instruction both efficient and reputable. The committee on the branches, charged with this duty, have encountered an arduous task in the management of the correspondence, the selection of principals and teachers, the examination of reports, and the pecuniary questions which required decision and adjustment, and the board owes to it much of the success which has attended the effort. It was conceived that the requirement of the act and the duty of the board in this respect would not have been fully performed by merely obtaining instructors of competent literary and natural abilities, disconnected from their moral influence, both in the branches and in the communities in which they are located. And it has ever constituted an object to find men, both as principals and subordinates, who united sound learning and apt judgment, and practical piety. And the confident hope is indulged that the importance attached to this principle in these selections for office, has produced a benign result.

" Of the seven branches established, five are under the direction of clergymen, and two of laymen, of various religious denominations. Two clergymen are also embraced among the assistants and tutors, the whole number of whom add to their literary qualifications those arising from religious considerations. The board can not, they believe, be mistaken in the importance they attach to the connection between learning and morals, science and religion ; and at any rate, they would be unjust to themselves not to express the belief that success can not permanently crown the institution committed to their management, after this ligament is severed."

In this report, Mr. Schoolcraft has stated the claims of piety as a qualification for an instructor's position, and the preference of the board for clergymen, in stronger terms than he could have used had he belonged to that profession.

These academic branches continued, more or less of them, from the time of their organization in 1837 until 1846, when, at the annual meeting in August, a select committee of three was raised in relation to the discontinuance of the branches. This committee reported, through its chairman, Mr. Redfield, in favor of discontinuance. He deemed it unwise to cripple the university by appropriations to these academies, and regarded it as almost necessarily leading to injustice and local jealousies, if the system in its partial application were continued, instead of the one originally recommended, of establishing a branch in each county of the State, which it was clear the fund would never admit, even if it should suffice for those already established. Perhaps this may be regarded as practically the end of these schools, though nominally they existed until several years later. At the January meeting in 1849, a resolution for their discontinuance was offered, but not acted upon, and a year from that time Judge Witherell introduced a measure designed to test the legality of appropriations from the fund to these or to anything but the university proper. The regents voted an appropriation of $10 to the branch at Romeo; the secretary refused to draw the warrant, and a mandamus was issued requiring him to show cause why he thus declined. No account is found of a decision; the case was virtually decided when the question was raised. The act appropriating seventy-two sections of land for a seminary of learning, could not be made to provide for such schools, scattered over the State, any more than for common schools.

There was, however, a decided influence exerted by the branches, and that, too, in just the right direction. They hastened the preparation of the first classes for the university, and kept up the succession as could not then have been done otherwise; they did much to beget the desire for schools in which preparation for college might be obtained, and when they were suspended, the people felt that the place must not be left vacant. Other points which had been applicants for branches, felt themselves now placed upon the same level with those which had been favored above them ; while others still felt in rapid succession the movings of a similar ambition. In this process the union schools came into being. They had become a deeply felt necessity, and the branches had generated this feeling. The common schools were free ; so was the university. There was a broad and impassable gulf between them. The former needed something above them, the latter must have something below it, in order that the whole system might be a regular gradation and a unit. The system being started, the cities and larger villages vied with each other in getting up this intermediate grade of schools. These city schools began to be wrought into a system, with graduates of our own or other universities or colleges to superintend them, and other graduates generally to teach the higher branches in them. Buildings, often fine specimens of architecture, varying in expense from $15,000 to $90,000, have been erected for them. As these have become the regular preparatory schools for the university, it has within a few years been proposed that they form some actual bond of union with it, which has been so far effected that such of these schools as provide for an examination in the presence of a committee sent from the university, have their students accepted by the latter, on their diplomas, without examination, and by a pleasant pun this class of students have been called the "diplomatic corps." This is now probably the most complete system in the country, though this last stage of development was not gained until the year 1870, and the union schools have arisen mostly within the past twenty years. Indeed, the connection is even more intimate than was that which originally subsisted between the university and the branches ; for the students from the latter were never received by the former without examination. The fact that graduates of the university are so generally at the head of the union schools makes the connection practically closer. The chief bond of union between the original branches and the central institution was that the branches were under the government and pay of the regents.*

With this system, of which the university seems as much a part as any other school, it is difficult to perceive how any one part, either less or more than another, can be regarded as entitled to the aid of taxation from the school district, the village or city corporation, or the State, as the case may be. In the school district, the primary school fund, supplemented by taxation, supports the school and gives it free to the families of the district. The principle is not different in the union schools of the cities and villages, and the system can not be consistently completed in any other way than to place the university upon the same basis. It must be expected to supply the full needs of the State in this highest grade of schools, and as often as its income shall prove insufficient for the education of all who shall demand admission to it on the prescribed conditions, it would seem that it should be supplemented by grants from the State. Such, indeed, has been the disposition shown by the most recent legislation as to almost justify the statement as a matter of history that this result has already been gained. In an experiment which led to the starting of these union schools, the regents spent, from

*The report of the commissioner of education for 1873 says: "In the West the experiment instituted in 1871, of admitting to the University of Michigan the graduates of State high schools without other examination than an inspection by the faculty of the course and methods of instruction in these schools, has been watched with interest. And as the report of the results of this experiment has been quite favorable, there has been a kindred linking of the high school with the university in Indiana and Wisconsin, though apparently without the careful guard'ng of it that prevails in Michigan. The educational reports and journals from Minnesota, Nebraska, Missouri, and Kansas indicate that the same system is either adopted or likely to be adopted in those States, the idea being that the State university is the climax of the State schools, and that in all these schools those who may be certified by competent authority to have mastered the studies which fit them for the university, should be admitted to it without further questioning."

1837 to 1846, $35,935, of course illegally. These schools, which grew out of the branches, now vie with the oldest and best preparatory schools in the United States, both in the number of pupils prepared and in the thoroughness of the work; indeed, from the union school in Ann Arbor, from thirty to forty enter the university annually—a number exceeded by very few schools in the entire country.

After the suspension of the branches, and before any progress had been made toward securing other schools of preparation for the university, suggestions were made looking toward other illegal uses of this fund for this purpose. It was suggested that the fund should pay premiums to the schools of the State, according to the numbers which should be received from them into the university.* This would seem to view the university as a business concern, which had some interest financially in the educational enterprise of the State, instead of being, as the highest school of the series, ready to complete the education of all who should come prepared for its course.

The view of the subject of the branches, as briefly given here, is one which has never been duly considered in the history of its relation to the present system. From the very starting of these schools, there was doubt as to the right of the board thus to use the fund. It soon became certain that the right did not exist, and the schools were suspended; but the existence of the branches had already laid the foundation of the union schools, and it is doubtful whether they would ever have come into being but for the preparation which the legislature and board had made for them in these branches, and in the unlawful use of the university fund. The desire had been kindled; the taste developed; a kind of model had been constructed and set up in about a dozen places in the State, and the suspension of the branches was a signal for getting up this new system of intermediate schools, which have gone on until they now stand in about the same relation to the university as

* See Dr. Whedon's letter to Senator Webb, printed in Michigan House Documents for 1850.

did the original branches, except that they are not supported by its fund, and the benefits of this movement, first made at the expense of the university, so far as they can be estimated in money, would even now mount up into the millions.

CHAPTER IX.

Preparations for the Opening of the University at Ann Arbor and the Actual Organization of its Working Forces.

THE organic law of the university is a good illustration of the imperfection of that legislation which precedes the lessons of experience. That it was ill-digested can not be said, for it presented a somewhat consistent system. Nor did it show any marked want of knowledge in educational matters in general, but merely in those lessons needed in order to adjust a system to the peculiar state of a community which had not yet assumed its definite form, so as to give intimation of its future dimensions. The problem was much like that of the tailor who should attempt to make a garment for a boy, from the measure and description of his father, who had favored him with his custom years before, and in distant parts.

The law originated with men who were never to have in their own persons the needed experimental lessons. The work of State legislation is, from the very nature of the case, seldom assigned to those who are to have the immediate responsibility of government and instruction in our universities and schools. It can therefore only be applied with safety to the most general provisions, leaving the details to be supplied by regents and professors, as the actual working of the system may reveal its wants. This general remark indicates the faults of the organic law; it was an attempt to provide for too many of the details, which should have been left to the immediate governing power of the institution. They had undertaken ‘to finish a garment for which they had only a portion of the materials, and were without an accurate measure; it was not found to fit, and it must either be worn as it was, or ripped and fitted anew, or else resort must be had to padding the body or the garment, or both, in order to produce a fit.

Reference has already been made to the constitution of the board, and its first meeting in June, 1837. The details of their action has not, however, been pursued as yet, except in relation to the finances and branches. It remains now to follow them in their arrangements for organizing the forces of the central institution. The legislature would seem to have designed to finish at once the whole work of legislation for perpetuity; so also the regents, judging from the record of their first session, seem to have desired to magnify their office, their chief regret being that the legislature had left no more for them to do. At this meeting, though not a branch had been established, not a student prepared, not a building erected, nor the site of one even selected—when the $100,000 loan, from which all the early expenses were to be paid, had not even been suggested, or deemed necessary—almost all the points relating to the new university were brought forward and discussed and many of them passed upon, some indeed a score of years in advance of any actual demand. They largely discussed, provisions for exigencies which were not yet present, and could not be definitely anticipated, and in providing for future glory and magnificence, they overlooked present necessity. The world has no wisdom equal to the task of planning in detail for the distant future. The genius of Locke attempted to put into the hands of a band of colonists about to sail for Carolina a plan of government to which it was supposed they might grow up. It was found, however, that colonies in a new country could not be made to develop according to a plan sent on from beyond the sea. So the attempt was laughed at, and never tried in practice. An ordinary sagacity, well schooled, will find a way out of a difficulty which has actually arisen; but until such crisis comes, and itself points out the needs of the hour, it is not easy to provide for them.

In all historical inquiries we have frequent occasions for

admiring how beautifully a higher wisdom supplements
that of man, or causes one' unwise human act to check
another, or in some way interposes a veto upon human
plans to the advantage of the planner. The retrospect of
this first board meeting shows us just such an occasion.
The legislature had withheld from the regents powers
without which it was impossible successfully to carry on
the university. They could not, for instance, appoint a
president or chancellor, as the chief executive officer was
to have been called. If they could have done this, it is
not improbable that the place' would have been provided
for at the very first meeting. The following record will
illustrate this statement :

"June 7, 1837. Dr. Pitcher submitted the following
resolution, which was adopted :

" ' *Resolved*, That the president of the board of regents
be a committee, whose duty it shall be to propose for the
adoption of the legislature such amendments of the organic
law of the university as shall be referred to by the board.'"

And later on the same day, "Dr. Pitcher submitted the
following resolution, which was adopted :

" ' *Resolved*, That the committee on amendments be instructed to procure, if possible, an amendment to the university law, so as to give to the board of regents the power
to elect and prescribe the duties of the chancellor of the
university.'"

Let the following record of the previous day—that is,
June 6th—be taken in connection :

"Judge Wilkins submitted the following :

" ' *Resolved*, That the arrangements of professorships,
until further ordered, be as follows: 1. Professor of mental
philosophy, who shall have in charge the instruction in
moral philosophy, natural theology, rhetoric, oratory,
logic, and history of all religions; 2. Professor of mathematics, who shall have in charge mathematics in all its
branches, civil engineering, and architecture; 3. Professor
of languages, who shall have in charge instruction in the
Roman and Greek languages.

" '*Resolved,* That the chancellor shall, in addition to his other duties, have charge of the law-department.

" '*Resolved,* That one of the tutors shall have in charge the grammar school of ancient languages, and the other the usual branches of an English education.'

" Then Mr. Crary introduced the following :

" '*Resolved,* That the committee on laws and regulations be instructed to inquire into the expediency of requiring certain of the professors of the university to deliver lectures from time to time in different parts of the State ; and, also, into the propriety of establishing a quarterly publication, and requiring each of the professors and tutors to write therefor, and report to this meeting of the board.'

" Messrs. Crary, Wilkins, and Farnsworth were made a committee on the appointment of professors, tutors, and other officers."

In the afternoon of the same day, so much of the above report as recommends the appointment of three professors was taken up. " Four " was inserted in place of " three," and then adopted ; it was decided that the salaries of professors should not be less than $1,200 nor more than $2,000 ; and, also, that one professor in the law department be appointed at a salary of $2,000.

The resolutions, as quoted above, had, before their passage, as the record seems to show, been freed from all provisions in regard to the chancellor and tutors, and in regard to requiring the professors and tutors to lecture through the State and write for a quarterly review. If the funds to pay these salaries had been on hand, if the buildings for the use of the university had been already erected, and if students had been crowding to their halls for admission, the provision contemplated in this action would have been sufficiently moderate ; but this was four years in advance of the completion of the first buildings at Ann Arbor and the final appointment of the professors of languages and mathematics, seven years in advance of the need of a professor of mental and moral philosophy, and twenty-two years before the services of a law professor were required ; and

provided for salaries—low as they were—double the amount
which the university found itself able to pay when the
work was actually begun.   There was doubt in the board
as to its right to appoint a chancellor, as the law then stood.
What would have been done if this doubt had not existed,
can not be with certainty known; but it is probable that
one would have been appointed, and that, as professor in
the law department, he would have been employed in a
service not needed, drawing money from the most pressing
necessities of the infant institution.

The principles stated in Mr. Schoolcraft's report, quoted
above, as governing the action of the board in relation to
the branches, are well supported in Dr. Duffield's suggestions of the following year in relation to the central institution.   The author of this paper, though others might have
had more influence than he over legislation, had no peer
in the board of that day, for the value of his counsels in
regard to the proper educational work of the university.
The portion of his report having reference to Christianity
in the university is of special interest, when viewed in
connection with the three names attached to it.   It is as
follows :

" The establishment of a collegiate institution in a free
State, and the conducting of its interests, should ever be
upon liberal principles and irrespective of all sectarian predilections and prejudices.   Whatever variations of sect
exist in the United States, the great mass of the population
profess an attachment to CHRISTIANITY, and, as a free
people, avow themselves to be CHRISTIAN.   There is common ground occupied by them all, sufficient for co-operation in an institution of learning, and for the presence of a
religious influence, devoid of any sectarian forms and peculiarities, so essential, not only as the most efficient police,
but also for the development and formation of the most
valuable traits of youthful character, and qualifications for
future usefulness.   Experiments made in other States, by
catering to morbid prejudices of sectarians, have only embarrassed the institutions of the State and matured the growth

of numerous and rival colleges, avowedly sectarian. Attempts made to exclude all religious influence whatever
from college, have only rendered them the sectarian en-
gines of an atheistical or infidel party or faction, and so
offended and disgusted the majority of the population
agreeing in their respect for a common Christianity, that
they have withdrawn their support, confidence, and patron-
age, and left them to drag a miserable existence, till they
invoked the presence and influence of the Christian religion in them.   The only security that can be had for the
avoidance of sectarianism, and the necessary and desirable
influence of Christianity, in the conduct of a collegiate institution intended to be the common property of the State,
is to be sought in the character and principles of the men
who are placed over it, and held responsible for its administration.   There are men to be found in all the different
Christian sects, of sufficiently expanded views and liberal
spirit and enlightened minds, devoid of the spirit of bigotry
and narrow prejudices of sect and party, that can be selected and deputed to such a work, whose public spirit and
philanthropy, and whose love of country, and attachments
to the interests of their State and its entire population, will
always furnish the best and only true guaranty against the
evils of sectarianism.   The board are happy to state the
fact, without meaning in the least to commend themselves,
that while they consist of gentlemen from almost, if not all
the principal Christian sects in our State, there has nothing
occurred in their individual intercourse, their deliberations
or debates, or any of their official acts, which has ever
elicited occasion for the expression, or even the existence
of jealousy and suspicion growing out of sectarian prejudices or attachments."

The board was first saved from the immediate appointment of a chancellor by the want of power ; and when the
power was given, the desire had subsided.   Furthermore,
the embarrassments of 1841—the $100,000 loan being
already exhausted, several of the branches being suspended
for want of resources—fortified the prudent counsels given in

Dr. Duffield's report, and led to the transfer of two able men from the branches to the university proper, and so perhaps the very straits of the governing body hastened its opening, and they certainly taught prudence in its management.

The paper given above was written, as we have said, by Dr. Duffield; but there were associated with him on the committee Mr. John Owen, at that time, and perhaps even now, the wealthiest and most influential layman of the Methodist Church in Detroit, and Rev. Martin Kundig,* a Catholic priest of that city, who of course concurred in it, as did also the board entire.

A conflict of jurisdiction, between the legislature and the board, has been hinted. This, with its bearings and results, needs to be briefly stated. All was not granted at once which the regents desired; indeed the changes when made at all, were slowly and reluctantly made. That constituting the governor president of the board, and allowing the appointment of a president *pro tempore* in case of his absence, was made immediately, as also one limiting the

---

* As Mr. Kundig was the first and last Catholic, either priest or layman, ever on the board of regents, the liberal educational policy which he adopted may seem to call for explanation. The lamented Dr. Houghton was nominated by the Democrats for mayor of Detroit, when absent from home, and inaccessible by correspondence. His friend, Dr. Pitcher, himself a Whig, ventured to pledge him to a certain policy in relation to the city schools which, though he might not have had the courage to make it, he was too honorable not to keep when thus made for him. Rev. Mr. Kundig undertook the task of bringing the Catholics of Detroit to the support of the scheme, with the hope that when they should ask a distribution to them of their share of the school money, the Protestant vote would be given for this measure. Naturally inclined to be liberal, he adopted also the same liberal views in regard to the university. He remained, however, but a short time in Detroit after he entered upon this course. It was the last time we ever saw Dr. Pitcher that the latter related, with no small manifestations of satisfaction, the story of his own part in persuading Dr. H. and Mr. K. to take the position which inaugurated the present school system of Detroit. It is generally supposed, also, that the displeasure of the authorities of the Catholic Church with the manner in which Mr. K. participated in this movement, and the failure of the expected result, were the cause of his immediate transfer to a field of labor beyond the limits of the State of Michigan.

agricultural departments of the branches. The relative powers of regents and legislatures were more or less discussed at the meetings of the board every year, from the very beginning until the adoption in 1851 of the present constitution, which modified essentially the relations of the board to the legislature. Indeed, the question still exists in some forms and applications. Previously, the regents were only petitioners for powers which might be given or withheld; subsequently, they claimed rights under the constitution, and, within the last decade of years, have resisted in the Supreme Court the application for a *mandamus* requiring them to carry out the act of the legislature of 1855 in regard to the appointment of a professor of homeopathy.

It will not be necessary to pass in review all the occasions and forms of this contest. The most distinct case of action in the board was at a meeting held in Detroit, January 7, 1840, when the following report was presented by Rev. Dr. Duffield, in behalf of a committee appointed on the revision of the organic law :

" The committee appointed to revise the organic law of the university, and to report such changes as may be desirable to be presented for the action of the legislature, by leave respectfully submit the following :

" Two things appear to be essential in order to the vigorous prosecution of the great and responsible duties devolved on the board of regents :

" 1. The first is the proper restriction of the responsibilities of the board themselves. At present, the regents, as by law provided, have not the sole responsibility in the location of the branches. The superintendent of public instruction shares it in common with them—nay more, has in effect the power by his veto of staying their procedure. This officer is not an *ex officio* member of the board, is 'not present at their meetings to hear and know what transpires in their discussions, and therefore can not be as capable as the board themselves of judging as to the propriety of establishing a branch in this or the other county. It does not seem reasonable, that to him should be given the power to

11

interpose his veto, and by withholding his concurrence, embarrass and prostrate measures which the board may deem advisable and necessary for the interests of education. Moreover, the board are directed by law to make report of their disbursements, as well as their general doings, to the superintendent of public instruction, to be embodied by him in his annual report of his proceedings to the legislature. Your committee think both these regulations exceptionable, and recommend such amendments of title 12, chapter 1, part 1 of the revised statutes of this State, as will throw the entire responsibility on the board, and require them to make a full report of their proceedings to the governor, to be laid by him before the legislature, instead of that responsibility being divided, and the board being made, as they now are, a mere appendage to another functionary.

" 2. The second matter of importance is the full trust and responsibility of the funds belonging to the university. The present law withholds from the board all agency whatever in the management and consolidation of the funds appropriated to the use of the university, and by making them the mere annual recipients of uncertain payments, depending in a great measure upon contingencies connected with the duties of the superintendent of public instruction, leaves them unable to adapt their measures to their means, or to project and execute such plans as the interests of education and the resources of the university may call for. The board have no power to sell any of the lands of the university, or to invest any means arising from the sale of lands by the superintendent, or to consolidate their capital and efficiently regulate their own fiscal interests and concerns. The right and authority to sell the lands of the university, and to invest the proceeds is vested solely in the superintendent of public instruction, and all the agency required of the board in reference to the same, except in specific dispursements of moneys from time to time paid over to them, is to submit an estimate of expenses for the ensuing year to another body, a board of visitors, consisting of five persons, to be appointed annually by the superintendent of public instruction, and who are to report to the superintendent. And your committee think that the duties of the superintendent of public instruction in relation to the primary school lands and funds, are sufficiently onerous without devolving on him those in relation to the university lands, which the board are competent to meet. They therefore recommend that such amendments of the law be made as will vest in the board the power of disposing of the university lands now conferred on the superintendent, and hold the board directly responsible to the legislature for the investment of the moneys arising from the sale of the same. They further recommend that the investment of the moneys arising from the sale of the university lands be paid into the hands of the State treasurer, to be invested and held in trust by the State for the use and benefit of the university, and that so much of the law as requires loans of such moneys to be made to the different counties be rescinded."

The action taken upon this report consisted in the passage of three resolutions moved by Chancellor Farnsworth and Chief Justice Fletcher for the adoption of the report and the raising of a committee to prepare a bill embodying its recommendations.

The embarrassments of the board referred to above, have been removed, perhaps more by the progress of events than by legislative action. The branches were long ago abolished. The sale of the lands was, from the nature of the case, but a transient work. The question of the investment of the university fund is one of perpetual interest. The board might, by investing the funds themselves, pay the expenses of their agency, and make them yield, at present rates, much more than is now paid by the State.

While it must be conceded that a State university, when in the full tide of successful operation, must be under the control of a board intrusted with almost unlimited powers, and charged with the entire responsibility of its management, it may still be questioned whether the board, at the time of its organization in 1837, was prepared safely to exercise these powers and meet this responsibility. They then asked the power to appoint a chancellor and assign him his duties. They suggested his duties in anticipation, making him the head of the law department, as well as chancellor of the university. On a subsequent occasion they determined that the incumbents of certain chairs should be deans of their respective faculties. This board consisted of the governor, lieutenant-governor, judges of the Supreme Court, and several other gentlemen, mostly of the same profession; but soon after this, other elements began to be introduced into the board. Several clergymen of different religious denominations, of whom Rev. Dr. Duffield was the most prominent, were appointed as regents. Instead of a chancellor to receive a large salary for presiding over the name of a university, and delivering law lectures without students to hear them, teachers were first employed to lay the foundation of an education in the branches, and two of these—Professor Williams, of the Pontiac, and Professor Whiting, of the Niles branch—were transferred to the central institution as soon as a class was prepared to enter it; and thus its present character was given to the university as a place where the elements of a thorough classical and scientific education should be given. For this turn of things we are probably indebted to the very fact that the board of regents, at the time of its organization in 1837, had not the power to appoint a chancellor and assign his duties as they desired. Thus Providence brought out of this conflict in regard to the proper jurisdiction of each, a result far better than the wisdom of the first board of regents or their contemporary legislators would have secured had either been left to itself; and while we may maintain that the regents ought to have this power, we ought also to feel profoundly grateful that it was not given them in the beginning.

Among the first things needed in order to gather the apparatus and assemble the forces for the work at Ann Arbor, were some kind of buildings. The erection of these, as a financial measure, was treated in a previous chapter, where it was shown how the system of checks operated to save the fund from entire dissipation in a grand architectural display. The first buildings, including four dwelling-houses and one dormitory edifice 110 by 40 feet, were either completed, or so nearly so, in the summer of 1841, as to allow the opening of the work of instruction. Governor Barry, who came to the chief executive chair of the State on the 1st of January, 1842, is said to have remarked that, as the State had the buildings and had no other use for them, it was probably best to continue the school, showing that the balance of the scale between suspending and going forward may have been turned in favor of the latter by the bare fact of having these architectural preparations. However this may be, it is true that no enterprise ever stood in more absolute indecision between advancing and retreating than did the University of Michigan from 1839 to 1843. The advance was ordered, and there has never been a retreat.

The apparatus for work began to be collected before the teaching was actually begun.

Dr. Asa Gray, who, as early as July 17, 1838, had been appointed professor of botany and zoology, was contemplating a visit to Europe, and the board, desiring to obtain the beginning of a library, placed, by a resolution of September 17, 1837, the sum of $6,500 in his hands—$5,000 of which was to be expended for books, and the remaining $1,500 was his salary for the year as professor. The result of this purchase was reported to the regents at their meeting on the 22d of December, 1840, as follows :

"The library committee have examined, with as much attention as the time would permit, the catalogue of books purchased in Europe by Dr. Gray, and derive satisfaction from being able to express to the board of regents the opinion that the trust committed to Professor Gray has been executed in a manner which reflects much credit upon his judgment and discrimination in the selection and cost. The collection numbers 3,700 volumes, embracing the various departments of history, philosophy, classical literature, science and art, jurisprudence, etc. A large portion of it consists of works which could not be obtained in America, and many of the editions are scarce and rare in Europe. We deem it fortunate for the interests of the institution, that such a basis has been laid for building up a library which shall do honor to the institution, and trust that its claims upon the funds of the board for annual and permanent increase may be steadily borne in mind.

"We have the satisfaction to add that the entire collection has been received and opened at the university buildings, at Ann Arbor, to which place the committee are about to forward the valuable but limited number of volumes elsewhere purchased. The invoices of books purchased by Dr. Gray amount to £1,036 18s. 7d., or $4,606.55, upon which have been paid $144.93 for freight and charges, and $35.75 for insurance."

There was an appropriation made at the meeting of the regents on the 28th of February, 1839, for Audubon's "Birds of America," which, by turning to the list of warrants, we find to have been $970. This was more than a year previous to the receipt of Professor Gray's purchase, and was probably the "valuable but limited number of volumes" referred to in the above report, as having been "purchased elsewhere." This celebrated work, obtained thus by subscription at the time of its publication, is worthy of remark here, as having been among the first, if not indeed the very first purchase ever made for the university library. It is now thirty-five years that the leaves of these ponderous volumes have been turned over constantly by students and visitors, excepting only a few years during which they were laid aside in the hope that by avoiding wear they might be transmitted as the property of the library to distant ages. But one edition was ever printed, and that was done in Edinburgh, simply because there was then no provision in this country for such work. There are, therefore, but few copies to be found. We knew of one in Boston in 1865, about as much worn as that of our library, which could have been bought for $1,200. We have since heard of the somewhat fabulous prices of about eight or ten times that sum as having been paid or offered, but know not whether the statements in regard to such offers 'are authentic. With these large volumes of plates there is a text in 8vo form, containing explanations accompanied with the exceedingly interesting incidents of Audubon's travels. The library copy of this text is imperfect—a fact which, so far as we know, was never discovered here until within five years past. There should be five volumes, we have but four. The fifth volume was published in 1839, probably after the purchase of the work by the regents, and no one thought to see that the remaining volume was purchased. This is a kind of oversight, which, without constant watchfulness on the part of librarians, will occur several times in the course of each year. But as the plates are the important part of the work, and these are perfect, this defect can not be deemed a serious one. The plates would be a work complete in itself, without the narrative.

Nothing of importance was ever done for the increase of the library from the time of the purchase by Dr. Gray until more than a decade later. The funds admitted of nothing. Scarcely any periodicals were taken, and of all that was done, scarcely anything is worthy of being noted as adding to the value of the library. The prudence of the board limited their expenditures to the first necessities of the young giant's nourishment and growth.

In referring to the election of officers for the central institution, the fact has been omitted that the first place ever filled was that of librarian, and this was done by the election, on the 21st of June, 1837, of Rev. Henry Colclazer, who received $100 a year on condition of residing in Ann Arbor. During the period of Mr. C.'s librarianship, from the time of his appointment till July, 1845, as also from that time to 1856, the work in the library was done mainly by some student acting as assistant to the nominal and responsible librarian, who, from 1845 to 1856, was some one of the professors.

There can be no great interest among the majority of readers, in a detailed description of collections of specimens in natural history ; and yet such is the general appreciation of the bearing upon science of well-chosen illustrations of the written or oral statements of its teachers, that the omission of an account of the origin of the university collections in this department, would rightly be deemed unpardonable. These much-needed helps to their work, gathered from nature's broad and beautiful fields, the regents took early measures to secure.

The first movement in this direction was made at the very first meeting of the board in June, 1837, by the appointment of a committee for the procuring of a library, cabinet of natural history, and philosophical apparatus. In less than six months after the appointment of this committee, and on its recommendation, negotiations were opened for the purchase of the collection of Baron Lederer, and the president was directed, at a meeting held in Detroit, November 18, 1837, to authorize Dr. John Torrey, of New York city, to examine this cabinet, report upon its value, and make preliminary arrangements for its purchase. On the 16th of January, 1838, the president of the board was authorized to complete the purchase. This collection consists of 2,600 specimens of minerals. It was first offered to the regents for $4,500 ; $4,000, however, was the amount finally paid.

In the account of the collections made under the general direction of the state geologist and deposited with the university, will be found some curious facts, showing that the large bestowments of the State upon its university may be credited to good fortune rather than to the well-formed educational plans of her early legislators, or to their full and hearty sympathy with the yet undeveloped institution.

The only legislation which we can find bearing upon the subject now under consideration, is embraced in three acts, substantially as follows :

1. "An act to provide for a geological survey of the State," approved February 23, 1837. This provides for the

appointment of a state geologist and assistants, for their collecting specimens, making maps and diagrams, and depositing the same in the State library. It allows also the deposit of similar specimens in such scientific and literary institutions as the governor shall designate. It appropriates, to defray the expenses which may be incurred by the act, sums not exceeding $3,000 for 1837, $6,000 for 1838, $8,000 for 1839, and $12,000 for 1840."

2. "An act (1838) relative to the state geological survey, and repealing the one of 1837." This act gives the details of the survey far more minutely than the former, prescribing with more or less fullness the organization of its corps. The only parts of it which need to be cited here are contained in sections eight and nine, as follows : "*First,* the State shall be supplied with single and good specimens ; *second,* if more similar specimens can be found, sixteen more, if possible, shall be procured, to be distributed by the regents amongst the university and its branches." Then, after appropriating $12,000 annually for three years, it adds : "*but, to entitle the university and its branches to any of the benefits of this act, of the aggregate amount herein appropriated, four thousand dollars shall be refunded to the state treasurer from the university fund, in the manner following:*" etc.

3. " An act relative to the department of natural history in the University of Michigan.

"SECTION I. *Be it enacted by the Senate and House of Representatives of the State of Michigan,* That the various specimens of geology, mineralogy, zoology, botany, and all other specimens pertaining to natural history belonging to the State and now deposited in the university buildings, be, and the same are hereby transferred to the board of regents of the University of Michigan, to be held by said board of regents in trust for the use and benefit of said university and its branches ; and the said board of regents are hereby authorized to take, have, and enjoy the right, property, possession, and control thereof, and make such disposition of the said specimens as may be most beneficial

for the interests of the university and its branches aforesaid.

" SEC. 2. This act shall take effect and be in force from
and after its passage.

"Approved May 11, 1846."

This last act is conceived in the true spirit of enlightened
legislation. It was enacted when a noble class of eleven
young men had already gone forth as graduates of the university, and four more classes, numbering sixty-eight in the
aggregate, were pursuing their undergraduate course. The
lineaments of the future institution could already be seen.

As we take in, however, the provisions of the act of 1846,
and then recur to those of the previous legislature, we very
naturally ask how there came to be any specimens deposited with the university, the proprietorship of which could
be thus transferred. The act authorizing the survey
did indeed allow the governor to deposit specimens with
such institutions as he might choose, but it was repealed
before the work had progressed so far that there could be
very much on hand to deposit.

The law of 1838 made a liberal appropriation for the survey. In accordance with its provisions, Dr. Houghton, who
had been appointed state geologist under the first act, was
able more fully to organize his corps of assistants for the
prosecution of the work. Soon after the passage of this act,
however, at a meeting of the board held April 7, 1838,
Major Kearsley, as chairman of a committee to whom
this legislative action had been referred, reported against
accepting the offer of the State. In his report he gave
utterance to some surprise, not unmingled with indignation, that the State should require such appropriation
from the university fund. He stated that the income of the
fund was not then more than $10,000 annually; that this
was but barely sufficient to redeem the pledges already
given for the support of the university and its branches,
and could not in justice be turned in the direction proposed
by this act. The report claims further that the university
is the proper guardian for the State of such collections;

that even the furnishing of a place for them, putting them up and keeping them in order, will involve very considerable expense, and that nothing more than an assumption of the responsibility of their safe-keeping could properly be required of the regents. The report closed with recommending the passage of the following resolution :

"*Resolved*, That the regents feel it their duty to withhold their assent to the appropriation contemplated by the act of the 22d of March, 1838; yet they hereby pledge themselves to provide for the preservation of such specimens as may be collected under said act and at any time intrusted to their care."

There was no action taken upon the report. The matter was, therefore, whether from oversight or forethought— and we may justly presume the latter—left in much better condition than could have been expected from definite action. The governor and heads of the scientific survey could proceed to deposit specimens with the university in the expectation that the regents would finally accept the terms of the act, or that the legislature might accede to the terms suggested in the report of the committee of the regents. At least whatever might have been the authority under which they acted, the head of the geological survey deposited large numbers of specimens with the university, and Professor Houghton did regard himself as authorized by the act of March 22, 1838, to collect these for the university, as appears from his report of February 4, 1839.

Under the law of 1837, Dr. Abram Sager was appointed chief in charge of the botanical and zoological departments of the survey, and it is evident from the action taken by the board in November of the same year, that he had already made no inconsiderable collection of specimens in zoology, which were designed for the university ; for, at a meeting held at that time, Dr. Pitcher presented the report of a select committee which had been appointed to examine the collection of zoological specimens made by the state geologist, and report in regard to measures for their preservation, and in regard to an appropriation to enable the state geologist to procure duplicate specimens of birds, so that the regents might, by exchange, obtain foreign specimens of the same class. This report recommended measures to procure, through the executive of the State, specimens of all the birds of Michigan, which it was supposed would require at least one thousand, in order that they might include one of each sex in both summer and winter plumage. From this action it will appear also how earnest the board were in their desire to have the work prosecuted, though we have no means of knowing whether anything further came of this action.

Dr. Sager made a report in 1839, accompanied by a catalogue of what he had collected, and the specimens mentioned in this are those which laid the foundation of the present zoological collection. Dr. Wright, who had the charge of the botanical branch of the survey, made a similar report with a catalogue, and the specimens procured by him formed the nucleus of the botanical collection.

All these acquisitions were first stored temporarily in a room hired for the purpose in Detroit; but when the professors' houses in Ann Arbor were finished, appropriations were made to fit up one of them for their reception. Here they were kept until the autumn of 1844, when that house had to be vacated to receive the newly elected professor of mental and moral philosophy, and the cabinet of natural history was put up in an apartment prepared for it in the fourth story of the building of which it now occupies the greater part. A single article belonging to the department of ethnology—an Indian canoe—was too long to be turned in the hall so as to enter the door leading into the cabinet, and so was left for several years suspended from the beams of Professor Ten Brook's wood-house, when the thought occurred to him that it might be drawn up into the cabinet through a window. To raise a thing of such size, though without great weight, and pass it into a fourth-story window, was quite an enterprise, and the work was probably enjoyed by the students who engaged in it just as well as many "college boys" enjoy an equally adventurous piece of mischief. It was a pleasant little episode in college life, probably remembered by many of the professors and students of the time, and we can not forbear to hint to the "boys" that such beneficent services are really better conductors for the discharge of their redundant electricity than those of another class sometimes resorted to for the purpose. Dr. Houghton's tragical death perhaps gave rise to the tradition that this boat was the identical one from which he was drowned, and that it is kept in memory of that sad event. This is now doubtless the prevailing belief among both students and professors; but the lamented professor was still prosecuting his adventurous explorations through the wilds, up the streams, and along the coasts of our lake-bounded State for years after he had deposited with the university this production of the mechanical skill and ingenuity of the original inhabitants of Michigan. This may still be regarded as a monument inscribed with the manner of Professor Houghton's death—for he was probably lost from such a craft—but it is one sent hither by himself when in the vigor of life, and cherishing the hope of ending his days in the university's service.

The foundation of our museum of natural history will, therefore, from the above account, appear to have been laid in the purchase of the Lederer collection, and in the early results of the State geological survey conducted by Dr. Houghton as geologist, Dr. Sager as zoologist, and Dr. Wright as botanist. The ornithological portion of the specimens was stowed away in a garret and not mounted for many years, and the results of the other branches of the survey may have lain long in comparative chaos, and large numbers of specimens are in that condition even now.

The further development of the resources of the university for the illustration of the various branches of natural history, we shall not at present pursue. The accessions by gift and purchase, and the labors in classification and arrangement, have been many and large, but they belong to a later period of our history, with which we are not at present concerned.

The opening of the work of instruction in the central institution took place in the autumn of 1841. In respect to the grade of preparation required, and the thoroughness of the subsequent work, it may be justly said that the literary department *started*, a full grown college. The first young man who matriculated in the university—Hon. L. D. Norris, now of Grand Rapids, Michigan—went afterward to Yale College, where he graduated long enough before the class he had left here, to be present with them at their graduation, himself already in possession of his own diploma from Yale. It is true that the course of study has been extended and varied in some directions since that time, and this has been made possible by increasing the requirements for admission; but in these respects the University of Michigan has rather led than followed other institutions.

Until years after the establishment of the university, there was little embraced in the course of instruction in the best American colleges beyond the following : The Greek and Latin classics, mathematics, natural, moral, and mental philosophy, astronomy, and political economy. Some few institutions had regular professors of chemistry and natural history, but many of them had only lectures for a brief period on these subjects from persons who served in other institutions in the same manner, or who volunteered to teach these branches in colleges in which they held other professorships. The university, however, set out with provision for instruction in several branches not at that time generally included in the college course. The French and German languages were provided for by the election of Professor Fasquelle to the chair of modern languages. But two classes failed of the benefit of his instructions. Professor Sager, elected professor of botany and zoology in 1842, gave instruction to them on these subjects. A course in chemistry, geology, and mineralogy was also given to the first class by Dr. Douglass, who, two years later, was formally elected to the professorship, which, with some modifications, he has held ever since.

It is really a matter of astonishment that this high class of college work should have been established and kept up through a period of depression in the finances of the institution, such that professors, who were working hard on a nominal salary of $700 per annum, must sell their warrants below par or wait for their pay, and through a period of such perplexity in discipline as will be briefly described hereafter; but this was nevertheless done, and never for a moment did the character of the work accomplished fall below that of the best colleges in the land. If, indeed, some studies pursued in Harvard and Yale were not found in the course here, we had their equivalents. It is true, there was then but one course of study; the scientific and engineering courses were of later origin, and optional studies had not as yet been introduced. The professors, however, met the financial difficulty as best they could. They trusted that the embarrassments of the board would be only temporary; and, besides, they did not wish to give up an institution which still had the prospect of splendid success.

The greatest trial of the university grew out of the questions of the presidency and the distribution of the labor among the professors, both of which questions were mixed up with various others, rendering their separate treatment quite impossible.

Tutors became here, as everywhere else, unpopular, and the board determined not to employ any more. Some professors had in their departments more and some less than the three daily recitations which had been deemed full labor, and the regents requested the professors to divide this extra work among themselves. Professor Agnew, of the department of ancient languages, chose to hear all the Greek classes, thus leaving the instruction in the Latin language entirely unprovided for. This work Professors Whedon and Ten Brook were requested to do, and rather than have it fail, they did it. Hard feelings, some disaffection, and an inconsiderable amount of imperfect teaching grew out of this arrangement.

Some who had theories to establish, or special wishes to

gratify, maintained that all the difficulties of the time came from the want of a head. Though the institution had been opened, and had achieved great success thus far with only a presiding officer of annual appointment; though most of the difficulties belonged to the period, and were common to the colleges of the land; though the great universities of Germany have only an annually chosen rector; though similar evils continued and at times multiplied under the administration of a strong president, who was elected soon after; and though we have since had a two years' vacancy in the presidency, which, under a temporary arrangement, had a success not at all below the average of past years—there will, doubtless, still be many who will sympathize with the feeling that the want of a head will sufficiently explain the facts.

Thus much for the organization of the forces. The routine of teaching affords no material for history. It is the revolutionary movement in which a nation comes into existence, or is renewed or perishes, that supplies the historian with the choicest and most abundant facts for his narrative. The period of unbroken prosperity yields him little. The planning and construction of the Niagara Suspension bridge was at the time matter of intense interest and extended descriptions, but the successive passage over it of thousands of trains furnishes no theme for narrative, nor will anything else but its renewal or its fall into the chasm below, which some future age may witness. So in our university history, the pangs of birth, the perils of infancy, the conflicts—internal and external—for existence, progress, and extension, and not the monotonous routine of instruction, graduation, and noiseless passing into the channels of active life, are the materials which will be used.

The first distinct movement toward the establishment of the medical department of the university of which we find any record, is in the shape of a memorial addressed to the board by Professors Seager and Douglass, and other medical men, which was presented at the January meeting for

1847. This was referred to a committee, which reported at the same meeting in favor of opening such a department with three professors ; that is, the two medical men already in the department of arts and sciences were to have duties assigned them in the school of medicine and surgery, and one additional professor was to be appointed. But at the meeting in August following, a committee was raised to report at a future day upon the expediency of organizing the departments of medicine and law. This was in effect a reconsideration of the previous action on a more comprehensive scale. The committee was composed of Messrs. Pitcher, Farnsworth, and Mundy, who presented an elaborate report at the meeting held on the 17th of January, 1848.

This committee recommended immediate action in regard to the medical, but further delay in case of the law school, for reasons which appear in the report itself—of the validity of which reasons we shall be satisfied when we remember that two of the three gentlemen constituting the committee were of the legal profession. They recommended also that instead of the ordinary method of teaching by lectures, text-books should be prescribed and studied, and the students should be required to bear daily examinations upon the portions assigned. This method, however, was not to be applied to the departments of chemistry and anatomy. They express the opinion that " a single professor could in this way more successfully teach practical medicine, surgery, and obstetrics, than they could be taught by the prelections of a more numerous faculty in the brief sessions now customary in medical colleges." The report enlarges upon the confessedly low condition of the profession in the West; mentions the ascertained fact that something like one hundred young men from Michigan were at this time attending medical lectures in other States; suggests the assignment of places in the medical department to the professors of zoology, botany, and chemistry, together with the appointment of a single new professor, viz., one of anatomy, and the extension of the session of the medi-

12

cal department throughout the entire year, as being all that would be necessary in order to place it upon a respectable foundation.

The report also takes up the question of a higher grade of preparation than had been required for admission to other medical schools, on which subject it states the action of a then recent convention of medical men held in Philadelphia, by which it had been agreed that a more thorough preparation ought to be insisted upon. It is worthy of remark that on the question of the location of this department of the university, the committee state that they consider its discussion precluded by the existence of a contract between the State on the one hand and the people of Ann Arbor on the other, fixing the site of the university; and when it is remembered that this committee of three embraced the chancellor of the State, and one of the justices of the Supreme Court, as then constituted, it may be fairly asked whether their opinion ought not to be regarded as practically and perpetually decisive upon the question of dividing the institution between different cities of the State.

The action of the board taken at the same meeting at which the report was presented, was in substantial accordance with its recommendations, as above stated, and was followed by a distinct set of rules for the government of the new department. This was, however, as yet like the paper-cities of a somewhat earlier day, in this respect at least, that it was only platted and not yet built, and during the two and a half years which were to intervene before the actual opening of the work of instruction, some changes of the plan were to take place. The intermediate steps need not to be stated with dates and details. In general, the laboratory, which was to be shared by two departments, was to be completed; the building, which was used by the medical school up to 1864, was to be built—the two together involving an expense of $14,000 to $15,000.

In anticipation of the opening, Dr. Moses Gunn was, at the July meeting of 1849, elected professor of anatomy and surgery, and in January, 1850, Drs. J. Adams Allen and,

Samuel Denton, were elected to professorships—the former to that of pathology and physiology, the latter to that of physic—while Professor Sager was transferred to the place which he held up to 1874, and Professor Douglass was to add *materia medica* and pharmacy to the chemistry and mineralogy which he had taught in the other department. With the above-named corps of instructors, and with a code of enactment modified from the original one, the school of medicine and surgery was prepared for active operations in the autumn of 1850, at which time the first medical term opened with a fair show of students.

It had been the desire of the members of the board and others, both professional and non-professional, to introduce into the professional schools, when they should be established, that closer relation of teacher and pupil which has always prevailed in college classes. On this subject a committee, of which Dr. Pitcher, one of the most prominent physicians in the State, and an old, highly respected member of the board of regents, was chairman, and Professors Sager and Douglass were members, reported to the board in July, 1849, recommending the adoption of the following provisions in relation to admission, instruction, and examinations in the medical school:

" Candidates for admission must furnish evidence of good moral character, and pass an examination satisfactory to the faculty, in English grammar, geography, arithmetic, algebra, geometry, and natural philosophy, and be possessed of such knowledge of the ancient languages as will enable them to read and write prescriptions with facility."

" All students and practitioners shall be required to enter upon the first term, or if they enter later they must pass examination upon the studies which the class shall have gone through with."

" The lectures and recitations shall occupy one entire year, to be divided into three terms, of fifteen, fourteen, and eleven weeks."

" The instruction to be by lectures and recitations, of

which there shall be three daily, Saturdays excepted, and all students shall attend unless excused by the faculty."

" Each professor shall examine the class daily upon the subject of his previous lecture or the assigned subject of the text-book."

" Theses shall be written by all the class once in two weeks, and these shall be read and defended before the class on Saturdays, as the faculty shall appoint."

The above statement, somewhat abbreviated from the committee's report, presents its main distinguishing features. The remainder consists chiefly of provisions common to other organizations, and necessary in carrying out the proposed system. As the time, however, for opening the course approached, various influences operated to modify the proposed plan. What these influences were, it might not be easy even for persons who were at the time familiar with the facts to state with confidence. This, however, must be evident to all, that a plan brought before the board by such physicians as Drs. Pitcher, Sager, and Douglass, and originally carrying to the minds of the regents a full conviction of its superiority over the prevailing system, must, with all the advantages which the board possessed for introducing an independent system, have encountered some obstacles of considerable magnitude to prevent its being put to the test of practice. The question at issue was simply this : Which is the better—a course of one full year upon which the student is required to enter with a respectable preparation, during which three professors shall be occupied in teaching and testing the results of their work by daily examinations of the classes, and by requiring frequent theses upon the various questions of medical science ; or a course of lectures crowded into three months, heard twice over at an interval of a year or two years, the students catching what they can without special help from the professors?

What the main consideration was which modified the original proposition, is clearly enough hinted in the words of Dr. Pitcher's report presented in July, 1850, a year later than the one quoted above and in the corresponding action of the board. He says, "the medical department can not be opened with any hope of commanding the public respect without at least three professors besides Professor Douglass." The committee then recommended *four* beside Professor Douglass, and the board elected, as already stated above, Professors Allen and Denton, making in all five.

The truth is substantially this : That the processes of medical education throughout the entire land had become so well established and so uniform, that the plan first proposed was finally deemed a more radical innovation than could be safely undertaken. Whether this apprehension was well founded, whether the department would have failed of that eminent success which it has so deservedly won, or whether it would have achieved still more decided triumphs if the first proposition had been finally adopted and rigidly carried out, are questions upon which equally candid minds, with all the facts before them, might differ. It will doubtless be admitted by all fair-minded observers on this theater, that this department of the university has, by a considerable extension of its session beyond those of other medical colleges, by its comparative independence of the numbers of students and the amount of fees paid in, and perhaps in other ways, favorably acted upon this branch of the work of professional education throughout the largest portion, if not the whole of our land. But, on the other hand, it was even then clear that both a higher standard of preparation and a more thorough and persistent drilling of students on the subjects of their lectures and text-books was demanded. If the board of regents had, from the beginning, persevered in that which seems to have been their original intention ; or if, still better, they had provided for two years—the first to be given to anatomy, physiology, and materia medica, relieved the junior class from other studies and held them responsible for a thorough knowledge of these ; then given the next year to the senior students for the remaining studies—they would have inaugurated the most important change ever made in the study of this profession in America. By releasing each class from the lectures belonging to the other, two hours daily now spent in hearing lectures repeated, would have been gained for close study, and the school permanently placed beyond successful rivalry.

The first medical building was ready and the course commenced in the autumn of 1850, with a class of ninety.

CHAPTER X.

Review of the Period from 1844 to 1852.

In looking over the whole field, from the opening of the work of the university to the closing scene of the drama enacted by the old board, occasion is found for observing or reviewing and generalizing great underlying facts, many of them never registered or capable of being registered, or, if briefly referred to, left unexplained, not understood, or misunderstood by contemporaries—generally of such nature that they could not find their way into the public prints, and their true solutions only hinted, and that in a fragmentary and enigmatical manner, and within only an exceedingly limited circle. These facts could not have been given in the previous chapters, without breaking the thread of the narrative.

This chapter but states the plan and the most material details of the university's battle for life, so far as its educational work was concerned.

This differs from the contest of ten to twelve years later, not indeed so much in its asperity and the wide-spread interest felt in it, as in the points at issue, and the number and character of the combatants, both of which will appear as the narrative progresses. The facts of this struggle have well-nigh faded from the memory of the most active portion of the present generation; those relating to Dr. Tappan, and reserved for succeeding chapters, are still fresh in a much larger number of minds.

State institutions, strictly such, had never prospered in this country. This fact was notorious, and was indeed regarded by almost all classes as decisive against the prosperity, and, of course, the life itself of this institution. This impression was varied in regard to the degree of pos-

sible success and the causes of final failure, but was in
some form more or less deeply fixed in the minds of the
people. The fund, however, had been given, and an obligation had been assumed, and rested somewhere, to build
up the school thus provided for. There was no definite
consciousness of ownership in the university and responsibility for its management. This consciousness existed everywhere, nowhere. The men officially charged with this responsibility harbored all shades of doubt, especially the
darker ones, in regard to the success of the enterprise.
What various motives may have led them on to action, it were
not easy to tell. The prevalent one, doubtless, was that it
had been made their duty to administer this trust, and they
ought faithfully to do so while it remained in their hands,
and then hand it over to others. Some, indeed, may have
hoped for incidental benefits from the dissipation of the
fund ; others may have expected to realize political or other
capital from the course which they should take in regard to
it. But whatever mixture of dishonest motives there may
have been in this enterprise, the doubts of success were
honest, and not groundless. On the contrary, all the successful institutions of this country were under the control
of bodies of religious men, strictly as such, or of close
corporations. Their leaders had been chosen with an eye
to their interest in the work, and their qualifications for it.
These were rarely changed, and only in order to bring
greater efficiency into the field of action. But from the very
nature of the case no class of men could thus fully identify
themselves with this university, at least in its beginnings.
The various religious denominations, and their members, as
individuals, looked upon it as quite foreign to themselves ; it
would of course, they thought, be managed by the politicians,
whose counsels would be divided by party and personal
strifes, making the institution powerless for good ; while it
existed, it would rather impede than promote the true work
of education, and only cause delay in the founding of colleges by the various Christian bodies of the State. Nay, the
feeling was more or less prevalent that the State belonged to

the so-called politicians, while Christians were citizens of
another kingdom, not of this world, and ought to have little
more to do with earthly governments than quietly to submit to those placed over them. The lower class of politicians, for their own private ends, encouraged this feeling
in various ways, and especially by trying to make the arena
of politics such that it would be somewhat perilous to the
true religious life of Christians to appear upon it, and many
of them practically followed this leading, not indeed as a
true theory, for it was never offered as such, but as a life
more accordant with their moral and Christian feelings.

A few leading religious men were indeed persuaded to
discourage a separate educational work, on the ground
that it would not be policy to exhaust themselves in doing
that which the State fund would do for them. But there
was nowhere any enthusiastic, or even hopeful feeling in
regard to the university. Such was, indeed, uttered in
public by those unacquainted with the true state of the public mind of the time, and these utterances may now be read
and used as a refutation of the view here taken; but the
gratulations vociferated over the magnificent university
fund and the prospect which it offered, were generally followed by whispers of earnest doubt and distrust from the
same lips, and it was not a little amusing to contrast these
undertones with the louder professions made in more public ways.

The men officially bound to administer this trust were, as
already hinted, moved more by a sense of present obligation, than by the hope of future and permanent results.
If the fund could have been legally transferred to other
purposes, and quite lost to the noble end for which it had
been given, many would have seen this without a sigh, not
a few with great satisfaction, none with disappointment,
few with regret. Petitions were sent to the legislature for
its transfer to common schools. But it had been accepted
as a trust, and for a particular end, and many of those responsible for it were too conscientious to neglect it. They

felt bound to do as well as they could, and then transmit the responsibility to others.

This general impression that the university would be managed by the politicians was quite natural, since no others attain to positions which give them control in matters of the State. Some of this class of men are conscious of not being able to run this kind of machinery very well; they feel that some other would answer their ends better, and some of them prefer to get rid of an engine which they do not understand, and have in its place one which they think they can run, and by which they may hope to profit. This element may not have been large, but when mixed in with other apathetic and antagonistic ones, it was indeed very considerable.

But the main element which supplies the ranks of the politicians, including in this term that small percentage of men who rise in character quite above its vulgar import, and might be called statesmen, comes from the profession of law. It will, therefore, but slightly vary the statement already made, if it be said that the people expected the university to be managed by the lawyers. There were, indeed, enough of these who had the intelligence, good sense, and integrity to carry on a university, but they were not so situated as to do it; and if they had been, and could have done it even better than others, still the institution in the hands of one profession alone would not have fulfilled the true idea of a university for the State. As the acrobat needs to give his whole attention to keeping his place on the rope, and can not do this and bear heavy burdens besides, so the politicians, to-day in places and to-morrow out of them, are too intent upon efforts to get and keep their unsteady seats to be safely relied upon for work of this kind.

This view as to the hands into which the management of the higher educational work would fall, seems to have been accepted by the State executive, and his early action tended largely to the propagation of this feeling; nor is there any evidence that this occurred otherwise than from a deep and honest conviction of responsibility resting upon this class of men, then called into this work. That Governor Mason's acquaintance was confined mainly to men in political life, and of his own profession, may have contributed to this tendency.

The first board of regents had on it as *ex officio*, by law, the governor, lieutenant-governor, and the justices of the Supreme Court, as then constituted, five in number. To these seven, the governor, with the concurrence of the Senate, added twelve, all of whom were in the first instance of the same class. They included all Michigan's representation in Congress, both Senate and House. The other members of the board were of the same general character, for although two of them were physicians, they were prominent in both state and local politics. At the first meeting of this board it was voted that the professor of law should be chancellor of the university. From this action, from the constitution of the first board, and from the known prominence of the legal profession in the State government and politics, and their power, if they should choose to do so, to control in this matter, there was seldom any opinion whispered around other than that the head of this institution must be professor of law, and this continued long after the introduction of the clerical element into the board, and its prevalence in the professorships of the branches and the central school. There are no traces of evidence that this profession itself ever held such opinion, or did anything beyond the action in the board referred to above to promote it; but the people thought so, and the professors of the university themselves mostly clergymen, thought so, and, so far as is now known, would have cordially accepted such a result.

As further testimony of this general class of facts, may be cited a memorial by Dr. Pitcher, addressed to the legislature in behalf of the board, in 1851, as follows: "On the first organization of the board of regents, it included no clerical members. For this reason the university, then *in futuro*, was stigmatized as an infidel affair, which it was predicted would fail to perform the functions for which it had been endowed. This prediction was uttered with much confidence in certain quarters, and an act for the incorporation of a sectarian college was urged through the legislature, partly by an appeal to the religious feeling of the members based upon this accusation, partly with a desire to disarm that kind of opposition, and more especially because they believed it to be a duty, irrespective of it, the board was careful to introduce the element of religion into the branches, which they did by the appointment of clergymen of the different religious denominations as principals thereof." This paper has a similar passage in regard to the central institution, only more full. The line of policy here indicated gradually conciliated the religious public, attached them more and more to the university, and inspired a degree of confidence which was wholesome in its influence.

In relation to religion, and religious men and clergymen in the board and faculties, things had taken a different turn from that which had been expected. This held the religious element among the people at least from a decision adverse to the university. But there was still an important question not yet decided, a great step not yet taken, and none could tell what would be its direction when taken. This was the choice of a president, the real dread of all the wise and honest friends of the institution. Nor was it easy to know whether men really entertained decided views upon this subject. Whatever might have been the nature of the questions agitated, the hints suggested, or the opinions supposed to be expressed, it might be taken for granted that in nine cases out of ten, the purpose of those speaking was rather to elicit the views of others than to utter their own. It was like the game of "twenty questions," with this difference, that one was not even informed if he guessed rightly the thoughts of another. Frank, honest and confidential conversations were indeed sometimes had between those members of the faculties who had neither personal nor party ends to gain. In these the name of Governor Felch is known to have been mentioned. But such talk could have been little more than amusement; for the university had no money to start the law department— the field in which he was expected to labor—scarcely enough to carry on the work, as already started. Moreover, Mr. Felch was at the time in the United States Senate, and was not likely to leave his seat there in order to accept so uncertain a place. There may have been other suggestions of the kind, but they can scarcely be seriously regarded as plans.

In our best American colleges it had become almost an axiom that the president must be of the clerical profession, as being more nearly related to this class of studies and to the disciplinary work expected of him, and also professor of mental and moral philosophy. Another view, as stated above, had indeed been suggested ; but in the meantime the college had been started, and was pursuing much the same course with the best Eastern colleges. The question was therefore fairly raised in many minds whether this almost unbroken line of precedents might not control the action here.

In anticipation of needing a professor of philosophy at the opening of the term in September, 1844, Edward Thompson, of Ohio, a minister of the Methodist Episcopal Church, had been elected and his entrance upon duty at that time was confidently expected, until near midsummer of that year, when he declined. Measures were at once taken to fill the place, and on the 12th of September, the names* of Schuyler Seager, a Methodist minister, and at that time a professor in the seminary at Lima, in Western New York, and Andrew Ten Brook, then pastor of the Baptist Church in Detroit, being before the board, the latter was elected, the ballot standing three—that is, all the Methodist members—for Mr. Seager and the rest, so far as present and voting, for Mr. Ten Brook. This meeting was the most excited of any which up to that time had

---

* Rev. Dr. Duffield, chairman of the committee to find and recommend a candidate for this place, had presented to him—by whom we not know— the name of Rev. Henry P. Tappan, but for some reason did not present it to the board.

ever been held. Language was used by the Methodist members severely reflecting upon the motives of the other members of the board in this action, and some of the regents retained ever after an unfriendly feeling toward the whole Methodist denomination in Michigan, growing out of this occasion. They seemed to regard the expressions of a few men, in the board and out of it, at this time and subsequently, as a claim set up by the entire church which they represented, to a certain position in relation to the university.

From 1848 to 1850, Rev. Elijah H. Pilcher was the only Methodist on the board of regents. He had several times intimated to regents, and to the assembled board, that there existed in his mind a plan by which the university might obtain a chancellor without much increase of expense. This plan he hinted at the meeting of January, 1849, in the following resolution :

"*Resolved*, That a committee of three be appointed to inquire into the expediency of appointing a chancellor, and of suggesting such changes in the duties now devolving upon the professors as they may deem proper, and that said committee report at the next meeting of the board."

The committee consisted of Messrs. Pilcher, A. E. Wing, and Justice Green, of the Supreme Court. No report was made, doubtless because the other two members did not concur in Mr. Pilcher's plan of making Dr. Wheden chancellor, and transferring him to the chair of philosophy. It was well known that Dr. Wheden did not like his place, and earnestly desired to exchange with the professor of philosophy ; but we have no evidence that Mr. Pilcher had his concurrence in this action. The only result of this resolution, so far as we know, was a private message from the regents to the professor of philosophy informing him that they did not desire the change to be made.

It will now be necessary to return over a period of about three years, and trace thence another stream of influences ; at first indeed a mere rill, but becoming a mighty volume before its final dissipation. The first reference to "*secret societies*" may awaken unpleasant reminiscences, and yet perhaps not. Few men are constituted with so singular a perfection, either real or conceited, as to perceive no wrong in the retrospect of their own lives, or to feel offended if the historian, in the true spirit of his calling and without transcending its proper limits, shall present a panorama in which many of his readers shall recognize themselves just as they appeared in the original transactions, though not to their highest honor. If the historic picture come to us without representations of the blots which disfigure the fairest pages of the book of human life, we lose our interest in it from the consciousness that it does not belong to us; and if the historian feel that he must eliminate from his materials all that can even give offense, it were well that he relinquish his task of writing.

Such scenes as are here reviewed, when the lapse of time has placed them in the somewhat distant past, should be surveyed by the philosophic eye in search of explanations, and such can almost always be found adapted to present real or apparent obliquities in a less glaring light than that in which they at first appeared. Such demonstrations will generally be found to be but violent and spasmodic efforts to set aside a state of things which, in process of time, had grown to be unnatural and out of harmony with the times.

American colleges are the natural growth of American society. They were all established upon the principle that their officers of instruction stood in the place of parents to the boys placed in their charge. Originally, a larger portion of students in college were minors than is the case at present. The course was less extensive, and could be completed during the period of minority. The few who entered college after the age of majority, and of their own wills, found no difficulty in placing themselves in this same relation to the college faculty. Among the small number of students, and in their personal relations to the professors, no objections were strongly felt to that system of gov-

ernment which presumed to watch over their habits in their
rooms, as nearly all roomed in dormitories erected and controlled by the corporations.   Time, however, was rapidly
producing changes which looked toward setting aside this
system ; and one class of influences especially, coming in
from abroad, was stirring up among students a desire to
set it aside even sooner and more suddenly than time itself
could do.

What in America is taught in the undergraduate course,
is in Germany taught mostly in the *gymnasia* to boys who
are under the care of either parents or guardians.   The
universities are founded on a different principle.   They
merely furnish facilities for professional and philosophical
study, and take no responsibility in the discipline of the
students or in instruction.   Professors lecture, and students
attend or not, as they choose.   They pursue studies either
within or without the range of the professors' lectures, or
pursue no studies at all.   They have their fraternities, and
attend their meetings, or not, as they may elect.   They
take rooms anywhere, occupy them as other tenants, and
are in every way free and irresponsible, except to a general
police authority, which in some instances is applied through
the city, and in others through the university, according to
the character of the latter.

The students in American colleges were, at the time of
which we write, of an age and maturity of mind on the
average above the boys in the German *gymnasia* who pursued the same studies, but below the German *university*
students.   The general prosperity of our country was
rapidly becoming such as to bring college education within
the reach of larger numbers who had passed the age at
which fathers usually send their sons to college.   Under
these influences the college system was expanding with
everything else.   The increase in the numbers of students
and in their average ages, the growth of the feeling of
manly independence and the modifications which had taken
place in the features of our civilization, were such that the
system gotten up for boys committed by their parents to

college officers was no longer appropriate to either party ; it could not be practically carried out by the professors, nor heartily concurred in by the students. If the secret society question had not come up and forced the issue, it might have been long before the other points of college law would have been changed, and the revolution might have been a silently progressive one, rather than a violent outbreak. But this question came just in time to bear the brunt of a general movement, the result of which is now wrought out, in this university at least, in relation to all the parties concerned. The professors are relieved from the responsibilities of that guardianship, then already little more than nominal, which had been exercised over students. Parents now understand that if they need persons to represent them in the care of their sons and daughters, they must themselves look these up and arrange with them. Students understand the extent of their obligations to professors to be less than formerly ; and even if the dormitory system should be restored here, as it still exists elsewhere, it would be under other rules than those which once prevailed.

The faculty of the university never took any action having reference to secret societies as such. Before the central institution was established, the board instructed Professor Williams, then in charge of the Pontiac branch, to prepare a code of laws for it, which was done so far as the earliest needs of the institution seemed to require. This code contains a provision in the following words : " No student shall be or become a member of any society connected with the university, or consisting of students, which has not first submitted its constitution to the faculty, and received their approbation." The framers of this code had in mind only such societies as those generally formed in colleges for literary purposes, and wished to provide against their undue multiplication. This rule, together with one to the effect that students' rooms shall at all times be accessible to the officers, another that " no organized meetings shall be held in the university without permission from the faculty," and still another that " students shall not absent themselves

13

from the college premises after 9 o'clock at night," was supposed to exist in all American colleges at that time, and all these were based upon general principles, without reference to those societies destined to come into existence some years later.

In the summer of the year 1846, while some nightly depredations were being subjected to inquiry by the faculty, some students were traced to a small house built and occupied by one of their number and his chum, on the edge of a neighboring wood; and the respondents refused to answer as to what had occurred there, on the ground that they were pledged to secrecy. In this interview, the existence of secret organizations in the university was brought out so clearly that the members of these fraternities thought best, for some reason, to reveal the facts as they were. They stated that two of these societies had already been organized in the university. They gave lists of their members, stated their affiliation with similar organizations in other colleges, and, with their statement, conveyed the intimation that their strength had become such as to make it difficult to deal with them.

On the day before commencement of the same year, 1846, a gentleman called upon the faculty as the agent of another secret society, and offered to comply with the law so far as to exhibit so much of the constitution as he had authority to reveal. The regents were in session, and their meeting, together with the necessary preparation for commencement, fully employed the faculty, and, instead of acting at the moment, they merely promised future attention to the subject. The third society was formed, however, on the same day, and without waiting to learn the result of the application.

The question of discipline, which arose in this way, was discussed in circles not immediately connected with the university, and two opposite views were taken. The one, that it should be immediately conceded to students to form themselves into societies and to hold meetings at pleasure in the university buildings with doors closed against the

officers, without special permission; the other, that all
students who persisted in keeping up these organizations
in the university, should be expelled at once. The faculty,
however, took what they deemed a middle course; they
allowed those already connected with these societies to retain their membership, but required of them a pledge to
receive no new members, and also required all new students
on entering the institution, in connection with the general
pledge to observe the laws, to give a special one to obey
this rule in regard to unauthorized societies.

At the opening of the college year in the autumn of
1846, the president of the faculty called the special attention of each student to this subject, and received from all
the required pledge, which amounted to an assurance that
all these societies would expire in 1849.

Some of the professors, indeed, hinted doubts as to
whether there would be any greater efficacy in this special
pledge than there had been in that general obligation to
obey the laws, which every student had acknowledged
himself under, and whether it would not be better to drop
the question of the mere existence of organizations of this
class, and deal only with overt acts of insubordination
among their members. The action, however, fixing a
special pledge was passed by the regents with the unanimous concurrence of the professors; and it is not easy to
perceive how a different action could well have been taken,
since the repeal of a law can not well be considered on the
demand of those who refuse to obey it even during the period necessary for the consideration of the question of repeal, and further, because the parties to be consulted, as
interested in the subject, were very numerous and their
relations complicated.

As to the students, the shrewd diplomacy, which followed the measures of the summer and autumn of 1846,
seemed to indicate mental reservations in the taking of the
pledge itself, though we must admit our belief that in many,
if not in most instances, this pledge was taken in good
faith, and that subsequent reasoning, under a very strong

pressure from the affiliations in other colleges, changed the purposes of those who had taken it. Indeed, not only the high personal character of very many of the young men involved, but also a distinct recollection of their action at the time, under the influence of impulses communicated from abroad, shows this to have been the case.

We will omit here, as requiring too much of minute detail,.all mention of the acts of the particular societies, and will only add, in general, that the reception of members went on with but a slight check from the special pledge of 1846. This had, indeed, been suspected, but was not positively known until near the close of 1849, when soon after the publication of the annual catalogue a loose leaf was found in a copy to be sent abroad, containing the names of all the members of one of these societies in the university, among which were found those of many new students. These all acknowledged that they were members. The plea by which they attempted the justification of this course was that their chapter, by an alteration recently made, was no longer styled a chapter in the "*University of Michigan*," but "*in Ann Arbor;*" that they did not meet on the university premises; and that they had recently admitted three members who were not connected with any college. They claimed, therefore, that their society could not be regarded as connected with the university, or as consisting of students. The defense set up by the other societies did not differ enough in principle from this to require a separate statement.

The defense was not deemed satisfactory, and on the last day of the term ending in December, 1849, the faculty announced to the members of two societies that their connection with the university would cease at the opening of the ensuing term, unless they renounced their connection with their respective fraternities. The evening of that day was occupied with the usual public declamations, and the occasion, it must be admitted, was not marked by quiet and respectful attention. As the audience retired and moved homeward, they did not fail to detect in the atmosphere those signs which generally betoken a storm.

A light was discovered about midnight by the president of the faculty, which was found to proceed from the burning of a pile of shavings which had been thrown into an outhouse and lighted, with the evident intention of getting up a fire. These were removed and extinguished before the solid wood had been ignited. A fire still raged, however, in some spirits which were promenading the grounds, and in half an hour it lighted up another heap of shavings, and, following the dictates of prudence, the families around the campus observed without interference the growing flames as they kindled upon the parts of some adjacent woodsheds, built of pine boards for temporary use, and then on the solid wood itself, lighting up the campus, rendering every tree, shrub, and fence-pale visible over the whole grounds, and then after an hour or two gradually dying down, so that before the sun had again lighted up the earth, after this long and snowless December night, darkness and quiet were allowed to reign for an hour or more over the landscape.

This was the culmination of those disturbances, which have, indeed, been so briefly described above as to give but an imperfect view of them, and yet with sufficient fullness to make clear the principle involved in the discipline. The members affected by the decision stated above, probably never actually dissolved their connection with their respective societies; but still they returned to their studies, remained inactive as far as was apparent in the work of their several fraternities, and waited for time to provide for their authorized existence. How this was finally brought about need not here be stated.

The obvious remark here in regard to this whole contest is, that whatever in the students' action there was that was wrong, and whatever there may have been in the course of the faculty which was unwise, they both appear to advantage as compared with their peers in Eastern institutions. It is absurd for the government of any one college to attempt the putting down of such societies without the support of other colleges. The faculty in Michigan supposed that they had this—that these societies had been exterminated in the East, while those with whom they were dealing all knew that their Eastern brethren were flourishing in secret. The faculty of the university had no desire to maintain such a law, but as the board kept it up, encouraged by the opinions of Eastern presidents, the faculty felt bound to attempt to carry it out while it existed, and the students behaved quite as well as, under all the circumstances which afterward became known, could with reason have been expected.

There was a general feeling, it might not be easy to tell upon what it was founded, that the contending forces were to be massed at another point—the State capital—under other leaders, the people's chosen legislators; and the profoundest apprehensions were justified by the violence of the events.

Preparations had been made by the regents to meet the emergency. Under date of December 29, 1849, the chairman of the executive committee, Major Kearsley, addressed a note to the faculty requesting "a detail of the recent occurrences, in consequence of which several students might by their own act sever their connection with the university." This paper was prepared and contained a recital of the facts substantially as given above, though more full, together with a statement of the grounds of objection to the existence of these societies, and accompanied with copies of letters from the presidents of six Eastern colleges, all deprecating the influence of these fraternities.*

This report of the faculty was laid before the board at a meeting held in Detroit, January 10, 1850, on which occasion a motion was made to authorize the publication of the report, to which an amendment was offered by Mr. Goodwin, that there be published with it "a statement of the expelled students in explanation of their views and conduct."

---

* See Appendix D.

Then followed a motion to suspend the rule for the violation of which this discipline had taken place. This was lost by the following vote :

Yeas : Messrs. Goodwin and Witherell—2.

Nays : Messrs. Ransom, Mundy, Green, Pitcher, Farnsworth, Taylor, Pilcher, Redfield, Kearsley, Allen, Atterbury, and the President (Chief Justice Whipple)—12.

A substitute for the resolution and its amendmehts was then offered by Judge Witherell, and passed, as follows :

"*Resolved*, That the whole subject of the late difficulties in the university, and the expulsion of a certain number of students, be referred to a select committee of seven, with power to make a full exposition thereof, and publish the same in their discretion, and that they report to the board at its next session."

Messrs. Whipple, Ransom, Witherell, Taylor, Redfield, Kearsley, and Pitcher constituted the committee. These gentlemen, or at least the chairman and several others, visited the university, saw not only the professors as a body and separately, but also the aggrieved students, and offered to the latter the opportunity to make such statements as they might desire to have accompany the reports of the faculty and this committee of the board, and promised them for this purpose access to the faculty's statement.

Two reports were made : one by the chairman, for himself and the majority of the committee, and fully indorsing the faculty's action ; the other by Mr. Redfield, also quite as fully sustaining the action, but on a somewhat different ground—the two reports, therefore, supplementing each other. The following passages, taken from Mr. Redfield's report, show well the spirit and tenor of both :

"The undersigned questioned the policy of the rule at the time of its adoption. He must, however, here admit that subsequent examination, reflection, and information have led him to distrust somewhat the correctness of the opinions he then entertained." This is in relation to the rule. In regard to the action of the faculty, he says : "The

undersigned, from all the evidence before him, can arrive
at no other conclusion on this part of the subject, than that
expressed by the majority of the committee in their report.
It appears clear, also, that the faculty have, in all their action upon the subject, manifested great wisdom and prudence, as well as great kindness and forbearance, toward
the offending students, and that the sentence passed upon
them is lenient and judicious. . . . "

In accordance with the promise of this committee, the
faculty's statement was returned to the president, where it
lay for some time subject to examination by all students who
should desire this, and called forth three different responses : *one* signed by seven young men who had been
affected by the disciplinary action and had returned to college; *another*, by five young men professing to act as a
committee of the students. These both, while they spoke
in high terms of the personal character of the professors,
took ground adverse to the action under the twentieth rule.
They claimed that the law itself was a nullity, because no
board had the right to pass, and no faculty the right to execute, a law thus abridging the natural rights of students,
and that such laws, though existing in other colleges, are
not executed. Neither of these communications was addressed, as was expected, to the board. Both, as memorials,
went directly to the legislature. The following passage
from one of these papers will show its author's view of the
remedy to be applied to the disorder :

"In conclusion, then, we would respectfully suggest
that the bill now pending in the Senate seems to us most
admirably adapted to accomplish the object it has in view.
Let the regents, and through them the faculty, be brought
nearer to the people, and more immediately amenable to
them, for the correct and faithful discharge of the responsible trusts they have assumed. Let some distinguished
man be placed at the head of the institution as chancellor
who can give it character and standing."

The *third* paper referred to was also in the form of a
memorial addressed to the legislature, and supported the

regents and faculty. The following passage will best set forth its ground :

" Your memorialists beg leave further to state that we believe that the measures which have been taken to influence your honorable body to take such action as is now contemplated, have been prompted by a vindictive spirit toward our faculty and the board of regents ; that we believe if the matter were left to take its own course, without legislative interference, it will soon be amicably settled ; that as the students who have been conditionally expelled are returning under the condition offered them by the faculty, we think that the *only thing in the way of a speedy adjustment of the whole affair to the honor and entire satisfaction of all who are rightfully concerned, is the probability that now exists of legislative interference.*"*

These memorials went directly to the legislature ; those emanating from the faculty and regents through the executive, and all of them appear as legislative documents of the session.† But they arrived too late, as the reader has been taught by the reference above to a bill pending in the Senate, to anticipate the beginnings of action.

One of those bold measures which, with a rapid execution are often successful, but if the first onset fails, insure defeat, was tried by those who sought a legislative remedy for the ills of the university. Two students contrived to get possession of the faculty's report and copied it, with slight changes ; then hastened with this to the capital, and had it printed and in circulation a week or more before the genuine report arrived. The changes were such as to make the faculty descend toward vulgarity and slang. For instance, where the genuine report says, " This assertion may be illustrated by the following specimen narrative," the spurious one says, " This assertion may be illustrated by the following *beautiful specimen.*" These changes occur in considerable numbers, and place the faculty on a plane quite below their true dignity. The greatest effect was designed

---

* In all passages quoted, the italics are in the originals.
† Senate Documents, 1850.

to be produced, and was produced, by a professed omission in the printed copy of something too bad to be printed. The tenor of the omitted words could be whispered round, and supply the imagination of some parliamentary orator with better aids to his eloquence than any printed words could furnish.   Indeed, this was so used; and it was declared in a speech that the honor of the university required the suppression of the passage.   The authors of this movement, of whom there were but two, and they were without the sympathy of the other students, did not wish to conceal their theft—it was indeed a part of their plan that it should be known; then it would show what the report would have been if the regents had not returned it to the faculty with a peremptory order for revision.   This view could be maintained even after the paper should be published by authority.

It was, however, clearly the design of these young men to hasten with this copy or caricature, whichever it may be called, to the capital, and make it effect its purpose, while the report itself was lying with the president of the faculty, whether, as they pretended, for revision, or, as the truth was, to be consulted at their leisure by students desiring to reply to its statements, and their plan worked well in the start.   ·

It is not easy to perceive or imagine just what these legislative agitators designed; their plans were not definite in their own' minds.   They were neither educators nor in any proper sense educated.   They had no plan of building up, except by first destroying all that had been done ; and they seemed to think that if all were but reduced to ashes, there would then spring up from these at once, and naturally, a new and glorious edifice.   And it was just this extraordinary looseness and recklessness of the plan of campaign, the questionable morality of some of the known means and agencies employed, and the precipitation consequently deemed necessary in the execution, which made defeat more certain in the end.   The bill reported in the Senate, not having become a law, is not now before us even in the journals; but its design was to place the university in as near connection as possible with the people, from which some expected and desired the immediate sweeping away of the existing board and faculty. The final form of this bill was not bad. Its main feature was the election of a board of regents by the people at the ensuing fall elections; but it was a movement made under the pressure applied by the aggrieved students, and was designed by its movers to break up the existing government.

The bill which embodied the plan of the disorganizers, was called " Finley's bill," from the connection with it of Hon. William Finley, of Ann Arbor, who was leader of the movement in the Senate. It was not unnatural that he should be depended upon for information in regard to the university; but he never in any instance sought it of the faculty's official organ, nor, so far as we ever heard, of any member of the faculty, but mainly of the young man who stole the report, or at least those who were unwilling to give their names. A main point was in regard to the numbers of students, the design being to prove that the institution was running down by reason of bad management.

The memorials of the aggrieved, radical as they were, did not materially understate the numbers of the students in the university. There was, indeed, an effort on the part of students affected by the faculty's action, and their friends, to hold out against returning for a time, in order to see what might be done for them; but those who served our radical legislators with their materials for agitation, were of quite another class, and but two or three in number.

There was a very quiet course taken by those who opposed this radical action. They were cautioned to keep still, as they could do nothing against so strong a current of feeling. They did keep apparently still, and let information come in gradually. This came in various forms. A letter from Dr. Whedon to Senator Webb, and published in the legislative documents of the session, states the case as it was, referring to the suspension of the branches, and the want of preparatory schools to take their place, and showing that relief was to be sought, not in the reorganization of the university, but in the rise of a system of preparatory schools. Hon. George Sedgwick, of Ann Arbor, a member of the House, kept up a correspondence with the professors of the university on the subject of this action. His earliest letters were desponding. But on the 2d of March he wrote that he thought that no action would be taken, and that Mr. Finley himself probably regretted his movement, and this is confirmed by the Senate journal. The bill notified on the 21st, and introduced with such flourish of trumpets on the 25th of January, in the midst of the whirlwind of excitement, inflamed by the arrival a few days later of the two disaffected students with the stolen report in their hands, was variously amended, not only by the committee on public instruction, but also by the author himself, and on the 13th of March, in the report of a committee, of which he himself was chairman, it is stated that the "committee doubt the propriety of making so radical a change, *particularly at this time*, in the manner of electing regents of the university," and then several amendments were added. The bill, as amended, was on the same day lost, by a vote of eight to thirteen.

Letters were received from Messrs. Webb and Sedgwick by the president of the faculty, stating that the matter of the so-called "original report" was understood at the capital. They doubtless thought so. The discovery of the trick made a profound reactionary impression on many minds. For twenty years and more, men who were in that legislature met members of the university faculty whom they had never seen before, and referred to their impressions, on the discovery of this trick, as never to be forgotten ; but they all supposed that it consisted in the stealing and publishing of a rough draft instead of a revised one. They did not suspect that the variations were manufactured, not copied, and this spurious report stands now unexplained in the Senate documents, as the "original report of the faculty."

Here this legislative history may be regarded as closing. It stands, however, to what follows, in a relation too intimate to be interrupted.

Several regents were at the capital during a portion of the session to which our narrative relates. Of these Mr. Redfield and Chancellor Farnsworth deserve special mention, as having had a conservative influence. On the other hand, many thought they discovered in the superintendent of public instruction, at that time Francis W. Shearman, a sympathy with the disorganizing movement. This suspicion had much the same effect as though it had been well founded. But there is nothing in Mr. Shearman's published reports to substantiate the charge against him. His compilation entitled "Public Instruction and School Law," published 1852, is probably the most important educational publication which has as yet appeared in Michigan. In his report for 1850, he says of the university, that "the standard of study and attainment adopted by the faculty is of the highest order, and is not second to that of any other similar institution in the country." All his references to the university are in the same strain of eulogy. If there is any implied abatement of this praise, it is in Mr. Shearman's earnest commendation of his visiting committee's report, inclosed with his own for 1850. This committee was made up of Isaac E. Crary, David A. Noble, and Joseph Penny. The two former were prominent in our early history. The last was a former president of Hamilton College—of which Mr. Shearman was a graduate—and had retired to spend his closing years in Michigan. These men speak in highest terms of the work done in the university, and quite specifically of each branch of it. Both superintendent and visitors speak of the want of preparatory schools since the suspension of the branches, and thus fairly account for the want of increase in the number of students, and the former, of the rise of union schools, as promising to supply this want. The visitors, however, *do* suggest that regents and faculty have, in the opinion of some of them, transcended the line of duty in attempting to put down

secret societies among the students, and this, doubtless, is
the suggestion which the superintendent designed to commend.

It is not improbable, therefore, that notwithstanding Mr.
Shearman's high and honest estimate of the university work,
he was carried along by the storm of the winter of 1849–50,
and showed more sympathy than he was conscious of with
the destructive movement at the capital.   Suspicions of his
unfriendliness seemed to be confirmed by the announcement of the names of his visiting committee for 1850.   The
name of William Finley was the only formidable one, and
the supposition was that the others were appointed to work
with him.   The professors, however, were doubtless misled
by their long existing apprehensions.   Mr. Finley did
nothing, so far as known, adverse to the interests of the
institution, nor did the committee in their joint action,
which was eminently wise.   They spoke of the employment of tutors, which was a provision for the greatest
internal need, and against the most fruitful source of bitterness in the university faculty.   Messrs. Whedon and Ten
Brook had been compelled to act as tutors, being taken
thereby quite outside of their respective fields of labor.
They referred very properly also to the want of a president,
and the approaching election as provided for by the constitution.

One member of this committee, however, collected
opinions of students, received some concurrent views from
three professors, and sent a messenger to the professor of
intellectual and moral philosophy advising him to resign.
This, so far as we know, was new work for a visitor.   Two
persons were mentioned, also, as thought of to succeed to the
place and the presidency, viz : Francis Wayland and Mark
Hopkins.   So, men for the place had been thought of before the movement was made for vacating it.

At the next meeting of the board, held in Detroit, on the
21st of January following, Mr. Foster offered a resolution,
which may be regarded as the result of this labor.   We
give it as follows :

"*Resolved*, That while such a memorial is in our opinion improper, and insufficient testimony upon which to base such action as it recommends, and that the board of regents ought not in the least to countenance a spirit of fault-finding and insubordination among the students, and while the communications * put into our hands express sentiments which we are all happy in possessing concerning the professor in that department, both as to his ability as an educated man and his affectionate and faithful bearing as an instructor; yet, on account of such an unhappy state of things as has come to our knowledge in taking the whole matter into consideration—a state of things for which we hardly know how to account, nor how to remedy—we deem it proper, having the best interests and the reputation of a professor in view, to recommend that it be the opinion of the board that said professorship ought to be vacated at the close of the present academic year, and that, as soon as may be, the board ought to have information of such fact."

We would not treat this performance facetiously, and think the reader can not but concur with us in regarding the following interpretation as severely logical; it is, perhaps, also logically severe:

"WHEREAS, It is, in the opinion of the board of regents, improper to receive from students such memorial as that which we have received, based as it is upon insufficient evidence, and encouraging as it does a spirit of fault-finding and insubordination; and, whereas, the communications put into our hands express sentiments which we are happy to possess in regard to the learning, ability, and affectionate and faithful bearing of the professor of moral philosophy as an instructor; yet, on account of an unhappy state of things which we can neither account for nor remedy—therefore,

"*Resolved*, That said memorial be cordially received and the prayer of the memorialists granted, in hope of

---

* A paper or papers from professors of the university.

thereby correcting that state of things which can neither be accounted for nor remedied."

From the sentence, "we deem it proper to recommend that it be the opinion of the board," etc., we learn that the members were not supposed to entertain such opinion, but that in passing the resolution they would merely recommend to themselves the making of an effort to attain to it.

On motion of Mr. Atterbury, the resolution was laid over to the April meeting. At most, it could have had but two votes. The only other action of Mr. Foster worthy of record was his vote for the dismission of the professors, whose communication is referred to in his resolution.

It was on the very evening of the above action that Dr. Pitcher distinctly shadowed forth the issue which came within a year. "It is," said he, "the beginning of the end; those professors who have shown their willingness to offer up an associate as a sacrifice of expediency with an eye to their own safety, have sealed their own fate."

On the following day, Mr. Ten Brook placed his resignation* in the hands of the executive committee—Messrs. Kearsley and Pitcher. The interview can never be forgotten, but will only be described so far as relates to subsequent action of the board. He was asked by them to name a person of his own religious views for appointment; he named Professor Boise,† of Brown University, not for the place which he was leaving, but for the chair of the Greek language and literature. He was proceeding to state that Dr. Whedon was well fitted for the chair of philosophy, and, as they well knew, had always desired it, but

---

* This was a great blunder, and an act of injustice to the university and to his associates. If it related to some other person, it would be explained by statements which we prefer, in this case, not to make.

† It is of interest to observe here the consequences of this. A little more than a year after this time, Professor Boise was elected; subsequently, at his recommendation, Professor Frieze was made professor of the Latin language and literature. He first named his friend, President Angell, for the presidency; all this, and an unknown series in the future, depending most probably upon this little occurrence in the executive committee.

was arrested by the remark that the regents would never entertain the thought of his election, and that he would not get a single vote in a full board besides that of Mr. Pilcher ; and more than this, that several professors, including him, would be removed.

The board had become deeply impressed with the conviction that it was essential to the highest prosperity of the university to attach the religious public to it by calling some of their prominent men into its service, though they never admitted the *claim* of any denomination either to a particular place, or to *any* place. Dr. Tappan, indeed, says in his historic statement, that he had been informed that " the regents designed to fill the chair of ancient languages from the Baptist denomination." So they did, but only because Professor Boise had been recommended as specially adapted to that place, as stated above.

It was not unnatural that leading men of the various religious denominations should be invited by members of the board to make suggestions. The position of the Baptists* was that they did not claim for themselves, nor would they concede to other denominations, as such, any rights in the university ; that, as individuals, their first wish was Mr. Ten Brook's stay in the institution, but that if this should not be accomplished, they would, if the regents should desire it, aid in bringing names before them. Several were accordingly suggested, the most prominent of which was that of Rev. Dr. Caswell, then a professor in Brown University, and since president of that institution. This name was offered with reference to the presidency and professorship of mental and moral philosophy. We have no means of obtaining a formal expression from others, but there is no doubt of this having been substantially the ground taken by the best representatives of all

---

* This statement is made on the authority of a letter from Rev. G. W. Harris, of Detroit, editor of the Christian Herald, to the author. It was written in 1851, and gave the names of the more prominent men of this denomination as having acted in concert with Rev. M. Allen, of the board of regents.

14

the different religious denominations, although utterances from some individuals of the Methodists had, unfortunately, seemed to justify a different conclusion in regard to them, and had led, as we think, the most prominent men in the board to treat a man of Dr. Whedon's marked ability with a degree of injustice.

Chief Justice Whipple, from a special committee on constitutional provisions, reported, at the July meeting of 1851, in favor of the immediate election of a president, but the report was not adopted. A motion was also made "that the board do proceed to fill the chair of intellectual and moral philosophy," pending which a motion to adjourn prevailed.

The board met according to adjournment, on the 30th of December following. After other business, not relating to the subject of this review, it was, on motion of Justice Ransom, voted "that the board proceed, at the hour of meeting to-morrow, to the election of a president of the university, and that the regents-elect be invited to be present and participate in the discussion." This was, however, reconsidered, and made the special order for the next morning at 9 o'clock, at which time it was lost by the following vote, viz : Yeas : Messrs. Pratt, Foster, Pilcher, Ransom— 4. Nays : Messrs. Pitcher, Redfield, Kearsley, Allen, and the President (Lieutenant-Governor Fenton)—5.

Justice Pratt, of the Supreme Court, then offered the following preamble and resolution :

"WHEREAS, The great primary object of establishing 'the University of Michigan,' as clearly expressed by the people, through the act of their legislature, was to provide the inhabitants of the State with the means of acquiring a thorough knowledge of the various branches of literature, science, and the arts ; that as such institution, it is worthy of the pride and fostering care of every citizen of the entire State, and whose duty it should ever be to watch and guard it assiduously, and to see that it is not by any means perverted, or directly or indirectly used for any other purpose, and *especially* that it is not used for the inculcation of political or religious dogmas :

" AND, WHEREAS, It is represented, and is undoubtedly true, that the Rev. D. D. Whedon, one of the professors of said institution, has, during a period of time past, not only publicly preached, but otherwise advocated the doctrine called ' the higher law '—a doctrine which is unauthorized by the Bible,—at war with the principles, precepts, and examples of Christ and the Apostles—subversive alike of civil government, civil society, and the legal rights of individual citizens, and, in effect, constitutes, in the opinion of this board, a species of moral treason against the government ; therefore,

" *Resolved*, That the Rev. D. D. Whedon, for the reasons aforesaid, be, and is hereby removed."

Major Kearsley moved the following as a substitute :

" *Resolved*, That in view of the duty devolving upon the board of regents-elect to reorganize the faculty of arts in the university, and to appoint a president, it is expedient that the board provide for that contingency by determining the terms of the existing members of said faculty ; therefore,

"*Resolved*, That the terms of office of the present professors of natural philosophy and mathematics, of logic, rhetoric and history, and of the Greek and Latin languages, in the university, respectively terminate and expire at the close of the present academic year, or at such other previous time as the board of regents-elect may determine to appoint their successors."

This substitute was passed by the following vote : viz : Yeas : Messrs. Foster, Pitcher, Ransom, Kearsley, and Allen—5. Nays : Messrs. Pratt, Redfield, Pilcher, and the President—4. The original resolution, as amended by the substitute, was then passed by the following vote : Yeas : Messrs. Pratt, Foster, Pitcher, Ransom, Kearsley, Allen, and the President—7. Nays : Messrs. Pilcher and Redfield—2.

Dr. Pitcher immediately asked his neighbor, Mr. S. N. Kendrick, the intimate friend of Mr. Ten Brook, to inform the latter, then in the State of New York, of the action, and state to him that its real ground was not that expressed in the resolution, but that which had been intimated to him at the time of his resignation.* But there was little need that a member of the board should reveal the ground of this action. Any one will perceive that it is not to be found in the terms of the resolution, and the sagacious inquirer will not fail to suspect where it is. Judge Pratt's resolution has indeed the merit of being consistent with his character and state of mind. Crude and illogical in thought, inexact and coarse in expression, the production of a man who had just come into the board and knew nothing of what an educational body should be or do, a true demagogue without culture, and used only to the stump, he has given in this resolution a skeleton of a stump-speech, but it expresses, when its true import is reached, the exact ground upon which he wished the action to be taken.

Major Kearsley's resolution, on the other hand, taken in its obvious and natural meaning, is utterly without consistency. There was no duty devolving upon the new board to reorganize the faculty of arts, except as the existing board should break it up, any more than that of medicine. But if this had been true, then the *whole* faculty of arts should have been removed, and not simply three out of six of its members. Nor can it be said that this is explained by the duty of electing a president. A place had already been made vacant for him, and he did not need three others any more than five others to choose from; nor would he be any more likely to choose the department of mathematics than that of chemistry or modern languages.†

Mr. Foster voted without hesitation for the removal of

---

* It is but just to say that Mr. Ten Brook had no thought that the intimation made to him would be carried out.

† There was in this meeting so much disposition to freedom of comment upon the characters and conduct of members of the faculty, that Dr. Pitcher made an attempt to have the remainder of the session with closed doors, but was not successful.

those professors who had aided him in the matter of his
resolution of the previous January. Messrs. Seager, Douglass, and Fasquelle were not involved in the ejectment,
because they had taken no part in the " conference." Professor Williams was not hearty in his participation in it,
and expressed regret that he had anything to do with it,
and so, although removed, he was restored. The catas-
trophe could have been avoided, and no professor would
have been disturbed, if Mr. Ten Brook had done as he
ought to have done—stood firmly at his post until the crisis
was past.

If we should go into a thorough criticism of the characters and conduct of all the professors of that period, we
should find that their merits would be magnified, and their
mistakes diminished, by a consideration of the complicated
and till then unknown difficulties with which they had to
contend. They were not, as in any other case that ever
occurred in the history of the successful institutions of our
country. In none of these have professors ever had any
such tribunals before which they might, under either original or appellate jurisdiction, be brought. Governed
either by close corporations or by boards of trust, having
generally a nominal dependence upon some religious denomination, the character of whose members and the prevailing
influences among whom the professors thoroughly understood, they have known what they might do without rational ground of fear that they would be brought to account
for it before any other tribunal than that of a well-known,
friendly, and independent board of trust.

Nor was the case of the University of Michigan then as
now. It is still, indeed, governed by a board dependent
upon the legislature and the people, and must occasionally
pass through a period of peril while an appeal suit is pending before the representatives of the people at Lansing, and
discussed through the State. But an educational policy
has been established and developed; a reputation has been
wrought out for the university, and thousands of eloquent
advocates have been retained for its defense in all future

suits, in its graduates and their friends. All have learned
each other's views of it, and these are, at least, tending
toward harmony.

On the contrary, during the period now under review,
no great name was established and spread abroad by the
university; no policy had been settled, or, at least, none
had been sanctioned by the people; the governing board
had no power which could be freely exercised, so that its
decisions would stand without appeal; and the appeal
must, in the end, come to a miscellaneous body, thrown
together from different sections, the most of them prejudiced
against higher education, and some of them exasperated
by having university lands near them and standing in the
way of their interests, or those of their constituents; and
the few of them who had any views on the subject had
never exchanged them with each other and wrought them
into harmony, and their reserved and cautious hints might
have given to them no meaning, or any supposable one, or
its opposite, all with equal ease. The university had indeed done a marvelous work, and this was appreciated by
the few who had kept along with it; but these felt that they
had no power over the whole mass of the people, and were
therefore backward in their efforts to exert any. The people might indeed be moved as a forest is shaken with a
mighty wind, but no one was sure whence the wind was to
come which should produce the movement. The presidential question had, from the beginning, been in the minds
of all who felt interested in the institution, though it had
but slightly moved the lips of any. It had been the end
of the contest, described in this chapter, over the chair of
philosophy. Some had been successful in vacating a place
for the president; but not one who had anything to do with
this was ever consulted in regard to a man for the place—
just as always in such cases, those who conquer by dividing are disqualified for any part in the work of reconstruc-
tion. The presidential question had breathed into this contest all its spirit and animosity, and yet the conflict closed
about midnight on the 31st of December, 1851, with no

president elected, and with no apparent progress toward the settlement of any principle to direct the choice.

Those who know little of our university beyond its present state, and who thoughtlessly deem it to have suddenly sprung into existence not far from the year 1852, may well contemplate the period here passed in review, in order not only to observe how the roots fixed and strengthened themselves in the soil, but how much more of growth and of fruit appeared than they had supposed. During the university's first decade, the State had less than a fourth of its present population, and perhaps scarcely more than a twentieth of its present wealth; the university had an income of less than $10,000, and no preparatory schools but those founded and sustained by its own fund; the institution had its battles with sects, infidels, politicians, and with indifference to fight, and all to do which is involved in winning a name to call students from abroad: when all which is taken into view, it may occur to the present workers in this cause to consider whether it were not as well to mingle with their self-felicitations on what they have accomplished, some self-reproaches that they have not accomplished more.

The influence of the financial management upon the work has been shown. Beyond this the power and vigor of the institution from 1841 to 1852 are explained by the strength of the faculty of that period. A stronger body of men of the same number was probably never associated in such an opening enterprise. This is true of each individual of the body, though all had weaknesses, some of which have been hinted as connected with the dissolution in 1851–52. Careful selection, not accident, had brought them together. Dr. Williams was not strong as a mere teacher, for he did not compel the reluctant mind to grasp the truth taught; but he had in what might be called the social elements of his nature a marvelous power. And if the names were all called out—Williams, Whiting, Seager, Whedon, Agnew, Douglass, Fasquelle—we would,

without forgetting that each lacked some desirable traits
and attainments, be responsible for pointing out elements
of great power in each.   We now pass to consider the
period of visible growth and expansion, the harvest of
earlier seed.

CHAPTER XI.

President Tappan's Administration.

THE board which entered upon duty on the 1st of January, 1852, consisted of the following gentlemen, viz: Michael A. Patterson, of Tecumseh; Edward A. Moore, of Three Rivers; Elon Farnsworth, of Detroit; James Kingsley, of Ann Arbor; Elisha Ely, of Allegan; Chas. H. Palmer, of Romeo; William Upjohn, of Hastings; and Andrew Parsons, of Corunna.

The attention of this board during its first year, besides carrying on the work as had before been done, was chiefly directed to the establishing of a financial system and the finding of a president. At the first meeting a finance committee was appointed, which has since been perpetuated. This provided for the principal branch of the work, which had previously been done by the executive committee. Dr. Patterson was placed at its head. There was found an outstanding indebtedness of about $10,000, to meet which a consolidated warrant was drawn, and negotiated at the Phœnix Bank, in New York, where the interest was paid semi-annually, until the income was sufficient to meet the principal.

At the very first meeting, also, a committee was appointed to obtain, by correspondence or otherwise, the information needed for the election of a president. This consisted of Messrs. Palmer, Farnsworth, and Kingsley, who were also charged with the finding of candidates for the vacancies caused by the action of December 31, 1851. On the 24th of April, notes were addressed to Messrs. Williams, Whedon, and Agnew, inquiring whether they desired to be candidates for re-election to their old places, or to any others.

The first candidate for the presidency of which the record has preserved the name, was Henry Barnard, of Connecticut. He had became known by his labors in the preparation, passage through the legislature, and final introduction into practical operation of a new educational system for Connecticut; then by similar work in Rhode Island. But his reputation was more widely spread by his travels, undertaken in order to qualify himself for the execution of a plan of educational history. Mr. Barnard was elected to the presidency, by what vote the record does not indicate, on the 22d of June, and promptly declined, though the minutes show no reason, and the regents had been led to expect his prompt acceptance.

The expenses of the university for the fiscal year ending June 30, 1852, amounted to a little over $12,600; while the interest on the proceeds of land sold was about $10,750, and the lands sold during the year were $1,117\frac{96}{100}$ acres, and brought $13,445.52.

On the 21st of July, Rev. Dr. Adams, one of the ablest and most prominent Presbyterian ministers of the city of New York, was elected to the same place, and also declined. There had doubtless been votes cast for some other person or persons in both instances, but the election in each case was declared unanimous. On the same day the professorship of anatomy and surgery was divided, and the former given to Dr. A. B. Palmer, while Dr. M. Gunn, who had previously held both, retained the latter. Alvah Bradish was also elected professor of the theory and practice of the fine arts, but without salary, and with the understanding that his expenses would be paid during the delivery of his brief course of lectures.

On the 12th of August, Henry P. Tappan was elected to the presidency by a vote of 5 to 3—the three votes having been cast for Chancellor Lathrop, then of the University of Wisconsin. The election of Dr. Tappan was declared unanimous. Dr. Williams was re-elected to his former chair of mathematics and natural philosophy without opposition; James R. Boise was made professor of the

Latin and Greek languages, by a vote of 5 to 3—the three being for Dr. Agnew. The remaining place, that which had been held by Dr. Whedon, was not filled until December 21st following, when Rev. Erastus O. Haven was elected professor of the Latin language and literature. The salary of the president was fixed at $1,500, with a yearly allowance of $500 for traveling expenses, and a house, which was soon after repaired and enlarged, so as to be an elegant one for the time and place. There were good houses for three professors, and those who occupied them received $1,000 a year, while the others were allowed $1,150. Though these houses cost originally $8,000 each, professors were unwilling to occupy them at any considerable reduction of the salaries which they would otherwise receive.

These men, whose election has just been mentioned, together with Messrs. Douglass, Sager, and Fasquelle, constituted the corps of professors who were to be the co-workers of the new president, so far as yet determined, and they filled all the chairs of instruction which had as yet been established. The reorganization was complete.

The president's arrival upon the field of his future labors was too late to modify to any considerable extent the courses of study for the year, the classes having already entered upon them, but his time was employed in forming his plans. Soon after his arrival he solicited of the people of Ann Arbor donations for the library, and the sum of $1,515 was raised, which purchased 1,200 volumes. He took immediate measures, also, for the founding of an astronomical observatory, by an application to the citizens of Detroit, and the latter responded in donations to the amount of $10,000. The whole expense was $16,000. Mr. Henry N. Walker was the largest donor, and the most active agent in this work. With the concurrence of Dr. Tappan, who was absent in Europe, mainly with reference to instruments for the proposed observatory, Mr. Walker, in March, 1853, engaged Mr. George Bird, of New York, to superintend the construction of the building. There was some difficulty about the location, and the one chosen never became quite satisfactory. Four acres of ground were purchased for the purpose, on the brow of a hill outside of the city, and overlooking the valley of the Huron, the cost of which was only $100 per acre.

The board presented a memorial to the legislature, at the opening of the session of 1853, accompanying the report of the finance committee, in which were stated the fact and manner of the payment of the $100,000 loan; viz., by the sale of university lands for certificates of State indebtedness, excepting $15,095 paid directly by the regents. It is interesting to observe how distinctly this board understood the fact and manner of this payment, which their successors seem to have entirely forgotten.

The lands sold during the year were 4,788$\frac{53}{100}$ acres, bringing $62,943.13. The expenses for the year ending June 30, 1853, amounted to $27,333.78, including the consolidated warrant, making the actual cost of the year's work something over $17,000.

The library received some attention, at least in the way of inquiry into its condition, as shown by a report of Professor Fasquelle, who had been made librarian. This states that 172 volumes were found to be missing, 86 of which were afterward recovered, making a loss of 86 volumes. It states that from January 8, 1850, to January 8, 1853, 30 volumes a year had been lost.

The new era of our university history was fairly inaugurated, and the announcement of the catalogue for 1852–53 will best show what was proposed. The regular classical course had the same terms of admission as all the first-class colleges, such as Harvard and Yale, as from the very beginning. To this was added a scientific course, the condition of admission to which was a rigid examination in English grammar, geography, arithmetic, and algebra, through equations of the first degree. Four years of study, the same as in the classical, were required to complete this course. A partial course was also provided for those who did not desire to become candidates for a degree. These might be admitted to any part of the classical or scientific course for such length of time as they might choose, in case they should exhibit satisfactory evidence of such proficiency as would enable them to proceed advantageously with the studies of the classes which they proposed to enter. An agricultural course was also entered upon the catalogue, in the hope that the legislature would make for it that provision which the constitution seemed to contemplate. There was also laid down a very distinct outline of a so-called university course, designed for those who should have taken the degree of Bachelor of Arts or Bachelor of Science. An engineering course was added in the catalogue of the next year.

At the meeting of the board November 15, 1853, President Tappan produced a letter from Regent Palmer, who had held the correspondence with him with reference to the presidency, in which he was given to understand that his salary would be $2,000 a year, and he was accordingly allowed that amount.

On the 4th of May, 1854, Alexander Winchell was elected professor of civil engineering, and an appropriation of $500 was made for instruments for this department. At the June meeting following, J. Adams Allen was removed from the professorship of therapeutics and materia medica, in accordance with a petition signed by the president and nearly all the professors of both departments. Professor Palmer was transferred to the vacant place; but soon after there was a new arrangement among the professors of the medical school, which modified their work throughout. At the same meeting Corydon L. Ford, M.D., was made professor of anatomy, and Rev. Charles Fox, professor of agriculture; Francis Brünnow was also elected professor of astronomy, at a salary of $1,150, and his traveling expenses from Berlin, and Professor Haven was transferred to the professorship of history and English literature, and Henry S. Frieze was elected to the place made vacant by this transfer. The expenses of the year ending June 30, 1854, were about $16,500.

At the March meeting of 1855, Professor Frieze was granted leave of absence for a year's residence in Europe, and was allowed to spend the difference between his salary and that paid for a substitute, in art illustrations of antiquity, for the museum of art. This amounted to nearly $800. During this year, Professor Winchell was transferred to the department of natural history, and William G. Peck made professor of physics and civil engineering in his place. Expenses of the year ending June 30, 1855, $23,000.

At a meeting of the board in May, 1856, the salaries of the professors in the department of the arts and sciences were raised to $1,500, and the president's salary was increased by $250. William P. Trowbridge was elected professor of mathematics in the scientific department. The first step, also, was taken toward the building of a chemical laboratory, by an appropriation of $2,500, to which, within the year, additions were made as needed, so that the cost was $6,459.

At the June meeting, in 1856, the medical professors asked for an extension of the term in their department to nine months, which was refused, on the ground that it would cost $2,500 more. At the September meeting of this year, the first steps were taken toward altering a dormitory building for the use of the library and museum, at an expense of $3,500. Professor Haven resigned soon after this meeting, and Datus C. Brooks was appointed assistant professor of history and English literature, and Dr. Lord was employed to lecture on history, and receive the same salary as other professors for such portion of the year as he should actually perform service. Alfred Du Bois was also made assistant in the laboratory, and John L. Tappan, librarian. The pay of these assistants and the librarian was $500 a year to each. The expenses of the year ending June 30, 1856, were a little over $28,000. During this year the museum of natural history received a donation from Professor Trowbridge of three hundred specimens in zoology. These were duplicates of the collection made by him on the Pacific coast for the Smithsonian Institution. Professor Peck resigned in December, 1856, and John E. Clark was appointed to his duties. An appropriation of $5,000 was this year made to the library.

Some action unfriendly to the university was taken at both the annual conferences of the Methodist Episcopal Church for 1857, which occasioned, at the December meeting of this year, the following action of the board of regents:

"On motion of Regent Patterson:

"WHEREAS, The following paragraph appears in the published proceedings of the Methodist Conference, comprising the eastern half of the State, which recently (September 2–9, 1857) met at Port Huron, viz:

"'The University of Michigan has heretofore received high commendation from the ministry of our church, in their annual assemblies, and the number of pupils has of late years increased at a rapid ratio; but we are sorry to say that many of its friends have their fears that its moral and religious condition is such as greatly to impair its usefulness. Whether this institution, so nobly endowed, so well organized in its courses of instruction, so directly under the guardianship of the citizens of the State, shall be a safe abode for the sons of Christian parents during the most important period of their education, it is for the future to show. Our earnest prayer shall be for its prosperity.'

"And the following in the proceedings of a similar conference for the western half of the State, held at Lansing, September 16, 1857, viz:

"'We deem it proper in this report to make a brief mention of some educational interests of the State. With respect to the Michigan State University, while we believe that in its facilities for thorough mental cultivation it is second to no kindred institution in the land, we are compelled to fear that it is so defective in those moral and religious restraints and influences which ought always to be thrown around students of literary institutions, that it can not be patronized by our citizens without imminent peril to the moral and religious character of those youths who may be sent there for instruction, and until there is a decided improvement in this respect, we must say to the Christian public, within the bounds of our conference, beware!'

" *Resolved*, That the president and faculties of the university be and are hereby requested to report to the regents, as far as practicable, the moral conduct of the students attending said university, and the means employed to impress upon them sound moral and religious principles."

The report called for by this resolution was made before the close of the session. It calls attention to the numbers of pious students; to the daily religious exercises of the university; to the weekly lectures of Sunday afternoon; to the students' weekly prayer-meeting; to the meetings of the Society for Missionary Inquiry; and attempts a comparison of the moral and religious condition of the young men of Michigan University and those of other institutions, quite to the advantage of the former. As several of the professors were from Eastern universities, they declared themselves qualified to make this comparison. This report was signed by the president and all the professors.

There was an effort made during the year 1857, by the appointment of the president and Regent Kingsley as a committee, to obtain from Congress a grant of three townships of land, in accordance with a joint resolution of the legislature of 1853; but nothing further was ever heard from it. De Volson Wood was appointed professor of physics at the last meeting of the year.

With the first of January, 1858, came in an entirely new board, composed as follows, viz: Benjamin L. Baxter, J. Eastman Johnson, Levi Bishop, Donald McIntyre, E. Lakin Brown, George W. Pack, Henry Whiting, Luke II. Parsons, John Van Vleck, Oliver L. Spaulding, William M. Ferry, George Bradley.

It was deemed worth while to follow, in the form of annals, the doings of the former board, inaugurating, as it did, an epoch in the history of the university. In the remainder of President Tappan's administration, it will only be necessary to notice such action as had some special bearing upon development. So far as can be discerned, the president had no policy but that which had been fully made known during the six years past. The new regents probably had none; for none of them had had any such experience as to have positive notions of what their duties might be. They doubtless relied upon their own powers of observation and judgment to determine what ought to be done when the occasion should arise. Nor is it to be questioned that they designed to follow the lead of the president, and render him aid and support in carrying out that general policy which had been introduced under their predecessors.

The important questions which came in issue during the period from 1858 to the close of 1863, were, *first*, that in relation to the removal of the medical department to Detroit. This had been urged on the ground that a clinic course was necessary, and could only be secured in a large city. Some of the professors were understood to favor this project, and especially the professor of surgery, Dr. Gunn, who had removed to Detroit, entered into a general practice there, and was editing the "Peninsular and Medical Independent," then published in that city, in which this view was warmly advocated.

A committee of the board, composed of Messrs. McIntyre, Baxter, and Bishop, reported exhaustively on the subject, the last mentioned making a minority report, in which he dissented from the view of the majority, that the board was legally restrained from the removal, but agreed with them that the removal at that time would be impolitic.

The report of the majority takes the ground that the act of the legislature providing for securing a title to land free of expense as a site for the university, is a contract which would be violated by removal; that the university property to an amount of about $100,000 would thereby be forfeited; that it would cost $30,000 to $50,000 to get the department into operation in Detroit, and $2,500 more, annually, for a professor of chemistry and an assistant in the new labora-

15

tory.   It claimed that the advantages to be derived from a
better clinic had been unduly magnified, and showed by
the most decisive proofs that country medical schools were
really doing best.   It blamed the discussion of the subject
by the professors, and especially the professor of surgery,
as having caused all the dissatisfaction which was felt;
stated that the people of the State did not desire the removal; that this desire was confined mainly to those who
had originated it—viz., some of the professors—and it advised them to attend to their duties and cease agitation.
The report went into a general view of the defectiveness
of medical education; the want of foundation for it in
previous discipline; the want of thorough teaching beyond
the lectures, and recommended stricter rules to be more
strictly enforced.   In all this there was a free use made
of the opinions of distinguished medical authorities and the
experience of other institutions.   This settled the question
of removal, and imposed a wholesome restraint upon agi-
tations of this kind.

Various memorials had been received for years past
praying for the establishment of a department of law, a
favorable response to which, on part of the board, had
been prevented mainly by the want of funds.   At a meeting, however, held December 21, 1858, a committee of
three was appointed to consider and report a plan for a law
school in the university.   This committee, consisting of
Messrs. Johnson, McIntyre, and Baxter, made inquiry into
the organization and management of the principal schools
of the country for the training of lawyers.   These they
found, some of them, under the instruction of a single professor, while others had two, and three, and a single one
five.   Those at Hamilton College, in Central New York,
and Columbia College, New York city, had each but one
professor; while the one at Poughkeepsie had two, those at
Albany, Cincinnati, and Cambridge, each three, and the
one connected with the New York University five.   In
cases where but one professor was employed, he gave his
whole time to lecturing and examining the students upon

the subjects presented in the lectures and text-books. Where the number of professors was greater, they were generally men actively connected with the judiciary or bar, and gave little beyond the time for their lectures. The applications for the starting of a law school in the university had generally spoken of but one professor, whose whole time was, of course, to be given to the work. The board, however, pursued the other plan and provided for three, in accordance with the committee's recommendation, which was adopted March 29, 1859.

At the same meeting Messrs. James V. Campbell, Chas. I. Walker, and Thomas M. Cooley were appointed professors of the newly established law school. The opening took place on the 1st of October, 1859, on which occasion Judge Campbell delivered an address, setting forth the lawyer's need of large culture beyond the range of his technical books, and explaining well the failure of those who have only the latter. On this view he based an argument for the general advantage to a law school of being in connection with a university.

At first the old chapel must be used for the law lectures. An appropriation of $2,000 was promptly made for law books, which the narrow space occupied by the general library must receive, until other provision could be made. As a larger room was needed for the university library, as also for a chapel, the economical plan was conceived of erecting one for the accommodation of the law school, which was also to be made to serve both the other purposes, while necessity for this should continue to exist. No time was lost in carrying this plan into execution, and the building was ready for occupancy at the opening of the law term of 1863, the expense being about $20,000. This occasion was made a festive one. An address was delivered by Professor Cooley, and a poem by D. Bethune Duffield, both of which were published, and, with what had appeared before, and that which has since been added, quite a body of literature of this kind has grown out of the special and anniversary occasions. But the best thing which can be said of the law school is, that it has no history. No differences of opinion as to its management have ever been brought before the public; its classes have matriculated and graduated in succession, and nothing has arisen to furnish matter of discussion.

The legislature of the State, by an act approved February 12, 1855, amended the statute which gave the regents the government of the university, by appending to it the following conditional clause : "*Provided*, That there shall always be at least one professor of homœopathy in the department of medicine."

Very soon after the passage of this act, Elijah Drake obtained an alternative mandamus, calling upon the regents to show why they did not appoint a professor of homœopathy; but it was not made peremptory, on the ground that the movement must be by the attorney-general, and not by a private citizen, and, further, that it had not been shown that the regents were seeking to evade the law. Neither of these reasons touched the merits of the case ; and, after various efforts on the part of the board to procure a decision upon the real issue, the question was handed over to be the torment of other administrations, where we shall again meet it.

The question of the admission of females was at various times brought before the board by application for such admission. A very carefully prepared report, from a committee made up of Messrs. McIntyre, Parsons, and Baxter, was submitted September 29, 1858. This argued the question, indeed, somewhat independently, but its chief feature was the bringing together of the opinions of the leading educators of the country. Of these, Horace Mann and Charles G. Phinney were in favor of the co-education of the sexes; the others viewed it mainly either with disfavor or doubt. The subject was adjourned for others to act upon.

The income of the university was never quite what has been needed, and measures for its increase have always formed a subject for the consideration of the board. At the meeting in June, 1863, there was presented a report on the propriety of a discrimination between the students from Michigan and those from elsewhere, in regard to the amount of their fees.   The proposed measure was not adopted.

There was no important modification of policy during the term of this board, except that which signalized its closing days, nor was there indeed then, for the want of harmony between the board and the president was mainly of personal origin.   But this want of harmonious co-operation and its almost tragic end are events too notorious not to receive something more than a mere passing notice ; it is fit that there should be here introduced a " *dramatis personæ.*"

Henry P. Tappan was born at Rhinebeck, on the Hudson, on the 23d of April, 1805, and was, therefore, at the time of his election to the university, forty-seven years of age.   He was graduated at Union College in 1825, and at the Auburn Theological Seminary, in 1827, soon after which he was settled as pastor of the Congregational church in Pittsfield, Massachusetts, where he remained but two years, and then retired on account of ill-health.   He visited the West Indies in 1831, and on his return, in 1832, was elected to the professorship of mental and moral philosophy in the University of the City of New York, in which place he remained until 1838, and then resigned, with the rest of the faculty, on account of difficulties of internal administration—any satisfactory statement of which now would be impossible, and certainly the purpose of this work does not require the attempt.   After this, he had for many years the management of a private seminary in New York, and occupied himself also with authorship. In 1839, he published a " Review of Edwards' Inquiry into the Freedom of the Will ;" in 1840, " The Doctrine of the Will determined by an Appeal to Consciousness ; " in 1841, " The Doctrine of the Will applied to Moral Agency and Responsibility ; " in 1844, " The Elements of Logic, with an introductory review of Philosophy in general, and a preliminary view of the Reason."   In 1851, he

published a treatise on university education. In the same
year he visited Europe, and, on his return, published " A
Step from the New World to the Old "—his last work before entering upon the presidency of the University of
Michigan.

It has been claimed, on the one hand, that Dr. Tappan's
name and labors made the university. On the other hand, it
was insisted that the university had made him ; that he had no
name until this place gave it to him ; that his books accumulated the dust of the publisher's depot and the dealers'
shops ; that they were brought forth to the light and found
a market only after his election to this place ; that he was
a theorist in educational matters rather than a man for the
practical details of the work ; that the difficulties which led
to the resignation of the faculty of the University of New
York in 1838, were due chiefly to his impracticable traits
and overbearing disposition, and other things of the kind.
These views will not be discussed, and neither side need
be taken. The facts in regard to the New York University
difficulties are not accessible ; it is in Dr. Tappan's favor, at
least, that he was re-elected to his old place there.

Dr. Tappan had large and comprehensive, and, in the
main, correct views of the whole subject of education. He
had studied it, and had also himself been an educator. He
had a just and laudable ambition to see carried into practice, under his own direction, those views of the plan and
work of a university which his studies had led him to
adopt, and he could scarcely have had a better field for
carrying out his cherished desire than was offered him in
his call to Michigan. He entered this field at a time when
the public mind was ready to give any man a fair trial for
the highest honors in the educational competition. He
came at the close of a fearful conflict of which all had become wearied and were unwilling that it should be renewed. He had been no party to this, was entirely ignorant of it, and could in no way be deemed responsible
for any policy growing out of it. The same was scarcely
less true of the board of regents, and it was to some ex-

tent true even of the faculties. The policy of predecessors, whether it were on the side of wisdom or folly, was alike available for his instruction, with no pledge on his part for or against it.

Dr. Tappan had written books, and their influence in his favor was none the less that they had been little read; for the dust which they had collected on the shelves of booksellers and libraries, private and public, was at once swept away, and brief references to them were made in periodicals, to the favorable character of which the fame of the authors of those great works he has attacked or noticed—for instance, Edwards and Cousin—has contributed much. His pamphlets and reports on education are, in general, unpretentious, but sound; his preliminary view of philosophy and logic is doubtless his most creditable work, because it contains a somewhat full and sufficiently accurate outline of the subject. His other metaphysical works, though more pretentious, are less satisfactory. His works on the will have been regarded by many as reasoning in a circle; which is indeed true of most works on both sides of the profound questions which they discuss.

But the favorable impressions made by his occasional reports and short articles in periodicals, and the much stronger one made by the references to his metaphysical works upon those who had never read them, was sustained, extended, and deepened by his wonderful power on the platform. Here he was at home. His personal presence was magnificent; he was graceful in action, with the single exception of a frequent winking of the eyes, and even this was quite in his favor, as the one trifling habit of a great man. Thoughts and words which would not obey his call in the study—for he was not one of those students whose combined talents and industry will pursue subjects, pen in hand, until they are finally compelled to surrender all their treasures— would come at his bidding in the presence of a popular assembly, though for want of close study it could not have extended itself over a wide range of subjects. This power availed him much, and the profoundly felt need of a head to the university, impressed by its trials, availed him more.

The manner in which Dr. Tappan was brought before the board is not without interest. The newly elected guardians of the State University perhaps supposed that the presidency of their institution might tempt the largest talents, culture, and reputation of the country. A letter was accordingly addressed to George Bancroft, doubtless modestly suggesting the question whether he would like the place. Mr. B. was not at the time in any public trust. He had published the earlier volumes of the most extensive philosophical and popular history of our country, and his laurels were fresh upon him in the eyes of all the people. Successively for a short time at the head of the Navy Department of the United States and the mission to England, who could doubt that his ambition might contemplate the presidency of our great western university as the next step of his ascent, as his friend Everett, after retiring from the English mission, had accepted that of the greatest of the New England seats of learning? Mr. B., however, viewed the matter otherwise, nor did he deem it worth while to encourage a call, hold it under consideration for a year, and then decline it; but in a very practical way he suggested the name of Henry P. Tappan, an account of whose election, with brief annals of his administration, has been given above.

It is no matter of wonder, if, at the end of this administration in 1863, the graduates of the ten years past felt that the first president had made the university; they knew nothing beyond his time. The former graduates were glad to see their alma mater risen to its immense power, and concurred in the favorable view of the president. Few had any definite knowledge of what had preceded. The pacification, achieved before he came, and with which he had nothing to do, was not unnaturally attributed to him. He had an almost unequaled opportunity.

It is quite clear, too, and no intelligent opposer of Dr. Tappan's course will deny it, that he had mental ability and attainments equal to his place; that he had an appreciative knowledge of every branch of science, and knew what place to assign to each in a university course; that his educational plans were well studied, and in the main correct; and that in some departments, of which the observatory is perhaps the most conspicuous instance, his merit is quite extraordinary. This is indeed high praise; but there was fault somewhere, and where was it? Was it all in Dr. Tappan? or all in those associated with him? or did they share it between them? These questions, notwithstanding their delicacy, demand a fair attempt at solution.

There is a class of men in the world more or less, by natural qualities of mind, adapted to leadership; none of these have *all* the necessary qualities in their perfection, and capable of adjusting themselves to all the classes and cases coming within the range of their influence. Among the traits of a natural leader, one of the most important is the power to inspire confidence in his fitness for his place among all the classes and persons embraced within the circle upon which he is expected to exert his power. One seems fitted to influence and control one class, and not another; but the demand is that a man in high executive place shall not only be ready to mete out to *all* classes their just dues, but that he shall also be able to impress them with the conviction of his readiness and ability to do this. He must be able to bring all classes to cordial co-operation, and hold all in harmonious action. In a kingly government the sovereign may act so evidently from an honest sense of justice to all his subjects as to impart to all a conviction of his fairness, and unite them in the feeling of loyalty to him; or he may so gain the good-will of nobility, clergy, or any other class, as to feel himself secure and care nothing about the common people; or he may fear the nobility, and in order to keep them down, ally himself with the common people.

To make the application to the case in hand. The president of a state university is related quite intimately to regents, faculties, and students; less nearly to the legislature and executive of the State; and then still less nearly—but the relation is by no means unimportant—to the people at large, including all its classes, ecclesiastical, political, and others. Dr. Tappan had perhaps in his nature and his education no small infusion of the aristocratic element. This need not appear in his intercourse with students, for they were so evidently below him in place, that nothing in his manner toward them could be interpreted as an acknowledgment of equality. The general fact was much the same in regard to his intercourse with the public, whether on the platform or in social life; he felt himself in no danger from infusing into it all that kindliness which is so grateful when coming from an acknowledged superior, and which it was doubtless, too, in his nature to show. He was paternal in his feelings and conduct, and would have been a kind father to all mankind; but he was deemed by many to lack the elements of a brother—an equal.

The relation between him and the regents and professors, or the State executive and legislators, was different. He was greatly the superior of most, if not all of them, both in natural ability and in attainments, as also in position, as head of the educational system of the State. This, almost every one would concede. The same would be true of any other man who should be worthily placed in the same position. Almost any man who has this superiority, is also more or less penetrated with a consciousness of it. This consciousness many a one can conceal from others, nay, almost from himself, so as cheerfully to occupy the same plane with his associates and fellow-laborers in the work, and bear these along with him, involuntary captives to his own views and plans. This Dr. Tappan did not succeed in doing. His manner was understood as a claim that his superiority must be acknowledged. The word arrogance has been applied to him even by some of his friends, and if it could be understood as not asserting that he ever arrogated to himself that which ought not to have been conceded to him, it would convey the true idea.

It belongs to the president that, whatever he, from his vantage ground of impartial observation, and with a just sense of his responsibility, deliberately recommends, should be first considered by the governing board, and never rejected without the best of reasons; but he should never, even by implication, lay claim to such consideration. Dr. Tappan, however, seemed to some always to have an air which carried with it this claim. This can be regarded as justifying only in part the course which was taken in regard to him, but it ought, in all cases, to be admitted in palliation.

This trait of the president led to no unpleasant consequences which became apparent, at least, during the term of the board which elected him. He had shown wisdom in his plans and energy in their execution, and the regents followed cheerfully his leadership, because they deemed it wise. In such case, the fierceness of a dozen lions might be slumbering in his nature and never show itself for want of something to arouse it. Nor did this board follow their leader blindly : they were intelligent men ; they had a deep sense of their responsibility ; they acted from their own understanding of the matters brought before them, and they left things in a good condition.

It was one of the infelicities of the constitution of 1851, that it provided for the election of an entire board at once, making it possible, at least, that every member should be new. This actually occurred in 1858. These men had no strong personal attachment to the president; they had not wrought with him in establishing his system; they had no sense of responsibility in him ; they did not elect him ; they had no knowledge of educational matters from the practical point of view; none of them had been teachers or trustees of collegiate schools ; none of them were prepossessed against the president's system from having any of their own. They doubtless designed cordially to work with him ; but they had to learn, and must naturally learn chiefly from him, and unfortunately he was not of the right spirit patiently to teach and lead such pupils—his superiors

in governing power, greatly his inferiors in the knowledge of matters pertaining to their work. His efforts to
teach and lead them, and theirs to hold him in check, all
ministered to growing alienation.

It must be further insisted in Dr. Tappan's favor, that the
traits referred to, which made him a favorite with the students and people generally, but rendered his relations with
regents and professors intolerable, are, after all, better than
a similar extreme of opposite traits. The president's true
work is to inform himself how all interests can best be har-
monized; how the burdens can be equally borne and the
services equally paid according to their nature, and to use
his best endeavors to bring the truth before the board and
secure the appropriate action. The office of president is
worth nothing unless it measurably effects this. The man
who does this in such way as to offend the whole board
and a majority of the professors, as did Dr. Tappan, sins
chiefly against himself, and may suffer for it, as he did;
but he who is so much in fear of doing or saying something not acceptable to the board of trust, as to be governed
in all he says and does by the hope of their favorable regards, and then expect cheaply to earn credit for courage
and independence by stemming the torrent of popular disfavor from students and others who can not touch him, is
really a more unsafe man. An earnest and fearless statement and recommendation of what one honestly feels to be
right, accompanied with the grace quietly to submit when
he finds the board against him, is the only true course.

Mr. Bishop, whether justly or not may appear in the
sequel, is generally credited with the chief part in procuring the breach with the president. His early education was
that of a common mechanic. At the age of, perhaps, a
little over twenty years, after his removal from his native
New England to Detroit, he lost a hand in firing on a fourth
of July, which turned his attention in quite another direction. He went into an office, and prepared himself for the
profession of law. Not content with this, he laboriously
struggled through more elementary studies, which had

been neglected in his earlier life. This all showed talents of no mean order, which, with early advantages, would have made him a scholar. He has, indeed, cultivated the poetic art, and, besides other things, has contributed to the literature relating to the aborigines of our country, an epic of twenty-eight cantos, under the title of Teusha Grondie, which is not to be despised. But even if he had received early culture, it is doubtful whether he would have acquired the higher graces and accomplishments of a man of letters, which his nature seemed rather to despise. He was impulsive, and yet strangely free from a certain kind of irritability; and, as he could utter his animadversions upon others, so he could receive theirs without showing permanent signs of irritation—they rattled harmlessly off, like buckshot from the scales of the crocodile. But still his impulsive nature brought him to the front whenever the occasion occurred to call any one out.

It will therefore be evident that Mr. Bishop was the right man to appear most prominent on all occasions of conflict with the president; but he must have been under the encouragement of men as decided as himself, if not even more so. Of these, Mr. McIntyre, a private banker of Ann Arbor, deserves special mention.

He was not a man to be greatly affected by public opinion, and, in the general interests of the university, he could carry out his own convictions with as little regard as any other man to what the rest of the world might think. His home being in Ann Arbor, gave him the title of " resident regent," connected with which certain special duties were assigned him. He was a prominent member of the Presbyterian church, to which Dr. Tappan also belonged, but this relation served rather to alienate than to unite them. The president seemed to act upon the mistaken view that his place rather required him in effect to renounce his relation to a particular church, and distribute himself to all the churches. He probably attended worship at the Baptist and Episcopal churches as much as at his own, and to both these his relations were always friendly, because, not being a member, no business transactions could come in to disturb them; while between himself and his own church there was much friction, and even bitterness, of which he gives some details in his "statement."

There was, indeed, one more decisive ground of alienation. Mr. McIntyre was one of the most earnest of the more advanced school of temperance. The president's table was well supplied with wines, and this practice was but a carrying out of his theory. When a young man once lost his life in a convivial scene into which he had been drawn by two students, an appeal, pointed by this fact, was addressed to him, which he consistently resisted, and the regent's feeling toward him became embittered, and the bitterness became a contagion.

The president was equally aggrieved by the course of the regent. In his "statement" he complains that McIntyre's banking-house was made a kind of headquarters of students and professors arriving in town—the center and source of information and authority—which he connects with other things of the kind, and represents as almost ignoring and nullifying the authority of president and professors.

When a cloud has once made its appearance upon the horizon, the eye can easily follow its course; but even the most exact science is but partially successful in finding the precise point in the earth's atmosphere, where it had its inception. So it is easy to tell how the university cloud accumulated, and how it finally discharged itself and gradually dispersed; but we shall not attempt to go back of appearances. Whether the origin was with regents or professors, or with what regent or what professor, need not be inquired. The president charged all upon Mr. Bishop. It is admitted on all hands that Messrs. Bishop and Boise formed one of the connections between the board and the faculties. What other connections of this kind there may have been, who formed them, and which of them were most effective, it is not material to inquire; the great majority of the professors were in the end with

the board—Messrs. Williams and Douglass of the older,
and Spence and Evans of the younger, being the only
ones known to have taken a decided stand with the president.

Besides the private rings formed between professors and
regents, as referred to above, there were two connections
which were formal and official—one by the placing of each
professor upon that committee of the regents which had
general charge of his particular department of work ; the
other through a body called the university senate, made up
of all the full professors in all the departments. What was
likely to occur through the former, the reader can readily
conceive. As to the senate, this body was constituted,
probably, by the board of 1852,* and its powers, which,
however, were only advisory, distinctly defined. One important effect of its existence and action was that the professors in the law and medical schools were brought into
nearer relation to the chief executive than they could otherwise have been ; for, as the president's connection with
these departments was little more than nominal, the influence of their professors could only become available by
some such provision. In this way, Professors Campbell
and Cooley, both skillful in those legal and semi-legal
questions which often came up, could make themselves
felt. And, in general, the opinions of the senate, expressed
by vote, after free interchange of views, would be justly
entitled to a respect from the board to which those collected
in private conversations could lay no claim.

Such were the organized means of exchanging opinions ;
the unorganized elements of influence were all the individuals composing board, faculties, committees, senate, and
all interested. The intentions of the regents were so carefully communicated to their friends as not to escape to the
public ; or perhaps there had been so much of bluster that
the escape of some words created no sensation—they were

---

* The records of the senate have within the past two years been lost.

not believed. The regents did the business of their June meeting for 1863 as usual—committees were appointed; duties were assigned to the president, which, according to the secret will of the board, he was never to perform.

The surface of the sea, in a few hours to be agitated by the most violent of tornadoes, was perfectly tranquil. The president appeared with his wonted grace and dignity on commencement day, and doubtless seemed to see through the vista of the future other and larger classes ascending the platform for the honors and the parting benediction of their *alma mater* under a new board then already elected, and including but a single one of that body whose course of action had so disturbed his peace. So it was not to be.

The ordinary business of the board was continued until the afternoon session of Thursday—the day after commencement. In the meantime, an intimation was conveyed to the president, through his friend, Professor Douglass, that his resignation would be acceptable. He declined to offer it. Regent Brown then moved the following resolution, which, with several others, had been proposed in secret session :

"*Resolved*, That Dr. Henry P. Tappan be and is hereby removed from the offices and duties of president of the University of Michigan and professor of philosophy therein."

The president retired, and Mr. Baxter was called to the chair, when the resolution was passed by the votes of all the members present except Mr. Baxter, who was excused from voting. Messrs. Spaulding and Ferry were absent. John L. Tappan was likewise removed from the librarianship, to which place Datus C. Brooks was transferred from the department of English literature. Rev. Lucius D. Chapin, of Ann Arbor, was made professor of mental and moral philosophy, and Rev. Erastus O. Haven, D.D., of rhetoric and English literature, and, by another vote, president, all the members voting for him.

The intelligence of this action was given to the winds, and seldom have those winged messengers made so great a clamor, or kept it up so long, as in the bearing abroad throughout the State, and even far beyond its limits, of this intelligence.

16

CHAPTER XII.

President Haven's Administration, and thence to the Present Time.

THE chief problem for the new president to solve, was whether he was really president or not; at least it took this form, for it was held by some that the election was void. On this theory, a writ of *quo warranto* was applied for by an attorney acting for Dr. Tappan, in order to test Dr. Haven's right to the place.

We do not know, of course, how far Dr. Tappan was himself responsible for this course. He had doubtless received legal advice which led him to take whatever measures he did take in this direction.

The great portion of the agitation, both in private circles and in the newspapers, was merely a venting of indignation or an expression of approbation, but mostly the former, though often without any practical end in view, and perhaps mostly with no definite purpose to affect the course of the regents; nay, perhaps it was even participated in by those who felt no great interest in the matter one way or the other, but thought they ought also to discharge their missiles in a cause which had aroused such feeling, though many were quite doubtful as to the direction in which they should aim.

There was, however, a class of men who had a definite purpose: it was the removal of the new president and re-election of the old one. The same power which had done a work—the board of regents—could undo it. Of this there could be no doubt. It was furthermore claimed that by the constitution it was made the duty of the board to elect a president soon after entering upon their term of service; that the place was, therefore, vacant by the con-

stitution of the State. It was supposed, and was perhaps
true, that most of the new board was with Dr. Tappan.
Whether they were directly approached on the subject or
not, it was kept before them in such way as to furnish all
the needed arguments and motives to action, by both sides,
though this was more quietly and cautiously done by his
opposers than by his friends. Indeed, this is true to such
an extent as to have given not a little point to the sarcastic
references which his friends made to the trifling nature of
the charges against him. The advantage was greatly on
their side; they dared to say, and even to publish, all they
thought and felt. Not so the other side. They were embarrassed. If they made no reply to the demand for the
grounds of the action, they seemed to justify the retort that
they had none but such as they were ashamed of; if they
said little, and only in a general way, it was regarded as
all that could be said, and as trifling; if they had told the
whole story, as they understood it, this would have been
treated as calumny and abuse to a great and good man.
They had, however, this advantage, that they were *in*,
their opponents *out*. Moreover, Dr. Tappan, called,
encouraged, and aided by injudicious counsel, came to
their support; he entered the conflict, and made its issue
certain against himself, if indeed there had been any doubt
before.

Dr. Tappan had the apparent advantage, as already
stated, except that he was out of place and another had
possession. It can not be deemed unnatural that those who
had become attached to him, should give vent to their feelings of sorrow and indignation in language somewhat ex-
aggerated, and even vituperative, and reasonable men on the
other side ought not to complain of this. Articles of this
kind did get into the papers, and those of Detroit were all
on the late president's side. The worst fears for the university were, no doubt, honestly entertained, and found expression, not only in conversation, but through the press.
It is, however, but just to all the Michigan parties who
participated in these utterances, to add that they generally

tempered them with the expression of a wholesome regard
for the best interests of the university; and if there were
exceptions to this, as indeed there were some, they should
readily be pardoned to that filial feeling which prompted
them. The most marked and least excusable instance of
this was the report of the majority of the visiting committee for the year 1863; but considering its source, the editorial article in Barnard's Journal of Education, for December, 1863, is most forgetful of the true character of a
/ dignified journalism.

It is perhaps better to give some official papers belonging to the period of conflict which ensued upon the
action of June 25, 1863, and let these speak for themselves.
It was not until the 18th of February, 1864, that the presidential question was fairly put to rest. The following extract from the regents' report, dated November 17, 1863,
furnishes their own explanation of their action:

" We long since saw, to our regret, that evils existed in
the university of a serious character. The senior year had
become of comparatively little value. Its high tone of
scholarship had fallen away. The philosophy taught
during that year was little more than a name. By-laws
adopted by the board for the government of the university
were rejected and their enforcement refused. Moral restraints were in many cases thrown off, and it became exceedingly difficult, if not impossible, to enforce discipline
for moral delinquencies. Habits of wine and beer drinking
to excess, and other improper habits, were not sufficiently
discountenanced. Dissensions existed between the professors and the president. The absence of the president from
the university during term-time occurred for extended
periods. A claim has been persistently asserted that a degree of power belonged to the president which was uncontrollable by any other body, and which would deprive both
regents and faculties of many of their most important pre-
rogatives in the external and internal management of the
university. Any difference of opinion on this subject has
been treated as a personal grievance, and has been re-

sented. Members of the faculties have experienced this jealousy to an extent which has caused them serious annoyance and inconvenience, and their usefulness has been impaired by assaults upon their character and motives openly made by the president. Others have abstained from expressing their views at faculty meetings, and on other occasions, from a well-grounded fear of exciting similar enmity and annoyance. It has been distinctly claimed that the views of the president should overrule those of the faculties where they should not be in unison; and the persistent assertion of this uncontrolled right of government, and the feeling known to be excited in him by any opposition to his views, has prevented any general or cordial interchange of sentiment upon university interests between him and the professors: and the complaints which he has made against regents and professors have not been confined to private circles or official intercourse; but his criticisms and attacks have been made most freely and publicly, without reference to the place or occasion, and have been made to students, and even in class exercises, to the manifest subversion of respect and discipline.

"Such a clashing of claims to authority, and such interferences with the rights and usefulness of others, could not but tend to destroy the university. All these evils were attributed mainly to the president.

" The extent of these and other defects and derelictions, the practical evils they produced—some of these obvious to every observer; others not so observable, but quite as injurious—convinced the board long since of the imperious necessity for their interposition to devise and effect a remedy; and we were as well convinced that the only effectual remedy was the one we applied—the removal of the president and the appointment of a successor. . . . We confidently trust that results will vindicate our action, and add to the prosperity and usefulness of the university."

The following extracts embrace all the material parts of the report of the visitors for 1863:

" Hon. John M. Gregory, *Sup't of Public Instruction:*

" The term for which the subscribers were appointed to serve as visitors of the University of Michigan being about at an end, they beg leave to report that they have discharged the interesting duty assigned them as faithfully as numerous other engagements would permit. The examinations attended were in the main highly creditable to the pupils and to their instructors. The public exhibitions witnessed have, upon the whole, done honor to the university and to the State, by the talent and training evinced. And the general aspect of the institution, its numbers keeping well up and the ordinary routine continuing, does not, as yet at least, present any marked symptoms of the transition which is going on, except a few discontented demonstrations on the part of the students, a certain anxious and restless disquietude among the professors, and the loss among them of some of the brighter lights, such as Brünnow and White.

" But the positive existence and pernicious character of this transition is a subject to which we feel compelled to call your attention, and through you that of the people of the State.

" For several years the interior management of our beloved and honored university has been gliding out of the hands of the president and professors, where it constitutionally and properly belongs, into those of the regents, who are of course, as a body, unqualified for this work, and were never elected for any such purpose. During this time the governing and directive functions, the administrative and executive control of its affairs passing gradually from the faculty appointed over it, has been largely usurped by the regents, and farmed out among themselves.

" Such a procedure was never permitted in connection with any college of standing, is directly subversive of the best interests of our State university, and was effected against the judgment, nay, in spite of the resistance of the ' chief executive officer.' This is, indeed, the very controversy which the regents had with that great and good man, Dr. Tappan. And this is the reason why, failing to entirely overmaster him, and being themselves excused from further attempts at it, by the people, they wound up with a final parting vote to remove him from his place. It was a fit termination of the disorganizing and revolutionary measures which they undertook to introduce. And a more deadly stab was never given to the cause of education, learning, high-toned refinement, and Christian culture in Michigan, and throughout the West. There is, in our judgment, no man in the United States, who combines so many strong points for a successful and illustrious head and front of the University of Michigan as he who, after years of faithful and most able and triumphant service in that capacity, has been discharged, and that by men who had themselves been repudiated by the people. But it is not the wrong done him, it is the tendency of such proceedings, and the effect of that consummating act upon the cause of sound learning, high scholarship, and elevated sentiment among us, that we here complain of. Our university ought to be conducted upon principles most conducive to the rapid development of its magnificent resources. And foremost among them, as every tyro in university matters well knows, is freedom for the faculty from meddlesome interference on the part of the regents. The latter, of course, are comparatively unfamiliar with such matters, and reside in different parts of the State, with affairs of their own to manage, while the college officers are ever there on the ground. Their work, their interests, their pride, their ambition, are there. In the study, the cabinet, the laboratory, the lecture hall and recitation room, do they live, breathe, and exult. And there should they be protected, there encouraged by generous and noble treatment, to do their very best to advance scholarship, elevate science, and fill the West with highly educated and refined young gentlemen. The people meant to say ' hands off,' let these men, and especially their chief executive officer alone, when they hurled those meddling

regents out of power. Whether they said so with emphasis
enough, remains to be seen.

" The only wise course is to have our university restored
as soon as possible, in all except monetary and outside interests of the most general character, and such restraining
or confirmatory action as may be necessary at very considerable intervals, to the entire control and management of
its own officers, with a chief executive over them fully
qualified by his talents and attainments, by commanding
personal and social advantages, by extensive knowledge
of books, art, and the world, and by intimate relations with
the learned and great of this and other lands, to hold that
position, make it resplendent, and extend the young re-
nown of the University of Michigan both at home and
abroad.

" All of which is respectfully submitted.

" AZARIAH ELDREDGE,
" E. H. THOMSON."

The above is followed in the superintendent's report by
the following from that officer :

"NOTE.—The foregoing report, sent at a very late date,
and reaching me still later by reason of being sent to Ann
Arbor rather than to this office, was accompanied by a note
from Mr. Eldridge, asking that the report should be presented to the third visitor, 'if he is at Ann Arbor,' but that
'otherwise it must go into your report as it is.' A letter
from Dr. Underwood, afterward received, is given here as
his expression of views as a visitor :

"*To* HON. J. M. GREGORY, *Sup't of Public Instruction:*

" SIR :—I have recently seen in one of the Detroit daily
papers a report made to you by two of the board of visitors
to the University of Michigan for the years 1862 and 1863.
As one of the members of the board, I wish to say that the
above-mentioned report was not submitted to me for my
approval or signature, nor was I consulted in any way
about a report. The following paragraph in the report has

my approval: 'The examinations attended, were, in the main, highly creditable to the pupils and to their instructors. The public exhibitions witnessed, have, upon the whole, done honor to the university and to the State by the talent and training evinced.' From the remainder of 'the report' I wholly dissent, for the following reasons. I do not believe it to be the proper business of the visitors to sit in judgment upon the acts and motives of the regents : I do not believe the allegations or charges against the late board of regents contained in the report to be true.

"Very respectfully yours,
" D. K. UNDERWOOD.

"ADRIAN, *February* 4, 1864."

The following action of the university senate relates to the point of complaint contained in the report of the majority of the board of visitors, as above :

"At a meeting of the senate of the University of Michigan convened January 14, 1864, present the President and Professors Williams, Sager, Boise, Palmer, Winchell, Frieze, Campbell, Cooley, Wood, Watson, Evans, Chapin, and Olney, the following resolutions were unanimously adopted :

" 'WHEREAS, It has been represented that the late board of regents have interfered with the interior management of this university by assuming the exercise of duties properly belonging to its educational officers, and by improperly meddling with their administration, thus impairing their usefulness and destroying their independence ; and,

" 'WHEREAS, These insinuations have, in some cases, proceeded from those who might be supposed to possess some means of knowledge and are calculated to have some degree of credit given them on that supposition, and for that reason it becomes proper that those who do know the facts should correct such erroneous impressions as may have arisen, to protect their own reputation as well as to certify the truth :

" '*Resolved*, That the late board of regents have uniformly treated the various faculties of the university with courteous consideration, and have, in no case that we are informed of, infringed in any degree upon their usual pre-rogatives, or attempted to interfere with them in the dis-charge of their duties ; and that in our opinion the internal management of this institution has in no respect been in-jured or diverted from its proper custody by the action of the late board.

" 'Resolved, That the foregoing preamble and resolu-tion be communicated to the superintendent of public in-struction.'

" THOMAS M. COOLEY,

"Secretary of the Senate."

. This whole interval between the end of June, 1863, and the 18th of February, 1864, was filled up with excitement, which was as yet almost unabated at the end of the time. Dr. Tappan remained for some weeks in Ann Arbor, where many friends paid him their sincere respects, including not a few who sympathized with the other side, and some pub-lic expression was made. Indeed, he occupied the presi-dent's house until it was needed for his successor, and the notice to leave served upon him by the university authorities, barbed some of the missiles of his friends. The sale of his household goods at auction, which took place after the family had left, and continued for several days, offered the occasion of many a joke, some arising from the display of glassware and cigar-stands. These, however, were chiefly from his friends, and none were reported which savored of disrespect to his memory.

In the meantime, he had retired to Berlin, Prussia. His account of his connection with the university was prepared, and, near the end of the year 1863, was published, so as to be ready for the new board when they should have entered upon their official term. This they read, as doubtless also much of other matter which might bear upon their decision. They had also much to hear, perhaps more than they de-sired, offered by way of qualifying them for duty. The final action was at a special meeting of February 16 to 18, 1864. On this occasion appeared a delegation from Detroit, bearing a numerously signed memorial, asking the restoration of the late president. This delegation was not merely respectable ; it was venerable. The Rev. Dr. Duffield and Right Rev. Samuel A. McKoskry were of it. The board felt deeply the responsibility of the moment, for in it were concentrated interests vast and enduring. Memorialists, whatever side they took, and however earnest and sincere, might be deemed to be advocates ; the regents were judges : upon *their* action all was to turn. The report of their committee, appointed to consider the subject, made through Regent Willard, was as follows :

"Your committee, to whom were referred certain papers and memorials, asking for the restoration of the Rev. Dr. H. P. Tappan to the presidency of the University of Michigan, beg leave to report :

"That the communications referred to, signed by eminent citizens of the State, and faithful friends of the university, have received that full and careful consideration on the part of the committee, to which, from their character and source, they were deemed to be entitled.

"Your committee regret that anything should have occurred in the history of the university, which should awaken the fears and apprehensions of persons of such distinguished respectability and influence as those whose names are appended to these memorials, and also sincerely join with them in the further regret that any circumstances should have arisen which should deprive the university and the educational interests of the State, of the services of one whose superior ability and attainments, and whose efficiency and success in the sphere filled by him with such rare distinction, have for some years past been an honor to our State.

"They appreciate, and believe that the people of the State appreciate, the labors of that eminent scholar and educator, and the impress which his influence has left upon our young and rapidly developing commonwealth.

" They recognize as fully as the memorialists the almost
unexampled prosperity of the university during the presidency of Dr. Tappan, and accord to him and to his coad-
jutors in the management of the several departments,
within that period, the distinguished merit of having placed
the institution among those of the very first rank in our
country, whether we regard its discipline, the character
and grade of the scholarship attained, or the number of
students whom it has yearly sent forth so well fitted for the
duties and responsibilities of active life.

" The action of the late board of regents, reprehended
by some of the memorialists, your committee would perhaps be stepping aside from their province if they should
presume, in this report, either to indorse or condemn.
They do not regard it to be the duty of the present board
of regents to sit in judgment upon their predecessors
in office, but believe that, accepting the university as
they find it, it is required at their hands to administer
the trust as the best interests of the institution shall appear to them to demand.   Such is the estimation in which
your committee hold the ability and scholarship of the late
president, they would be glad, if consistent with these interests, they could recommend his recall to his former position.   But, after the most careful deliberation, they have
come to the conclusion that it is impracticable, and believe
that in the posture which affairs have assumed, such an
act would prove injurious to the real welfare of the university, which welfare they deem to be the legitimate subject
of consideration for the board of regents, on the question
presented by the memorialists.

" The assumption made by a portion of those who have
memorialized the board, that the university is not at present
in good condition, and does not give promise of success,
appears to your committee to have been made without sufficient knowledge of the facts.   The pressure upon the
board from the different departments for increased facilities
for the accommodation of students, is a proof that the institution is not languishing.   The law and medical depart-

ments especially, under the more immediate direction of their several faculties, are flourishing to a degree not before paralleled since they were established. The literary and scientific departments give no signs of that decadence mentioned by the memorialists. Apparently, the institution is prosperous; and there is a good degree of harmony in the several departments, and among the various faculties, and, from what we can learn, after the most deliberate examination and survey, the conviction is forced upon us unanimously that, under all the circumstances of the case, such a change as, is sought by the memorialists would be attended with a disturbance of that harmony greater than has yet existed in the university.

"The charge is made in several of the papers referred to your committee, that the rules and regulations of the board of regents confer duties and prerogatives belonging to the different faculties and to the president, upon committees appointed by the board, and consisting mainly of members of the same. This objection can no longer be urged, as the revised rules meet the unanimous approbation, it is believed, of all the faculties of the institution.

"Your committee feel constrained to recommend that the request of the memorialists be not granted. In making this recommendation, they submit the grave and important question to the board, and would here express the hope that the conclusion which shall be finally reached, may be such as shall secure the acquiescence of every true friend of the university, and that, all strife and contention being laid aside, the spirit of peace, and harmony, and mutual concession may prevail, and that the institution which has justly been hitherto the pride of the State, may go on, in its career of usefulness, dispensing its blessings, and imparting a beneficial and gracious influence to all."

The report was adopted by the following vote :

Ayes : Regents Walker, Willard, Gilbert, Johnson, Sweezey.

No : Regent Knight.

Absent : Regent Joslin.

This report was adopted with substantial unanimity; for, although Mr. Knight voted against adoption, on account of some views expressed in the report, he declared himself as cordially concurring in the result, and Mr. Johnson voted for adoption, but dissented from some parts of the report.

Mr. Willard has himself been heard to express the opinion that Dr. Tappan would have been restored but for his " statement." Nor is this remark to be understood as implying that this statement changed the views of the regents as to the late president's fitness for his place, but rather in regard to the policy of his restoration; for it seemed to indicate that his triumphant return must sweep away nearly all that remained, and inaugurate a new contest, of which the end could not be foreseen. This board had not the responsibility of the excitement called forth by his removal, and would not incur that which his restoration would be likely to introduce. Their action was eminently wise; by acting otherwise they would have opened what might have become an endless series of retaliatory acts. The wisest and most ardent friends of Dr. Tappan have long since viewed the matter in this light. Those of them among the alumni who knew that his return would cost the university almost an entire faculty, expressed serious doubt of the wisdom of his proposed recall at such expense. Their justly honored friend is in dignified retirement with ample means. He has escaped the trials and torments which would inevitably have attended his return to the university. His monument in Michigan is a noble one, and both that and his happiness were more likely to be marred than mended by his coming back. The successors of those who removed him did him sincere and ample honor, and the public praise which his successor in the presidential chair gave him in his inaugural, was proved to be sincere by all the utterances he ever made in the confidential intercourse of private friendship.*

---

* At the meeting of the board in October, 1874, Regent Grant submitted the following, which was unanimously adopted:

To indicate, as is done above, the general traits of Dr. T.'s character, which made his stay unpleasant, is doubtless wiser in a work like this, than, on the one hand, to pass the whole subject over in silence, or, on the other, to bring forward the trifling details of the long-continued strife. The former course would have left the reader unsatisfied, and invited his imagination to supply something worse than the reality, while the introduction of numerous details would have been a descent below the dignity of history. If we have erred, we have erred honestly.

"Recognizing the distinguished ability of Henry P. Tappan, LL.D., formerly president of the university, and the valuable services which he rendered to the interests of the university in its early history and to the cause of education in this State, and desiring again to welcome him among us, therefore,

"*Resolved*, That we do hereby most cordially extend to him an invitation to be present and participate in the exercises of our next commencement."

At the meeting in February, the following letter from Dr. Tappan was read:

"BASEL, SWITZERLAND, *November* 12, 1874,
"LEIMEN STRASSE 41.

"*President Angell,*—

"DEAR SIR:—It affords me sincere pleasure to acknowledge the receipt of your very courteous and kind letter of the 26th ult.

"Please present to the board of regents my cordial acknowledgment of their invitation to be present at the next commencement of the university, and assure them that nothing would afford me more heartfelt gratification than to meet them and my old pupils and friends on that occasion.

"The intervening years have passed away as a dream and although my health is generally good and my mental vigor unimpaired, as I trust, this flight of years has brought with it indisputable signs of advancing age, which admonish me that long journeys and sea voyages are not to be accepted so lightly as formerly. While, therefore, I do not decline the invitation, I can only hold it in abeyance, and leave my decision to maturer consideration and to what the coming months may offer.

"Accept my thanks for your hospitable invitation to become your guest in the 'old house' consecrated by so many tender memories. Believe me, Mr. President, with sincere respect,

"Truly yours,
"HENRY P. TAPPAN."

The enthusiastic expressions which the bare hope of a visit from Dr. Tappan has called forth have been such as to indicate that it would be a jubilee participated in alike by all, without reference to the views which they took of the action.

After the meeting of February, 1864, Dr. Haven was fairly established in his place, though the recollections of the classes which had personally known his predecessor sometimes found expression in comparisons which might wound sensitive hearts. But the predictions of decay in the university were so far from being realized, that greatly increased numbers sought its benefits.

Details being mostly omitted and chronology little regarded, the main points to which effective action was directed from the establishment of President Haven in his place to the present time, will be passed in rapid review.

Though the president was firm in his seat, yet the unpleasant effects of the change were not all removed. There were persons who did not deem it prudent to attack the head of the institution, who were nevertheless willing to incur the hazards of opening a campaign against a subordinate, and chose Professor Chapin as most easily assailable. He had been pastor of the Presbyterian church of which Dr. Tappan and Regent McIntyre were members, and unfriendly relations had long subsisted between the president, on the one hand, and both the pastor and the regent, on the other. There were those in the board, and also among the professors, who would have made Mr. Chapin president. This would have been indeed a grave offense, and doubtless, too, a great error of judgment; and indeed it was offensive to the friends of the late president that Mr. Chapin should have been elected to even a part of his place. Bad motives were ascribed to Mr. McIntyre, who was supposed to have favored Mr. Chapin's election to the presidency. It would be giving too much dignity to this gossip to even mention it. He doubtless thought that Mr. Chapin would make a good president and professor of philosophy, for he was a man of good character, and an instructive, sound, and by no means dull preacher. By dint of close application to study and attention to his classes, he was successful in acquiring clear and sound philosophical views, and imparting them to his students. But he was not specially quick of apprehension, and when

plied with hard questions, and in rapid succession, he became confused; and with a persevering effort to stir up
students to put him to this test, it is not a matter of wonder
that he finally had to yield. In 1866, he asked leave of
absence for a two years' residence in Europe, whither he
went with his family, confidently expecting to return and
resume his duties at the end of this period. He did return to the university, but listened to the advice of friends
and resigned, instead of resuming the duties of his professorship in it, and is now doubtless more useful and happy
than he could, at least for a long time, have been in returning to the work he had left. The president had discharged
his duties during his absence, and about a year after his
resignation the place was filled by the election of Rev. B.
F. Cocker, D.D., who still holds it.

The most difficult question by far which this board had
to solve, was that of the want of funds, complicated by the
hostility of the homœopathic school of medicine to the
medical department of the university as then existing. The
increased attendance of students demanded more instructors ; the advance in prices of the necessaries and comforts
of life, caused by the depreciation of the currency and
the increase of the precious metals, called for higher salaries. Plans had been laid upon the supposition that the
existing salaries would be permanently adequate. This
was no longer true. Further than this, the university had
acquired a reputation which it had not the means of sustaining. This was a view familiar to all connected with it,
unsuspected abroad. The praises of the young institution
had not only reached every part of our land, but had
crossed the Atlantic. With the funds as they were, its
friends were rather alarmed than cheered by its growing
fame. In course of the year 1866, this state of facts had
become so apparent as to make it evident that something
must be done.

At the September meeting of this year, measures were
taken looking toward an application to the State legislature
for relief. With the action taken on this occasion as their

17

warrant, the president and some members of the board visited the capital during the session of 1867, in order to solicit legislative aid for the university.

The question of a school of homœopathic medicine had been long and much agitated. Its first assumption of a definite form was in the State legislature of 1855, in the amendment to the revised statutes of 1846, which was given in a previous chapter, providing " that there should always be at least one professor of homœopathy in the department of medicine." This law had been during this interval warmly contested ; memorials had been sent to the board urging the action contemplated by it. In 1859, a committee of the regents was raised in regard to it, and the final result of various efforts to bring the matter to a judicial test was the decision on a collateral issue, which has been stated already, and the bringing of the case before the court, as " *Drake et al.* vs. *The Regents of the University of Michigan*," where it was still lingering at the time of which we write.

It was a time for the homœopathists of the State to renew their claim, which they did with great determination, and were so far successful that the act of the session of 1867, which offered the university about $16,000 a year from the State treasury, contained a proviso that at least one homœopathic professor should be appointed in the department of medicine. This brought on one of the most exciting contests of recent university history. Should the aid be accepted or rejected? It was argued on the one side that the teachers of the two rival theories could be made quite independent of each other, so that neither should become responsible for indorsing in any way the other's teaching. It was even suggested that their lectures might be at different seasons of the year, the one course beginning at the close of the other. Separation in place as well as in time was mentioned, and a plan for this seemed at once almost to have been matured; for the location of a homœopathic school in Detroit, as a part of the university, was substantially agreed upon. But various difficulties arose besides that very essential one, the want of funds. It was doubted, too, whether a school at any other point than Ann Arbor would answer the demands of the law. The so-called branches of the university had been discontinued, on the ground that the institution could not be legally thus separated—that it must be a unit in place as well as in organization. The question was also agitated as to the effect which it might have upon the regents' government of the university if the precedent of legislative prescription should once be fairly established. It was never doubted that the State could make donations to the university and connect the same with conditions ; but it was claimed that if the conditions should be such that either in their own nature, or in their probable influence as precedents, they would embarrass the future action of the board, then such donations should be declined.

Uninfluenced by any pressure from outside of the board itself, it is probable that the members would almost all have thought that they could make the professors of the two schools so independently responsible for their respective teachings, that no clashing could reasonably be feared. So thought many of the wise men who were consulted in the matter, and no one could have thought for a moment of requiring them to indorse, either in diplomas or otherwise, the antagonistic portions of each other's systems.

The above are the general arguments which were advanced on this subject, without reference to any times and occasions on which they were presented.

But the board could not act freely. They must pay some regard to the opinions of the profession chiefly concerned. They took their time. At a special meeting on the 9th of April, 1867, a resolution was offered by Regent Walker, to the effect that the subject should lie over for one year. The preamble to this resolution recited the facts of the case, and sets forth the difficulties of action upon it.

The excitement was increased by the resignation about this time of Dr. Gunn, the first professor ever elected in this department, at first occupying the chair of surgery and anatomy, and later that of surgery alone; Dr. Lewitt, demonstrator of anatomy, and Dr. Armor, of the chair of materia medica. The last named consented to remain for a year longer; the two former went to places in the Rush Medical College, at Chicago.

It was said that all the medical professors wrote their resignations, and that efforts were made by some to have them act as a unit, and present these in a body. To some, this looked too much like menacing the board, and it was not done. Some other resignations besides those accepted were said to be in the hands of the regents; but if so, they were not beyond the reach of those who wrote them, and were recalled, or at least never acted upon. Some of these professors did not hesitate to express their conviction that the days of prosperity in the medical school, if not in the entire university, were numbered. An attempt, also, was made to remove, with the two men who went to Chicago, some of the eclat of the school, and a large portion of its provision for the opening of the next year's work in the department of anatomy—a species of property so delicate in its nature and the means by which it is acquired, as to make it an unpleasant subject for inquisition, and give ground for the hope that the regents would lose all rather than make any stir about it. The latter, however, claimed that they had never either directed or justified any illegal or improper measures for obtaining subjects, and the matter was settled without becoming more public. This offers a proper place for the remark, that, so far as known here, the regents have always paid for subjects, and obtained them in a legitimate way, however great the distance which this principle might require them to send. *

The year's interval contemplated by the resolution of Mr. Walker offered in April, 1867—all filled with agitation on this subject—had passed away, and at the meeting of

---

* There is in the "Zeitschrift für die gesammte Staatswissenschaft," published at Tübingen, in the second number, for 1874, an exhaustive article on the supply of subjects for the university medical schools. It is well worth the reading.

March 25, 1868, Regent Walker presented the following resolutions, which were voted on separately and adopted :

"1. *Resolved*, That the board of regents accepts the aid proffered by the legislature of Michigan, by the act approved March 15, 1867, with the terms and conditions thereof.

"2. *Resolved*, That in order to comply with the conditions imposed by said act, there be organized in the department of medicine a school, to be called the ' Michigan School of Homœopathy,' to be located at such place (suitable in the opinion of the board of regents) other than Ann Arbor, in the State of Michigan, as shall pledge to the board of regents, by June 20th next, the greatest amount for the buildings and endowment of said school.

"3. *Resolved*, That two professors be appointed for said school, one at this time, and another prior to the opening of said school, and others as may be necessary.

"4. *Resolved*, That the sum of $3,000 be appropriated, besides the salary of the professors, out of the State tax, so donated to the university, to be expended in establishing said school of homœopathy.

"5. *Resolved*, That Dr. Charles J. Hempel be appointed professor of the theory and practice of homœopathic medicine, in the Michigan School of Homœopathy, at the salary of $1,000 per annum, from this date, to be paid out of said fund so donated."

This provision was declared by the Supreme Court not to be in compliance with the law, which might indeed have been foreseen, as it could not be regarded as the appointment of a professor in the department of medicine of the University of Michigan.

A portion of the members of the medical faculty entered into negotiations preliminary to the establishment of a medical school in Detroit, to which should be transferred all that was specially valuable in the existing school—the reputation of its professors. This is not matter of record, and the exact time, which is not indeed important, can not be stated. Exasperating influences were multiplied. In December following, a professor gave out a notice of some lectures against the homœopathic system, and the board being in session, and having learned the fact, Regent Sill presented the following, which was adopted :

" WHEREAS, It has been announced in the public press, that a professor in the medical department of the university proposes to deliver a course of lectures on homœopathy to the medical students ; and,

"WHEREAS, It is believed that the delivery of such a course of lectures, would be justly regarded by the friends of homœopathy as an unfriendly act, for which the university and its management would be held responsible; therefore,

" *Resolved*, That this board forbids the delivery of such a course on the university grounds, and strongly disapproves of the same being delivered elsewhere to the students of the university, as such, by any professor in the medical department."

The lectures were nevertheless delivered, though not on the university grounds, and answered by a homœopathic physician.   Both the lectures and answer were published.

At the same meeting, the president called attention to the growing practice among the medical professors, of charging students fees for private instruction, and expressed his disapprobation of it.   The matter was referred to the committee on the medical department, for a report at the next meeting, and at the meeting on the 1st of April following, it was resolved that all fees for private instruction during term time be disapproved and prohibited.

The board felt that in assuming an attitude of intimidation, the professors were not treating their authority with due respect, and that by any measures calculated to exasperate the public mind, they had not acted wisely.   But there was, on the other hand, a profound apprehension of incompatibility in the proposed plan of connecting rival systems which foreshadowed the downfall of the existing school.   The ground was also taken, verbally correct, though it was claimed, on the other hand, to be sophistical, that the board recognized no schools in medicine; that they had established one medical department without acknowledging the existence of any school or party, expecting that all which had been confirmed as true in medical science should be taught in it, holding its instructors responsible for bringing out everything which belonged to the branches assigned to each by the titles of their respective professorships, and maintaining that this was not, therefore, an allopathic school, but a school of the true science of medicine. This was admitted to be *verbally* true. Was it *really* so?

The friends of homœopathy were differently situated. They had no risks to run; their triumph would be clear gain; their defeat no loss. If they should destroy the existing school—and some maliciously ascribed to them this motive—they would be rid of a great enemy, even if they should fail to establish a school of their own; and if a prosperous school of their own system should rise from the ruins, their gain would be immense. But they were not united; and some claimed that it was but the more radical and less rational and prudent among them who pressed an affirmative decision of the question of a rival school connected with the university, while the great body were doubtful of this policy, did not court an exterminating war, feared reaction against extreme measures, or for other reasons preferred another course.

There seems to have been a peculiar class of difficulties in this department growing naturally out of the history and state of medical schools in the country, and affecting indirectly the whole university. In the schools of this profession there have been two classes of professors—those who reside in or near the place of the school and have their professional practice undiminished or perhaps increased by their positions as instructors, and those who deliver their lectures in several different schools, and consequently must either limit or relinquish other professional labor. This latter class would naturally desire to hasten through their course as soon as possible, so as to have time

for engagements elsewhere, while the former would prefer to extend their lectures through a longer period.   The
original practice here was to pay salaries according to the
length of the terms of study in the different departments,
on the supposition that each professor would be occupied
throughout the term ; and then if any one should so arrange
with his associates as to satisfy all the claims of his particular branch of study in a shorter time, he was entitled to
use this advantage, and this was allowed, whether the time
spent in actual service should be the entire six months of
the term or but half that time.   Thus a medical professor
could receive two-thirds of what was deemed the full pay
of a professor, and only be employed one-third of the
time.   Some of the professors in the department of literature and the arts attempted similar arrangements for double
duty : Professor Winchell, with the University of Transylvania, at Lexington, in the State of Kentucky, and
Professor Boise with the University of Chicago.   This,
however, was not allowed, and as the result, Professor
Winchell gave up his lectures in Lexington, and Professor
Boise resigned his place in Michigan and went to Chicago.

Professor Ford, of the medical school, has no medical
practice.   He is one of the ablest, most popular, and most
instructive lecturers among the professors, and has held
positions in two other places.   In December, 1868, the
general wish that his whole time should be given to the
interests of the university found expression in the following :

"Ann Arbor, *December* 19, 1868.
"*Honorable Board of Regents:*

"Gentlemen :—At a meeting of the medical faculty
held this day, the following preamble and resolution were
adopted, viz :

" Whereas, The interests of the medical department of
the university require and demand that Professor Ford
should become a resident professor at Ann Arbor, devoting
himself solely to the work of education and the cultivation
of science at the university ; and whereas, the salary of

$1,000 is inadequate to the support of any professor and family; therefore,

" *Resolved*, That the board of regents be requested to provide such additional duty for Professor Ford as will occupy the entire time of a professor, and enable the board to advance his salary and make it equal to the pay of the professors in the department of science, literature, and the arts, and of equal time of service in the university.

" Respectfully, etc.,

" A. SAGER,

" *Dean.*"

This was referred to the committee on the medical department, and at the March meeting, in pursuance of the recommendation above, Professor Ford was made curator of the medical museum and instructor in microscopy, and his salary made the same as that of a full professor in the department of literature. He, however, only remained in actual service about the same length of time as before, perhaps in obedience to engagements already made.

With these discussions and attempts at action, the period between the legislative sessions of 1867 and 1869 was filled up, and in the latter year the grant was made unconditional, and the accumulations of two years—somewhat over $30,000—paid to the university treasury. There remained a law for a homœopathic school, indeed, and there is such a one to this day, but not as a condition of any grant. If no further legislation shall be had, if the regents shall take no decisive action themselves, which, indeed, they are not likely to do, and if the homœopathists shall press the matter, the only resort will be the courts. The subject was recently brought before the circuit court of the district in which the university is situated, and the result was a decision that this tribunal had no jurisdiction, and it has been taken to the Supreme Court, where it awaits an early decision.*

---

* It is understood that the Supreme Court, at the October term of the present year (1874), decided against the application of the homœopathists, by an equal division.

Immediately after the first payments under the new act, there was an advance of salaries; that of the president to $3,000 and a house, those of the professors and the librarian to $2,000, and others at about the same rates. This was a unanimous vote, and the advance did not exhaust the income; the expenses were paid, and no embarrassment was felt with the increased rate of expenditure.

There was one further fact in connection with the movement for legislative aid, which, on account of its bearing upon the educational policy of a State, ought not to be passed over in silence. Michigan's part of the Congressional grant of 1862 for industrial education had been given to the State Agricultural College, which had already been partially provided for; but it did not create a fund at all adequate to the entire support of the institution, and large grants had to be made each year from the State treasury. The question had been often raised as to whether the results were such, or were likely to be such, as to justify the expenditure, and the public feeling tended strongly toward a negative answer. The discussion of university aid naturally brought this question before the legislators and the people. The Detroit papers participated largely and warmly in it. Educational men exchanged views in a more private way upon the subject. The elements expressed and unexpressed which entered into the result, can perhaps be best introduced in this place.

The constitution of 1850 provides that the legislature shall, as soon as practicable, establish an agricultural school, and for this purpose may appropriate twenty-two sections of salt spring lands for the support of such school, and may make the same a branch of the university, for instruction in agriculture and the sciences connected with it, and place it under the supervision of the regents of the university.

The school was established by legislative act in 1855. It was located near Lansing, the capital of the State, and placed, not under the regents of the university, but under a State board of education. Besides the salt spring lands, the legislature had given it 6,000 acres of swamp lands, and, as mentioned above, the 240,000 acres which Michigan received in the general provision made by Congress for education in agriculture and the mechanic arts in the different States, in 1862. Besides this endowment, annual appropriations were made from the State treasury for current expenses, and occasional ones of larger amounts for special purposes, such as buildings.

There were not a few of the educators of the State, if not even a majority of them, who had always thought that agriculture would have been better, more largely, and far more economically taught, if that which the State had to bestow from its own funds and lands, and the large gift intrusted to it by Congress, had been given to the State university, where all the needed instructors, libraries, buildings, and apparatus, except those for the industrial arts alone, were either already on the ground or in a short time must be there. But there is no better material for demagogues to put into appeals for popular suffrage than allusions to agriculture and agricultural colleges, though few of those affected by such an appeal would ever send their boys to such a college. The idea that colleges are for the sons of merchants and professional men, and that farmers' boys feel themselves away from home in such company, is one which finds an easy currency at first suggestion, though none could be more absurd. It was ever escaping to notice that country boys were not only not embarrassed and abashed in the presence of their city fellows in study, but quite as often as otherwise occupied a proud pre-eminence above them.

But whatever the influences which led to this, there was in the legislature of 1867, which gave to the university the twentieth of a mill tax, a feeling which, if the friends of the university had felt it wise to make use of it, might have been employed to secure the transfer of the funds of the agricultural college to the university. President Haven, always inclining to peace, and as politic as the convictions of his judgment and a very sensitive conscience would allow him to be, advised his friends in the legislature not to favor the measure, and it was lost. When it comes to be considered how strong a conviction in the public mind is required in order to disturb an institution established as was the agricultural college, and having its prescriptive rights, it will be evident that there had been much and wide-spread doubt in regard to the wisdom of sustaining this as a separate institution; for the wisest will generally hesitate, as did Dr. Haven, to destroy that which they may have even deemed it unwise to build.

A brief reference to the library can be more appropriately thrown in here than elsewhere. There was no librarian whose time was given up to this work until the appointment of Mr. Tappan, son of the president, in 1856, and he retired with his father in 1863. Datus C. Brooks, who had been in charge of the department of English literature, which place was desired for the president, was made librarian; he remained, however, but one year, and resigned to accept a place on the editorial staff of a Chicago journal, and Mr. Ten Brook, who had just returned to Michigan after an absence of eleven years, was elected to the place. In 1866, measures were inaugurated for a complete system of catalogues, embracing, first, a journal, in which is entered the title of every work received by purchase or presentation, with date, description, source, and price, and also with the number of the entry, which is also entered upon a fly-leaf of the book, so that a book being taken down, this will guide the inquiry back to the entry in the journal, where date of purchase and price may be found. Secondly, a card catalogue of authors' names, with titles, arranged in drawers alphabetically, so that an author's name being given, it can be ascertained whether the work is in the library as readily as a word can be found in a dictionary. On these cards is also indicated the place of the work on the shelves. Thirdly, an index of subjects, with a reference to the works in which they are discussed, written on cards like those of the nominal catalogue. These cards have reached the number of about

80,000, and embrace the subjects, not only of books, but of all the more important review articles. They occupy, at present, forty drawers.

As to the value of the library, it may perhaps be safely said that there is not another in the country of its number of volumes, which is equal to it. It is, however, comparatively small, numbering but a little over 22,000 volumes, with 7,000 to 8,000 pamphlets. This collection of books is indebted to Hon. Philo Parsons, of Detroit, for a donation of about 4,000 volumes and 6,000 pamphlets, the library of the late Dr. Rau, of Heidelberg, in the Grand Duchy of Baden. Mr. P. has continued to add, each year, something to this gift, and in the same line of subjects—chiefly political economy, government, and diplomacy.

The library is kept open for consultation ten and a half hours daily, and six hours during the summer vacation, and the use of it has become so large, that the room is often but a poor accommodation for those who try to crowd themselves into it.*

There are taken somewhat over one hundred and sixty periodicals in the library, about half of which are supplied by the Students' Lecture Association, which appropriates several hundred dollars yearly to this purpose.

Among the pressing needs of the university, all unite in regarding a new building for this purpose as one of the first.

The museum, embracing collections in the natural sciences and the fine arts, is constantly accumulating specimens in all its branches. The origin of this was duly noticed in its proper place. Nothing further can be added, without entering into details which would be tedious. The collections in the natural sciences have grown to be exten-

---

* It had always, until within the present year, been closed on Friday evenings, on account of the meetings of the literary societies. The interest in these, however, has greatly declined, and the president, in proposing to open the library on that evening, remarked that "it was the greatest civilizer on the ground."

sive and choice, and that of the fine arts* and ethnology is not to be despised. The museum is the resort of all visitors. There is also a medical museum, the most considerable portion of which was a purchase from Professor Ford.†

There had been an effort to induce President Haven to accept the presidency of the new institution, then recently founded by the Methodists, at Evanston, near Chicago, and called the Northwestern University. He had, however, intimated no intention of accepting the place; rather the contrary. But just before the June meeting of the regents for 1869, he went to attend some meeting at Evanston, and returned having accepted the presidency of the institution there; and on the 29th of June of this year, offered his resignation to the board. The only motive which he assigned for this action was that he had a desire to engage in another enterprise. It would not, however, be difficult to make out the feelings, positive and negative, which controlled him. He had fought triumphantly through all the contests which had thus far disturbed his administration. The financial problem had, for the time, been solved.

---

* President White, of Cornell, when a professor in the university, did very much for this branch of the museum, by personal contributions, as did also Dr. Tappan, both in this and in other ways. Mr. C. C. Trowbridge, of Detroit, presented, in 1871, a marble medallion, nearly life size, of Randolph Rogers, the sculptor, by the American artist, Cushing, in Rome. Governor Bagley presented, in 1873, a case of silver and bronze medals, ninety in number, struck by the United States, in honor of our principal naval and military commanders and presidents. The most considerable current additions to the specimens in natural science and ethnology, are those made by Mr. Steere, who has been for about two years making the circuit of our globe, for scientific purposes. His specimens already number more than 17,000.

† The following is an estimate of the value of all the collections of the university, in every department:

General library,	$44,000	Zoological collection,	$5,000
Observatory apparatus,	20,000	Botanical collection,	2,000
Chemical apparatus,	20,000	Miscellaneous do. for museum,	3,000
Fine art collection,	15,000	Dep't of physics apparatus,	2,000
Mineralogical collection,	10,000	Dep't of engineer'g apparatus,	1,000
Anatomical collection,	10,000	Law Library,	6,000
Geological collection,	8,000		
		Total,	$146,000

There had never been a day when the condition of the work, and the state of feeling toward the president among regents, professors, students, and the public generally, were so favorable as from the spring of 1868 to the time of his resignation, in 1869. He had lived upon a salary of $2,000 and a house, afterward $2,250, and then $2,500 and a house. An advance to $3,000, offered him by the board, he had once declined, on the ground that this sum would be out of proportion to the salaries of professors which, at that time, were $1,725, and his salary had just been raised to that amount at the same time with the advance of professors' pay to $2,000. If he was ever in a condition when his stay might have been deemed desirable to himself, it was. on the day of his resignation. He was indeed a Methodist, and perhaps preferred to labor among his brethren of his own church, as his acceptance of the place at Evanston would seem to show; but he had raised himself quite above the suspicions which had been felt toward some of his denomination, of which some views have been given in a previous chapter, and his desire not only to *be* but to *seem* impartial, had carried him quite beyond any reasonable demands of other denominations; for, during his whole presidency, he never recommended a Methodist * for appointment, and never showed any special favors to those in places. He did, indeed, preach more in Methodist churches than in others, but only because he was invited to do so; his fault, if it was a fault, was that he knew not how to answer negatively a request for service.

Arrangements were at once made by the board, the president aiding in them, to secure a successor. A committee of regents was appointed, who made a journey to the East in discharge of their duty. What other men may have

---

* The professorship of moral and intellectual philosophy was to be filled in 1869. With reference to the following year's work, Dr. Haven had spoken with Mr. Ten Brook in regard to accepting the place, and an understanding was had as to the division of labor. Soon after this, he resigned; and, in the following autumn, Dr. Cocker, his intimate friend, whom he would gladly have seen in the place, was elected, on the suggestion of others.

been in their minds besides those who were successively offered the place by the committee, is not known, except that President Anderson, of Rochester University, it is said, would have been the unanimous choice of the board, but gave not the least encouragement to hope that he would accept the place, if elected to it.   The offer which the committee was authorized at this time to make, was no temptation, so far as salary was concerned, being but $3,000 and a house.   Professor Julius H. Seelye, of Amherst College, and President James B. Angell, of the University of Vermont, were successively offered the presidency, and both declined.   The negotiations occupied no little time, as both visited the university, were not very prompt in making up their minds to do so much as that, nor in deciding after their respective visits whether to accept or not.

But before any other definite action in regard to the presidency, Professor Henry S. Frieze was made president *pro tempore*.   This arrangement was really at first against his own feelings, but he nevertheless held the place for two years.   This period passed without any drawbacks on the continued prosperity of the institution, and with no exciting contests.

One event, however, occurred during this time which marks, and will ever mark, an era in the history of the university.   The question of the admission of females had often been discussed in the board and outside.   In the legislature, too, it had frequently been brought up in such a way as to make it doubtful whether aid would be very freely granted from that source unless females were permitted to share the benefits of the fund.   At the January meeting of 1870, the following action was taken :

"*Resolved*, That the board of regents recognize the right of every resident of Michigan to the enjoyment of the privileges afforded by the university, and no rule exists in any of the university statutes for the exclusion of any person from the university who possesses the requisite literary and moral qualifications."

This unpretentious resolution, expository rather than

legislative, inaugurated a revolution which may prove the greatest of any single one during the existence thus far of the university, though it is as yet by no means certain how far it will proceed or what its effects will be. There are now about seventy ladies in all departments.

It is understood that at one time, after the two gentlemen named above had successively declined, the regents unanimously called Dr. Haven to return to the presidency, and that Regent Gilbert visited his home, in Evanston, with reference to this subject. Though this is not a matter of record, there seems to be no doubt of the fact.*

Some time in the winter of 1871, it was suggested that the friends of President Angell had advised him, in case the offer from Michigan should be renewed, to accept it. It was renewed and was accepted, and he entered at the opening of the next year upon duty.

This was the occasion of another advance of salaries. That of the president was fixed at $4,500, and the use of the president's house, which was extensively repaired for his reception. That of the full professors of the department of literature was advanced to $2,500. Other advances were made in expenses, and the limits of the income were soon found to have been again transcended by the provision for increased expenditure.

When females were admitted to the university, and $500

---

* After the above paragraph was written, it was deemed wiser to verify this fact, and a note of inquiry was addressed to Dr. Haven, without intimation of its purpose, and the following was received in reply:

" COLLEGE OF LIBERAL ARTS OF SYRACUSE UNIVERSITY, }
" SYRACUSE, N. Y., *September* 16, 1874. }

"*Rev. A. Ten Brook:*

" DEAR SIR :—In reply to yours of September 10th, I would state that I was informed, by telegram and by letter, that the regents wished me to return to the presidency of the University of Michigan. The letter was from Regent Gilbert; the telegram was destroyed, and I have forgotten who sent it. Regent Gilbert also called at my house, at Evanston, during my absence, and expressed his earnest wish that I would not decline the proposal. That is all my information on the subject. The letter just now is not accessible; but I could find it after my papers are once more in place. Yours truly,

" E. O. HAVEN."

18

additional given for separate lectures to them in the medical school the salaries in this department became from $1,800 to $2,500, the latter sum being $500 more than was received at that time by any other professor, while the period of actual service was much less. This inequality was probably used as a principal lever in the subsequent raising of the salaries in the department of literature.

Another question has still more recently been settled, if indeed it is settled, not quite identical with the above, and yet kindred with it. Can a professor in the medical school of the university be allowed to hold a place in the similar school in Detroit? The modifying circumstance in this case is, that the professors would receive salaries quite independent of the attendance upon their lectures in the university, and then could accept fees according to the attendance in Detroit, which might build up the Detroit school out of the ruins of that in the university.

At the time of the excitement referred to above, when the university was menaced with the resignations of most of the medical professors, it was understood to have been a part of the plan formed in Detroit to gather such as they might choose of the Ann Arbor professors around their newly formed school, and thus create a reservoir to retain the departing glory of the university school. The main cause of this expected rupture—viz., the Michigan School of Homœopathic Medicine—did not go into effect, and so the carrying out of the plan remained in abeyance. It was not, however, abandoned, but the only reason for it which was even plausible, was found in the supposition that better arrangements could be made for clinical instruction in Detroit than at Ann Arbor.

During the latter half of the year 1871 and early part of 1872, some excitement in undertone was abroad growing out of the rumor that a lecture term would commence in Detroit soon after the close of the one in Ann Arbor, for which two or three of the university professors had been engaged, and that the juniors of the university school might there immediately take their second course and graduate. It is scarcely necessary to inquire as to the amount of truth contained in the rumor, since it is quite certain that it had a truthful basis, and occasioned an extended and animated discussion in the board meeting of March, 1872.

Having been referred to the committee on the medical department, the report of that committee will best set forth all the aspects of the question. It is as follows:

"*To the Honorable Board of Regents, University of Michigan:*

"The following resolution was referred to the committee on the medical department, at the last meeting of the board:

"'*Resolved*, That the committee on the medical department be and are hereby instructed to report at the next meeting of the board, whether, in the judgment of said committee, professors holding positions in the medical department of the university, may hold similar positions in the Detroit Medical College compatibly with the best interests of the university.'

"Pursuant to the requirements of the above resolution, your committee have had correspondence with Professors Palmer and McGraw, gentlemen who are advertised as holding the double relationship to which reference is made.

"These gentlemen claim that the university is laboring under great disadvantages from lack of proper clinical instruction; that the small percentage of graduates—students in many instances going East to finish their medical education—is due to the absence of such instruction; that they have effected an arrangement by which many of these students will be retained to finish their course in Ann Arbor, and that 'the Detroit Medical College will also gain, in getting a great number of students who otherwise would go to Eastern schools.' It is also claimed that the appointment of Dr. McGraw as lecturer on surgery commits the regents to the arrangement.

" On the other hand, we are advised—and we trust that
no confidence is betrayed in bringing such advice to the attention of your honorable board—that certain members of
the medical faculty think the ‘ arrangement’ hazardous to
the university, and beneficial, if at all, to the Detroit school.
Eminent members of the profession in the State, outside of
both institutions, assure us that the partnership proposed is
not only injudicious, but unwise; that the university can
not afford, and does not need, the formation of entangling
alliances; that professors can not well serve two masters who live in immediate proximity, and that the best interests of the university demand an immediate dissolution
of any relationship which interested persons may have
been laboring to effect.

" Your committee, in approaching the consideration of
this question, do not wish to impugn the motives of any
gentleman who may have expressed an opinion on the subject, or who may have been more intimately associated
with the arrangement under which the double relationship
has been thus far permitted. Our object is to candidly present such facts as may have a bearing on the case, advise
such a course as will, in our judgment, maintain the integrity of the university, preserve its unity, and best promote
those interests which we are bound to protect, not only by
our individual pride in the institution, but also by the solemn
official obligations which we have assumed.

" The medical department has certainly labored under
serious disadvantages during the last few years, by the too
frequent changes which have occurred in the *corps* of instructors. Persons of marked reputation and long experience, who had contributed their full quota to the success
of the department, have severed their connection with the
institution, and are now engaged in other fields of labor.
An unsettled and unhappy state of feeling has existed,
growing out of the acrimonious discussion of the homœopathic question. Notwithstanding these drawbacks, however, we find that the number of students since the session
of 1863–1864, has averaged considerably more than double

the attendance prior to that date; that the percentage of graduates has not only increased from six to twenty-six, but the whole number of graduates for the last six years nearly equals the total number of students who graduated during the first sixteen years, and, further, that public confidence has been steadily growing in the men who have been honored by securing diplomas from an institution distinguished by the establishing and maintaining of a course of instruction, which, for its thoroughness, is without parallel in this country.

"The objection is now made that we do not afford suitable clinical advantages. We think that this disadvantage has been unduly magnified, not only by parties interested in rival schools, but also by some of our own people. The great majority of our students enjoy, before coming here, and also between lecture-terms, the best kind of clinical instruction under the direction of practitioners who are generally persons of eminence in the profession. It is generally conceded that the advantages which are thus afforded are preferable to those offered in hospital practice as usually conducted. The student in private practice monopolizes all the facilities which careful diagnoses, the judicious application of remedies, and a decent regard for the good-will of the people afford. Every practitioner of experience knows that the crowded hospital, with the hurried method of observation, and the too often stereotyped prescription, is not well calculated to beget correct, careful, painstaking investigation in the student whose ideas and habits are formed under such vicious and demoralizing influences.

"Hospital practice affords a striking contrast to that which exists in the field of the private practitioner. The student who has enjoyed the thorough course of elementary instruction which the university enforces, and, in addition to this, has been carefully drilled in the application of great fundamental principles at the bedside of the sick, under the watchful eye of the experienced practitioner, is admirably adapted to the work of humanity in which the medical profession is engaged.

" Our students are being prepared for private practice. If the saying of the old Spartan king be correct, that 'boys ought to learn those things which they expect to practice when they come to be men,' then certainly the best field for the acquirement of such practical knowledge as may be needed is under the direction of the private practitioner. Experience proves this ; the most eminent educators admit it. The unparalleled growth of the medical department of itself furnishes no weak argument in favor of the points which we have briefly made.

" If it were desirable to secure enlarged clinical advantages, your committee entertain grave doubts of the propriety of accepting such facilities through the questionable source of a rival school, and by an arrangement which transfers the time and talents of our instructors to the service of such rival. You would not certainly permit professors in the literary or scientific departments to devote their time, talents, and influence, through a portion of the year, to the colleges now existing in Albion, Hillsdale, Kalamazoo, or Adrian. Why then discriminate in favor of medical gentlemen who, besides the emoluments of private practice, are certainly quite as well paid as our professors in the other departments of the university. Self is, to a certain extent, the spring of most men's actions. Medical men are not wholly exempt from this necessary ingredient. In the university a certain fixed salary is paid whether there is a medical class of ten or ten hundred. In a private school—such as Detroit, for instance—the professors' fees depend on the number of students in attendance. Permit this double relationship, and you afford unusual facilities for building up the Detroit school at the expense of the university; opportunity is given for intrigue; the unity of the institution is endangered; the faculty is divided, while no adequate compensation is afforded even prospectively, other than that which the Detroit institution expects by 'getting a great number of students who otherwise would go to Eastern schools.'

"Furthermore, if two members of the faculty be permitted to hold this double relation, why may not every member of the faculty be permitted the same privilege, and thus while receiving a liberal salary from the university, conduct a school in a neighboring city of our own State for their own private emolument?

" Your committee have no desire to wage a warfare with the Detroit Medical College. While we would extend the courtesies of the university to this and every other institution of learning in the State, we are strenuously opposed to effecting a partnership when nothing can be gained and much may be lost.

" The best interests of the university demand that the various faculties shall serve in their respective departments with *undivided* loyalty; that the very best results attainable shall be produced with such advantages as we now possess or may be enabled hereafter to control, and that a spirit of enthusiasm for the university may be communicated from professor to student. In this way, and this only, can the institution meet the reasonable expectations of a generous people. Your committee, in view of all the facts involved, respectfully report adverse to any professor in the medical department of the university holding a similar position in the Detroit Medical College."

A long and animated discussion is supposed to have occurred in secret session on this subject, and we are not permitted to know what was said. The resolution was not directly voted upon, but Dr. McGraw resigned his place in the university, and Dr. Palmer his in the Detroit Medical College, and the end of the passage of the resolution was, for the time, practically, and it is to be hoped permanently, gained.

Advancing somewhat beyond the period here reached, so as to show the tendencies in the medical college up to the moment, it will suffice to say that Dr. Rynd, chairman of the committee of the board on this department, is vigorously urging, with the support of the board, both a higher standard of preparatory study and a closer attention on the part of professors to the attainments of their students during their course.

By the legislature of 1871, there had been made an appropriation of $75,000, for the erection of a central building, to be called University Hall, which was to contain lecture-rooms for the accommodation of the academic department, and a large hall for commencements and other public exercises. The plan was agreed upon, and the work begun, with as much regard as possible to the amount of the appropriation. It was to fill the entire space between the two buildings originally erected as dormitories—one of which, now occupied by the museum, and the other used as recitation-rooms, would form its wings. These were each 110 feet in length, and the space between them was 127 feet, making an entire front of 347 feet. The central edifice is surmounted by a dome, and the wings having received a front finish to correspond with the new part, the whole offers an imposing appearance. But the appropriation fell short by about $25,000, which the legislature made up, together with a deficiency of about $13,000 in the income for current expenses in the session of 1873. The same legislature provided also for an increase of income, to be realized after the year 1875, by the raising a twentieth of a mill on the dollar, provided the same should not exceed $50,000 a year. The existing deficiency already, however, anticipates to a great extent this increase, and leaves no room for expansion without still further increase of income.

The new building was dedicated in November, 1873, but all except the main hall itself had been previously used. This latter, including the portions, which may be occupied by temporary seats, accommodates about 3,000.*

---

*This may be a proper place to insert an estimate of the value of the entire real estate of the university, which was somewhat carefully made at this time:

Forty acres of land, - - - - - - - - - -	$30,000
North and south buildings, - - - - - - - -	40,000
University Hall, - - - - - - - - - -	105,000
Law building, - - - - - - - - - - -	25,000

It had not been designed to pursue this history further than to the end of President Haven's administration. That of Dr. Angell lies, it were to be hoped, still mainly in the future. It has just been signalized by some disciplinary action in regard to hazing, the results of which can not be foreseen, though the action has been very generally applauded throughout the country. Some few of the facts already stated belong to this period, but they will not be further pursued. The annual expenses, in the beginning, were less than $10,000 upon the university and all its branches. They are now about $118,000 a year.*

As " he that girdeth on the harness should not boast as he that putteth it off," so his friends should not boast for him. That President Angell may long wear the harness, and, together with his co-workers, accomplish so much for the university that he shall have the best of eulogies in the perpetual remembrances of some thousands of graduates, is the honest and earnest wish with which we take leave of him in this direct narrative.

Medical building, - - - - - - - - - $35,000
Astronomical observatory, - - - - - - - - 20,000
Laboratory, - - - - - - - - - - - 20,000
Four dwellings, - - . - - - - - - - 32,000

The laboratory was estimated at $10,000 on the occasion referred to, but has had additions since, costing about $10,000. It has accommodation for 190 students. It is 146 by 90 feet.

* The incomes of Oxford and Cambridge, England, according to the report of a commission, in 1871, were as follows: Oxford University, £47,000; halls and colleges, £366,000. Cambridge University, £34,000; colleges and halls, £306,000. Making an aggregate for Oxford of £413,000, or over $2,000,000; and for Cambridge of £339,000, or over $1,600,000. On the other hand, the University of Berlin, with 180 professors, and about 2,500 students, has only an income (including students' fees) of about $150,000. The work done by the various colleges of Oxford and Cambridge is by no means according to the ratio of their incomes. Exeter, with an income of £14,000, has 170 to 180 undergraduates; Merton, with £17,000, has 54 undergraduates; and Baliol, with £8,000, has 145 undergraduates. The education of a pupil at Merton thus costs about six times as much as at Baliol.—*Vide London Athenæum*, of October 24, 1874.

Since this was in press, the legislature has made appropriations for several new schools in connection with the university, considerably increasing the annual expenditure, for a statement of which see Appendix E.

CHAPTER XIII.

Conclusion of the History of the University of Michigan.

IT has been quite impossible to introduce all the facts of interest in our university history at just the points where they either chronologically or subjectively belong. There must, therefore, be brought together in a closing chapter, whatever may be deemed worthy of note which has been omitted, and as this is a kind of gleaning process, the unity of this concluding chapter as a composition need not be expected.

The relation of religion to the university will be among the most important and interesting of this class of facts and questions. By this is not meant simply the policy of the regents in regard to the choice of religious men, or men connected with the various religious denominations, to professorships. This subject has been treated, and the general principle can be stated in very few words; for it has never changed since it became fairly settled, and that was very early. It is simply an application of the rule that measures should be taken to draw all classes of the people into sympathy with the institution, and give them confidence in it, and thus make it a congenial place for the assembling of the young people of all classes for instruction in the higher branches of learning. This has also been modified by the conviction that religion is a wholesome influence in college life, and that religious men have some advantages as teachers. But there can probably be no instance found in which regents determined beforehand, if indeed they ever suggested, that a particular place should be filled with a man of a particular denomination of Christians. Nor do they make any effort to keep the confessions evenly represented; although if they should ever find any one decidedly predominating over others, they might perhaps, in a quiet way, check the tendency.

The regents have not, indeed, by any very distinct action explained their policy, though the papers of Dr. Pitcher and Mr. Schôolcraft, from which extracts have been introduced, seem clearly to indicate it. But the board could not put its policy into words any better than could a close observer outside ; and yet it would be quite safe to say that they have probably regarded the so-called orthodox denominations as embodying all of that religious sentiment which it is necessary to consider in their action ; for with these all the people are by some members of their families identified, and all are brought more or less into sympathy with them, if, as in some instances, at no other times, yet certainly on occasions of marriages and funerals.

As to the so-called liberal Christians, they are, without any conscious effort on the part of the board, naturally represented in faculties in nearly the proportion of their numbers among the learned. They have very few organizations in the West, numerous as they are among the people, and have shown no disposition to establish denominational centers of their own in the form of educational institutions. It can not be said, therefore, that the regents have disregarded any religious sentiments known to any considerable extent to exist.

Nor are we left without unequivocal expressions from the people indicating that the great body of them are better pleased, whether they are themselves pious or not, to have their sons and daughters under the instruction of pious men. It brings anxieties to parents to have their children away from home at that perilous period of life which is generally occupied with college studies, and numerous and touching letters testify of their preference for having them under religious influences, even where they have not themselves obeyed their own religious impulses.*

* Dr. Porter, of Yale College, in his little work, entitled " The American Colleges and the American Public," does not state too strong views in regard to religion in college, and yet these views can not well be fully

There are not wanting occasional instances of that intense negation of all particular religious teaching, that preternatural dread of Church and State, which refuses to be satisfied with anything less than the ejectment of all distinctively religious men from the service of the State. In the minds of men of this class, the employment of clergymen as teachers in a State university, is a connection of Church and State. One of these contrived to get a resolution through a branch of the legislature of Michigan, in its session of 1873, appointing a committee of inquiry into the teaching of religion in the State university. It was the occasion of many a jest that men, some of them not specially inclined to piety, should be sent on such an errand. and the report that they did not find any just ground of complaint on this score, might perhaps be interpreted in a way not complimentary to the piety of the institution. They had professors upon the witness-stand, and especially those of mental and moral philosophy, and history, and it was not enough for the originator of this movement, who, although not a member of the legislature, accompanied the committee, to have the question settled as between the sects of Christians, and see that no sectarianism in this narrower sense was favored; a broader view must be taken; it would be unfair to the followers of Mahomet and Confucius, and especially to unbelievers in Christian lands, if the Christian system should be allowed an advantage over them. This action seems, however, to have given the impression that the people of Michigan desired to have the Christian religion acknowledged in the univer-

realized in a State institution. There is, however, a compensation in the latter. In the denominational colleges, a more distinct and perfect system of religious teaching and worship can indeed be established, so as to include in it all the professors and students, and consequently, in some instances, in effect exclude the pastors of churches in the place from any participation in the religious work among the students. This can not with any uniformity be done in State schools; but the students can, through their own organizations, carry on their religious meetings, and the religious professors can labor with them with quite as much freedom, and the city pastors doubtless with less impediment, than if those exercises were under the control of the governing board.

sity, and that they were even quite willing that it should go further than it had as yet gone in this direction.

It is but just here to remark that this inquiry never could have been instituted but for another which had long been agitated. University aid was under discussion in the legislature; the homœopathic claim had again come up, and was leading not only to animated, but to heated discussion. In the heat of this debate, and perhaps for the purpose of avoiding hasty action, and gaining time, a committee was appointed to visit the university on the homœopathic question. Under the protection of this latter committee, the one for inquiry on the subject of religion was appointed. It had a salutary influence, though probably not a member of either house would have entertained this subject, as a matter of independent action.

The class of facts, however, really intended in referring here again to the subject of religion in the university, is that developed by students and professors in their character as persons thus thrown together. If professors were Christians when elected to their places, it is of course presumed that they may remain such. It is indeed expected that the subjects assigned them severally to teach, will be first attended to; that the teaching of these will be their main business, and in their several class-rooms, their sole business. But aside from this, both professors and students have their relations to the churches, where they may labor together as they may feel inclined, and so anywhere outside of class-rooms. Students and professors lose no rights which they before possessed, except those which are distinctly given up in their contracts with the university. These contracts involve nothing but a good moral conduct, and faithful discharge of their duties in the class-room, and other exercises actually laid down in the programme of duties. They may have arrangements for literary, and social, and why not for religious improvement, outside of their college work. The board have granted to the literary societies, rooms for their special use. They have done the same for the Christian association. In this room they have their library; here

they assemble when they choose—and for a part of almost
every year it has been daily—for worship, conducted by
whom they may appoint. Thither go the professors, pastors of city churches, and all who wish. If students and
professors connect themselves with the congregations of the
city, they become subject, both actively and passively, to
labor in those congregations, just as any other members.
They neither lose nor gain any rights religiously by their
relation to the university. The Christian pastor, or other
person, who may choose to perform missionary labor in the
city, may regard those connected with the university as
being just as much within his field as those in business occupations, and the president and professors have no right
to forbid this on the plea that the students have been placed
especially under their care.

The principle involved in this free religious work outside
of class duties, is one which ought never to have been
questioned; and yet it has not always been understood.
It is well remembered that there was an extensive religious
awakening, affecting not only the city, but the university,
in 1846, and there was no little apprehension felt that the
intelligence would spread, and be used by enemies to the
prejudice of the institution. It was mentioned to Major
Kearsley, of the board, who was an active member of Dr.
Duffield's church, in Detroit, and also an active politician,
and he replied, in effect: " Do what you can for the work,
but say nothing about it; there are people everywhere to
use it against the university."

This subject, and all others on which different opinions
prevail among the people, have come to be better understood than formerly, and, under anything like prudent
management by those chiefly concerned, can produce no
difficulty. Indeed, it is much the same as in the denominational schools in this respect; for if, in these latter, professors should in the class-room forsake their proper work to
teach any peculiar religious dogmas, patrons would have
occasion to find fault, and this, so far as we can ascertain,
is seldom done.

Lists of names are dry reading, and viewed by themselves, would generally, if not always, be quite valueless. It was not, therefore, intended to offer any such but as woven into the history itself in their natural places. There have been very important names, however, which could not so be brought in, and it would seem scarcely right to bring this volume to a close without introducing them.

Nor are these names without a certain argumentative value in relation to the whole enterprise of the university; for not until the reader shall have run through with such list, finding here and there the names of those personally known, oftener those of men known by their reputation and their works, and finds in general what classes of men have been connected with this work, will he have in possession all the helps he needs in forming his judgment in regard to the institution.

The following are the names of the old board of 1821, omitting those which are to be more specially referred to hereafter: Charles Biddle, N. Baldwin, D. Leroy, C. Clemens, W. H. Puthoff, John Anderson, John Hunt, C. Larned, G. Richard, J. R. Williams, Solomon Sibley, John Monteith, H. I. Hunt, Charles L. Leib, I. J. Desnoyers, B. Stead, P. Lecuyer, William Brown, A. Edwards, A. Welton, Thomas Rowland, N. M. Wells, Luther Humphrey, Richard Berry.

The governors of the State were *ex-officio* presidents of the board from 1837 to 1852. Of these—

Stevens T. Mason was the first. A brief notice of him will be found in connection with his veto of the "bill for the relief of certain settlers on university and school lands." He was governor from 1837 to 1840, and died in 1843, in his 31st year.

William Woodbridge was elected governor in 1840, but was sent the next year to the Senate of the United States. Mr. Madison had made him secretary of the Territory of Michigan in 1814; 1819 to 1821 he was delegate to Congress. Mr. Woodbridge's father settled in the colony, at

Marietta, Ohio, when he was 11 years of age. He died in 1861.

James Wright Gordon, lieutenant-governor under Mr. Woodbridge, served the remainder of the latter's term as governor. Mr. Gordon died at Pernambuco, South America, in 1853.

John S. Barry served three terms as governor, viz: 1842–46 and 1850–52. He was born in Vermont, in 1802; died in 1870, at Constantine, Michigan.

Alpheus Felch was born in the State of Maine, in 1806, and graduated at Bowdoin College. He emigrated early to Michigan, and was in the State legislature in 1836 and 1837. His position in relation to the so-called wild-cat banks exposed him to much censure at the time, but yielded him a better harvest when the results justified his action. He became one of the justices of the supreme court of Michigan in 1842, governor in 1845, United States senator in 1847, and at the close of his term, in 1853, was sent as land commissioner to adjudicate claims in California, as provided by the treaty of Guadalupe Hidalgo. He now lives in honorable retirement in Ann Arbor. He is still occasionally drawn into a little professional practice, and has recently argued the case for the board of regents, in the supreme court, against the application of the homœopathists for a mandamus.

William L. Greenly, born in 1813; graduated at Union College in 1831; elected lieutenant-governor; served the short remainder of Mr. Felch's term as governor after the latter's election to the United States Senate in 1847. Mr. Greenly is still living.

Edward Mundy, as lieutenant-governor, was a member of the board of regents from 1837 to 1840; by appointment, from 1844 to 1848, and as justice of the supreme court from 1848 to his death, in 1851.

Origen D. Richardson was on the board, as lieutenant-governor from 1842 to 1846.

William M. Fenton was lieutenant-governor and *ex-officio* regent from 1848 to 1852.

Elon Farnsworth, as chancellor of the State, was in the board from 1837 to 1842, and again from 1846 to 1847, from which time until 1852 he was a regent by appointment, and thence to 1858 by popular election, according to the constitution which came into force in 1852. He still lives to see the fruit of much labor and care in this service.

Randolph Manning, as chancellor of the State, was in the board from 1842 to 1846. He was a justice of the supreme court at the time of his death, which was about 1863.

William A. Fletcher was the first chief justice of Michigan, and *ex-officio* regent from 1837 to 1842, and thence by appointment, to 1846. He prepared the first code of laws of the State. He settled in the Territory about 1820, and died about 1855.

George Morrell, a native of Massachusetts, and graduate of Williams College, as justice of the supreme court, was *ex-officio* regent from 1837 to his death, in 1845.

Charles W. Whipple was a justice of the supreme court from 1837 to 1852, and most of the time chief justice. He was, during this period, an active member of the board of regents. He died in 1856.

Daniel Goodwin was appointed to the bench of the supreme court in 1843, and retired in 1846. He is still in the judicial service in the State.

Warner Wing, born in Marietta, Ohio, in 1805, was regent *ex-officio*, as a justice of the supreme court, from 1845 to 1852. He is still living.

George Miles, as justice of the supreme court, was *ex-officio* regent, from 1846 to his death, in 1850.

Sanford M. Green, *ex-officio* regent from 1848 to 1852, as justice of the supreme court.

Abner Pratt, appointed to the bench of the supreme court in 1850, was *ex-officio* regent thence to 1852.

George Martin, appointed to the bench in 1851, ceased in 1852 to be *ex-officio* regent; died in 1867.

John Norvell was regent by appointment from 1837 to 1838. Mr. Norvell was made postmaster at Detroit, by
19

President Jackson; he was one of Michigan's senators in Congress from the admission of the State into the Union until 1841. He died in Detroit, in 1850.

Ross Wilkins was regent only from 1837 to 1838. He had been for a time in the old board of trustees. Mr. Wilkins has been United States district judge for Michigan during most of her existence as a State.

John J. Adam, regent only from 1837 to 1838, has been, at different times, treasurer of the university, and of the State, as also auditor-general of the State. He is a Scotchman by birth, and was graduated at one of the universities of Scotland. He is now living in retirement at Tecumseh.

Lucius Lyon, regent only from 1837 to 1838, and appointed in 1839, but did not serve; was one of Michigan's last delegates in Congress as a Territory, and one of her first senators in Congress as a State. He was also a representative in Congress from 1843 to 1845. He died in 1851.

Isaac E. Crary, regent from 1837 to 1843, has had honorable mention in this work, as connected with the Constitutional Convention of 1835. He was one of the last delegates which Michigan as a Territory sent to Congress, and her first representative in that body. Mr. Crary was a graduate of an eastern college. He died in 1854.

Thomas Fitzgerald was appointed regent in 1837, but did not serve. He was senator in Congress from 1848 to 1849. He died in 1855.

John F. Porter, regent from 1837 to 1838.

Jonathan Kearsley, regent from 1838 to 1852, had been on the old board of trustees. His eminent services have been already noticed. Major Kearsley lost a leg, above the knee, in the war of 1812. He never had an artificial limb, but walked on crutches. He was, a great portion of his life, register of the land office in Detroit. He received a pension, and is said, on good authority, to have been, up to the time, the only man who ever received one from the war department for a brevet rank. This was effected by his determination in urging his claim to it. He showed this trait in the management of his own affairs, and of all his public trusts. Major K. was a native of Pennsylvania, and a graduate of one of her colleges. He died at an advanced age, in Detroit, in 1855.

Samuel Denton, a physician in Ann Arbor, and afterward a professor in the medical school of the university, was regent from 1837 to 1840.

Gideon A. Whittemore was regent from 1837 to 1840.

Michael Hoffman, regent from 1837 to 1838.

Gurdon Leach, regent from 1838 to 1840.

Zina Pitcher, regent from 1837 to 1852, served the university with a persevering fidelity which is very rare. Dr. Pitcher was a surgeon in the army, and when stationed in Detroit he became attached to the place, and resigned rather than leave it. In that city he spent the remainder of his life, where he died in 1872, at the age of 75 years. He was a brother of Nathaniel Pitcher, so well known in the politics of New York, acting governor of that State during the remainder of DeWitt Clinton's term, after the death of the latter, and several terms in Congress.

Henry R. Schoolcraft, regent from 1837 to 1841, has a name known throughout the civilized world, on account of his various works and services in connection with the North American Indians. Born in 1793, and died in 1864. Mr. Schoolcraft was educated at Middlebury College.

Robert McClelland, made regent in 1837, did not serve at that time, but was in service from 1850 to 1852. He was one term governor of Michigan, and was secretary of the interior department of the United States government during the administration of Mr. Pierce. Mr. McClelland is a graduate of Dickinson College. He has since been in retirement from the public service.

Seba Murphy, regent from 1837 to 1839.

Joseph W. Brown, regent from 1839 to 1840.

Daniel Hudson, regent from 1840 to 1841.

Charles C. Trowbridge, regent only from 1838 to 1842, had performed valuable services in the old board of 1821 to 1837. He was also treasurer in 1837.

The following letter, the autograph original of which the librarian of the university has pasted on the inside of the cover of one of the volumes referred to, may be of interest here :

"DETROIT, *March* 18, 1869.

"*Rev. Andrew Ten Brook, A.M., Librarian of the University, Ann Arbor.*

"MY DEAR SIR :—About half a century ago, I had the honor to be appointed secretary of the board of trustees of the then existing University of Michigan, which office I held for several years. During that period, a few books fell into my hands as secretary, and as there was no library* belonging to the institution, they were marked and consigned to the dark corners of my house. In clearing out an old closet they have been *exhumed*, and although you will hardly think them worthy a place in your catalogue, I send them to you as per subjoined bill.

"Yours truly,   .

"C. C. TROWBRIDGE."

" List of books belonging to the old University of Michigan, found in an old closet in C. C. Trowbridge's house, and sent, March 18, 1869, to the librarian of the present university :

"Seybert's Statistical Annals,   -   -   I vol.
Secret Journals of Congress, -   -   4
Practical Education,   -   -   -   I
Pamphlets on Education,   -   -   I
Parent's Friend,   -   -   -   I
Introduction to Arithmetic,   -   -   I
Academician,   -   -   -   -   I
Manual of Teaching, -   -   -   I

———

11 vols."

Seybert's Annals, the volume in which the above is

---

* Mr. Monteith, in an extract from his journal, inserted in a previous chapter, speaks of a library in connection with the "catholepistemiad." As there was none in Mr. Trowbridge's time, it will furnish good work to some antiquarian to find out what became of it.

pasted, has also pasted in it an autograph letter of Governor Woodbridge, dated June 14, 1823, and stating how he obtained the book, he being then Michigan's delegate in Congress.

Mr. Trowbridge was born in 1800, and is now enjoying in Detroit a quiet and happy old age.

George Duffield, D.D., regent from 1839 to 1848, was the most prominent and influential minister of the Presbyterian Church in Michigan. His services in the interests of the university were at a time when just such a man in the board was a necessity. Born in 1794, in Lancaster county, Pennsylvania, and graduated in 1811, at the University of Pennsylvania. He died in 1868.

William Draper, regent from 1840 to 1844.

Francis Higginson, regent in 1841.

Samuel W. Dexter, regent in 1840–41.

John Owen, regent from 1841 to 1848, was and is among the most prominent and wealthy merchants of Detroit.

Lewis Cass, regent in 1843–44, did inestimable service in the old board, but was never in Michigan enough to be depended upon as a regent of the present university. Governor of the territory from 1813 to 1831, secretary of war from 1831 to 1836, minister to France from that time to 1842, thence to 1861 either in the senate of the United States or at the head of the state department, his work in Michigan was mainly done. He was at the commencement of the university in 1848, the only occasion of his attendance at commencement of which we have any recollection, and this was at the time that the whole country was agitated with the canvass between Cass and Taylor. He dined with us privately, and his observations in the Orient, and questions of that kind rather than the more exciting ones of the day, were the staple of his conversation. Those who examine the records of the old board, will fail to find the interest of General Cass in the work. His views and his desires, however, were expressed through his friend, Austin E. Wing. Born in 1782 ; died in 1866.

Martin Kundig, regent from 1841 to 1845, was a Catholic priest, and the only one ever on the board.

George Goodman, regent from 1841 to 1843.

Dewitt C. Walker, regent in 1843–44.

Robert R. Kellogg, a Congregational minister, regent in 1844–45.

Andrew M. Fitch, regent from 1842 to 1846. Mr. F. is a Methodist minister, and still, as we believe, lives in Michigan.

Elisha Crane, same period as the last mentioned, and also a Methodist minister. These, and some others, were put upon the board in deference to that feeling among religious people which has been referred to elsewhere. Mr. Owen, whose name has been given, was a layman of this church, and probably this motive had an influence also in his appointment.

Marvin Allen, regent from 1843 to 1852, was a prominent and influential Baptist minister, and valuable member of the board. The motive suggested in the cases of the last named had its effect also in this appointment. Died in 1861.

Alexander H. Redfield, 1844 to 1852. References will be found to his services in Chapter X.

Austin E. Wing was on the board from 1845 to 1849, the date of his death. Mr. Wing was on the old board of 1821 to 1837, and, altogether, rendered services scarcely excelled by those of any other member. He was a graduate of a New England college—Williams, we think; the family were connected with the colony at Marietta, Ohio. Mr. W. was Michigan's delegate in Congress from 1828 to 1832.

Minot T. Lane, 1845 to 1849.

Charles C. Taylor, 1846 to 1850, Episcopal clergyman in Ann Arbor.

Elijah H. Pilcher, 1846 to 1852, a Methodist minister, still in active service, which he began in Michigan in 1830.

John G. Atterbury, regent from 1848 to 1852, was educated for the legal profession, and practiced it for a time, but afterward entered the Presbyterian ministry.

Justus Goodwin, 1848 to 1852.

Benjamin F. Witherell, 1848 to 1852, was son of James Witherell, who was made one of the Federal judges of Michigan in 1808, at which time he was serving in Congress from his native State of Vermont. The son adopted the profession of his father, that of the law, which he practiced in Detroit to his death in 1867, except as his practice was interrupted by several periods of judicial service.

Edwin M. Cust. 1849, never served.

Gustavus L. Foster, 1850 to 1852, is a Congregational minister, still in active service in Michigan.

Michael A. Patterson, Edward S. Moore, Elon Farnsworth, James Kingsley, Elisha Ely, Charles H. Palmer, Andrew Parsons, Henry H. Northrop, and William Upjohn, formed the board of 1852 to 1858. Of these, Mr. Patterson, a physician of Tecumseh, had been a member of the board from 1838 to 1842, and Mr. Kingsley had been on the old board which expired in 1837. This is the board which elected President Tappan, and co-operated with him in his organizing work.

The board of 1858 to 1864 was made up of the following:

Benjamin L. Baxter, J. Eastman Johnson, Levi Bishop, Donald 'McIntyre, E. Lakin Brown, George W. Pack, Henry Whiting, Luke H. Parsons, John Van Vleck, Oliver L. Spalding, William M. Ferry, and George Bradley. This is the board, though all its members did not stand through from the beginning to the end of the term, which dismissed President Tappan. Some of the members have been specially referred to.

The following is the list of regents from January 1, 1864, with the dates of their entering the service and retirement from it. This includes, of course, the present board:

Edward C. Walker, 1864 to 1874; George Willard, 1864 to 1874; Thomas D. Gilbert, 1864 to 1876; Thomas J. Joslin, 1864 to 1868; Henry C. Knight, 1864 to 1866; J.

Eastman Johnson, 1864 to 1870; Alvah Sweetzer, 1864 to 1865; James A. Sweezy, 1864 to 1872; Cyrus M. Stockwell, 1864 to 1872; J. B. M. Sill, 1864 to 1872; Hiram A. Burt, 1868 to 1876; Joseph Estabrook, 1870 to 1878; Jonas H. McGowan, 1870 to 1878; Claudius B. Grant, 1872 to 1880, and Charles Rynd, 1872 to 1880.

John D. Pierce, the first superintendent of public instruction—1837 to 1841—has been sufficiently noticed in this work. He is a Presbyterian minister, and is now living in Ypsilanti, about 78 years of age. He is a graduate of Brown University.

Franklin Sawyer was superintendent of public instruction from 1841 to 1844.

Oliver C. Comstock, regent from 1841 to 1843, and superintendent of public instruction from 1843 to 1845; was educated for the profession of medicine, but forsook it first for politics, and served in the New York legislature as early as 1810, and in Congress, as representative from the State of New York, from 1813 to 1819. While in Congress, having changed his views of duty, he began to preach, and from that time forth was generally pastor. Among other churches of his denomination—the Baptist—he served those of Rochester, in the State of New York, and Detroit, Michigan. He died at Marshall, Michigan, in 1860, aged 76 years.

Ira Mayhew, superintendent from 1845 to 1849, and from 1855 to 1857. Has published several works, among which is one on practical education and one on book-keeping. His official reports, too, are valuable.

Francis W. Shearman, superintendent from 1849 to 1855. A reference to his services will be found elsewhere.

John M. Gregory, LL.D., superintendent from 1858 to 1864, is a Baptist minister. In 1864, he accepted the presidency of Kalamazoo College, and was called thence, about 1866, to that of the Industrial University of Illinois, where he still remains. He was educated at Union College.

Oramel Hosford, superintendent from 1864 to 1872, was,

at the time of his election, a professor in Olivet College, which place he retained, and has returned to its duties. He is of liberal education, and by profession a clergyman.

Daniel M. Briggs, an alumnus of Williams College, is the present superintendent.

The reports of the superintendents furnish the best published materials for the history of education in Michigan. Those of Mr. Shearman for 1852, and Mr. Gregory for the several years of his service, are specially valuable.

The presidency of the university was never filled until 1852. There was a resolution of the board which made it the duty of the faculty to constitute one of the professors occupying the university houses their organ, each for a year in turn. Joseph Whiting, a graduate of Yale College in 1823, a minister of the Presbyterian Church, and for many years an efficient pastor, had been called to one of the branches of the university, and in 1841 transferred to the central institution, being then in service as professor of the ancient languages, was president of the faculty for the years 1844–45, but died a few weeks before the commencement at which the first class graduated, and Mr. Williams served in his place during those few weeks. Mr. Williams was also president of the faculty during the years 1848–49.

As Mr. Williams was the first man ever appointed to a place in a branch, and the first also in the central institution, and still survives in nominal connection with the university, it seems specially appropriate that he be more fully noticed here than others have been.

George Palmer Williams, LL.D., was born in Woodstock, Vermont, in the year 1802, and is now 72 years of age. He was graduated at Burlington, in his native State, in 1825, and was afterward one year (1827) at Andover Theological Seminary. From 1823–31, he was tutor in Kenyon College, at Gambier, Ohio; 1831–34, professor of languages in the Western University of Pennsylvania, at Pittsburg; 1834–37, again at Kenyon College, and in 1837 he entered upon the service of the board of regents of the University of Michigan as principal of the Pontiac branch—the first appointment of the regents to an instructor's place. His was also the first appointment to a professorship in the university proper, having been made July 22, 1841, to the department of ancient languages. On this work, however, he did not enter, having, at the earnest request of Professor Whiting, exchanged this place for that of "mathematics and natural philosophy," or "physics," as now called. In 1854, the department of physics was otherwise provided for, leaving him only mathematics, which, in 1863, was again exchanged for physics, the department in which he still labors.

The words which we shall use in this brief estimate of Dr. Williams' character as a teacher, college officer, and man, will be but slightly influenced by the thought that they may fall under his own eye. We shall simply state our convictions, matured by time and mellowed by the recollections of thirty years of intimate acquaintance. For seven years he was our next-door neighbor. We were at home in each other's houses; we walked and drove together; together on Saturdays amused ourselves in hunting the game of the neighboring forests—doubtless more to the amusement than the danger of the game itself; and this estimate of him is formed quite as much from the unguarded and incidental utterances of his mind and heart as from our official intercourse in the work of education, and the following statement will be hazarded.

Dr. Williams thoroughly understood what he attempted to teach, and though he never felt himself called upon to force the reluctant mind into a thorough understanding of that for which it had no liking, he helped those who desired to study in attaining to the established standard, and, in a private way, he loved to aid those who desired his help in transcending that limit. Astronomy, though not nominally in his professorship, he taught until the revision of the course in 1854, and a great enthusiasm was annually awakened among the students as they came to the calculation of eclipses. So also of some other special points.

When the occasion, in his view, called for firmness, whether in his own recitation-room or in the general government of the university, he was not wanting in that quality, and ground once taken was held with special tenacity.

But his highest character is not that of a mere teacher, or disciplinarian. Born a gentleman, improved by culture; with keenest wit, controlled by good feeling and a quick sense of right, cutting like the Turkish executioner's blade, so that the victim must attempt to shake his head in order to find that it was severed from his body—all united with true Christian principle and emotion, he has for thirty-three years past diffused an influence which has been far more than a compensation for the want of a little "mathematics" and "physics."

Dr. Williams was not in the ministry until the year 1847, when he had reached the age of 45 years. His religious sense, however, was delicate and active, and his religious character was his most prominent one; but he placed a low estimate upon his powers of public speaking, which he seldom attempted, and even after his ordination, though he preached often, preaching was his only form of public address, and in many ways it was apparent that he entered upon this work late in life, under a sense of duty which had remained till then unsatisfied. He served at one time for more than a year as rector of St. Andrew's church, in this city, and by a donation of his salary relieved the church of a debt. His health impaired, his mind in sympathy with his declining bodily vigor, he awaits a call to a higher and purer service, for which, in the estimation of all but himself, he is fully prepared.*

Andrew Ten Brook, graduated at Madison University and the Theological Seminary connected with it in 1839 and 1841; professor of moral and intellectual philosophy from 1844 to 1851; was president of the faculty for the years 1845–46 and 1849–50.

J. Holmes Agnew, D.D., was the faculty's organ for the years 1846–47 and 1851–52. He was called, in 1845, to the

---

* Dr. Williams' friends are subscribing for the endowment of a professorship to bear his name, the income to be his while he lives.

professorship of ancient languages, and served in that place until the breaking up in 1852. Dr. Agnew did much in the way of editorial work, both before his connection with the university and after his retirement from it. He died in 1865.

Daniel D. Whedon, D.D., was president of the faculty in 1850–51, though the usual statement is not found in the catalogue for that year. He had been professor of the ancient languages, and for a time acting president of the Wesleyan University of Middletown, Connecticut. Dr. Whedon has published "Collegiate and Popular Addresses," "A Commentary on the Gospels of Matthew and Mark," and a work on the "Freedom of the Will." His labors, however, as editor of the Methodist Quarterly have been his most important. On this work he still labors. Few men in his denomination have exerted a more salutary influence, and won a better or more deserved reputation.

These men received no extra pay for their services as executive officers. If they went to Detroit to meet the executive committee, they paid their own expenses. Their labors have been elsewhere noticed.

The presidency, since the date to which the above sketch brings us, has been held by the following :

Henry P. Tappan, D.D., LL.D., 1852–63, who has been already noticed so far as our purpose requires. The same may be said also of

Erastus O. Haven, D.D., LL.D., president from 1863 to 1869.

Henry S. Frieze, LL.D., acting president from 1869 to 1871, professor of the Latin language and literature since 1854, has, in addition to what has already been said of him, done valuable service by way of preparing editions of the Latin classics, especially Virgil and Quintilian.

James Burrill Angell, LL.D., president since 1871, has been so short a time in his place that any further notice of him than has been already given would scarcely be proper. He belongs, we trust, to the future. Dr. Angell graduated at Brown University, in 1849. He was editor of the Providence Journal, in time of the war. From this place he was called to the presidency of the University of Vermont, and thence to the University of Michigan.

Asa Gray, professor of botany and zoology from 1838 to 1842, has been, since the latter year, connected with Harvard College. His connection with the university is referred to elsewhere in this work. His services to the science of botany have been large.

Douglass Houghton, professor of chemistry and mineralogy, 1842 to 1845, never entered upon the duties of his professorship, but did other valuable service already noticed. He was drowned while prosecuting his work for Michigan, on Lake Superior, in October, 1845. (See Memoir in the American Journal of Science, 2d series, Vol. V., page 217.)

Abram Sager, professor of botany and zoology, 1842 to 1855, and obstetrics, with some other subjects, from 1850 to 1874, has resigned during the present year on account of failing health. He has been a close and successful student, and retires to the less laborious duties of such extent of professional practice as he shall choose to perform, still retaining his deanship of the faculty of medicine, with the title of emeritus professor.

Silas Hamilton Douglass, then just entered upon medical practice in Ann Arbor, was first employed to teach in place of Professor Houghton in 1844, and was made professor of chemistry and geology in 1846. The geology was dropped in 1855, and the chemistry has been retained, the title of director of the chemical laboratory having been subsequently added. The laboratory has been a very successful branch of the university; has been frequently enlarged, and is now again undergoing very considerable enlargement, under Professor D.'s direction. It is probably the largest in the United States.

William S. Curtis, provisional professor of moral and intellectual philosophy for one year—1851–52—was successively afterward a professor in Hamilton College, and president of Knox College, in the State of Illinois. Mr. C. is a minister of the Presbyterian Church.

James R. Boise, LL.D., professor of the Greek language and literature from 1852 to 1868, had formerly been in the same place in Brown University, and now since 1868 has still the same in the University of Chicago. He has done good work in the editing of Greek classical authors—an edition of the Iliad among these—and in the preparation of educational books. An edition of "Xenophon's Anabasis," and "First Lessons in Greek" are best known. He is regarded as a perfect teacher in his department.

Charles Fox, professor of theoretical and practical agriculture in 1854. Mr. F. was a clergyman of the Episcopal Church.

Lucius D. Chapin, professor of moral and intellectual philosophy from 1863 to 1868 ; now president of a college owned by the Presbyterian Synod of Western New York, at Leroy.

William P. Trowbridge, professor of mathematics from 1856 to 1857. Mr. T. made the most valuable present ever made to the museum of natural history.

Edward Olney, LL.D., professor of mathematics since 1863. Professor O. has published the most of a series of works in the higher mathematics, which have been already introduced into colleges and high schools, and is now adding a series of arithmetics. His works are making him a name throughout the country.

Alexander Winchell, LL.D., professor of physics from 1854 to 1855, and thence of botany, zoology, and geology to 1872. Dr. Winchell has been of late years somewhat prominent in the field of authorship. His most considerable work is that entitled "Sketches of Creation." This is a combination of the scientific with the popular, and has had a large sale. He has published several yearly reports of the geological survey of Michigan, and in 1870 a geological chart of the State. He has just published a work on the doctrine of evolution. Dr. W. accepted the chancellorship of the University of Syracuse in 1872, and resigned the same in 1874, but remains in that institution as professor of geology.

Martin Luther D'Ooge, graduated from the University of Michigan in 1862 ; professor of the Greek language and literature since 1868. He has an edition of Demosthenes on the Crown now passing through the press.

Elisha Jones, acting professor of Greek in 1870, during the absence of Mr. D'Ooge. University of Michigan, class of 1859. Author of First Lessons in Greek Prose.

William G. Peck, professor of physics and engineering in 1855 to 1857, is in the same department in Columbia College, in New York. He has recently published a work on Mechanics.

De Volson Wood, professor of civil engineering, from 1859 to 1872. Mr. Wood has published several important works, among which are one on the resistance of materials, with an appendix on the preservation of timber, 1871, and one on the theory of the construction of bridges and roofs, 1873. He is now a professor in the Stevens Institute, in Hoboken, New Jersey.

Louis Fasquelle, LL.D., professor of modern languages from 1846 to his death, 1862. Born near Calais, in France, in 1808, pursued his studies in Paris and in the German universities. Having taught some time in England, where he married, he came in 1834 to America, bought a farm in the interior of Michigan, and divided his time between the care of it and his occupation as a teacher until his removal to take his place in the university. His authorship of works for the study of the French language, has made him known throughout the entire country. Few men used the English language with more accuracy than he, and yet he always retained his French accent.

Eugene W. Hilgard, Ph.D., University of Heidelberg, professor of geology, zoology, and botany, since 1873, was called from the same chair in the University of Mississippi, in which State he has rendered important service in this department. He has contributed not a little to the literature of his field of study. Dr. H. has accepted a place in the University of California.

Edward Payson Evans, professor of modern languages and literature from 1863 to 1870. Graduated from the University of Michigan in 1854.

George S. Morris, professor of modern languages and literature since 1870, has contributed to literature various critical articles on metaphysical subjects, and a translation of Ueberweg's History of Philosophy, published in two volumes octavo, in 1872. Mr. M. is a graduate of Dartmouth College.

Andrew D. White, LL.D., professor of history from 1857 to 1867, a graduate of Yale College, has been since its organization president of Cornell University, at Ithaca, in the State of New York. His much greater prominence since his retirement from the University of Michigan makes him belong more to New York than Michigan, and more to the future than the past.

Charles K. Adams, graduated from Michigan University in 1861, successively instructor and assistant professor, has been professor of history since 1867. He has been a contributor to the critical literature of the quarterly reviews, and has a work on the conflicts of democracy and monarchy in France, from the great revolution to the close of the second empire, which has now just passed into the trade, and is very favorably noticed by reviewers. It is a clear and impressive statement of the leading facts relating to this period, so far as they bear upon his theme. A second edition has appeared since the above was written.

Moses Coit Tyler, professor of rhetoric and English literature from 1867 to 1872, and recalled to the same place in 1874, a graduate of Yale College, published, in 1869, a little volume entitled the "Brawnville Papers." During his absence he was in the editorial department of the Christian Union. Professor Tyler is a Congregational minister.

Francis Bruennow, professor of astronomy and director of the observatory from 1854 to 1863, except during the year 1860. Dr. B.'s "Lehrbuch der Sphoerischen Astonomie," first published in 1851, has a preface by the celebrated Encke, which gives it very high praise, and regards it as a fortunate supply of a long existing desideratum. A translation was published in England, in 1860. A new edition of the original appeared in 1862. He published also, in 1855, "Tafeln der Flora," and "Tables of Victoria," in the same year. Dr. B. is now director of the Royal Observatory, at Dublin. His connection with the Observatory in Michigan has already been noticed.

James C. Watson, Ph.D., professor of astronomy in 1859–60, transferred to the chair of physics in 1860, and back to that of astronomy in 1863, which he still holds. Mr. Watson has, by his discovery of planetoids, in which he has no competitor but Mr. Peters, of the Hamilton College Observatory, and by his work on theoretical astronomy, gained for himself a recognition throughout the world of science. Mr. Watson graduated from the University of Michigan, with the class of 1857.

Alvah Bradish, professor of the fine arts 1852 to 1863.

Benjamin Franklin Cocker, D.D., LL.D., professor of moral and mental philosophy since 1869, is a native of Yorkshire, England, whence he went in 1850, with his family, to Australia, to engage in mercantile pursuits. His operations were large, but he was in the end unsuccessful, and started with his family for America, where he arrived in 1857. During a visit with the missionaries in a Cannibal island of the Southern ocean, he narrowly escaped being sacrificed to the appetites of some ferocious natives. On his way up the Mississippi, he had to sell his clothing, to pay the expenses of himself and family through to Adrian, Michigan, where he hoped to find friends. Not long before reaching this place, a sick child died, on the train, in its mother's arms. In this state of destitution, and bearing the remains of their child, they reached Adrian, were helped to what they needed, and the people were not long in discovering his ability as a preacher of the Gospel. To his eloquence Dr. C. adds clear discrimination as a metaphysician. He published, in 1870, a work entitled "Christianity

20

and the Greek Philosophy," an octavo volume of about five hundred pages, and has a volume now passing through the press, entitled " Theistic Conceptions of the World." Dr. C. is about fifty-seven years of age.

Charles E. Green, graduated at Harvard College, professor of civil engineering since 1872. Mr. Green has just published a little work in his department.

THE MEDICAL SCHOOL.

Moses Gunn, professor of anatomy and surgery from 1850–52, and of surgery to 1867. He was elected in 1848, two years before the opening of the medical department.

Samuel Denton, professor of pathology, and theory and practice, from 1850 to his death, in 1860.

Jonathan Adams Allen, professor materia medica, physiology, and therapeutics, from 1850 to 1854.

Alonzo B. Palmer, elected in 1852 to the professorship of anatomy ; has been transferred several times, but since 1860 has been professor of theory and practice and pathology. Professor Palmer has made numerous. contributions to pamphlet literature, and to the medical periodicals, but has published no work.

Corydon L. Ford, professor of anatomy since 1854 ; has had physiology added since 1860. This veteran professor, notwithstanding his long connection with the work, and his popularity as a lecturer, has never attempted, so far as we know, to add anything permanent to the literature of the profession.

Henry S. Cheever, professor of materia medica since 1869, University of Michigan, literary department, 1863.

William Warren Green, professor of surgery, 1868–69. Alpheus B. Crosby, 1870–72.

Albert B. Prescott, professor of organic and applied chemistry since 1871 ; previously assistant professor of chemistry, University of Michigan, medical department, 1864. Dr. Prescott has just published two small works, viz., " Outlines of Proximate Organic Analysis," two hundred pages duodecimo, and "Chemical Examination of Alcoholic Liquors," ninety pages duodecimo.

Edward S. Dunster, a graduate of Harvard College, and descended from its first president, professor of obstetrics and diseases of women and children, 1874. Dr. D. has done important editorial work.

Donald McLean, professor of surgery since 1873. Dr. McL. has edited "Symmes' Surgery."

Frederic H. Gerrish, graduated from Bowdoin College, lecturer on therapeutics and materia medica since 1873.

LECTURERS, ETC., IN THE MEDICAL SCHOOL ASIDE FROM THOSE ALREADY MENTIONED.

Henry Francis Lyster, surgery, 1868-69, University of Michigan, 1858, literary department.

George E. Frothingham, ophthalmology, University of Michigan, 1864, medical department.

Charles P. Farmer, demonstrator of anatomy, 1855-57.

Albert M. Helmer, demonstrator of anatomy, 1857-58, University of Michigan, 1858, medical department.

William Lewitt, demonstrator of anatomy, 1857-58.

William F. Breakey, demonstrator of anatomy, 1868-69, University of Michigan, 1859, medical department.

Theodore McGraw, lecturer on surgery ; graduated from the literary department of the University of Michigan, in 1859.

ASSISTANT PROFESSORS.

Allen J. Curtis, 1865-68. University of Michigan, 1861. This promising young man resigned in 1868 ; traveled in Europe and America ; contributed to the periodicals, both in prose and verse. He died at his father's, in Michigan, about 1872.

Adam K. Spence, 1865-67. Univ. of Mich., 1858. Now president of Fiske University, Nashville, Tennessee.

Edward L. Walter, since 1868. Univ. of Mich., 1867.

John E. Clark, 1857 to 1859. Univ. of Mich., 1856.

Albert H. Pattengill, since 1869. Univ. of Mich., 1868.

George B. Merriman, since 1868. University of Michigan, 1864.

Alfred Dubois, 1857 to 1863. University of Michigan, 1848.

Charles DeWitt Lawton, 1870-71.

Stillman W. Robinson, 1867-69. University of Michigan, 1860. Now in the Industrial University of Illinois.

Mark W. Harrington, since 1872. University of Michigan, 1868.

Joseph B. Davis, since 1872. University of Michigan, 1868.

Wooster W. Beman, 1874. University of Michigan, 1870.

Harry B. Hutchins, since 1873. University of Michigan, 1871.

INSTRUCTORS AND ASSISTANTS.

Fitch Reed Williams, 1858-60. University of Michigan, 1858.

Cleveland Abbe, 1859-60.

Elmore Horatio Wells, 1864-65. University of Michigan, 1862.

William B. Morgan, 1865-66. University of Michigan, 1863.

Jules Deloulme, 1870-71.

Jules Frederic Billard, 1870-71.

George Maasberg, 1870-71.

Jonathan Beach, 1843-45.

Burritt A. Smith, 1844-47. Yale College, 1844.

William Henry Brückner, 1862-63.

Dexter Valvard Dean, 1863-64. University of Michigan, medical department, 1865.

Preston B. Rose, since 1865. University of Michigan, medical department, 1862.

P. R. B. De Pont, since 1871.

Chas. S. Dennison, since 1872. University of Vermont.

Francis A. Blackburn, since 1872. Univ. of Mich., 1868.

Alfred Hennequin, since 1873.

Frank Austin Scott, since 1873. Yale College.

John L. Gilpatrick, 1873-74. Now professor in Dennison University, Ohio.

Seneca Haselton, 1873-74. University of Vermont.

Otis C. Johnson, 1873-74. University of Michigan, pharmacy department, 1871. Oberlin College.

Wm. H. Smith, 1873-74. Kalamazoo College.

Robert Harbison, 1871-73. Princeton College.

Edward L. Mark, 1871. University of Michigan, 1871.

Raymond C. Davis, 1868-72.

Rufus H. Thayer, 1871. University of Michigan, 1870.

Henry F. Burton, 1874. University of Michigan, 1872.

C. N. Jones, 1874. Oberlin College.

LAW DEPARTMENT.

James Valentine Campbell, LL.D., Marshall professor of law.

Charles Irish Walker, LL.D., Kent professor of law.

Thomas McIntyre Cooley, LL.D., Jay professor of law.

These three gentlemen were elected at the same time—1859—when the law department opened, and all continue in the service. Messrs. Campbell and Cooley are justices of the supreme court of the State. Mr. Walker is a lawyer, formerly of large practice in Detroit, from which he has latterly somewhat withdrawn himself. Messrs. Campbell and Walker have given no attention to authorship. Their professional work, and fugitive pieces, chiefly relating to pioneer history, have occupied them.

Judge Cooley, on the contrary, with a mind naturally clear and quick in its discriminations in the language of law, had, besides his previous law studies, a special schooling in the same direction in the compilation of the laws of Michigan for 1857; then in his Michigan Digest, published first some years earlier, and in a new edition, with a continuation, in 1866. He has published also a volume of reports of supreme court decisions. His chief work, however, is that on "Constitutional Limitations," which seems to be everywhere regarded as having satisfactorily filled a place where something was greatly needed in what may be called the philosophy of fundamental law. The first edition, which appeared in 1868, has been followed by two others, respectively in 1871 and 1874. He has also published an edition of Blackstone, with notes, and of Story's Commentaries on the Constitution.

The Fletcher professorship, so called from Hon. Richard Fletcher, of Boston, who made to this department a donation of a large part of his own library, was filled from 1866 to 1868 by Ashley Pond, a graduate from the literary department of the University of Michigan in 1854, and since the latter year has been held by Charles A. Kent, a graduate of the University of Vermont, both in the practice of their professions in Detroit.

It is just to all to add here that there are graduates of college in the above list in regard to whom this fact has not been stated, sometimes even when it was well known. It was not deemed important in case of regents. It would often have been unjust to other men, of whom it could not be said that they were graduates of college, although equally well qualified for the places they have held. In case of all officially connected with the university who have been also its alumni, this fact has been stated. This has been done in order to show to what extent the university is carried on by its own graduates.

The various associations among the students may deserve a passing notice, and would indeed deserve more but for the general similarity of these in all institutions. The minds of students have, within a few years past, been so diverted by other attractions, that they have been less interested in those literary societies which were once an important means of rhetorical and elocutionary culture. There are two of these societies, which have their rooms neatly fitted up and furnished with libraries. These are called the Alpha Nu and the Literary Adelphi. The debating clubs are too numerous to be mentioned. These are connected with both literary and law departments. The secret societies, of which there are seven—viz: the Chi

Psi, Alpha Delta Phi, Delta Kappa Epsilon, Delta Phi, Sigma Phi, Zeta Psi, and Psi Upsilon—form the basis of some of the social life of students, but they are little known to the general public.

The two societies of most public interest are the Students' Lecture Association and the Christian Association. The former of these provides a series of entertainments, generally lectures, extending from about November to some time in March, of each year, and numbering not far from a dozen. After paying·their lecturers and other expenses, and obtaining for the members some of their tickets free, they have often more than a thousand dollars at the close of the year, which they put to various uses—one of the most important of which is the furnishing of the reading-room connected with the university library with several hundred dollars worth of periodicals. This has been said to be the best attended course of the kind in the United States. Until the last year, this association has obtained the·use of the Methodist church, which will seat an audience of 1,200; for the last year the university hall, which seats 2,500 or more, has been used.

The Christian Association has been already referred to. It is the center of all the social religious interest of the students. This body has been accustomed, several times in the course of each year, to hold public meetings, addressed by men of more or less eminence.

There was formed by the students of the university, about the year 1847, a society for missionary inquiry, after the model of one then existing in Madison University. This gave way, in 1858, to the Christian Library Association, which in a short time yielded the religious work in the university to the Christian Association as it now exists.

In regard to the admission of females, the results are decisive, so far as this at least, that young ladies are.found able successfully to study the subjects of a collegiate or professional course—if this, indeed, was ever a question. They are supposed to average about the scholarship of their classes; if they had an average standing above that of the young men, it would not decide their superiority, much less that of their sex, for they are supposed to be under stronger stimulants, so soon after the institution of this test, and their numbers being so much smaller, they may be regarded as representing those who pursue studies from their own internal impulses, rather than from the desire of parents, which is often not true of the young men. The question of equality of powers could only be fairly settled when about equal numbers of the sexes from the same average classes of mind should have been brought for a length of time together in study. Some stories of the superiority of the young ladies have gone forth from the university, which were not sustained by facts. These are found to have been circulated without the knowledge of the ladies concerned, and not a little to their discomfort and chagrin.

There was an attempt made, in 1869 and 1870, to create a feeling of unity among the students of all the departments of the university by bringing them together once a year in a fête, to be called " university day." The result was much like that of bringing together several strange herds of cattle ; they spend the first few hours, or days, perhaps, in a series of combats, in order to settle their relative positions, which once done, they become one herd, and the most orderly social life prevails among them. It is much the same with the human animal. The departments of a university should never be brought together unless this is done to such extent as to have time to unify the whole. If a fine large organ were placed in the great hall of the university, and all the appointments tending to make the worship impressive were added, and all the students of the several departments were required to comé together there at a fixed hour of each day for a period of ten to fifteen minutes of worship, there would be secured a greater power for the social culture and government of the students than could possibly be realized in any other way. The difficulties of discipline would mostly disappear before such a system of united worship, in which all should come together. Some have been sorry to see the recent tendency toward giving up the chapel worship of college; we should prefer to see the tendency the other way—that is, toward bringing all the departments of the university together in worship. This arrangement would have a wonderful effect aside from its character as worship.

The first class graduated from the department of literature and the arts in 1845, not yet thirty years ago. The medical and law schools are respectively twenty-four and fifteen years old. The catalogue of the past year gave for the first-named department 484 names; for the other two, each 314—leaving, after deducting 7 names found in more than one department, an aggregate of 1,105 * students. There was a period, just after the close of the war, when the professional schools, and especially that of medicine, showed considerably larger numbers of students. Some had formed a taste, or rather laid a foundation for this latter profession by having been nurses in army hospitals, and had saved from their pay money enough to carry them through their studies. These schools have in former years shown sometimes considerably greater numbers. The department of literature and the arts has also sometimes had a few more names on the catalogue, though the last year shows some increase upon the previous one, and it may in general be said that there has been a constant progress, making altogether the University of Michigan a marvelous phenomenon in the history of education. May those who have its management never allow it to lose its prestige by standing still to contemplate and proclaim the wonderful successes which it has already achieved.

---

* The aggregate for 1874–75, is 1,191.

CHAPTER XIV.

The Prospective University.

ALL higher education, including that of the university system, in this country, and at no distant day, has yet to pass through a period of revolution, involving considerable changes. Various questions pertaining to this subject are in an unsettled state. The relation of the university to the colleges, and of the colleges and intermediate schools as they now exist to each other, then that between the parts of a university—the schools of law, medicine, theology, and technology, and those of the arts, sciences, and philosophy—must be revised. The relative value of different studies claiming places in the course will never cease to be discussed. This will not only be true of new branches of science, but the old established tenants of the course will have to submit to a readjustment of their claims. Whether the ancient languages ought to hold the place which they have long held, is still, as ever, an unsettled question, and can not be excluded from the discussion. The extent and character of the control which the university faculties shall exercise over the studies and conduct of the students, must come up for a new decision as connected with any rise of our universities above their present rank. The relation of the State to this work, and the rank of its schools relatively to the denominational institutions, are questions not yet settled. These are but hints of what is involved in the further development of the university system. And a question, too, logically antecedent to all these, and long ago settled in the old countries of Christendom—the question involved in the phrase "self-education"—is still practcally unanswered and demands our first attention here. There is, perhaps, no better way to set forth the idea of the phrase self-education, and terms of equivalent import, than by taking an account of what enters into the conception. The division of this subject is naturally that indicated by the parts of the compound *self*, and *education*. The word *self* designates the original capital; *education* that which is acquired: the result is the original self, or person, and his education. This, however, is not the idea generally sought to be conveyed by this phrase; for it is used to point out that particular kind of education in which the same mind is supposed to be both teacher and pupil. It conveys also, as used by some, the hint that those thoroughly taught in the schools are all *education* without any *self*—a hint to which it might be retorted that those *not* so taught are mainly the *self* without the *education*. The phrase will here be used in its popular sense, abating the undue praise connected with it, and considering the relation of the self to the educational means and processes.

To state just what is contained in the self, would be to write a system of mental philosophy; only the self-determining or self-directing power of the mind in its own education will be considered.

Even the infant is active in its own development, though not from any purpose of self-improvement, but from its own internal impulses. Its eyes are turned to objects pleasant to behold; its hands lay hold of those which are near and wield them as instruments of its will, and thus it exercises, tests, and develops its powers of mind and body, not from premeditation, but from its instincts, directed by an ever-growing intelligence. From the very beginning, one of these instincts is curiosity, or love of knowledge.

Early education is mainly directed by others. Objects are placed within the infant's reach, by which even its plays are controlled. Its society is not of its own choice. The results determined by its own personality are confined within a very narrow range; and yet there are such, and precisely the same surroundings, living and inanimate, would not resolve all mankind into absolute uniformity.

The very germ of being often strongly asserts its individuality—its self.

In attempting to measure this self-directing power of the mind, we find ourselves floundering in one of the deepest mires of metaphysics. We are conscious of a power of election between things already in part known. On the other hand, the mind can not choose to make the acquaintance of things as yet utterly unknown, but must simply select from those subjects which are, already partly in it— those first thrown in its way without its choice. By these things and its own constitutional predilections, the mind is shut up to a certain course which it has but a limited power to modify; a kind of wriggling motion may throw it a little more this side or that of the current which bears it along, but never quite out of that current, though the elective power widens its range with progress.

This power, be it more or less, is the basis on which our responsibility for self-education rests. The will is so far determined by the bent of the mind itself and the force of circumstances without, as to give not a little point to Jonathan Edwards' sarcastic illustration of the self-determining power of the will. He represents a learned philosopher as saying that 'he had been to Terra del Fuego, and there had seen an animal which he describes as having begotten and brought forth itself, and as having at the same time a sire and dam distinct from itself; as having an appetite and being hungry before it had a being; as led and governed at pleasure by its master, who was always governed by it and driven by it where it pleased; as always when it moved taking a step before the first step; as moving head first, and yet always tail foremost, and this though he had neither head nor tail.'

But the question between Edwards and his opponents was the theoretical, not the practical one : whether the will does not always and necessarily act in accordance with that which, in the view of the mind itself, as led by its own internal impulses and impelled by external influences, is the strongest motive; and this question seems really to be a purely verbal one, turning upon an ambiguity in the word strongest. Does the word mean that which, under all circumstances, *ought* to be the strongest motive, or that which, by its prevalence in a particular instance, *proves* itself such in the mind which is swayed by it?

In the machinery of the human mind the intellect and sensibilities are but the means to a higher end; they are the powder and the spark, which, brought in contact, produce the explosion; the act of the will constitutes the definite aim toward an execution. Not that the volitions do not have for their direct object, quite as often as otherwise, some still further intellectual achievement or emotional result; but yet in that endless succession of the mind's affections and actions, volition is the end to which all else tends.

The range of the mind's absolute power of election is certainly somewhat narrow; and this makes it beyond conception important that all existing educational forces should be brought in to the aid of the young in the choice of their studies and in the pursuit of those chosen.

There is no question that the earliest development should be under strict direction. But even in the cradle, the teacher—that is the parent—can not absolutely extirpate all independent processes of mental development, much less can this occur in the later stages of education. At what point and how far the pupil is qualified to elect his studies, how far to pursue them without systematic aid and superintendence from teachers, are the questions to be settled.

Whether food suits the palate is decided by tasting, but there is no such summary process for testing even the agreeableness of a study. The declension of " penna " or " μοῦσα " does not even foreshadow that which may be enjoyed in an ode of Horace or Pindar, or an oration of Cicero or Demosthenes. These studies can not be tried much short of a mastery of these languages. Testimony must be taken. Those who have pursued the studies must be consulted, and they will generally recommend them; those who have no knowledge of a subject are not the persons generally called to bear testimony in regard to it. The student can beforehand but inadequately weigh the arguments offered to him.

The question is but slightly modified in case of other studies. An intelligent boy would know in general what the engineer's work is, and that he must study engineering if he wished to qualify himself to do that work ; but he would be ignorant as to what specific branches pertained directly or collaterally to the study, and could not fully appreciate the considerations which ought to determine these. Nor are young persons generally prepared rationally and intelligently to choose a course for themselves until they have made some proficiency in those philological and scientific studies embraced in the college curriculum, still less can they successfully pursue it without a teacher's aid. In other words, it is easier to appreciate the arguments for and against a course, than to pursue it without the help of a living instructor. The attempt to do the latter would almost always fail for want of the necessary decision and perseverance to carry out the plan, and the attainments would, of course, be imperfect. A scholar whose habits of study have been fully formed can pursue studies lying in the line of his previous course, or even outside of it, but this is not self-education, in the popular sense of the phrase, but the very work for which all school instruction tends to prepare the mind.

There have, indeed, been many and marked successes in what is called self-education—successes, however, generally in the mastery of some one branch of knowledge and successes in life, but never in exact and general scholarship. Many well-balanced minds have entered upon the practice of their professions with little knowledge except professional, and but a scanty supply of that, and have yet achieved eminence. But they have done this by picking up in later life, and in a fragmentary way, the elements of that general information which they had at first wanted, correcting by the aid of a strong will and a vigorous common sense the errors and defects of even their profqssional training, and whatever such men succeed in achieving is at double the expense which a thorough schooling would have cost them. More than this, such successes are only made possible at all by that atmosphere which has been formed by the prevalence of schools, scholars, and books. Those who have thus succeeded have converted all the learned men and literature within their reach into teachers, and thus have acquired later in life a part of what they might have better learned earlier. They are indebted as much as others to the prevalence of learning and learned men, though they have never employed and paid the latter as teachers, but have stolen here and there, as they could find them the needed helps, and then have received credit for acquiring their education by dint of personal exertions of a more independent character than others.

The so-called self-educated, however, are too seldom of this high class. There is more hobby-riding among them than among the thoroughly trained; for, although school education can not give balance to a naturally defective mind, it is nevertheless remedial so far as it goes. No one who has observed largely and closely in this matter, has failed to find men who have really won a reputation for much greater ability in some particular fields of study than the same men could have gained had they been liberally educated. The reason is obvious. All truth forms one whole or system. The parts are more or less nearly related to each other, and consequently more or less modify each other. The man of liberal culture and large general attainments perceives this, and thus is imparted to all his statements a moderation and modesty which many interpret as indicating mediocrity of intellect as compared with him, who, from perceiving only his one great truth and expressing it without limitations or modifications, obtains credit for a more vigorous intellect than that of his more cultivated brother.

In an important sense all education is self-education; the self is the basis of it, and is to be chiefly active in the work.. The men and books seized upon by the way, are but the crutches needed to help one along while his limbs are acquiring the strength to move more freely. Whether one orders regular crutches made, and keeps up a succession according to his needs, or runs the risk of being able to pick up just the stick he needs, and just at the time of his need, is not so much a question of greater or less dependence upon helps, as of the best system of providing them.

The breadth of the field allowed for the expansion of the self, or individuality, is ever the same. The teacher should guide the mind, and neither cram nor cramp it in its work. The educator true to his trust will lead his pupil in the best, if not indeed in the shortest way, to the highest destiny of which he is capable. Knowing the way himself, he makes it his business to save his pupil the toil, weariness, and perplexity of trying this path, and that and another, with the constant hazard of failing in the end to find the right one. Some think this toilsome and half successful labor a good discipline, strengthening the mind and inuring it to hardships in the contest with difficulty; but this discipline is really no better than the same amount of well-directed exertion attended with double the success in the acquisition of knowledge and culture, and the latter has an encouraging effect which the other wants.

The popular impression that this self-education, which often means little more than the want of college learning, is more meritorious than liberal culture in the schools, must bear a large share of the responsibility of precipitating such multitudes without the needed training into the professions. If they *were* self-educated, it would be well; but many are *un*educated. The blunder is a double one. It is a mistake to attribute merit to self-made men, as though they mastered greater difficulties than those educated in college, since they often really seek to escape the way of difficulty; and the error is still greater to call those *self*-educated who are scarcely educated at all. The young man who overcomes the obstacles which poverty and toil interpose in the way of a full course of study, is the man of merit, and will generally be the man whose merit will be rewarded.

The mind needs to form a purpose of systematic labor, directed to an end, and then it needs something to hold it to its purpose. The bees hived near a clover-field, need no other systematizing of their labor than that which instinct and sense supply. They pass from flower to flower, just as senses draw them, until their load is obtained and nature's purpose is accomplished. But in the case of a young man, nothing could be done worse than to turn him loose into a large library, with the direction that he obtain an education in four or six years, and come out with it ready for use at the end of that time. If he could even know—which he would not—the books best adapted to serve this purpose, the barrier to keep him from those which would yield most of present gratification would be too feeble, and not one in a thousand would have the decision, thus unaided, to neglect all the other attractions, and confine himself steadily, even so far as he knew them, to the books best adapted to his purpose. The only way which has ever been found uniformly to answer this end well, is that the pupil have a contract with other persons to meet him daily and aid him in mastering the subject assigned for study, only using such intervening fragments of spare time as may be at command, for excursions into those fields of independent inquiry, which he expects in future life to traverse without the aid of a personal guide.

The difference is immense between the best mentally, morally, and religiously educated in civilized and Christian lands, and the more neglected classes in the same, and yet a general likeness of ideas and modes of thought marks both of these extremes, as descended through modern Europe, from classical and christianized Greece and Rome, with modifications derived mainly from Hebrew, Teutonic, Celtic, and Scandinavian elements—forming a result so unlike the Indian, Chinese, or Tartar ideas and modes of thought, that ours could not in a single person

21

be displaced by theirs, short of sending that person in earliest childhood, to be brought up unattended by any of his own people, in one of those countries. The ruts worn by the revolving wheels of time through fifty generations of men, have become too deep and fixed to be entirely obliterated in any other way. This indicates our work as educators. Our universities are but the heads of systems which embrace every child in the States to which they belong, and these systems should compel their attendance in its first stages, and invite it in all the others. This exactly corresponds with parental government, which begins with an affectionate compulsion, which gradually passes into counsel. The extension of such plan to all lands, and their acting in correspondence with each other, will realize the result. This is foreshaded in the enterprises of missions and of commerce, and responses from even pagan lands are not wanting; Japan has quite a large company of students who have come to bear the fruits of our system to their own land, where each one's self or individuality, and the education furnished among us, will work together to bring America and Japan to a common standard, and it may soon be so of other nationalities.

It will be obvious to every enlightened educator that our country occupies a vantage-ground for the settlement of the university question. The European universities sprang up in the middle ages, and have attained their present growth with no models elsewhere in advance of them to suggest what should be adopted and what avoided. They were like trees, indigenous in the soil, having but their own organizations and the elements supplied by the soil and atmosphere to form them. We, on the other hand, are nearing the close of the nineteenth century without a university. We have a few great schools, or more properly clusters of schools, which have outgrown the rank of the college, and can at once be advanced to that of the university when their governing powers so determine. We are in full connection and sympathy with the world's progress in this respect. We have long been observing the institutions of other lands with a freedom from prejudice which should qualify us to judge what parts work well and what ones do not, with no such pre-occupation by any system of our own as need prevent us from selecting or rejecting or building anew, according to the light elicited by inquiry. Harvard, or Yale, or Michigan, or any other institution, can determine each for itself what ought to be done, and their boards being agreed, can carry out their determinations. Any one having made the movement, others will follow, according to their funds and the demands of the public.

The long-agitated question of the place which the Latin and Greek languages should hold in education, the University of Michigan settled originally by giving them the same prominence which they had in the old colleges of this country, and the State universities generally have inclined to this course. This action needs no comment or defense beyond a statement of the reasons which have been supposed to justify it. The relation of the study of these languages to that of other subjects, has been greatly changed by the introduction of new branches of study, but not by any special change of views in regard to the value of the languages themselves.

Language is the instrument of thought. Even our internal processes of thinking can never be well carried on and bring us to trustworthy conclusions, not to speak of expressing those conclusions to others, without accuracy and precision in the use of language. Almost the whole inner work of study consists in the employment of words in order to inform and convince oneself in the same sense in which they are used to convey information and conviction to others; and according as one has first convinced his own mind, whether rightly or deceptively, will he lead others into truth or error. This is equally true whether applied to the study of books; that is, to thought guided by printed pages before the eye, or to thought without such aids. We call it perhaps a critical process when the mind is occupied with the words of an author, and a logical or reflective one when it reasons without such help; but our

epithets do not change the fact.   The whole life of the man
of study, whether he operate reflectively within himself, or
in the way of narration, description, argument, or persua-
sion, is one continued logical process, of which language
is the instrument; and if a word is used in the conclusion
in a sense slightly differing from that given it in the premises, error must be the result.   There is little danger of expending too much labor in putting this instrument in order
for effective use; and it may fairly be assumed, in case of
a candidate for a literary or scientific career, that in his
preparation, time and labor ought to be given to the per-
fecting of his acquaintance with it in the proportions in
which they are to be given to its use in study and reflection and in his intercourse and transactions with the world;
for instance, in the study of botany and zoology, there
is, to say the least, fourfold as much time spent in the
prosecution of these studies through the medium of language as in direct contact with specimens from the world
of plants and animals.   May not this indicate to us the
amount of time which ought to be devoted to language
relatively to that to be given to the natural sciences?

Language is, of all studies, the most practical.   The
useful and sublime sciences, such as chemistry, botany,
geology, and astronomy, are of little immediate use even
to the learned.   Their main facts and generalization are
indeed well employed in literature, in philosophy, and in
social life; but beyond these they are only to be pursued
by the special student who can not, indeed, after having
acquired the prerequisites for their study, give them too
much time.   On the other hand, there is no person to whom
the greatest skill, precision, and facility in the use of language would be without its practical use for a single hour
of his life; none who would not be hampered and crippled
in any other study without these attainments.

The instances in which we use only words in our processes, either of reflection or communication, as compared
in number with those in which we go back to the things
represented by those words, might be reduced to almost

absolute exactness. In the professional labors of the lawyer and clergyman, language is almost the sole instrument, the going back of them to the things they stand for is only in conception; or, at least, the cases are so rare that this statement is substantially true. The physician, the naturalist, and the chemist must indeed sometimes go back to things, in order to learn or teach well their respective branches of science. They must offer with the verbal statement illustrative facts. But it is safe to say that both in their reasonings with themselves and in their statements to others, the words are used a thousand times where the things they represent are actually once produced. So the simple artisan, because he does not comprehend your abstract words, must be shown by diagrams, or pieces of wood or metal placed together, what you wish him to do; the lawyer may even have to employ a diagram in order to bring testimony before a jury. All of which rather confirms our rule, that language is the great and almost sole instrument of thought, and all its confusions arise from the ambiguities and other imperfections of its use.

It is admitted that the main purpose in the study of language is to acquire the most exact and facile use of one's own mother tongue. If foreign languages are learned, it is not in order to inspire admiration for having surmounted difficulties, as the pianist is admired without having produced one strain to touch the soul, for feats on a level with those of the circus-rider and acrobat. If one should learn to speak and write Attic Greek, as did Euripides or Demosthenes, or Latin as did Horace or Cicero, he would do a marvelous thing, for he would overcome impediments tenfold greater than any which Demosthenes ever encountered in acquiring his matchless power of oratory; but he would still have performed an almost useless task. The mastery of the particular language or languages to be used for our own purposes of study and of public and social life, is the true end of this study, and this will be chiefly our own mother tongue.

What part shall foreign languages act in this acquisition?

To present this subject to those who have never pursued these studies, seems a little like dilating on the beauties of the landscape to one born blind, or discoursing on the exquisite emotions to be enjoyed from the combinations of musical sounds to one born deaf, only rather worse; for the blind and the deaf will believe that those who see and hear have pleasures unknown to them, but a man's reason seems to forbid his admission of any great utility in the study of a language, except as the direct medium through which intelligence is to be acquired or disseminated.

The study of foreign languages is like foreign travel; it is liberalizing. The man who has never been from home, regards other people somewhat as did the ancient Greeks; they are all barbarians. He may indeed admire, and perhaps, under the enchantment which distance imparts, excessively admire some specimens of his race, of which he has heard as produced in other lands; but he will, in general, regard most foreigners as barbarians : and if books teach him better, the feeling is but little changed until changed by travel; and by this he learns to view the peoples much as botanists do the plants of the same species, as found in other lands—they are all the same thing with but the variations produced by climate, soil, and cultivation. So, when the traveler comes to view the men of other lands in their native homes, he learns to regard them as brothers formed under other influences.

The study of foreign languages is next, in its liberalizing effects, to intercourse with those who speak them, indeed much better than travel with no knowledge of foreign languages, which is much like an attempt to explore a mountain by passing through it in a railroad tunnel.

Nor is this reasoning applicable to modern languages alone. The learning of an ancient language is a kind of visit to a distant age. You find the people indeed from home, and never to return; but in their languages, you explore, as it were, their empty habitations, and walk over their deserted fields, finding apartments, furniture, and implements all as they left them. If any deem these visits to the dead past as of little use compared with those to the living present, let them reflect on the beautiful and profound significance of the proverb: "It is better to go to the house of mourning than to the house of feasting." They show whither all forms of civilization are tending—to death and a resurrection to some new form of life. Nor is it inappropriate to remark that, while the claims of natural history have been readily admitted, though they require the study of the minutest details of the changes which have transpired in the earth's crust for innumerable ages before the birth of language, the claims of philology for the study of the most important structures of our race, though the oldest of them are recent compared with geological periods, have been persistently challenged.

Antiquity had but two highly cultivated peoples, who left behind them polished languages and extensive literatures. These dwelt on the shores of the Mediterranean. They received, at an advanced stage of their development, and transmitted, the Christian religion, the world's great civilizing and regenerating power. These languages, and their inestimable treasures, entered into the nations of modern Europe, and made them what they are, and we of Europe and America now stand in indissoluble connection with them. The blood is no more certainly forced through the animal system by the impulses of its central organ, than have been the elements of our civilization by influences descended through this channel. To study these peoples and their languages, is to visit the homes of our literary, scientific, religious, and political ancestors.

There are those who deem it a kind of long-standing and deep-rooted superstition to continue to perform these pilgrimages to ancient shrines; but if we had indeed lost all respect for the long line of our antecedents in this wonderful history, it would be strange if we did not seek to know the process of our own development through it. The substratum of our language is indeed the Anglo-Saxon, the Latin being merely the largest contributor to its development into modern English. The Anglo-Saxons, too,

are our natural ancestors.   But they offer us no history,
and no literature to study.   Taking all together—language
and history, including religious, civil, political, judicial,
and domestic institutions, and manners and customs, and
more especially science, literature, and the arts—and all
other contributions to our civilization are small compared
with the Greek and Roman, and those which have come to
us through these languages.   The Angles, the Saxons,
the various tribes of Celts, Goths, and Sclaves, have furnished indeed some of the material which Greece and
Rome have wrought into shape.

But whether these languages must be studied in order to
keep up this connection and secure the benefits of this history, still remains a question.   The languages form the
strongest cord in this historic connection.   This severed,
the intimacy of our union with Greek and Roman antiquity
is disturbed, and in the way to be finally lost.   This line
once broken, what others shall we pursue?   Shall they be
those of the ancestors of the various nationalities of Europe?
By what vehicle can we follow these lines?   That of the
Greek and Roman geographers and historians, to be sure;
and yet perhaps not entirely at the present day, but we
must go to other sources, against which still stronger objections will be raised—viz., to what is involved in the science
of ethnology, among the branches of which comparative
philology greatly outweighs, in value and extent, all else
put together.   Those who would have us drop these, recommend in their place, to no small extent, other studies
which every scholar knows can not be successfully pursued without them.

Unsound arguments and extravagant demands have indeed been put forward for the ancient Latin and Greek
languages.   They have been joined together as though
they must not be separated.   There is no good reason why
one, and especially the Latin, might not, by those who do
not design to teach them, be pursued alone.   There will
long be in our country young men needing this philological basis of an education, whose beginning will be too

late, and their means too small, to admit of their taking a respectable course in both, and who may with advantage take Latin without Greek. The interests of education, too, may well spare that pedantry which desires to exhibit the power of writing and speaking these languages with facility; they may be pursued only to the extent deemed necessary in order to read and translate them: Nor need it be insisted that the person who has studied Latin and Greek must ever after eschew all translations of their classics, since the finding of new mediums of investigation was neither the sole nor the most important object in their study. Hence those who reproach the student of the ancient classics with making use of translations from them, may spare the breath employed in this way.

Recurring to the position taken above, that the chief object in this study should be the greatest attainable perfection in thought and in the use of one's own language, the study of the classics in their originals may be shown to be the best means to this end. It will doubtless be admitted that the languages chosen for this disciplinary study should be those of cultivated and refined peoples; that they should contain a body of literature of considerable extent and polish, and characterized by logical and stimulating thought, and that they should have some near kinship and historical and philological alliances with our own language. If so, there seems to be but one resort.

It is not easy to make evident to the mind which has not had this training, or having had a little of it has not reflected upon its processes, the method of its working; and yet nothing could be more clear. Let the study of the Latin language be taken, and let the problem in its study be to give in the mother tongue the exact equivalent of the author examined. Here the thought is furnished, and it is the best thought of mature minds—of the representative men of the most cultivated age of antiquity. The pupil is to render this, with all possible exactness, into his own language. Let this process be continued from the age of twelve to that of eighteen or twenty years, and the two

greatest educational problems have been solved—the young
mind has been supplied with thoughts, and these have been
engraven upon it and rendered clear and distinct by the
necessity of expressing them in the mother tongue. Let
this be compared with any other process for reaching the
same end—for instance, that of giving out subjects to be
written upon. The pupil wants both thoughts and language,
and directly or indirectly he must go to some one else for
both, or he must draw upon his own resources. In the one
case, the result is not his own production; in the other,
though his own, it amounts to nothing. In neither case is
his mind anchored and held to any fixed point; he floats
simply whither winds and currents chance to bear him; he
goes where it seems easiest—where words are most ready
at hand—following perhaps the vague and indefinite suggestions of parents or friends offered for his relief, having
no fixed point of beginning, progress, or end. But in a
paragraph of a foreign language before him, the problem
is definite; the sense must be given in his own language,
which, in a course of years of such training, must become
the supple agent of his will in the expression of his own
teeming thoughts, by this process quickened into life.
Nothing is so eminently practical, and with all the complaints which boys and girls and young men and women
utter in regard to their tasks, there are none to which they
can be held so easily. The natural sciences—geology,
botany, and chemistry—are admitted to be important. Education is defective without their main facts, ideas, and principles. But no student, unless his life is to be spent in their
prosecution, can be forced beyond these elements. Students
complain of the ancient languages because these require
much study, which, however, they render; they complain
of the natural sciences, because they require little and do
not reward that which they require.

But must the languages thus pursued be the Greek and
Latin? In regard to all other dead languages, we have
but to name them in order that their claims may be dismissed. They are the languages of barbarians, and are

without literature. Hebrew could best sustain its claim, and ought, if possible, to have a place as an elective study in our colleges. But the languages of our Anglo-Saxon, Gothic,* and Celtic ancestors could not be thought of as a disciplinary drill. The living languages of modern Europe, and especially the German and French, are the only rival claimants for this place. Can they fill it? Their claims will not be argued here in detail. The elements of the argument will be found mainly in the above suggestions. If this change is made, the same kind of drilling in the preparatory schools and in the lower classes in college must be applied in the French and German as now in the Latin and Greek.

We lose, then, the most perfect language ever used—the Greek—and another equal to it in the most important characteristics. We begin to loosen our connection with the original sources of our civilization, and instead of taking in its whole range in its spirit and elements as crystallized in the ancient languages of Greece and Rome, we are ever more and more confining our view to its modern aspects. It was the ancient classics, and the Hebrew and Greek scriptures in their originals, which awakened Europe from the sleep of the middle ages. They are adapted to just that kind of work, and they will probably hold their place, contested though it may be, for ages to come, as for centuries past, in the course of higher education.

The mathematics, pure and applied, furnish another kind of discipline, giving strength, precision, and direction to the reasoning powers, and while students murmur at them as their great dread, they can be brought to expend two or three times as much labor upon them, as they can be coaxed or driven to give to the natural sciences, or even to the modern languages. They seem, indeed, to have an instinctive impression of their value.

As to the time to be devoted to these studies, it is difficult to perceive how the period between childhood and that for

---

* Gothic has, indeed, one remarkable poem—the Niebelungen Lied.

entering upon professional study can be filled up to any
advantage with those which any one would approve, without giving to the ancient languages about the time now bestowed upon them in our best American colleges. The
objections are all abstract. They apply with even greater
force to almost any other studies, and, if carried out to
their final results, would clear the educational track of
everything which intervenes between reading, writing, and
common arithmetic, on the one hand, and the commencement of professional study on the other, and would thus
reduce themselves to an absurdity.

Nor is this statement too strong. Let it be formally
tested whether the argument which erases these studies
from the list would leave anything beyond reading, writing,
and common arithmetic as a foundation to professional and
business education. It is indeed true that many men with
even this slender preparation, having good powers of per-
ception and reasoning and strong wills, have risen to eminence in the professions. They have been able to do this,
because the prevalence of higher education has multiplied
learned men and books. A lame man of great energy
and muscular power might make his way without artificial
aid better than a weaker and less resolute one in like
manner unfortunate could do with a well-constructed
crutch, or still another of sound limbs; but all this does
nothing toward proving that lameness is an advantage or
a chance stick better than a well-made crutch, and no one
should attempt to persuade the world to adopt his misfortune as their law of action.

There are indeed minds that do not need the discipline
which most require; they are, so to speak, born disciplined. We can not agree with those sticklers for even the
best course of study, who would refuse to admit to the circle of the educated all who had not been driven through
it. Nor do any go really so far as this. They content
themselves with saying that some men not systematically
educated are great men, indeed, but how much greater
would they have been with a better education. But even

this is not true. Let Franklin be taken as an example. A different line of studies, largely and rigidly carried out, might have permanently diverted him from that in which he was so eminently successful. This may be often true, and the error of burdening the mind and taking the time for the acquisition of numerous languages in adult age, with no definite purpose, is as real, though not so common, as the opposite one.

Most educators would perhaps, at the present day, agree that the drilling of boys and girls in the languages and mathematics should be left mostly to schools below the rank of the proper university. As the two lower classes in our American colleges need but a continuation of the same kind of instruction which they had received in the preparatory schools, they should be left for two years longer to those schools. During this time the method of instruction by immediate contact of teacher and pupil, the former calling out by direct questions what the latter has learned, can not be relaxed without peril to the highest interests of education. But while this kind of instruction should be continued to some extent, even to the completion of the professional course, it may properly be modified on the introduction of philosophical studies in what is now called the junior year in college, and a freer range given both in the selection of studies and the prosecution of investigations.

The provisions for teaching the classics and mathematics in the preparatory schools—the union schools of Michigan and the academies of New England and New York, may be taken as examples—would need but little, if any, extension in order to cover these two years, so as to relieve the universities of that which does not properly belong to them. The preparatory course being thus extended and raised toward the standard of the German gymnasia, ought to have its satisfactory completion marked by some more formal testimonial—some degree. This being deemed in some sense a graduation instead of a mere preparation for college, would determine many a candidate for professional study, who otherwise might not enter upon it at all, to take the course entire. In this way, in a few years, the whole body of those looking forward to the professions might, without any unnatural pressure, be induced to take this course. This will be a great point gained.

The preparatory schools can, as suggested, easily rise to this demand. On the other hand, will not the small colleges, which are struggling in vain to rise, content themselves with this rank? If they should do this, most of them would have resources sufficient for their support, and might do their work easily and thoroughly. On this plan, the graduates of those which are connected with the various religious denominations, would be prepared to enter their theological seminaries, if they should choose to do so, or they might still spend a year or two at a university before entering a professional school. This would make a completed education possible in thousands of instances where a fragmentary one must now be made to answer.

Among the studies now comprehended in our university course, which ought to be handed over to preparatory schools or to private teachers, mention of the rudiments of the languages of modern Europe must not be omitted. They ought to be studied. It would be well if the body of university students had made themselves so familiar with these as to be able to read appreciatingly some of the chief works in French and German literature, and hear critical lectures upon the range of subjects embraced in these literatures; but it has now become quite unnecessary to provide for this initial work in our universities. To take the State of Michigan for an example, there is probably not a union school in it which is without provision for teaching them; certainly not one which could not easily, and without much expense, make such provision; and there is scarcely a city or large village in our whole country where private instruction in these languages can not be had.

It is therefore no longer necessary for the university to furnish instruction in the rudiments of the French and German languages. Those who desire to begin these studies after they enter upon university work, should find private instructors, which will always gather, according to demand, and only to those who are willing to pay for this instruction, is it of any value. Of those who take it in the university at the public expense, scarcely one in fifty ever reads a French or German author. Since, therefore, these languages are studied in order to open their literatures, and not for mental discipline, which purpose will have been already subserved in most cases by the study of Latin and Greek, and especially as these modern languages are not pursued far enough by those who depend upon the university for their teaching, to answer the purposes of either opening their literature to the student, or of disciplining his mind, the time devoted to this work in college is more completely lost than that given to any other branch of study in the course. While there ought to be a professor for French and one for German literature in every university, it should certainly not be their business to teach the mere rudiments of those two languages.

In such an institution as the University of Michigan, scarcely more than about twenty students out of a thousand ever call for French and German works in pursuing investigations in the library; of these, one-half find that they have overestimated their attainments in those languages, and seldom try again, and some of the other half prove to be of foreign parentage, or to have been previously led by some favorable circumstances to these studies. It is very seldom that an instance has occurred of any real value from the study of the rudiments of a modern language in the university. The time is all lost, and such a loss in the midst of a university course is a serious one. The mind which should be grappling with the great problems of history, metaphysics, political economy, government, and the higher generalizations of natural history, is diverted from these, to busy itself with the alphabets of languages which it will never master.

There are, in general, two purposes to be subserved by university lectures and instruction. These may be set

forth by the example of any single branch pursued. Professors of the ancient languages, for instance, may lecture
on the literature of these languages, and read the classic
authors with their classes in illustration of their lectures, and
as a part of them, and thus aid in that general culture
which most students seek. Or they may prosecute the
study of the more occult principles of those languages,
with greater minuteness of detail than the general student
requires, and so meet the demands of those who desire to
become teachers. So also in every branch of science and
literature. For this higher teaching there are established
in the German universities what are called seminaries, for
each of the more important studies, as philology and physiology (philologische und physiologische Seminäre). A
course of special teaching can therefore be had in almost
any branch of study.*

---

*We could earnestly desire to set forth in few words the difference
between the higher education of our country and that of Germany, if this
could be done without creating the impression that we cherish an entire
approbation of the German system, or wish to substitute it for ours.
Theirs has become established, and is not in any rapid process of transition. The whole country is full of schools of all grades. The gymnasia,
which are of about the grade proposed above for our colleges or schools
preparatory to the universities, are in every part of the land, there being 330
in Germany proper, and with the progymnasia, 544, in which are included
none of the real or polytechnic schools. The system is so uniform and so
well understood everywhere, that it can be carried out, there being no new
and undeveloped schools dragging heavily on the skirts of the system to keep
the standard depressed. The *esprit du corps* is one which penetrates the
country, and not merely a small section here and there. Social and
domestic arrangements are such that the educational process scarcely
ever needs to be suspended in deference to the demands of social life. The
effect of this one fact is beyond the calculation of those who do not know
it from actual observation. The American literary gentleman spends
nearly all the time which he can spare for social life in the company of his
own family or of others who are not in sympathy with his studies, and
from the time he leaves his study until he enters it again, all reference to
the subjects of his investigations must be shunned. As a student, he is
a kind of hermit. In Germany, on the other hand, if one goes to the café,
where most of the studious and many others are always seen after dinner,
he will soon observe that the gentlemen are grouped in a way to favor
conversation upon the subjects which they have pursued in private; he
will find that they talk familiarly of the condition of their ancestors as

There are other subjects embraced in the courses of American universities, which do not belong there and should be in whole or in part omitted, as elementary botany, and perhaps also zoology. These could as well be taught in lower schools, even to children, and should not consume the time of learned professors, who have enough of higher work if they must indeed conduct their pupils in even the most cursory explorations of those illimitable fields which these sciences spread out before them. The course should be cleared of all elementary studies which can as well be taught earlier.

It is not proposed to discuss any of those theories of a university which are quite beyond the limits of probable

pagans in the reign of Charlemagne, or earlier, and so of all subjects of history, natural science, or philosophy. Go, as we have done as a matter of curiosity, to some great brewery—the court brewery at Munich, for instance. You hear the din arising from the conversation of a thousand voices mingled with the clatter of glasses, and you may suppose yourself in some peasants' bedlam; but turn your attention from the general aspect to particular groups, and you may hear the last discoveries in astronomy or polar exploration, or the Chinese or Sanscrit language, history or philosophy, or something else equally unexpected, subjected to discussion. We were once where we met occasionally during a summer the wife of one of Germany's most distinguished historians, with her two boys of ten and twelve years of age, and saw the evidence of their being already familiar with the outlines of history, and aided by their mother in this work. Another lady, wife of a well-known diplomatist, we were accustomed to meet often under similar circumstances, and hear her talking to chilren of nine to twelve years in two languages foreign to them and to her. The natural process of immigration does not bring many Germans to this country who impress us favorably of their education. Most of their able men find places at home, and many who reach our country find none here. Revolution has, however, driven a few to us who may be used for illustration. It was by this educational process that Francis Lieber became an authority equal to any in this country on any subject which he chose to take up, and especially as a publicist. It was probably by this that Carl Schurz obtained much of that power by which in a single term in the United States Senate, he became "*facile princeps*" of that body in many of its discussions. That part of this educational process illustrated above by reference to cafés and breweries, or anything which tends to the disintegration of the domestic circle, we should regret to see promoted in this country; and we think that with the good that Germany has done us, she has also done us some evil in this way, and would discriminatingly distribute to the Germans both the credit and the blame which they deserve.

22

realization, but rather to suggest the best system which it can be rationally hoped to realize by some natural process of evolution from our present condition, first considering that general range of studies which, in the German system, would be called the faculty of philosophy. From this were eliminated above those elementary studies which ought to be pursued in the lower schools. This should also be relieved of those which are pursued in immediate preparation for business or professional life. The so-called professions, though ever deemed parts of a university, have always been assigned to special faculties.

This subject may be more minutely discussed by those who have a liking for questions which are rather formal than material. The grounds of many divisions which have been suggested are not definite. Probably no better can be found than that which should include in this one faculty all the pure sciences and their speculative applications, as also all speculative philosophy, the natural sciences and chemistry, political economy, and, in fine, all except the studies immediately preparatory for special professions or occupations. In other words, this faculty should include all provisions for the studies designed to lay a broader and firmer foundation, either for general culture or for special professional training, without itself being a part of such training. These latter should be provided for by separate faculties, though their general connection with a university may be important.

The three so-called learned professions have long been so treated. The same should be done for the fine and the useful arts—the former of which, in Europe, are assigned to the art academies, and the latter, as also in this country, to the polytechnic schools. In the universities of Germany the practical arts are not taught, though they are traced historically in lectures, which belong, however, to the history of civilization and not to art study; for neither their manual operations, nor the immediate scientific principles in which those operations are grounded, are made the subjects of this instruction. This may be applied to engineering in all its applications, as also to all the other industrial pursuits and the fine arts.

The Germans seem to think that the literary and scientific atmosphere of a university is neither necessary nor important to those who look forward to the practice of these useful arts. It is indeed a fair question whether they might not offer themselves in such crowds as to overload it with numbers not in the full spirit of its studies, and thus corrupt that spirit. We, in this country, are not, however, in sympathy with this view; we are tending to the largest possible penetration of all classes with the spirit of science and literature, and would never consent to provide against such a result. With us the question would be, whether these arts are better taught in connection with the universities or in separate schools. The general verdict would doubtless be in favor of giving the students of the arts whatever advantages there might be in a connection with the universities, though under separate faculties.

For the faculty now under consideration, the following subjects and groups of subjects, each to be assigned to one professor or to several, are suggested: Philosophy, including ontology, psychology, ethics, æsthetics, and metaphysics; the natural sciences—geology, botany, and zoology; philology; history, with geography and ethnology; mathematics, astronomy, and physics; political economy; principles of government. Within the field here indicated more minute divisions may be made to almost any extent, and professors may be multiplied as necessities arise.

This forms the nucleus of every university. It is the bond of union of the other faculties, holding them together and investing them with the respectability of an institution in the interest of discipline, culture, and scientific progress. Disconnected with such a center, law and medical schools can scarcely maintain a respectable standing.

The line which ought to separate this from all the other faculties of a university, as intimated above, is that which forms the boundary of distinct professional or industrial study. Hitherto, but three occupations have been distin-

guished as professions; whether we should in our modern
system advance others to that rank, is a question. The
tendency is to such advance, and there are indeed other
pursuits of equal dignity, of which journalism is an example; but it is doubtful whether any of them offer fields so
distinct as to call for separate professional schools.

The teacher's profession comes nearest to it; but a little
reflection will show that this requires rather a thorough
teaching of the subjects to be taught, than how to teach
them, and is therefore better made an incidental attachment
of every school, than assigned to a special faculty. A provision like the seminaries in the German universities is
best.

The enthusiasm over the marvelous educational progress
of our country has awakened extravagant ideas in some
minds, mainly those a little defective in education or birth,
or having private ends to gain. To suit them, everything
must be taught in the schools, nothing left to be supplied
in practice. It is much like the boy in the fable, who resolved never to touch the water until he learned to swim.
If the idea were not quite absurd in itself, it would at
least require that the human race be divided into two nearly
equal divisions, chiefly according to age, one of which
should be rehearsing in the schools precisely the parts
which they were afterward to enact in real life. We once
asked a great stickler for agricultural colleges what he
would have taught in these institutions. He promptly replied : " *Everything which belongs to farming. I would,
for instance, have the professor take his pupils into the
field, and teach them the mechanical pulverization of the
soil.*" This in better English, is nothing else than either
plowing or crushing clods. A great revolution is involved in
such suggestions. It proposes to send the whole youthful
population from the farms, mechanic shops, artists' studios,
and the business bureaus of government and private corporations, into schools, where all the manual, arithmetical, and
other operations are to be anticipated by lessons and re-
hearsals. But the common sense of the masses will

generally decide against this, and will not sustain it in practice.

Notions not unlike those just referred to have even found their way into the national legislature. A bill was reported in the Forty-second Congress of the United States, making provision for a great university, with at least the following faculties, viz:

"First, a faculty of philosophy; secondly, a faculty of the social and political sciences; thirdly, a faculty of jurisprudence; fourthly, a faculty of commerce and finance; fifthly, a faculty of education; sixthly, a faculty of letters; seventhly, a faculty of natural history; eighthly, a faculty. of medicine; ninthly, a faculty of agriculture; tenthly, a faculty of mining and metallurgy; eleventhly, a faculty of applied chemistry; twelfthly, a faculty of the mathematical and physical sciences; thirteenthly, a faculty of topographical and hydrographical engineering; fourteenthly, a faculty of civil and mechanical engineering; fifteenthly, a faculty of navigation; sixteenthly, a faculty of architecture; seventeenthly, a faculty of art."

The State universities are the highest grade of State schools, all on the same general plan, and so far as they realize their ideal, each is a kind of repetition of the others; while the national institution is to be, as is supposed, from the provisions of this bill, of a higher rank.

Now, a university, not only in the etymological sense of the word, but in the view of all men of high culture, and as realized historically in those of Europe, is a place where the principles of all sciences are taught. If our highest grade of State schools then become universities, the great national institution must either be the same, or differ only in extent. If this is the thought, there can be no ·objection raised to it except its uselessness; but it is to be suspected that the minds which prepared this bill did not in every instance make out to themselves exactly what is involved in their terms. The only other supposition, which is not indeed a charitable one, is that some men are planning for places for themselves or their friends.

Let this list of faculties be considered here a little in detail. "*The faculty of philosophy*," as known in the European universities, embraces generally the whole course
except what belongs to the faculties of theology, medicine,
and law.   But in this plan these professional departments
are left undivided and expressed by the words : "*Thirdly*,
a faculty of jurisprudence ; *eighthly*, a faculty of medicine."
What shall the faculty of philosophy mean then? Perhaps
ontology, psychology, æsthetics, and ethics ; but why should
these, any more than a scientific view of social life and politics, be comprehended in the word philosophy? The de-
signation of a faculty as that of the "*social and political
sciences*," is scarcely defensible.   What does it mean?
The principles upon which society is constituted and governed, ought to be regarded as simply one science, and
called the social science, or the science of society ; or else
the idea ought to be extended to take in all the details of
men's relations as social beings—such as ethnology, history, politics, government, law, beneficence, and other
subjects.   As history is left out of this list, we are left in
doubt whether this most extensive of all the sciences is to
be omitted as unimportant, or whether it is to be included
in some other ; and if so, whether in " philosophy " or in
the " social and political sciences."   Political economy is
not   mentioned in this list; of course, its elements are
mainly involved in commerce, finance, and agriculture,
but the division indicated by " a faculty of commerce
and finance," is so minute as to leave no room for the assignment of chairs.   Agriculture is extensive enough, and
could be divided up into work for several men ; but how
could this be done with commerce or finance as matter of
scholastic teaching? These subjects are exceedingly simple in their principles, but illimitable in their details.   If
the principles are to be taught, they can be brought within
very small compass ; if the details, they embrace the entire
course of men's business lives in all departments.   If this
latter is the thought, it presupposes that a man shall not
enter upon a practical life until he shall' first have gone

through with a theoretical one, embracing the machinery of all its motions—in other words, that one shall not enter upon the labor of his life until he shall first have exercised himself in it for a time.

All of these designations are subject to similar criticisms ; the whole looks much as though some educational adventurer, perhaps in search of a place, had urged his services upon a Congressional committee, and brought out this result. They have proceeded from the affected thoroughness of half-educated men. Designations of these faculties, so different from those ordinarily employed, seem to have been selected as a device in order to prove that something quite above the ordinary idea of a university was meant, and thus justify its endowment.

Universities should be in an important sense a growth, and not a construction. They should spring up naturally, or be extended in exact accordance with existing demands. We can not assign to some expert the work of planning one from the beginning to the end, as we do to the architect his task of planning a building. We do not destroy all that exists and begin anew, but build to an existing structure. What admirable institutions some men could build, if their way were once cleared of all that exists ! How systematic and beautiful a work could be reared from the material if it had not been spoiled in putting up, or if it were torn down and put into the hands of these great builders ! Alas ! it is perhaps a weakness of all men to conceive what they could have done if they had only had the management in the beginning. Experience cures this, if the disease is not too deep-seated. If the genius for making repairs and building additions is not indeed the higher, it is the more useful of the two, for it covers most of the work of man. We make our little additions to the structures of our predecessors, and then leave all to those who are to follow ; the whole work of ages is but a growth. An educational plan formed anew would need much more mending than one which had grown up with demand.

The educational problem of the general government of this country is an important one, and it is solving this satisfactorily. It has given, and may still give, its wild lands to the States and Territories for this purpose. It has established a bureau of education which is doing much in the way of furnishing needed information to educators. And it is doing what only a government can do, in its reports of scientific expeditions, explorations, and surveys. These, the professors of other institutions can use as well as could those of a great university which should be established at the national capital. Indeed, it is not easy to resist the impression that the great institution proposed would be but an ornamental appendage to other and better provisions which the government has made for the cause of science, and that its professors would be but a set of figure-heads, whose services would be inversely as the cost of their support.

Whatever other occupations rise to the dignity of special provision, should have it. The only ones which have plausible grounds for this claim are the fine arts, the technical arts, agriculture (including horticulture and forestry), and the state service. But a university should only teach these in their scientific principles, not in their details. The fine arts are in their grounds but a branch of æsthetics, and only as such can be a subject of scholastic lectures. Their manual operations are only to be taught in the art academies and the studios of artists. The basis of gardening and architecture as fine arts is in æsthetics; as business occupations, the one belongs to agriculture, the other to the technology in general, to which civil engineering is fundamental. Except where special demands exist for something more extensive, as a school of mines, or one of architecture, it is better in a university to combine all in one faculty, just as medicine and surgery are assigned to one. All that approaches the mere manual part of the art is better confined to the mechanic's shop or the studio of the artist. So also the technicalities of the state service are better learned in their proper bureaus.* For instance, engineering and architecture are to be taught in theory, but not in such details as to involve the manual work of masonry and carpentry. So in general of agriculture. Model shops and model farms would be desirable; but no one would go to the university to learn plowing and hoeing, sawing and planing.

In some of the sciences no definite limits can be set as to the extent to which they may be pursued in a university, except as determined by the funds and the importance of the subject itself. All have their peculiarities. History, for example, has this distinctive feature, that it is so extensive in detail as to make it the most difficult of all subjects to be compressed into a satisfactory outline, and hence such outlines are the driest of all books, while among the most fascinating of all are the narratives of the events of particular periods, with philosophical statements of causes and principles, and even the examination of documents is attended by many an agreeable surprise.

Political economy is the opposite. Its generalizations are large and satisfactory; its principles, when once perceived, simple and clear, and a system can be compressed into a moderate-sized volume with sufficient illustration to give it interest. The first man who attempted the reduction of these details to a science came nearer to the perfection of a scientific system than was ever done in any similar instance. But the details are endless, and apart from their uses, are the most dry, confused, and uninteresting possible, embracing the whole range of commerce, finance, manufactures, and agriculture, with all their endless statistics.

Mental philosophy, and in general metaphysical studies, are distinguished from both of the above mentioned, in that they are capable of being divided up and presented in detail, for the benefit of the special student, or an outline of their main facts may be thrown together in one general

* Some European governments teach diplomacy by giving to young men unpaid places in their foreign legations, from which they are gradually promoted to places of trust and emolument.

view and in very small compass, and they lose none of their interest by the expansion or the compression.

Of course, in a university proper, the studies are to be largely elective. Whether the desire to prosecute those which students may elect, and the necessity of passing a rigid examination for degrees, should be solely relied upon as the motives to secure attendance at lectures and recitations, is a question which we shall not here discuss. Certain studies, with some variations in detail, should be made conditions of degrees, and this will somewhat limit the range of election.

In regard to the professional schools, it was suggested above that the great evil of so many entering them unprepared might be much abated, if not entirely removed, if there should be somewhere a reduction of two years provided for in the full course. This would so increase the number of candidates for the professions who would take this preparatory course, that the unprepared, finding themselves in the minority, and feeling the disadvantages of their want of class-room drill, would offer themselves in ever-diminishing numbers, until they would quite disappear from these schools. The students of these departments, by gaining what time they could from their professional lectures for needed philosophical studies—perhaps one exercise each day—and then remaining the period by which the philosophical faculty's work is extended beyond the term of the law and medical schools, might, during the two years of their professional lectures, acquire much philosophical culture, and, by adding a year, they might take most of the philosophical course.

Nor can there be any doubt that political economy, that the philosophy of mind and of morals, the very fountain from which all law springs, and by which it is justified or condemned; that history, presenting the theater upon which all laws have played their parts, would ultimately be chosen by all law students. Of these, psychology would be equally necessary to the medical profession, and all the others would have their value, while some of the natural sciences would be needed to greater extent than they are offered in medical lectures ; and even if no change were made in the terms of the professional schools, their students might be invited and encouraged to avail themselves of these helps, and where they had entered these schools with the preparation which this plan provides for, they would doubtless be largely inclined to do so.

But this subject requires to be treated with some discrimination as to the present state of the professions and professional schools in this country. In this view we shall include the three professions of theology, medicine, and law. Each has its marked characteristics, distinguishing it from each of the others, and these differences must be noticed in order to show the provisions which need to be made for them. The ministers of the Christian religion are, from the nature of their work, teachers. Their original commission was, " Go, teach all nations." They have been the world's teachers ever since, and that quite beyond the demands of the commission.

Teaching, both in its subject-matter and in its form and spirit, is more in harmony with the work of this than with that of other professional callings. This tendency has been still more powerfully aided by the natural action of the law of supply and demand. Aptness to teach, involving, as it does, aptness to learn, is, as a rule, the highest order of mind. This, so far as it depends upon native talents, we may suppose to be about equally represented in all the professions ; but while the average pay of ministers may be nearly as much as that of lawyers and physicians, the salaries of the first class of minds in the ministry probably does not exceed half of the income with which first-class talents would be rewarded in the practice of medicine or law.

The bearings of this fact are plain. A minister of first-class talents can be called to a teacher's place—and here the kindred nature of the teacher's and preacher's work helps to move him—at a salary which would move no lawyer or physician of his talents and learning. Of the same class is also the fact that theological schools have their endowments, buildings, and libraries, and their professors of the highest order of mind and culture, who, for salaries which would not move a lawyer or physician of the same talents, with liberty to practice their professions besides, spend their whole time in the care of these seminaries for the preparation of future ministers.

Almost the whole body of this profession, too, are in favor of full college and theological courses. It is true that large numbers of them have not taken this full course; but those who have not, generally speak of their inability to do so as a matter of regret, and advise all to take it who can; and yet it is clear that for very many this course is too long, whether viewed in relation to its expense or the absolute demands of the fields of their future labors.

Now, our plan for a university course would, in case of this profession, relax the stringency of the rule, and make it possible for those who desired this, to lengthen it by one year; while those who might feel pressed for time and money, or feel that the full course, as it now stands, was beyond that demanded for the fields they were to occupy, could shorten it by a year or two years, as they might desire; that is, students designing to study theology could go directly from the college or preparatory school, whatever it might be called, to the school of theology; or pursue university studies for one, two, or three years before going thither; or if the theological school should be connected with a university, enough of the philosophical course could be elected and taken during the three years of theological study. But if the three parts of the course should take the student to three different institutions, even this might have its advantages. Thus is obtained a natural elasticity, which stretches or shrinks to variations of demand without leaving the education incomplete.

The profession of law is distinguished in many respects from the clerical. The lawyer is not by profession a public teacher. He may, as a man, do much designedly; and if his moral principles are right, will, by his professional practice, do much incidentally to improve the community in which he lives; but his contract for service embraces, primarily and directly, but the interests of his client. Not having prepared himself for teaching, and not being connected with a profession which has been historically identified with the teacher's work, he is less naturally drawn to those branches, such as the languages, natural history, mathematics, and natural, mental, and moral philosophy, which are the staple of the teacher's work; and he is apt to look upon these subjects for the purpose of estimating in dollars and cents their value to his profession.

This profession differs from the other two in that it has no positive, or, at least, no very definite boundaries as to its practice. If strictly professional business fails, the lawyer can easily and naturally slide off into agencies, or become the medium of any transactions between parties, or pass into politics, and is still never beyond the confines of his profession, which is not true in any proper sense of medical men or ministers.

The lawyers and the clergy have one thing in common, in which both are distinguished from physicians—their practice subjects them to public tests of ability and skill. Lawyers are so pitted against each other, and brought into such relations to court and jury, as quickly to show their merits or defects, and determine their several ranks and incomes; and hence it is that while their average pay is probably much below that of physicians, the most successful of them receive far higher incomes than do the most successful physicians.

Ministers are not indeed directly and formally placed against each other; but still, such is the public nature of their labors as to place them in the balances and show whether they are wanting, and in what respects.

In this particular the physician stands in decided contrast with both. He is subjected to no trial except that by which his professional brethren receive him into their ranks, which a man of pleasant and plausible address in social life, with little medical knowledge or skill, might not pass as readily as the thorough-bred physician ; and as opposite experiments can not be carried on at the same time with the same patient, the public can never know with certainty whether other treatment would have been better or worse. Hence the more fearful responsibility which rests upon medical faculties.

The studies of medicine and theology have one feature in common—they are divided into well-defined and distinctly named schools, each teaching its own peculiar doctrines, which is not true of lawyers, whose differences of opinion come up and are fought through in each individual case. Though decisions of courts are sometimes appealed from, and reversed, yet these differences of opinion can never, from the nature of the case, give rise to schools or sects in law.

As to the province of medical study, aside from the obvious fact already mentioned, that tests of skill and knowledge are not within the reach of the public, it is one of the most difficult successfully to explore. Symptoms, even when observed most closely and by experienced men, are often ambiguous, if not as to the causes, certainly as to the extent of the disease. It is scarcely easier, often more difficult, to reason and act in regard to remedies. And the obvious doubt and perplexity in which we frequently see the acute and experienced physician, operate as a caution not to trust the medical tyro with these difficult processes of observation and reasoning. Nor can the trial be put off from term to term, according to the wish of the professional man concerned, as in case of lawyers. The decision which places it forever beyond his reach may be made within a day or an hour after the case had been put into his hands.

The conclusion from all this is that the candidate for this profession should not be allowed to come with undisciplined powers to these most obscure and intricate processes of observation and reasoning. Languages, mathematics, natural science, and psychology, in which he may exercise and discipline his powers innocently and without peril to human life, should for years be the theater of action of the candidate for medical practice before he enters his proper field of the studies of his future life. But the tendency of medical students to study the history which connects our age with enlightened antiquity, and seek information and discipline through the two ancient languages which have mainly brought this history to us, is still less than that of the students of law, perhaps almost exactly in the proportion that medicine is less than law wrought into that history.

In view of this state of things, it is greatly to be hoped that all medical students will ultimately be brought to take the full course of preparation indicated in our proposed plan; and then, instead of merely hearing a brief series of lectures, to be either verbally or substantially repeated after an interval of a year or two, they will be subjected to three, or at least two full years of systematic study, under the constant guidance of able teachers, with one course for juniors and one for seniors, and with time to add other studies in the philosophical department of the university course, such as the various branches of natural history and psychology, and that they may be no longer sent forth to experiment upon human life in the practice of a profession of the qualifications of which the public has so imperfect means of judging, and are so peculiarly dependent upon the high sanctions of a medical faculty.

Briefly to recapitulate: We have in our plan the preparatory schools, taking their pupils to about the middle of our present college course; then the university, with the department of the general sciences which are not studied in direct preparation for a professional or industrial pursuit, for its nucleus; then, clustered round this, departments or faculties of theology, law, medicine, the technical arts, the fine arts, and agriculture. These, or as many of them as shall in any case be desired, will form our university.

We are on the subject of *State* universities, and just here arises an important, and indeed a delicate question, which ought not to be passed over in silence : *Ought the State to give in all these departments, and in all equally, a free education?* We shall give the elements which enter into a decision of this question, without drawing any conclusions.

We proceed upon the supposition that education for general culture should be made substantially free by the State. This will include everything from the common school to the end of the college course or the university, so far as the department of general science is concerned. Should strictly professional and business education be made free? Should there be any exceptions to the rule that each person chooses his own business and pays the expense of learning it?

The State, on our supposition, carries every person just so far in that way of general culture and discipline which it has provided as he desires to go. When he chooses to stop and enter upon an occupation, if he elect the life of a merchant, mechanic, or farmer, he prepares himself for it in the shop or on the farm, and at his own expense. Is there any ground on which the professions can be made exceptional? Can not candidates for law, medicine, and theology prepare themselves as well for these professions in professional offices or studies as boys can, in a similar way, for farmers, mechanics, and merchants?

It would seem that so far as the professions are sought as mere occupations for a livelihood, they could not be distinguished from other industries. The only ground of difference will be, that professional men are in such sense public benefactors as to refund to society the expenses of their professional instruction. Do they so regard themselves, or are they so regarded?

There is still a possible case not included in this supposition—viz., if the State wishes to institute investigations in order to enlarge the boundaries of the sciences on which the professions and pursuits are founded, and thus give to a few an education quite beyond what would be possible in a private office, this may be deemed a public good which it ought to pay for. Under this head might come the highest experiments in agricultural chemistry, or inquiries into the occult causes which affect the sanitary condition of a city, or questions of law, constitutional or otherwise, which no lawyer's office affords the means of investigating. If it should be admitted that the common routine of instruction for professional and industrial pursuits should not be at the expense of the State, it might still be reasonably claimed that the actual enlargement of the boundaries of science by these higher investigations should be at public cost.*

We are so accustomed to look to Germany as the land of university study, that it would seem a just demand upon any one who touches this subject to suggest at least to what extent and in what respects the German universities should be taken as models in any new departure. In one respect these institutions are above all praise—that is, in the thoroughness, minuteness, exclusiveness, and perseverance, not to say obstinacy, with which the professors prosecute original investigations and experiments in their several departments, bring out the results in their lectures, and publish them in their books to the world. They do not choose a branch of science, accept a professorship with reference to its investigation and elucidation, and then set

---

* Professional education has rarely been at the expense of the State in this country; theological, never. Michigan is quite exceptional. The facts are substantially these: Besides the candidates for the professions of law and medicine, those for civil engineering and pharmaceutical chemists or druggists are prepared in the university. As to the civil engineers, they are so mixed up with the literary department that it is difficult to determine whether they actually make the support of the university cost more than it would without them. A similar remark may be made in regard to the pharmacy school. The students probably about pay their way. The law school cost a considerable amount in the starting; but the fees are understood now to pay the expenses, and even a little over. The medical school has always cost the fund largely beyond what it has brought in; and of late this excess has been increased by the advance of salaries. It amounts to about $8,000. These schools are all founded on the theory of being supported by the university fund, though some of them, as it appears, approach a self-support, not charging them with their participation in those provisions which are common, or with the interest upon the real estate.

23

themselves to getting up popular lectures, articles, or books on other subjects. Few exceptions would be found to the statement, that whatever they publish in periodicals or books is first brought out in their lectures for the class-room. Liebig did not find time outside of his laboratory work to write popular letters for the Allgemeine Zeitung on chemistry and agriculture—these are all the result of exclusive and obstinate devotion to one class of studies in the laboratory. Ranke did not write his great works, the history of the popes of the 17th and 18th centuries, and his history of the Reformation, outside of his university work, but as a part of it, and so of all his works. So his most distinguished disciple, Sybel, did not write his work on the French Revolution as extra to his scholastic labors, but as a part of them.

But German professors in the universities do not feel their responsibility to see that students actually learn that which is taught them. There should be some kind of daily examination upon the subjects gone over, and it is to be hoped that no plan for a new system of proper university work will be introduced without adequate provision for this want. But with even this abatement of Germany's merits, it is the best place in the world for those who are disposed to study in order to prepare themselves for special fields of labor as teachers, and is fast becoming the school of American professors.

At those forks of the road which individuals and na-tions are constantly meeting in the journey of their de-velopment, it becomes them to know as well as pos-sible the direction which they should take in order to reach most speedily their truest and highest destiny. It is not proposed here to furnish a chart in which shall be marked all the turns and windings and wayside objects of the path of progress, but only to indicate its general direc-tion—its leading incidents—and suggest a few cautions, which, whether they arise from well or ill founded appre-hensions, may aid in securing our safety. Some of these have been fairly indicated above; a few more remain, which may all be comprehended in one general proposition, viz : *That the course taken will be successful in the ratio, and* ONLY *in the ratio of its conformity to the Creator's purpose, known or unknown, in the constitution of the human mind, and its habitation, the world.*

No law will absolutely remit its claim, or indeed any portion of that claim, or its penalty; for all apparent instances of such remission are but the checks which one law interposes to the action of another. The taking of poison is followed by its natural effect in the loss of health or of life ; if taken in order to produce death, a moral law is broken, and we call the act suicide whether the purpose was effected or not. Sound theology will make even the divine act for saving the world but another law of the Creator interposed as a check to the natural workings of sin—the law of divine mercy limiting without violating justice.

Most minds have an impression so strong that it might almost be deemed a divine prophecy recorded in the human soul, that the world is destined to some grand result to be obtained in the way of perpetual progress. This may be the growth of blind hope ; it may come from an observation of the tendencies shown in history, from the feeling that a wise and beneficent Ruler of the universe must in the end produce perfection in the working out of His purposes, from revelation, or from all these combined. This hope of all humanity is doubtless in some way to be realized, and partly indeed in the present state of being.

But this conclusion does not involve the realization of the theories of those who prate of the destined progress of particular nations. Nations have risen from obscurity and barbarism, and have fallen again into decay and returned to barbarism. History shows the causes of all this in what may be called the world's *education*. So far as shall be introduced into education elements discordant with the Creator's plan, as shown in human nature and the world in general, the results will be imperfect and pernicious ; this plan being perceived and followed, they will be increasingly glorious.

If Christianity is a true and divine system, its author will not allow it to be rejected or corrupted without testifying his displeasure. This has been realized in parts of Western Asia, Northern Africa, and Eastern Europe, where another system has supplanted it, and in those parts of Europe and America, where its growth has been cramped by the substitution of a mere ritual service for its spirit.

There is in our country little to complain of in this respect. Our teaching has been largely done by those whose characters have been decidedly Christian. Our institutions have been mostly endowed and carried on by such, and they have everywhere had at least a fair field for free action. If theological education has been excluded from State support, it has not been from hostility to religion. States would doubtless like to repair this apparent injustice if they could, by allowing the sects to establish chairs of dogmatic theology around their universities and enjoy common provisions in their aid. There are many things common to the professions and to the whole world of letters, and these things make us wish that the clergy and the other professions should not be separated by that impassable gulf which has often lain between them—that ministers, lawyers, and physicians should be side by side in their preparation, as they are to be in the practice of their professions.

Several features at least of this antagonism between the clergy and the other professions and pursuits should be removed. They ought not to be ever mutually serving notices upon each other to keep off from their respective grounds; they should rather welcome each other. Man is a unit; truth is a unit: no one can suppress any function of the one or the other without causing a mischief which will vary as the value of the suppressed function.

God's teaching in material nature and in special revelation, if indeed He has given us such, are but parts of one system of truth, which must confirm, support, and supplement each other. Nor can we make any such division as into material and immaterial existence. Revelation can not reach us without becoming mixed up with nature, nor can the world of matter be studied without justifying conclusions reaching quite beyond its limits. God will not be satisfied with those who neglect either of these branches of study as not concerning them, and content themselves with but a part of His system of truth.

The Christian minister may indeed leave the details of natural history to those who have chosen this field as a specialty; but he should inform himself in regard to their accepted conclusions, and even their conjectures, and give them their true value in his course of teaching. On the other hand, the naturalist may relieve himself of the details of the philological, critical, and historical study of those books which claim to be divinely inspired; but no one may neglect to make a fair and honest effort to settle practically for himself the claims of these books, so as to give them their relative importance in the great system of truth and life. The parties need to get nearer together, and occupy more common ground, to make the labors of the one supplementary to those of the other, each accepting and incorporating into his system all the established conclusions of the other. We have had too much evidence of the one-sidedness of all systems which leave out either nature or revelation. The hope of greater harmony in this respect is not visionary, and there is no place so important as a university to provide for it.

In the State universities the question of religion may always be embarrassing. It can not, however, be regarded as differing in principle from any other upon which men think variously, unless it be on the ground of its transcendent importance. If nothing is to be taught upon which men do not think alike, then teaching may be suspended, for no subject can be traced far in any direction without ramifying into disputed territory. Religious thought may be seldom expressed in scientific teaching, but it can never be ruled out of a university short of employing teachers who do not think, and these seldom prove successful.

The truth and claims of revealed religion can not be excluded from historical inquiry. Christianity has been the greatest factor in the world's progress; at least, it has *appeared* to be so. It is so interwoven with all history that the inquirer can not take a step without encountering it in some way. If the historical teacher should ignore the career of Alexander the Great, or Julius Cæsar, or Mahomet, or Charles V., though each of these careers except that of Mahomet was brief and of uncertain influence, he would justly be deemed unworthy of his place. How if he ignore a history and doctrine which meet him at every step of inquiry, from the opening to the closing scene in the world's historic drama?

Nor can the teacher of philosophy in a university escape the question of religion and do justice to that which is in his own mind, and that of every pupil who visits his classroom. It is better that it be met fairly and honestly.

The most important question which remains to be discussed in connection with this general subject, relates to the part which the female sex shall have in this progressive work. The difficulty which has hitherto beset this inquiry has grown mainly out of the prejudiced and heated feeling with which it has been pursued. And this feeling has arisen very naturally from the course which the discussion has more recently taken. In the *first* place, it has brought into antagonism parties which, from the delicate nature of their mutual feelings, had never before met upon the polemic field. Hence, not only the preliminary skirmishes, but the opening of the real conflict, has shown many of the features of the mock heroic. The case has been not unlike that of the little boy whose father has sportively invited him to a gladiatorial contest. The former, feeling no responsibility for his own defense, and the latter having no disposition to strike, finds himself, with the growing excitement and earnestness of the boy, forced to a precipitate retreat.

Upon this serio-comic combat of the sexes, the world of spectators has looked with an interest ever deepening and countenances ever changing according as the serious or comic has seemed to prevail. And the case has, too, been greatly complicated and the mutual animosities increased by the parts which great portions of each sex have either quietly or openly taken in direct opposition to the claims of the champions of their respective sexes. Perhaps the most intense feeling has been among that large body of women who deem themselves misrepresented by those who have professed to speak for them; and this has breathed itself quietly forth in the social and domestic circles, and found its utterance through a few of their own sex, and more of the other; and their frown has rather exasperated the claimants of an advanced position for women; while men who have joined in the advocacy of these claims have, in various ways, subjected themselves to the suspicion of other motives than that of honest conviction.

Further, intelligent and strong-minded women have expended their strength unduly upon formal efforts to prove their equality with men. If such men as Plato, Aristotle, Descartes, and Locke, or Kepler, Newton, and Laplace, or Homer, Dante, and Milton, had each announced the proposition that he, in his own department, was the greatest man of his age, they would have excited a just indignation against themselves, been diverted from their true missions, and failed to prove the very thing of which the general admission has made formal proof needless. But a large share of the literary efforts of women has been bestowed upon the formal proof of the equality of their sex with the other, or questions on this general subject, such as co-education and the right of voting or holding office. They have availed themselves of sarcasm and other advantages which the gallantry of men has offered them, instead of keeping distant, as Sherman did in his grand march, from the points which he would force to surrender. The effect of all this has been bad; but the general voice is so decided that the peril is probably past.

We can perhaps now dismiss party feeling, and unite upon a course which shall refer the whole subject, so far as education is either directly or indirectly concerned, to the free arbitration of the universal law of supply and demand.

This would require : 1. That so far as public provision is made for education, it shall be with reference to the equal education of the two sexes together, in the same institutions, and according to the free demand of each, as expressed by themselves or parents; or, in other words, this provision shall ignore the distinction of sex, and be offered freely to both sexes upon the same conditions. 2. It would be unjust to those who believe that woman's peculiar sphere calls for a peculiar and separate education, if no provision were made for them; it might oppress the larger class in an attempt to meet the wishes of the smaller. On the other hand, it may be a question whether those who have insisted upon co-education and female equality have not thereby unwittingly renounced all claim to separate provision in medical schools.

Legislation, whether by the State or by school boards, should not attempt to forestall or coerce public opinion, but should, so far as it is decided and legitimate, provide for it, leaving the social question as to the pursuits and professions which are proper for women to society itself. Then those who prepare for labors which the public do not demand at their hands, will make just the mistake which thousands of the other sex have made, and those of them who accept the verdict of society somewhat quietly, will fare better than those who dedicate the remainder of their lives to complaining that the world is out of joint, and to efforts to set it right.

As to the mental improvement of women with reference to its happy influence upon personal, social, and domestic life, there is no reason why it may not be obtained to the same extent as in case of men, and in the same schools, where the sexes may as properly meet as in churches or public lectures.

Women will not continue to prepare for avocations in which they will not be employed; but the question will arise whether the public ought to bear the expense of the professional education of a class whose services will not be required. It will suffice to answer, that their services not being called for, few will be educated and the cost will be small; it will be worth while to expend a little in the settlement of such a question; and, furthermore, in some fields of labor once occupied only by men—the medical profession, for instance—women will, to some extent, find an appropriate field.

It is safe to predict that the verdict upon which the public mind will finally settle on this subject, will not ignore all distinction of employment as founded upon sex. That which has its support in physiology will remain; life-long public occupations will be nearly all in the hands of men, for the marriage of a woman will always be deemed to disqualify her for such, and as this will be looked upon in almost every instance as possible, few women will be called to such places. It may be doubted whether the relative occupations of the sexes will ever be essentially changed. Woman's less physical strength and power of endurance speak the will of the Creator in a language not to be safely disregarded. She can not perform the same amount and kind of service with man. There are exposures which would interfere with a woman's response to professional calls, where traveling by night and in solitary places should be necessary. A feeling of gallantry on the part of men would forbid them to call for certain services of women, and this will never be extinguished until we return to a lower order of civilization.

There is, too, a sentiment in all civilized society, which provides for the want of more paying employments for certain classes of women. In but few domestic circles would a male relative, even a son or brother, without occupation, be tolerated as a permanent guest or pensioner, while in many families a female friend so living would be regarded as conferring an obligation on the family rather than incurring one herself. So far as women desire to find employments to relieve this sense of dependence, they ought to

have them, and no prejudice should stand in the way of
this; but it would be sad if this should be carried to the
extent of annihilating the class of females who are blessing
so many households by their presence, and obtaining in
return a free and honorable living.

But physiology does in some respects fix a permanent
and impassable boundary between the sexes as to occupations. The burdens and cares of maternity can not be
shifted at will from one sex to the other; she who accepts
the condition which makes her a mother, should cheerfully
submit to the natural consequences, and these, if they do
not necessitate a life-long seclusion from public and official
labor, must subject its performance to interruptions which
must often continue for months in succession. Nor can it
be concealed that there exists in society generally a feeling
that the great body of the female sex would, on receiving
eligible offers of marriage, enter into that relation, and
having done so, would renounce all steady occupations
which might take them away from domestic duties. This
feeling must from the nature of the case be perpetual, and
will prevent both individuals and boards of trust from giving permanent and responsible places generally to females.
This will fall in with that feeling toward the weaker sex
which would prevent employers from requiring of them what
they would of men in the same positions. Women, too,
without being conscious of it, will always continue to expect some consideration of their sex.

It were easy to show that differences of mental endowment, though less obvious, are, when sought out and placed
in the scales by which this general question is to be settled,
quite as decisive as the physiological grounds, and taken
together, they are convincing that the general assignment
of parts in civilized society to the sexes ought never to be
substantially different from the existing one. For mental
improvement, they will have the same chance and in the
same schools and universities; in a limited number of instances where they choose to renounce domestic life, or
Providence has not burdened them with its cares, women

will be received and employed in professional labor ; but their sphere will never be essentially changed until the world shall turn to go backward, and the great body of women themselves feel most deeply hurt by the persistent attempt now being made to force them, or admit their sisters to more prominent public or business positions.

The importance of a library as connected with a university, is so universally admitted as to make its discussion here scarcely worth while. But this subject is not viewed with due discrimination. There is scarcely a library in the world of which the complaint is not daily heard of its utter inadequacy to meet the demand for which it was gotten up. Professors often have books ordered as indispensable, and then never look at them or direct others to them. Indeed, this might be said of most professors, and the better class of them too. Many books can not be used to advantage in their work either by professors or students. The latter must occupy but a third part of the time for a term upon a subject represented in the library by a thousand volumes. How many of them can each examine to advantage? Certainly but two or three typical ones on each general subject of study. These should be of the kind which furnish the best stimulants and guides to thought ; they should be clear, exact, and spirited expressions of fundamental thought, and each should be a complete discussion of the subject which it takes up.

Hence the inquiry is naturally made : What is the use of so great libraries as are generally deemed necessary in connection with universities? The books which now give inspiration and direction to thought will in a few years be dropped from all ordinary use, and take their places upon the shelves to mark permanently the steps of development in their respective branches. Then those books which belong to all ages, though they be less than one in ten thousand of those which have been published, have become not a few in the course of 3,000 years. Here are the elements of large accumulation. Further, books never designed to be read, and others never worth reading, become often indispensable in processes of investigation, and sometimes the want of one such is the want of a link in the chain. The largest libraries in the world are often insufficient to relieve special inquirers from the necessity of going elsewhere for aid. There is scarcely any limit to the amount to be expended upon libraries, even with the most careful selection.

Students, after getting their lessons thoroughly, have little time for investigation ; but it would be a very defective scholastic education which should be closed without several opportunities of trial in this kind of work ; and where the numbers are thousands, the fields over which their inquiries spread embrace the whole empire of science and literature, the collection of books should be the largest and best. The professors need still larger provisions. And then the great attraction which brings men of leisure for literary pursuits to either settle around a university or visit one, is its library, and such men really add to the value of a university by helping to create its atmosphere.

When a university has such supply of books, with provision for perpetual increase, and has placed over it as librarian a man whose mental and moral traits command general respect—whose varied learning and administrative skill are such that he can guide all inquirers to such of these collected treasures as each may need to consult, and who can do all this so quietly and unostentatiously as not to make the impression that he does anything, or merits any praise, then that institution has in its library a crowning glory. This forms a center of attraction which must bring to it all who have the true spirit of inquiry. It should be kept nearly all the time open, even in vacations. Here, at all hours, until long after the voices of teacher and pupil have ceased in the class-rooms, whether by sunlight or gaslight, the beneficent influence of reading and study is exerted, and is in value immensely beyond the ratio of the expenditure upon it. It is not merely a source of good—it is an antidote to ills.

As to the pay of the teacher's profession, it has formerly

been much less than it should be, and the tendency has been for some years to an advance, which has in some places probably reached its limit. Indeed, extravagant ideas have prevailed in some sections; the remembrance of the meager allowance of teachers in the past, together with a recognition of their eminent services, has given rise to better views, and sometimes led to an extreme, and schools have vied with each other in raising salaries. Our expectation is not that this will continue in sections where education has reached its most advanced stage; but in a large portion of our country, it is in an incipient, or rather a transition state, and until these sections are better supplied, the demand will exceed the supply, and salaries will be good.*

The presidency of a university is of such importance as to merit notice in any view of what such institution ought to be. Its true purpose, and the best way of accomplishing it, are the points to be considered. In the German

---

*All have heard of the almost starving salaries of German professors. One would, however, get a different idea from Mr. Hoyt's " Education in Europe and America." He says (page 331) that he has often " been surprised to find the incomes of some German professors amounting to from $5,000 to $8,000 per annum—the equivalent of at least $10,000 in this country." He states the income of the University of Berlin, including students' fees, at $150,000—only $102,000 of which, he says, is expended upon salaries. The number of professors he gives as 180; and, of course, their average pay must be less than $600 a year. This would not support 13 professors at $8,000 a year. What becomes of the remaining 167? We should be surprised to find that the salaries of German professors averaged $500. The salaries of rectors in the first-class gymnasia—they have more labor and responsibility than university professors—are 1,800 thalers, about $1,300. From this, they range down to 1,200 thalers—$867. The other teachers receive from $360 to $750. The largest pay we have ever personally known in case of a university professor in Germany, was that of Baron Von Liebig, in Munich, whom the King of Bavaria called thither at a salary of 9,000 florins—$3,600—after he had gained his immense reputation. If he received an additional $1,000 in the way of fees and otherwise—and that is quite too much to suppose—it would give him but $4,600. We should be surprised to learn that the average pay of the professors in the University of Munich in 1860—the time of our acquaintance with it—was as high as $400 a year; and this, after reducing it by paying the salaries of Liebig, Sybel, Lassaulx, Pötzl, Pettenkofer, and others, would make some next to nothing.

universities this office is an annual appointment, made by vote of all the faculties, and the incumbent is called rector. It passes from one to another of the different faculties, unless, as sometimes happens, one renounce its right in favor of another. It is there little more than nominal.

This officer is, in our country, generally president of the board of trust, and of each faculty, and the united faculties, if they ever meet. Thus he unites the whole. He is the natural medium of communication between the parts, and especially between trustees and professors. If he is absolutely impartial, of quick and perfect discernment, capable of appreciating all branches of the work placed under his supervision, of selecting the men who can do it best, and seeing that it is done; if he is honest and fearless, and, at the same time, conciliatory in stating his convictions to all concerned, especially to the board, so as to bring about the needed action, then this office works justly and beneficently. But when a president fails in any of these points, the office fails accordingly to realize its true end. If the president has his favorites, or if some of the officers of the institution doubt their right to go directly to members of the board with their wishes, and others do this freely in private, and the true office of the president is practically ignored while it still nominally exists, anarchy often ensues; and it is still worse if the president retains the full confidence of the board while he fails to meet his own responsibilities. If the university system should be modified, as suggested, by advancing the preparatory schools so as to make them include the freshman and sophomore years in college, some modification of the office of president might naturally follow.

The infelicities hinted above as possible, might perhaps be partially obviated by a rule that all matters pertaining to the work of instruction, and to cabinets and libraries, should first be discussed in a university senate, composed of all the faculties, and agreed upon there before they should be presented for action by the board.

There is a point here more likely than any other to be

in some future day the occasion of revolutionary movements in State universities. It has caused all the difficulties thus far; it will cause them still. It is not, on the one hand, safe that men should be elected to places by regents, without consulting the existing corps of workers as to their probable adaptation to those places; nor, on the other, that existing faculties *alone* should be consulted as to the persons to fill their vacant places. On the first supposition, uncongenial elements would be thrown together; on the other, any faculty could perpetuate the class of men whom it might for any reason desire, while equally good or better judgments outside would be neglected. There is one great fact which would scarcely be believed, if the examples were not everywhere to be found, that professors, and even presidents, without being conscious of it, are shy of introducing men of marked talents, culture, and honest independence of character, into their number, and prefer those who are sure to be sufficiently unambitious and obsequious; and hence the perpetuation of faculties made up of men who never rise above the pure pedagogue. We know of no cure for this but that trustees thoroughly inform themselves of the facts and act accordingly. This is what they seldom do. They do not give the necessary time. There might be professors in a university who did nothing, or nothing to any good purpose, and the board be quite ignorant of it. But it would be still worse if boards of trust, becoming in general satisfied of such a state of facts, should commence hasty action without concurrence and advice from the really working part of the university corps." No university could possibly survive such action. This whole class of subjects is only suggested, without any attempt at solution, with the hope that they may attract attention in any reformatory movement which may arise.

The equalization of labor and pay offers a question of no small difficulty. Grounds of discrimination in pay are sometimes found, which indeed seem just; but when distinctions are once made, they furnish a lever which others will continue to use, until they raise themselves up to the

level of those who receive higher salaries, and the cases are
not infrequent of professors quietly favoring plans for raising the salaries of their fellows, in the secret hope of soon
being able to use this precedent in their own favor. A salary
is sometimes raised to save a professor, generally without
success, but others are glad to see it, for their own purposes.
The true way is to put salaries where they ought to be,
and not raise them, either to save or obtain a desirable man.
No endowment fund is large enough to stand a process of
this kind, when once fairly inaugurated.

The contrast between this country and Germany is, that
there the highest order of learning and talent is mainly
collected in the universities. Those who have traveled
there will probably remember to have been asked such questions as : " *With what university is Emerson connected?*" As
if it could not be otherwise than that such a man must be a
professor. In this country the highest order of mind is not
so sure of these appointments. There they are substantially
made as the result of impartial examination in some form.
Here it is simply the choice of some one professor, who
inquires what young man can best assist for a year or two
in teaching some branch of study for which he must provide, and one so started is too likely to be shoved along on
the track upon which accident gave him his start.

There is much which might be said in regard to the
prospects and perils of the government, external and internal, of our State universities. Whether there is danger
of their being seized and held by parties and sects, and
perpetuated in their interests, or thrown into anarchy by
some of the changes to which universal suffrage shall lead,
involves the most important questions, and perhaps all that
need to be inquired into here. That such results are
at least possible, all will admit. The former of these has,
indeed, occurred in case of Harvard College, which is now
held, with power of perpetuating their hold, by those who
do not at all represent the average religious opinions of the
educated and intelligent classes of the State as now existing, much less of early patrons and friends ; and the find-

ing of examples of anarchy in the early management of
the affairs of our State universities, may be left to the
reader ; for he can not go amiss of them. It will in general be true, that at the very point where an institution
passes beyond the danger of the latter of these results, it
becomes more exposed to that of the former. These points
call for more minute inquiry, and irl making this it will be
better to take a rapid survey of the whole field.

There is an instinctive sense of right which calls for the
perpetuation of all funds to the uses for which they were
given. This applies alike to those which have arisen from
private munificence and those which owe their crigin to
State grants. The latitude allowed in the use of these gifts
will be greater or less, according to the stipulations originally connected with them. The fund which Congress
has given for a university in any new State may not be diverted to the support of common schools, or mere academies ; but this principle will not require that the idea of a
university which prevailed when any particular grant was
made, shall be crystallized, and remain in defiance of all
progress the unchangeable model of the institution to which
the income of the fund must be applied. Every kind and
amount of development and progress is admitted in the
terms of such a grant. An endowment given in general for
a professorship of geology can not limit the teaching of its
holder to what that science might have been at the time when
it was made ; but if its income shall be applied to teaching
chemistry, it is diverted from its purpose. If a fund is raised
for the distinct purpose of ministering to the interests of a
sect of Christians, it can not rightfully pass out of their hands,
at least if that sect shall still exist. If a legacy should be
left to endow a lectureship on Christian evidences, it might
indeed be plausibly maintained that a course of lectures
against the truth of the Christian system came within its
scope ; but the inquirer's mind goes instinctively back to
the views of the testator and determines accordingly as to
to its being a just or unjust use of the fund. Diversions
of endowments from their original design have doubtless

24

been frequent, especially when they have occurred by a long series of progressive steps. The judiciary has seldom been invoked in such cases, and mainly because no party has had interest enough to institute a process. In cases, however, of proposed *removals* of institutions from places where they had been established as the conditions of donations, this has been done, and with uniform results. Nor could judicial decisions be more uncertain in other cases involving diversion of funds from their proper uses. The well-known decision of the Supreme Court of the United States, delivered by Chief Justice Marshall, in the Dartmouth College case, is a typical one, involving the entire principle. It declares the inviolability of the original contract by which the college had been endowed and chartered, as against a law of New Hampshire, by which an attempt had been made to annul this contract. It restored the president, trustees, and professors who had been removed by this new State legislation. This decision was founded upon that clause of the constitution of the United States which declares that, " No State shall pass any bill of attainder, *ex post facto law or law impairing the obligation of contracts*,"* and could be applied to nothing but the interference of State legislation with the execution

---

* It must be admitted that much of the legislation of Michigan having reference to the university fund has been in violation of this clause of the constitution of the United States. It might be maintained that this language would not forbid a State to release a party from the obligations of a contract, to which it was itself the other party. Let this be admitted. Will it then follow that the State might accept $12 per acre for university lands for which the purchaser had contracted to pay $20? It is first to be inquired whether the State is really a party, or only the trustee of a party to this contract. Congress gave the fund, and the State accepted the trust, involving all the obligations of faithfulness in its management. But let it be admitted that the State would have a right to act as though the fund were its own and not a trust, the legislation which accepts $12 instead of $20, violates a contract made with the board of regents, upon which they inaugurated their action. On any supposition, the legislation which releases an obligation to the State, violates one which the State has entered into with the regents. This legislation has much of it been " *ex post facto*," and has impaire d the obligation of the State itself to fulfill its own contracts.

of this trust; but in principle it carried everything with it. If a sovereign State can not interfere with a trust corporation which it has once chartered, much less can any other power rightfully do so. In this decision the highest judicial tribunal in the land has but spoken out that which the popular conscience everywhere firmly holds; indeed, Mr. Webster's argument in the case will be regarded by every reader as little more than the utterance of a universal conviction—a trust or grant is to be administered accqrding to the expressed or known purpose of the grantor. It is his own property, to be applied by the grantee for him..

The application of this principle to State universities is not distant nor difficult. Nor is there any difference growing out of the fact that a fund was given by Congress, or by a State legislature, or by a private donor, except as the original stipulations differ, and there is no right in any case to revoke the grant or modify its terms after it shall have been made and accepted.†

The State of North Carolina once repealed a grant to the university of that State, and one of its own courts declared the repealing law unconstitutional and void. If a State can not repeal, modify, or divert its own grants, much less can a State or any other power rightfully divert a fund of which it is a mere trustee, in any respect whatever from the purpose of the grantor.

The main question here will be in regard to what will in any case constitute a violation of the real design of a grant to a State institution. If Congress has granted lands in any State or Territory for the use and support of a university, with no conditions, leaving the State to determine all except the general design of the grant, then the legislature of such State has the largest possible responsibility; it has entire freedom of choice as to the agencies by which its university is to be managed, and is therefore responsible for choosing the very best, unless this is forbidden by some principle which is justly deemed mandatory in the case.

---

† This precedent may doubtless be abused, but the cases will seldom be those of educational corporations, generally those of a commercial nature.

Let, for instance, the general conviction of fifty years
ago, that the organizations of a religious denomination are
best adapted to choose and execute plans of literary institutions, be supposed to prevail in the legislature of the
State, is there any principle which forbids this legislature
to commit its trust to some religious body to be administered
for the State? Or if it were indeed admitted that this
course would produce the most economical and efficient
government, should the undue advantage which it would
give to such sect, and its consequent failure to represent
and summon to its support all other sects, classes, and
interests among the people of the State, be decisive against
it? A State should, as nearly as possible, provide for all
classes of its people, and it may be justly doubted whether
it should ever permanently and irrevocably delegate its
trusts, even to a body which at present may promise their
best management.

If, in any case, the United States grant should not be
sufficient to support a university, and the State should not
be inclined to make appropriations from its own treasury in
aid of such grant, the latter might pass the institution over
to some similar one of sectarian origin, which should carry
on the two institutions thus united. The right acquired in
this way would not be easily revoked; but any stipulations
which the State should insert in such contract would be
inviolable.

The danger that a university governed by a board
elected by the people, or appointed by the State executive,
may fall into the hands of a sect or party, is not obvious.
It has generally been deemed hazardous to the harmonious
working of an institution if its officers shall be appointed
without the recommendation of the existing faculties, and
especially the president; so the president is seldom appointed without some, at least, informal recommendation
or concurrence on part of the faculties. It is easy to conceive, that in case of a very long presidential term, the
professors might become mostly of the party or sect of the
president, and this might lead to a perpetuation of the

same in the faculties and presidency. This is suggested
as a possibility; but the danger in most directions is remote. No board of trust originating with the State executive or the people would concur in such nominations.
They would, at least, veto those which looked too much
like perpetuating a sect or party, and ask for others. And
even in case of the most complete success in the installa-
tion of a sect, their course would be most damaging to
themselves. They would stand before the people as objects of suspicion and jealousy; they would be more
strictly watched than if they had been so selected as fairly
to represent the whole people, and perhaps they would be
forced to do better work, and so the State would derive an
incidental advantage from this injustice.

The greatest danger is that evangelical Christianity will
be quite driven out of this class of institutions; but this is
not so imminent as some might think. The State naturally
desires to meet the views and wishes of all classes of the
people; and none have been better patrons of learning
than those who are most truly Christian. This class may
combine and draw off with them all they can, and assert
their rights through the press and at the polls. If beaten
finally, they could withdraw to the schools of their several
denominations, which are numerous and well endowed;
and these would thrive, and State institutions, in spite of
large endowments, would decay. The danger which we
have attempted to appreciate is therefore remote, and the
people hold a guaranty against it.

It would be a great calamity to extinguish the colleges
and other institutions in this country which have been
founded upon the funds of religious bodies. They have
done our best work in college education; they are to do
much yet, and to be important regulators of the whole educational enterprise, whether directly carried on by them
or not. It indicates little judgment, and the want of a
duly grateful remembrance of the past, to depreciate these
schools. It is an attempt to kick away the ladder by which
culture has reached its present stage of elevation, and that,

too, long before the day when we shall be no longer in need of its use can be anticipated. With the strongest desire to see State universities at the head of State systems of schools prospering wherever there is a chance for them, we should regret the accomplishment of this result at the expense of a war upon denominational institutions. It is an error to suppose that these schools teach sectarianism. Those which do this are exceptional, if such exist at all. The only tendency in this way is by indirect influences. It is an error also to regard them as too exclusively favoring the ancient languages and mathematics in disregard of the just claims of the natural sciences and the arts. They have done what they could do. When higher education without them would have utterly failed, they kept its wheels revolving. They secured quite as well as is done now, the best men, and all the men within the reach of their meager resources, and these few did the best work, and all the work they could do, and nearly all that was done.

Those, too, who compare our earlier with our later college training, very greatly to the disadvantage of the former, so far as sound learning and mental discipline are concerned, are gravely at fault. Jonathan Edwards, Timothy Dwight, Eliphalet Nott, Daniel Webster, Edward Everett, Francis Wayland, and others of their class, earlier, and even later, received their college training when the course embraced, besides the two ancient languages and some pure and mixed mathematics, scarcely more than rhetoric and mental and moral philosophy; and we should hardly wish to consider these men and the generation of college-trained men to which they belonged as sadly deficient in sound learning in comparison with those of our more favored period. Indeed, the multiplication of studies—and all have not yet been introduced into the course which ought to be—has had the effect, by extending culture over a larger surface, of making it more superficial, and of giving it less of strength and depth, and fully justifies the growing conviction of all wise educators, that the range of elective branches must be largely extended.

We have reason to rejoice that the increased resources of our present universities have enabled them so to multiply the branches taught in them ; but a little better acquaintance with that which the earlier colleges effected in the way of genuine culture would check the tendency to exuberant self-gratulation over our progress.

We can not better close the consideration of this subject than by an expression of the profound conviction that much is lost in power by an attempt to spread the mind over too wide a range of subjects ; that in order to remedy this evil, the general plan suggested in this chapter should be inaugurated, that the elements of all the natural sciences and all the languages which are to be acquired at all, should be secured before entering upon the university course, leaving this to be devoted entirely to that higher sphere of philosophical study in which the mind develops its power of thought and utterance, and to the closer and more detailed study of those particular sciences which are more or less nearly allied to the student's chosen field of life-labor. Those skeletons of the sciences which are not to be made specialties, which students have early formed in their minds, will gradually gather a body of flesh, and become without special application, all that the purposes of general culture require, and all this may be made the facile instrumentality to be employed in the mind's narrower sphere of special study and work.

How far the field of inquiry and experiment with reference to discovery, and beyond the needs of actual teaching, will be entered by university professors, can not be foretold with certainty. This must, however, take place to some extent. In Germany, most of this field is occupied by professors in the schools, which is not strictly true in England or America. It is not always, however, in their character as professors that those in Germany are occupied in original investigations. They are members of the various ducal, royal, and imperial academies of science, in which character they sometimes have special appropriations made to aid them in these inquiries. We think it would be found generally true in Germany that the work of special original inquiry is united with that of teaching in the professors of the universities. Pettenkofer, Bischoff, and the late Baron Liebig, at Munich; Bunsen, at Heidelburg; and Virchow, at Berlin, may be given as instances. It remains to be seen how far this field will open to our American professors. It has never been very systematically occupied in our country. While labor for invention, where the hope of p ivate gain has impelled to exertion, has been exceedingly active, there has been less stimulus applied to original scientific inquiry. The geological and other surveys provided for by the state and general governments have been the chief exceptions. Whether, with increase of resources, our universities will ever become, to any extent, places for this kind of work, remains to be seen. Individual munificence may make special provision for this purpose, and the general government may do it with far better prospect of achieving desirable results than by endowing and attempting to carry on a national university for purposes of instruction. Perhaps this may occur.*

---

* Since the completion of this chapter we have read the admirable little book of Dr. Porter, of Yale College, on "The American Colleges and the American Public," in which nearly all the subjects of this chapter, and not a few others, are discussed from another point of view. The book is commended to educators who have not yet seen it, and to whom this may come, as treating questions a discussion of which would have borne us beyond our purpose. The subjects of Dr. Porter's chapters are as follows: 1. Historical and introductory. 2. The studies of the American colleges. 3. The prescribed curriculum. 4. Text-books and lectures. 5. The enforcement of fidelity. 6. The evils of the college system, and their remedies. 7. The common life of the colleges. 8. The dormitory system. 9. The class system. 10. Laws and supervision. 11. The religious character of colleges. 12. The guardianship and control of the college. 13. The relation of colleges to one another. 14. The relation of colleges to schools of science. 15. Educational progress and reforms.

CHAPTER XV.

Conclusion.

WHETHER there is any good ground for expecting an early realization of something like that which we have presented in outline in the preceding chapter, and something corresponding to it down to the primary school, is an appropriate question for the conclusion of this work.

The state of culture in our country up to a certain time, was surveyed with reference to our educational prospects. We found prospective funds for education put into the possession of most of our new States and Territories, at periods far in advance of their readiness to use them. This state of things could not be presented by statistics, for no such existed; but the case was nevertheless made clear: and indeed in the utter failure, in most instances, to realize for a long time any substantial results, would be found sufficient proof that the country had not reached such condition of intelligence and wealth as to be able to use these funds.

Is the case different now? The greatest civil war that ever visited a civilized land, has been followed by but ten years of peace. It has left sad financial, sad social consequences, sad memories. It arrested in some parts the progress of scholastic culture; and yet there is now but one State in the Union without a school system; but two which have as yet made no provision for the education of colored children; and, as this is taken from the report of the commissioner of education for 1872, perhaps these exceptions may no longer exist. Here is progress!

All the new States and Territories have bases of action in their Congressional grants. These not only invite their attention to the subject, and aid them in making their beginnings, but operate in a compulsory way—necessitate action. If they have these grants, they feel compelled to use them; if they have squandered them, they feel bound to restore them. The agricultural gifts of 1862 have in some instances enabled the delinquent States to recover themselves, and in some, to establish a kind of State university where none existed before. It has made feeble ones strong; as the Vermont State University, endowed originally by the State with 29,000 acres of land, yielding but $2,500 income, which had been pieced out with donations and bequests, has been started anew by this grant of Congress. Whether the funds of State universities originated with Congress or the State legislatures, they come at last to the same thing—they are under the fostering care of the State. Those in North and South Carolina, Georgia, and Virginia were endowed by State grants. Those in all the States west of the Alleghanies, Kentucky excepted, arose from Congressional appropriations. In the latter, State aid has been already mixed in with the original fund, bringing all to much the same level.

And what do those who speak for the people say in regard to the establishing of State systems which shall embrace all in one, from the primary school to the university? The report of the superintendent of the schools of Illinois for 1872 says: "I would see every American State add to the elementary school, the grammar school; to the grammar school, the high school; to the high school, the State university; and to the State university, I would see the American Congress add a grand national university, as the fitting top-stone to the whole magnificent edifice." What the verdict of intelligent educators throughout the land west of the Alleghanies might be in regard to a great national university, may be doubtful—the subject has been discussed elsewhere in this work; but there is no doubt as to what the general voice would be on the other points of the passage quoted. This whole region, if not the entire country, is moving in the direction indicated, as rapidly as it is in the constitution of human society to move.

We have treated the University of Michigan as having been placed, by happy combinations of circumstances, in advance of all the institutions which have grown out of Congressional land grants. So it is. But, notwithstanding this, the success of several others, and perhaps to the keener gaze of eyes adjusted to greater distance of vision, of all the others, is as well assured as that of Michigan. Some States have appropriated much more largely relatively to their resources and the age of their universities than has Michigan. Some have recognized more fully than Michigan the principle that the State university is to be supported by State appropriations. The first college grant of Missouri was either squandered, or left unused for a generation ; but success there, is now placed beyond doubt. The States referred to in our preliminary sketch, as having founded their universities from their own funds—North and South Carolina and Georgia—have been held back by difficulties of which we at the North know little, and they have still, in the presence of the colored race, a problem by no means easy of solution ; but, considering all the circumstances, they are making most satisfactory progress, and their movements, first inaugurated nearly a century ago, will now be taken up where they were left, and urged to completion as rapidly as the rubbish which obstructs their way can be removed. It is but a question of time as to the rise in all our States of universities, in the sense indicated in our last chapter ; the preparatory schools will be advanced, and the small colleges will fall back to the rank there indicated, and become the feeders of these universities. We shall not attempt, however, to predict the length of the time which must intervene before this shall be accomplished.

The elements involved in the question as between State and denominational schools, have been incidentally brought into our work, and we can not well omit a contribution to this discussion. We shall not, however, take up the subject in a controversial way.

It can scarcely be seriously argued that governmental

provision, whether State or national, has as yet effected as much for higher education in this country as private donations.   In our first chapter it was claimed, indeed, that the principle of State support to these institutions was generally held in the colonies and the States formed from them from the beginning.   The State benefactions to Harvard and Yale were adduced in proof of this.   But then the State aid to these schools has been trifling in comparison with the private gifts and legacies.   So take our whole country through, any results as yet realized from governmental endowments as compared with the fruits of private munificence, have been small.   And if this question were applied to the future, it would be by no means certain which side could bring forward the soundest reasons for its claim.   On the one hand, the private donations for the last few years for higher education have been immense.   Not to go into particulars, the commissioner of education, in his report for 1872, gives over nine millions of dollars; the one for 1873 gives over eight millions for colleges and universities alone ; and this seems to be an increasingly popular form of beneficence in some quarters, perhaps most of all in the Methodist Episcopal Church.   What this tendency, falling in with prejudices which as yet largely prevail against State institutions, will finally effect, it is as yet impossible to predict.   On the other hand, Congressional grants have been large.   Some have indeed been squandered or injudiciously used ; a great portion of them lie dormant : but they have in them an immense power, if waked into activity by a strong public feeling and a right action in the States to which they have been made ; for in this way, where they have been wasted, they are likely to be restored, and where they remain in their integrity, to be supplemented by State grants, and from time to time, as confidence in these schools shall be acquired, by private benefactions.   The probability is now that this tendency will rule.

But these two classes of institutions will rather aid than injure each other.   They may, to some extent, even grow

into each other. State universities may have private benefactions, as has already occurred even in case of such as
are, like the University of Michigan, of purely governmental origin. Institutions, too, the birth and growth of
private munificence, may have State aid. This has been
true of Harvard and Yale. The so-called University of
the State of New York has no other purpose than the aid
of all the colleges in that State, so far as they shall attain to a certain rank. Some of the States placed their
agricultural grants of 1862 under the direction of the
trustees of institutions which originated in private gifts.
Cornell University, in New York, may be given as an example. Perhaps it has occurred to few that a process has
been begun which may possibly unify, whether for weal or
for woe, our whole system of higher education throughout
the country; indeed, this may occur by some turn in
either direction. All may be drawn more and more into
the hands of the State by a kind of mutual arrangement
and consent, as in the instances given; or States may
show, as some predict, that they are incapable of managing this branch of education, and gradually yield it to independent boards of trust, private benefactions to State institutions coming in to aid in bringing about this result.
Some one who can look a few centuries into the future
may take up this subject here where we leave it.*

---

* The report of the commissioner of education for 1873 came to hand
since the completion of this work; but it has been cursorily examined and
found to show a very rapid progress in the direction of a complete public
school system. All the Territories have adopted such system, and all will
have their universities. In the cities of the old States, the free school system is being extended and the property of various incorporated schools
being purchased and turned over to the city authorities for this purpose.
It will probably soon be satisfactorily proved that no private or denominational schools, unless they are prepared to furnish a nearly free education, can compete in the West with the free school system. Especially
will this be true of the academies or schools preparatory to the universities, though some Christian denominations are endeavoring still to establish such academies. We know, at least, that the Baptists are laboring,
to some extent, for this end. It is a question whether the money given for
this object is not really diverted from that evangelical work in which the

In this age of the world, the light of history has made it clear that a State can never safely deny or neglect the just claims of any important element of its population. The Roman empire did attempt this in case of the early Christians; but these claims forced their way to recognition. A hierarchy grew up which repeated this attempt in regard to Christians of a modified faith. This power did, indeed, succeed in keeping down the Paulicians, Albigenses, Waldenses, and the movements of Wyclif and Huss, only, however, to gather their elements as subterranean fires to break out with uncontrollable violence in the time of Luther. The ages in which accounts can be so long accumulating for settlement, seem to be past in nearly all lands. The day of retribution comes quicker now. If any government, whether under religious or anti-religious dictation, shall fail to regard all its popular elements in dispensing its favors, those elements will in the end enforce their claims. Our State institutions have, so far as we know, made a commendable, if not indeed an entirely successful effort, to treat with proper respect all the elements of the population for which they have been provided. If this shall be continued, it is safe to predict for them success and permanency; and if it were worth while, in this work, to express an opinion of the future school system of our country, it would be that the one indicated above is destined to prevail. All things are looking in this direction, and nothing but a series of great blunders on the part of the States can prevent such a result.

In the history of the University of Michigan, we trust that we have given that of a score of others, which, with fewer embarrassments, will soon attain to the ample meas-

---

donors would prefer to see it expended; whether it were not better to strengthen the pastorate in those centers where the higher schools are established, and thus labor for the conversion and Christian education, in their churches and Sunday-schools, of the young people whose education will be otherwise amply provided for. These academies will probably, when about half endowed, fall mostly into the hands of the public for union schools.

ure of its success, and that in our outline view of the future university, we have truly foreshadowed what the generation of students now pursuing their college studies will live to behold and enjoy in their children.

APPENDIX.

A.

REPORT RELATIVE TO APPROPRIATIONS OF PUBLIC LAND FOR THE PURPOSES OF EDUCATION, MADE TO THE SENATE OF MARYLAND, JANUARY 30, 1821.

The committee to whom was referred so much of the governor's message as relates to education and public instruction, beg leave to report:

That they concur with his excellency in believing education and a general diffusion of knowledge, in a government constituted like ours, to be of great importance, and that " in proportion as the structure of a government gives weight to public opinion, it is essential that public opinion should be enlightened." Your committee consider our government as emphatically a government of opinion. A general diffusion of knowledge, which is essential to its right administration, can not be effected, unless the people are educated. No high degree of civilization, of moral power and dignity, or of intellectual excellence ; no superiority in science, in literature, or in liberal and useful arts, which constitutes the noblest national supremacy, can be obtained without the aid of seminaries of learning. The establishment of literary institutions, then, of all grades, from the common school up to the university, becomes the first duty of the legislature of a free people.

Your committee are well aware of the difficulty, in the present embarrassed state of our pecuniary concerns, of providing the means of making education general. They are fully sensible that, at this time, large appropriations out of the public treasury for this purpose, all-important as it is, can not be expected. They deem it, therefore, their duty to recall to your notice a report and certain resolutions, presented to the senate at the last session, by a committee of a like nature with the present, which has been referred to your committee, as a part of the unfinished business. The object of those resolutions was to call the attention of Con-

25

gress and the legislatures of the several States to the public land as a fund from which appropriations for the purposes of education may with justice be claimed, not only by Maryland, but all the original States, and three of the new ones.

One thirty-sixth part of all the States and Territories (except Kentucky) whose waters fall into the Mississippi and the Gulf of Mexico, has been appropriated by Congress, wherever the Indian title has been extinguished, and provisions made for further appropriations, according to the same ratio, wherever the Indian titles may hereafter be extinguished, for the support of common schools, and other large appropriations have been made for the support of seminaries of a higher grade. Your committee are of opinion that the States, for whose benefit no such appropriations have been made, are entitled to ask them of Congress, not as a matter of favor, but of justice. That this may more fully appear, especially as the right of those States to an equal participation with the States formed out of the public lands, in all the benefits derived from them, has been doubted, your committee have deemed it proper to take a cursory view of the manner in which they have been acquired.

Before the war of the Revolution, and indeed for some years after it, several of the States possessed, within their nominal limits, extensive tracts of waste and unsettled lands. These States were all, at that epoch, regal and not proprietory provinces, and the crown, either directly or through the medium of officers, whose authority had been prescribed or assented to by the crown, was in the habit of granting those lands. The right of disposing of them was claimed and exercised by the crown in some form or other. They might therefore, with strict propriety, be called the property of the crown.

A question arose, soon after the declaration of independence, whether those lands should belong to the United States, or to the individual States within whose nominal limits they were situated.

However that question might be decided, no doubt could be entertained that the property and jurisdiction of the soil were acquired by the common sword, purse, and blood of all the States, united in a common effort. Justice, therefore, demanded that, considered in the light of property, the vacant lands should be sold to defray the expenses incurred in the contest by which they were obtained; and the future harmony of the States required that the extent and ultimate population of the several States should not be so disproportionate as they would be if their nominal limits should be retained.

This State, as early as the 30th of October, 1776, expressed its decided opinion, in relation to the vacant lands, by a unanimous resolution of the convention which framed our constitution and form of government, in the following words, viz: "*Resolved, unanimously,* That it is the opinion of this convention, that the very extensive claim of the State of Virginia to the back lands hath no foundation in justice, and that if the same or any like claim is admitted, the freedom of the smaller States and the liberties of America may be thereby greatly endangered; this convention being firmly persuaded that if the dominion over those lands should be established by the blood and treasure of the United States, such lands ought to be considered as a common stock, to be parceled out at proper times into convenient, free, and independent governments."

In the years 1777 and 1778, the General Assembly, by resolves and instructions to their delegates in Congress, expressed their sentiments in support of their claim to a participation in these lands in a still stronger language, and declined acceding to the confederation, on account of the refusal of the States claiming them exclusively, to cede them to the United States. They continued to decline on the same ground, until 1781, when, to prevent the injurious impression that dissension existed among the States occasioned by the refusal of Maryland to join the confederation, they authorized their delegates in Congress to subscribe the articles; protesting, however, at the same time, against the inference (which might otherwise have been drawn) that Maryland had relinquished its claim to a participation in the western lands.

Most of the other States contended, on similar grounds with those taken by Maryland, for a participation in those lands.

By the treaty of peace, in 1783, Great Britain relinquished to the United States all claim to the government, property, and territorial rights of the same and every part thereof.

The justice and sound policy of ceding the unsettled lands, urged with great earnestness and force by those States which had united in conquering them from Great Britain, strengthened by the surrender on the part of Great Britain of her rights of property and jurisdiction to the United States collectively, and aided moreover by the elevated and patriotic spirit of disinterestedness and conciliation which then animated the whole confederation, at length made the requisite impression upon the States which had exclusively claimed those lands; and each of them, with the exception of Georgia, made cessions of their respective claims within a few years after the peace. Those States were Massachusetts, Connecticut, New York, Virginia, North Carolina, and South Carolina; the charters of which, with the exception of New York, extended westwardly to the South Sea or Pacific Ocean. This circumstance gave to Massachusetts and Connecticut a joint claim, with Virginia, to such parts of the Northwestern Territory as came within the breadth of the charter of Virginia. New York, indeed, had an indefinite claim to part of it. Cessions, however, from all these States at length completed the title of the United States, and placed it beyond all controversy.

The State of North Carolina ceded its claim to the territory which now constitutes the State of Tennessee.

Georgia, whose charter also extended westwardly to the Pacific Ocean, at length, in 1802, ceded the territory which now constitutes the States of Mississippi and Alabama, except a small part on the south side of them, which was acquired under the treaty ceding Louisiana. The conditions of that cession were that the United States should pay $1,200,000 to Georgia, and extinguish the Indian title within the limits, which she reserved.

The United States have in this manner acquired an indisputable title to all the public lands east of the Mississippi.

All the territory west of the Mississippi, together with the southern extremity of the States of Mississippi and Alabama, was purchased of France for $15,000,000. This sum, as well as the sums required for the purchase of the Indian title to the public lands, was paid out of the treasury of the United States.

So far, therefore, as the acquisition of the public lands has been made by purchase, it has been at the common expense; so far as it has been made by war, it has been by the common force; and so far as it has been made by cessions from individual States, it has been upon the ground expressly stipulated in most of the acts or deeds of cession, that the lands should be "considered," to use the words of the act passed for that purpose by the State which made the largest cession, "as a common fund for the use and benefit of such of the States as have become, or shall become, members of the confederation or federal alliance of said States, according to their usual respective proportions in the general charge and expenditure, and shall faithfully and *bona fide* be disposed of for that purpose, and for no other purpose whatsoever."

In whatever point of view, therefore, the public lands are considered—whether as acquired by purchase, conquest, or cession—they are emphatically the common property of the Union. They ought to inure, therefore, to the common use and benefit of *all* the States, in just proportions, and can not be appropriated to the use and benefit of any *particular* State or States, to the exclusion of the others, without an infringement of the principles upon which cessions from States are expressly made, and a violation of the spirit of the national compact, as well as the principles of justice and sound policy.

So far as these lands have been sold, and the proceeds been received into the national treasury, all the States have derived a justly proportionate benefit from them. So far as they have been appropriated for purposes of defense, there is no ground for complaint, for the defense of every part of the country is a common concern. So far, in a word, as the proceeds have been applied to national, and not state purposes, although the expenditure may have been local, the course of the general government has been consonant to the principles and spirit of the federal constitution. But so far as appropriations have been made in favor of any State or States, to the exclusion of the rest, where the appropriations would have been beneficial, and might have been extended to all alike, your committee conceive there has been a departure from that line of policy which impartial justice, so essential to the peace, harmony, and stability of the Union, imperiously prescribes.

Your committee then proceed to inquire whether the acts of Congress in relation to appropriations of public lands have been conformable to the dictates of impartial justice.

By the laws relating to the survey and sale of the public lands, one thirty-sixth part of them has been reserved and appropriated in perpetuity for the support of common schools. The public lands are laid off into townships six miles square, by lines running with the cardinal points; these townships are then divided into thirty-six sections, each a mile square and containing 640 acres, which are designated by numbers. Section No. 16, which is always a central section, has invariably been appropriated (and provision has been made by law for like appropriations in future surveys) for the support of common schools in each township.

In Tennessee, in addition to the appropriation of a section in each township for common schools, 200,000 acres have been assigned for the endowment of colleges and academies. Large appropriations have also been made in Ohio, Indiana, Illinois, Mississippi, Alabama, Louisiana, Missouri, Michigan, and the Northwestern Territory, for the erection and maintenance of seminaries of learning of a higher grade than common schools. Your committee have not had an opportunity of ascertaining the exact amount of those appropriations; but, from such examination as they have been able to make, it is believed that they bear a smaller proportion to those of common schools than in Tennessee. Tennessee, in Seybert's Annals, is stated to contain 40,000 square miles, which is equal to 25,600,000 acres. One thirty-sixth part of this number of acres, which is the amount of the appropriation for common schools, is 711,111. The appropriation for colleges and academies in that State is, as above stated, 200 000 acres, being something less than two-sevenths of the common school appropriation. It is believed that the appropriations in the other States and Territories, for seminaries of a higher grade, do not amount to more than two-tenths or one-fifth of the appropriations for common schools. Your committee think they will not be far from the truth in estimating them at that proportion.

The States and Territories east of the Mississippi, which have had appropriations made in their favor for the support of literary institutions—that is to say, Ohio, Indiana, Illinois, Mississippi, Alabama, Michigan, and the Northwestern Territory—are estimated in Seybert's Statistical Annals to contain of unsold lands.. 200,000,000
Of lands sold... 11,697,125
To which add Tennessee................................... 25,600,000

And the aggregate number of acres in those States
　　will be........ 237,297,125
One thirty-sixth part of that aggregate number, being the amount of appropriations for common
　　schools, is... 6,591,586
Add one-fifth part of the common school appropriation as the appropriation for colleges and academies..:.. 1,318,317
And the aggregate number of acres appropriated for the purposes of education in Ohio, Indiana, Illinois, Tennessee, Mississippi, Alabama, Michigan, and the Northwestern Territory, will be..... 7,909,803
At two dollars per acre, which is less, according to

Seybert's Statistical Annals, than the average price of all the public lands which have heretofore been sold, the amount in money will be $15,819,806

Seybert estimates the lands purchased of France by the United States is 1803, at acres.................... 200,000,000

By the laws relating to the survey and sales of lands in Louisiana, Missouri, and Arkansas, appropriations of lands for the purposes of education, have been made after the same ratio as in the new States and Territories on the east of the Mississippi, and it is presumed the same policy will be adhered to in relation to the whole of the public lands on the west of that river. On that supposition the appropriations for the common schools—that is, one thirty-sixth part of 200,000,-000 acres—will be............................ 5,555,555

Add for colleges and academies one-fifth part of the appropriation for common schools 1,111,111

And the aggregate number of acres will be.......... 6,666,666⅔

At $2 per acre the amount in money will be $13,333,333⅓

To the aggregate number of acres appropriated for the support of literary institutions on the east side of the Mississippi...................................... 7,909,903·

Add the aggregate number of acres, which, if the system heretofore followed should be (as it ought to be) adhered to, will ultimately be appropriated for literary purposes on the west of the Mississippi.. 6,666,666⅔

And the total literary appropriations in the new States and Territories will be, acres.................. 14,576,569⅔

At $2 per acre the amount in money will be......... $29,153,130⅓

Such is the vast amount of property destined for the support and encouragement of learning in the States and Territories carved out of the public lands. These large appropriations of land, the common property of the Union, will inure to the exclusive benefit of those States and Territories. They are appropriations for state and not for national purposes; they are of such a nature that they might have been extended to all the States: they, therefore ought to have been thus extended. All the other States paid their full share for the purchase of the region west of the

Mississippi, and for the extinguishment of the Indian title on both sides of that river. Massachusetts, Connecticut, Virginia, North Carolina, South Carolina, and Georgia, beside paying their proportion of those expenses, ceded all their vacant territory on the east side of the Mississippi. All these States, therefore, might with great propriety complain of partiality and injustice if their applications to Congress for similar appropriations for like purposes should be refused.

But of this refusal they need have no apprehension, if they are true to their own interests, and are united in asserting them; for if, contrary to all reasonable expectation, the States which have already received the benefit of literary appropriations, should be opposed to the extension of them to their sister States, the latter are more than two-thirds in number of all the United States, and have a still larger proportion of representatives in Congress. These States are Vermont, New Hampshire, Maine, Massachusetts, Rhode Island, Connecticut, New York, New Jersey, Pennsylvania, Delaware, Maryland, Virginia, North Carolina, South Carolina, Georgia, and Kentucky, and together have one hundred and sixty-nine representatives in Congress. The favored States, on the contrary, have only seventeen representatives. The excluded States have, therefore, an overwhelming majority in Congresss, and have it completely in their power to make appropriations for the benefit of their literary institutions, upon the improbable supposition that the representatives of the favored States would oppose them in Congress; a supposition too discreditable to their character for justice to be admitted.

The magnitude of the appropriation that would be required to place the States which have not yet enjoyed any, for the purposes of education, upon an equal footing with those in whose favor they have already been made, can afford no just ground of objection. For, superior as the population of those States is, yet if the ratio of population be observed with regard to them which has been adopted in relation to the others—*i. e.*, one thirty-sixth part of the number of acres in the territory of each for common schools, and one-fifth part of that thirty-sixth for colleges and academies—the number of acres required will be much less than has already been given to the favored States and Territories; it will indeed amount to a very small portion of the public lands. For, according to Seybert's Statistical Annals, those lands in 1813 amounted to 400,000,000 acres. The amount required for all the excluded States would be less than two and one-half per centum of that quantity. To show which more clearly, your committee beg leave to submit the following statement, founded upon calculations made upon the extent of territory in each of those States, as laid down in Seybert's Statistical Annals:

New Hampshire contains 6,074,240 acres.

One thirty-sixth part of that extent, being the number of acres of public land to which that State is entitled for the support of common schools, is.................................... 168,728

One-fifth part of that thirty-sixth, to which New Hampshire is entitled for the support of colleges and academies, is 33,745

Total for New Hampshire.................... 204,473

Vermont contains 6,551,680 acres.

One thirty-sixth part for common schools is.... 181,909

One-fifth part of one thirty-sixth, for colleges and academies..................................... 36,398

Total for Vermont............................ 248,389

Massachusetts (including Maine) contains 28,990,000 acres.

One thirty-sixth part for common schools is.... 805,277

One-fifth part of the thirty-sixth, for colleges and academies 161,055

Total for Massachusetts and Maine......... 966,332

Rhode Island contains 1,011,200 acres.

One thirty-sixth part for common schools is.... 28,088

One-fifth part of one thirty-sixth, for colleges 5,617

Total for Rhode Island....................... 33,705

Connecticut contains 2,991,360 acres.

One thirty-sixth part for common schools is.... 83,093

One-fifth part of one thirty-sixth, for colleges and academies 16,618

Total for Connecticut......................... 99,711

New York contains 28,800,000 acres.

One thirty-sixth part for common schools is.... 800,000

One-fifth part of one thirty-sixth, for colleges and academies 160,618

Total for New York............................ 960,000

New Jersey contains 5.325,800 acres.
One thirty-sixth part for common schools is.... 144.557
One-fifth part of one thirty-sixth, for colleges
and academies...................................... 28,917

    Total for New Jersey   173,494

Pennsylvania contains 29,872,000 acres.
One thirty-sixth part for common schools is.... 829,777
One-fifth part of one thirty-sixth, for colleges
and academies....................... 165,955

    Total for Pennsylvania.........................   995,732

Delaware contains 1,356,800 acres.
One thirty-sixth part for common schools is.... 37,688
One-fifth part of one thirty-sixth, for colleges
and academies 7,537

    Total for Delaware...........................   45,225

Maryland contains 8,960,000 acres.
One thirty-sixth part for common schools is.... 248,888
One-fifth part of one thirty-sixth, for colleges
and academies........ 49,777

    Total for Maryland..............................   298,665

Virginia contains 44,800,000 acres.
One thirty-sixth part for common schools is.... 1,244,244
One-fifth part of one thirty-sixth, for colleges
and academies 248,888

    Total for Virginia   1,493,332

North Carolina contains 29,720,000 acres.
One thirty-sixth part for common schools is.... 825,555
One-fifth part of one thirty-sixth, for colleges
and academies..................................... 166,111

    Total for North Carolina......................   990,666

South Carolina contains 15,411,200 acres.
One thirty-sixth part for common schools is.... 428,088
One-fifth part of one thirty-sixth, for colleges
and academies 85,617

    Total for South Carolina   513,705

Georgia contains 39,680,000 acres.
One thirty-sixth part for common schools is....1,102,222
One-fifth part of one thirty-sixth, for colleges
and academies.. 220,444

    Total for Georgia   1,322,666

Kentucky contains 32,000,000 acres.
One thirty-sixth part for common schools is.... 888,888
One-fifth part of one thirty-sixth, for colleges
and academies 177,777

    Total for Kentucky....................   1,066,665
Total amount of literary appropriations neces-
sary to do justice to the States which have
not yet had any...................................   9,970,760

The Senate will perceive from the foregoing calculations that if the ratio of appropriation for the purposes of education which has hitherto been observed, be adopted with respect to the sixteen States which as yet have received no appropriations of that nature, a much smaller number of acres will be required than has already been assigned to the western region of our country. It would be an inconsiderable portion of the aggregate of public lands; a much less quantity, indeed, than now remains unsold in any of the States which have been formed out of them, with the exception perhaps of Ohio and Tennessee. The magnitude of the appropriations, then, which equal justice now requires, can not be considered as a reasonable objection to them; and as the literary appropriations that have heretofore been made, have been granted for state, and not for national purposes, according to the just principle set forth in the beginning of this report, similar appropriations ought to be extended to all the States.

The circumstance, that the lands which have heretofore been appropriated for the purposes of education are a part of the territory of the States for whose benefit they have been assigned, can furnish no reasonable ground for the preference which has been given them. The public lands are not less the common property of all the States because they are situated within the jurisdictional limits of the States and Territories which have been formed out of them. Such States have no power to tax them; they can not interfere with the primary disposal of them, or with the regulations of Congress for securing the title to purchasers. It is, in fact, Congress alone that can enact laws to affect them. The interest which a citizen of an Atlantic State has in them, as a part of the property of the Union, is the same as the interest of a citizen of a State formed out of them. But hitherto, appropriations of them for State purposes have only been made in favor of such States; and the citizen on the eastern side of the Alleghany may well complain that property in which he has a common interest with his fellow-citizen on the western side, should be appropriated exclusively to the use of the latter. That this is the fact, with regard to that part of the public lands which have been assigned for the support of literary institutions and the support of education, can not be denied.

Your committee do not censure the enlightened policy which governed Congress in making liberal appropriations of land for the encouragement of learning in the West, nor do they wish to withdraw one acre of them from the purposes to which they have been devoted; but they think they are fully justified in saying that impartial justice required that similar appropriations should have been extended to all the States alike. Suppose Congress should appropriate 200,000 acres of the public lands for the support of colleges and academies in New York; and Virginia, who gave up and ceded a great portion of those lands to the United States, on the express condition that "they should be considered as a common fund for the use and benefit of all of them, according to their usual respective proportions in the general charge of expenditure," should apply for a similar grant, and her application should be refused, would she not have a right to complain of the partiality of such a measure, and to charge the federal government with a breach of good faith and an infringement of the conditions on which the cession was made? It can not be denied that she would. Congress has already made a grant of 200,000 acres of land for the support of colleges and academies, not, indeed, in New York, but in Tennessee. Would not Virginia, if she now made an application for a like grant, and were refused, have the same reason to complain as if New York, instead of Tennessee, had been the favored State?

Your committee beg leave to illustrate, by another example, the equity of the principle which it is the object of this report to establish. Foreign commerce and the public lands are alike legitimate sources from which the United States may and do derive revenue. Foreign commerce has fixed its seat in the Atlantic States. Suppose Congress should pass a law appropriating one thirty-sixth part of the revenue collected from foreign commerce in the ports of Baltimore, New York, Boston, Norfolk, Charleston, and Savannah, to the support of common schools througout the States in which they are situated. The other States, every person will admit, would have a right to complain of the partiality and injustice of such an act. And yet in what respect would an act appropriating one thirty-sixth part of the revenue derived from foreign commerce to the use of schools in the six States in which it should be produced, be more partial or unjust than an act appropriating one thirty-sixth part of the public land in Ohio, Indiana, Illinois, Tennessee, Mississippi, and Alabama, the six States in which the public lands, on this side of the Mississippi, are chiefly situated, to their exclusive benefit in the maintenance of schools?

Your committee are aware that it has been said that the appropriation of a part of the public lands to the purposes of education, for the benefit of the States formed out of them, has had the effect of raising the value of the residue by inducing emigrants to settle upon them. Although, in the preambles of such of the acts on this subject as have preambles, the promotion of religion, morality, and knowledge, as necessary to good government and the happiness of mankind, have been assigned as the reason for passing them, and no mention has been made of the consequent increase of the value of the lands that would remain as a motive for the appropriation, yet the knowledge that provision had been made for the education of children in the West, though other motives usually influence emigrants, might have had its weight in inducing some to leave their native homes. If such has been the effect, the value of the residue of the lands has no doubt been increased by it. This increase of value, however, has not been an exclusive benefit to the Atlantic States, but a benefit common to all the States, eastern and western, while the latter still enjoy exclusively the advantages derived from the appropriations of land for literary purposes. The incidental advantage of the increase in value of the public lands in consequence of emigration, if it is to be considered in the light of a compensation to the old States, must be shown to be an advantage exclusively enjoyed by them. That this, however, is not the case, is perfectly obvious; because the proceeds of the lands thus raised in value by emigration, when sold, go into the United States treasury, and are applied. like other revenues, to the general benefit—in other words, to national and not to state purposes.

It is, moreover, most clear that this increase of the value of lands, in consequence of emigration, produces a peculiar benefit to the inhabitants of the new States, in which the inhabitants of the other States, unless owners of land in the new, have no participation. The benefit consists in the increase of the value of their own private property.

On the other hand, it is undoubtedly true that emigration is injurious to the Atlantic States, and to them alone. While it has the effect of raising the price of lands in the West, it has, in an equal ratio at least, and probably in a much greater, prevented the increase of the value of lands in the States which the emigrants have left. It is an indispensable principle in political economy, that the price of every object of purchase, whether lands or personal property, depends upon the relation which supply bears to demand. The demand for land would have been the same, or very nearly so, for the same number of people as are contained within the present limits of the United States, if they had been confined within the limits of the Atlantic States. But the supply, in that case, would have been most materially different. It must have been so small, in proportion to the demand, as to occasion a great rise in the value of lands in the Atlantic States; for it can not be doubted that it is the inexhaustible supply of cheap and good land in the West which has kept down the price of land on the eastern side of the Alleghany. If the Atlantic States had been governed by an exclusive local and selfish policy, every impediment would have been thrown in the way of emigration, which has constantly and uniformly operated to prevent the growth of their numbers, wealth, and power; for which disadvantage the appreciation of their interest in the public lands consequent upon emigration can afford no adequate compensation. It appearing, then, perfectly clear to your committee that emigration is exclusively advantageous to the new States, whose population, wealth, and power are thereby increased at the expense of those States which the emigrants abandon, the inducement to emigration furnished by the appropriation of public lands to the purposes of education in the West, instead of affording a reason for confining such appropriations to that quarter of the Union, offers the most weighty considerations of both justice and policy in favor of extending them to the States which have not yet received them.

Your committee beg leave to present one further reflection for the consideration of the Senate, drawn from the effect produced by encouraging learning in the Western States alone, upon the relative moral power of the Atlantic and Mississippi States. They are far from wishing to make any objection to the augmentation of the intelligence and mental improvement of the people of the West. On the contrary, they sincerely desire the advancement of their brethren in that quarter of the Union in everything that can strengthen, dignify, and embellish political communities. But, while they entertain these sentiments, they can not shut their eyes to the political preponderance which must ultimately be the inevitable result of the superior advantages of education there, and they must therefore ardently desire that the same advantages be extended to the people of the Atlantic States.

Your committee are persuaded that, from the views which they have thus presented on the subject of appropriations of public lands for the purpose of education, the Senate will be satisfied that Maryland, and the other States which have not yet had the benefit of any such appropriations, are entitled to ask of the general government to be placed on an equal footing with the States which have already received them. They believe that no one, convinced of the justice of such a measure, can question its expediency ; nor can they entertain any apprehension that an application to Congress, supported by the combined influence of all the States which are interested, would fail of success. For the purpose, therefore, of drawing the attention of the national legislature to this important subject, and of obtaining the co-operation of the other States, your committee beg leave to recommend the adoption of the following resolutions :   .

Resolved, by the General Assembly of Maryland, That each of the United States has an equal right to participate in the benefit of the public lands, the common property of the Union

Resolved, That the States in whose favor Congress have not made appropriations of land for the purposes of education, are entitled to such appropriations as will correspond in a just proportion with those made in favor of the other States.

Resolved, That his excellency, the governor, be requested to transmit copies of the foregoing report and resolutions to each of our senators and representatives in Congress, with a request that that they will lay the same before their respective houses, and use their endeavors to procure the passage of an act to carry into effect the just principles set forth therein.

Resolved, That his excellency, the governor, be also requested to transmit copies of the said report and resolutions to the gov-

ernors of the several States of the Union, with a request that
they will communicate the same to the legislatures thereof respectively, and solicit their co-operation.

All of which is respectfully submitted.

V. MAXY, *Chairman.*

B.

EXTRACT FROM GOV. HULL'S LETTER TO PRESIDENT JEFFERSON ON THE BURNING OF DETROIT.

" The few titles granted by the government of France, were of
three French acres in front, by forty in depth, subject to the feudal
and seigneurial conditions which usually accompanied titles in
France.   The ancient French code, called ' *la coutûme de Paris,*'
was the established law of the country, and the rights of land
were made strictly conformable to it.   All these grants, however,
required the grantee, in a limited period, to obtain a confirmation from the king ; and, with the exception of a very few, this
confirmation has never been made.   On the conquest of the
French possessions by Great Britain, in the war which terminated
by the treaty of Paris, in the year 1763, as well as in the original
articles of capitulation in 1759 and in 1760, as in the subsequent
treaty itself, the property of the inhabitants of the country is confirmed to them.   The expression in the original is ' *leurs biens,
nobles et ignobles, meubles et immeubles.*' It is therefore conceived to comprehend these lands."—*American State Papers,
Public Lands,* Vol. I., p. 248.

In regard to the burdens to which these lands were
subject, the same volume (page 282) contains, in a letter
of Judge Woodward, the following : " As an example of their
policy, I will only refer you, sir, to the earlier claims which
appear on the files of the committee.   The first is the grant
of the nobleman, De la Mothe Cadilac, to an inhabitant of
Detroit, François Faford de Lorme, in the year 1707 ; the conditions of which are nearly similar to that of the Marquis de
Beauharnais, governor and lieutenant-general of New France
and Louisiana, to St. Aubin, which is the next on the file.   That
of De la Mothe contains two arpents of front by twenty of depth,
about thirty-two American acres, for a colonist and his family in
an American wilderness.   But what are the conditions of these

grants contrasted with an American estate in fee-simple. They are no less than these: 1. To pay a rent of fifteen livres a year to the crown forever. 2. To begin to clear and improve the concession within three months from the date of the grant. 3. All the timber is reserved to the crown whenever it may be wanted for the fortifications, or for the construction of boats or other vessels; that is to say, when reduced to plain language, it may be taken by any military officer who may happen to have the command of the country. 4. The property of all mines and minerals, if any be found, does not pass by the grant. 5. The privilege of hunting hares, rabbits, partridges, and pheasants does not pass. 6. The grantee is to come and carry, plant or help plant a long Maypole before the door of the principal manor-house, on the first day of May in every year. 7. All the grains of the grantee are to be carried to the *moulin bannal,* or mill of the manor, to be ground, paying the tolls sanctioned by the *coutûme de Paris.* 8. On every sale of land a species of duty is to be paid, termed the *lods et vente,* which, in the English law, might bear the name of a fine of alienation, but is more intelligible to an American ear under the appellation of *a tax on the sale of the land.* This tax, by the *coutûme de Paris,* forms no inconsiderable portion of the value of the whole. 9. Previous to a sale, the grantee is to give information to the government, and if the government is willing to take it at the price offered him, it is to have it. 10. The grantees can not mortgage it without the consent of the government previously obtained. 11. For ten years the grantee is not permitted to work, or cause any person to work, directly or indirectly, at the profession and trade of a blacksmith, locksmith, armorer, or brewer. 12. All effects and articles of merchandise sent to, or brought from Montreal, must be sold by the grantee himself, or other person who, with his family, is a French resident, and not by *engagés,* or clerks, or foreigners, or strangers. 13. The grantee is not to sell to a foreigner, without special permission. 14. If he sells to a foreigner, with permission, the rent reserved is greatly increased; and the duties of the *coutûme,* in such cases, are to be paid. 15. He is not to sell or trade brandy to the Indians, on pain of confiscation. 16. The public charges and servitudes, and royal and seigneurial rights of the *coutûme de Paris,* are reserved generally. 17. The grantee is to suffer on his lands the roads which may be thought necessary for the public utility. 18. The grantee is to make his fences as it shall be regulated. 19. He is to assist in making his neighbors' fences when called

26

upon.   20. He is to cause his land to be delineated—that is, surveyed—at his expense.   21. He is to obtain a brevet of confirmation from Europe within two years."

C.

*AN ACT concerning a seminary of learning in the Territory
of Michigan.*

*Be it enacted by the Senate and House of Representatives of
the United States of America, in Congress assembled,* That the
secretary of the treasury be, and is hereby, authorized to set
apart and reserve from sale, out of any public lands within the
Territory of Michigan, to which the Indian title may be extinguished, and not otherwise appropriated, a quantity of land, not
exceeding two entire townships, for the use and support of a university within the Territory aforesaid, and for no other use
or purpose whatsoever, to be located in tracts of land corresponding with any of the legal divisions into which the public
lands are authorized to be surveyed, not less than one section ; one of which said townships, so set apart and reserved
from sale, shall be in lieu of an entire township of land, directed
to be located in said Territory, for the use of a seminary of learning therein, by an act of Congress, entitled " an act making provision for the disposal of the public lands in the Indiana Territory, and for other purposes," approved March twenty-sixth, one
thousand eight hundred and four.
    Approved May 20, 1826.

D.

SECRET SOCIETIES.

From President HITCHCOCK, of Amherst College :
    " So far as their moral influence is concerned, their effect is de-
cidedly bad. Indeed, a large part of the difficulties we have in
managing the college grows out of these societies. They produce a large amount of prejudice, jealousy, and enmity among
the students, and contain rivalries and clanships that are very
hostile to harmony and religion. The principal objection to them
lies in their moral influence, which is decidedly bad.
    " I hope your wisdom will guide you to measures that shall

conquer this great evil, which in secret is blasting the hopes of so many parents.

" We have a law which requires every society in college to present its constitution for the inspection and approval of the faculty, and we have hitherto enforced it."

From President WOOLSEY, of Yale College :
" Their influence on the larger societies, and in producing divisions into cliques, is not good. Their influence on scholarship, on morals, by keeping up secret treats, and on Christian character by mingling religious students in one close body with others of a different stamp, is either not good or questionable."

From President NOTT, of Union College :
" Their tendency is to evil, and it requires great care to prevent the evil to which they tend.

" We have such a rule (requiring college societies to submit their constitutions to the faculty), but it avails little, in so far as secret societies are concerned, as it can not be known what articles are concealed or subsequently added."

From President NORTH, of Hamilton College :
" While the influence of some of them has appeared to be favorable to the scholarship and discipline of the college, that of others has been manifestly the reverse. They differ widely in the character of the young men of which they are composed, and there is a corresponding difference in the influence which they appear to exert.

" On this general subject, I have received frequent communications from the officers of other institutions. I believe the feeling to be a growing one, that this feature of our college system is connected with many evils—evils, too, which are becoming greater as the associations in question are becoming more numerous."

From President FRELINGHUYSEN, of University of the City of New York :
" We believe them to be of no use, and often of great injury, furnishing occasion and excuse for the youth that are prone to vice and indolence.

" By a standing law of our faculty, no society can be formed in the college without submitting the constitution to the faculty, and obtaining their consent."

From President CARNAHAN, of Princeton College :

"Some two or three years ago, some of our students, in consequence of correspondence in some of our Eastern colleges, formed a secret society distinct from the old societies (the authorized college societies), with which the faculty and trustees were not connected, and of whose doings they had no knowledge. As soon as the existence of this society was known, the faculty directed that this society must be dissolved, or its members would be dismissed from the college. It was accordingly dissolved, and no attempt to institute another has been made. My opinion is, that no society among the students should be tolerated, of which the faculty and regents have not directly or indirectly the control."

E.

RECENT LEGISLATIVE APPROPRIATIONS TO THE UNIVERSITY OF MICHIGAN.

Since this work has been passing through the press, the legislature has made the following appropriations for the university, viz :

One of $13,000, to pay outstanding interest-bearing warrants, the most of which were issued for the extension of the chemical laboratory.

One of $5,000, to procure a supply of water for the university grounds.

One of $6,000 annually, for the support of a school of homœopathic medicine. It is not doubted that the regents' action in establishing this school will make it so independent of the existing medical department, that the professors of the two schools will not be compelled to indorse each other's systems, and therefore no conflict between the two need arise.

One of $21,000, for two years—that is, $10,500 for each year —for the support of a school of mining engineering.

One of $3,000 a year, for two years, for the support of a school of dentistry.

A bill has also been passed for the building of a State hospital, for which purpose the sum of $8,000 has been appropriated on the condition that the citizens of Ann Arbor shall add $4,000 to this sum. The conditions being fulfilled, this hospital is to be under the care of the existing medical school.

By this legislation three new schools are established in connection with the university, viz., one of homœopathic medicine, one of dentistry, and one of mining engineering; and the acts which found these involve, by implication, a promise of their perpetuation.

NAMES OMITTED.

Edward Thompson, elected professor of mental and moral philosophy in 1843, but never entered upon duty. He was a Methodist minister, and at the time editor of a periodical in Cincinnati.

Datus C. Brooks, graduated from the University of Michigan in 1856, assistant professor of rhetoric 1857-1863, and librarian to 1864.

Edmund Andrews, graduated from the University of Michigan, Literary Department, in 1849, professor of comparative anatomy 1854-1855.

INDEX.

www.ingramcontent.com/pod-product-compliance
Lightning Source LLC
Chambersburg PA
CBHW032309280326
41932CB00009B/752